Wilson's War

Sir Henry Wilson's Influence on British Military Policy in the Great War and its Aftermath

John Spencer

Foreword by Professor Gary Sheffield

To Stephen, with gratitude & best wishes

John Spencer

November 2023

Helion & Company Limited

For Jean

Helion & Company Limited
Unit 8 Amherst Business Centre
Budbrooke Road
Warwick
CV34 5WE
England
Tel. 01926 499 619
Email: info@helion.co.uk
Website: www.helion.co.uk
Twitter: @helionbooks
Visit our blog blog.helion.co.uk

Published by Helion & Company 2020
Designed and typeset by Mary Woolley (www.battlefield-design.co.uk)
Cover designed by Paul Hewitt, Battlefield Design (www.battlefield-design.co.uk)

Text © John Spencer 2020
Images open source or as individually credited
Maps designed by George Anderson © Helion & Company 2020

ISBN 978-1-912866-27-4

British Library Cataloguing-in-Publication Data.
A catalogue record for this book is available from the British Library.

For details of other military history titles published by Helion & Company Limited contact the above address or visit our website: http://www.helion.co.uk.

We always welcome receiving book proposals from prospective authors.

Contents

List of Illustrations

Acknowledgements

This book would not have been possible without the support and assistance of a large number of people. In particular, my thanks go to Professor Gary Sheffield, my PhD supervisor who first suggested this subject. I am grateful for his wise counsel and for providing the foreword here.

I am particularly grateful to Dr Paul M. Harris who was kind enough to share with me his database of Staff College graduates. Thanks are also due to Dr Andy Simpson for his insight into the daily routine of corps commanders, and to John Hussey for sharing his research on Henry Wilson at the Supreme War Council. Others, who at one time or another have offered valuable counsel, information or simply a listening ear, include Professor Stephen Badsey, Professor John Bourne, David Bugden, Dr Tony Cowan, Brian Curragh, Jonathan Grun, James Halstead, Timothy Halstead, Dr Spencer Jones, Phil McCarty, Paul Potts and Professor Peter Simkins.

My thanks to the Trustees of the Imperial War Museum, London, for permission to quote from the diaries and papers of Field Marshal Sir Henry Wilson and of Field Marshal Lord French of Ypres. Thank you also Trustees Liddell Hart Centre for Military Archives at King's College London for permission to use the papers of Field Marshal Sir William Robertson, and to the Trustees of the Churchill Archives Centre, Churchill College, Cambridge for permission to quote from the papers of Lord Hankey of the Chart and those of Lord Rawlinson of Trent. I am also grateful to the National Archives (TNA) for permission to quote from the documents cited in the text, the Parliamentary Archives for permission to quote from the papers of David Lloyd George and Andrew Bonar Law and the National Library of Scotland to quote from the diaries of Field Marshal the Earl Haig.

Finally, and most of all, my gratitude goes to my wife Jean, for her graceful and unflinching support for this, the latest in a lifetime of obsessions.

Abbreviations

AC	Army Council
ADC	Aide-de-Camp
AEF	American Expeditionary Force
AG	Adjutant General
BEF	British Expeditionary Force
BGGS	Brigadier-General General Staff
BLO	Bodleian Library Oxford
CB	Companion of the Order of the Bath
CAC	Churchill Archive Centre
CIGS	Chief of the Imperial General Staff
C-in-C	Commander-in-Chief
CoS	Chief of Staff
DCIGS	Deputy Chief of the Imperial General Staff
DMO	Director of Military Operations
DMI	Director of Military Intelligence
EEF	Egyptian Expeditionary Force
EWB	Executive War Board
FM	Field Marshal
GHQ	General Headquarters
GOC	General Officer Commanding
GQG	*Grand Quartier General*
GS	General Staff
IWC	Imperial War Cabinet
JN	Joint Note
OH	Official History
LHCMA	Liddell Hart Centre for Military Archives
MGO	Master General of Ordnance
MP	Member of Parliament
NLS	National Library of Scotland
PA	Parliamentary Archives
PMR	Permanent Military Representative
PPS	Parliamentary Private Secretary
QMG	Quartermaster General
SWC	Supreme War Council
TNA	The National Archives
WO	War Office

Foreword

Over the years my path has crossed with that of Field Marshal Sir Henry Hughes Wilson, or at least his historical reputation, on numerous occasions. As an undergraduate studying the First World War in the early 1980s, I picked up on the then standard interpretation of Wilson as a glib, unscrupulous intriguer, a political general in the worst sense. A little later I bought a second-hand copy of *Brasshat*, Basil Collier's early 1960s biography, a not entirely convincing attempt to rehabilitate Wilson. It at least gave me a glimpse of something other than the stereotype. When writing a research Master's thesis, I discovered that the battalion I was studying, the 22nd Royal Fusiliers (Kensington), had in May 1916 briefly come to the attention of Henry Wilson, and not in a good way. A German attack near Vimy Ridge had seized some trenches, and a counterattack involving the 22nd RF and the 1st Royal Berkshires was called off at a local level at short notice. Wilson, an acting Army commander was incandescent, not least because Haig used this failure as a stick to beat his rival. I well remember checking the relevant entries in Haig's manuscript diary and discovering his fury. This was the first - but far from the last - time that I was to use this source.

The late Keith Jeffery's early work was an important influence on my thinking about Wilson. His study of *The British Army and the Crisis of Empire 1918-22*, and even more, the 1986 volume of Wilson's papers as CIGS that Jeffery edited for the Army Records Society, revealed both the range and sheer complexity of problems and issues that he faced, and gave depth to a man often depicted almost in two-dimensional form. Much later, I began to specialise in studies of British high command in the First World War. While working on the edition of Haig's diaries and letters that was published, jointly edited with John Bourne, in 2005, I read the letters that the C-in-C of the BEF exchanged with Wilson, then Chief of the Imperial General Staff, in 1918. I was struck by the fact that they had obviously forged a reasonable working relationship, whatever they privately thought of each other. This view was strengthened by research for my biography of Haig, which first appeared in 2011.

Keith Jeffery's fine biography of Wilson, which appeared in 2006, was a game-changer. Based on a lifetime of research and thinking about Wilson, it was at long last the sort of weighty, scholarly 'Life' that a figure of his significance deserved. I leaned on it when working on by Haig biography, and returned to it again when writing *In Haig's Shadow*, an edited collection that of original sources concerning Hugo De Pree and Douglas Haig. De Pree served as Chief of Staff of IV Corps when Henry Wilson was its commander, and Wilson's diary afforded glimpses of his CofS at work. Some correspondence showed that the two men had a warm, friendly relationship and worked well together. This is significant given that De Pree was Haig's close kin and friend. There is a hint that Wilson was jealous of De Pree's easy access to Haig, although he did not allow that to affect his relationship with his CoS.

By the time I began work on *In Haig's Shadow,* I knew a great deal about Henry Wilson thanks to my supervision of John Spencer's PhD. When John proposed this subject, I agreed to act as supervisor because I believed that in spite of Keith Jeffreys's biography, there was still areas of Wilson's career to explore in greater depth, and new things to say. In particular, John concentrated on the period in 1917-18 when Wilson finally had real power as a strategist and decision-maker. He produced an excellent PhD, which was passed with no corrections - for those not in the know, that is a rare event indeed! This book is an expanded version of that thesis. It is an important piece of work, supplementing Jeffreys's book in a number of ways. As it turned out, John struck a rich seam of material for 1917-18, and so some of his original ideas for topics to cover had to be sacrificed. I am pleased to see this book has allowed him to broaden his scope beyond the artificial boundaries imposed by a PhD.

If Keith Jeffery consigned Wilson's reputation as a mere lightweight intriguer to the dustbin, John Spencer's achievement is to push on from this firm base and establish that 'Wilson's great contribution to the British war effort was his skill, not as a "political soldier" dabbling in domestic political "intrigue", but as a "soldier-diplomat". As he convincingly argues, Wilson's relationship with French generals and politicians was of great importance. Coalition warfare is difficult, conducted by endless inter-allied meetings, negotiations, arguments and compromises. The policies and aspirations of allies may be very different, but if a coalition is to survive, let alone thrive, there must be understanding of each other's position, and a willingness to give and take. In the circumstances that Britain found itself in during the First World War, Henry Wilson was a valuable asset in dealing with the French. In every sense, he spoke their language. Not that he was a slavish admirer of the French, as some of his detractors charged: Wilson never forgot whose commission he held. But his understanding and empathy for Britain's principal ally, and the strong personal relationships that he built with people like Foch, were of very great importance.

A second pillar of Dr Spencer's case concerns Wilson's understanding of the 'frocks', Britain's frockcoated politicians. He is persuasive that Wilson was the right man in the right place at the right time. The Prime Minister, David Lloyd George, was frustrated that there was no meeting of minds with the likes of Haig and Robertson. Dr Spencer makes the important point that Wilson was no credulous admirer of politicians. Rather, he took 'as dim a view of most "frocks" and their motives as any other "brasshat"'. Wilson's key asset was that he was able 'to "see the bigger picture"'. Reversing Haig and Robertson's intransigence, he worked with, rather than against, the political grain. Therefore politicians listened to him, although in many ways Wilson's views did not differ greatly from those of his predecessors (Lloyd George's denunciation of Wilson as 'Wully redivivus' when Wilson argued for the centrality of the Western Front in British strategy is ample testimony to that).

Perhaps the most important theme of *Wilson's War* is Henry Wilson's strategic vision. He saw clearly that a purely national stance on strategy was inadequate. Only by adopting a holistic, pan-Allied approach could defeat be averted and victory assured. His domination of the Supreme Allied War Council was an important, if flawed, step in that direction, and John Spencer's detailed analysis of Wilson's views form a very significant contribution to our understanding of this facet of the history of the First World War.

The Henry Wilson that emerges from these pages is, in some respects, a very recognisable one. He did indeed have a silver tongue, and his light-hearted demeanour endeared him to some and infuriated others. He was obsessed with his native Ireland, and his stubborn determination to force through conscription on the island in the teeth of Nationalist opposition was politically disastrous. But the protagonist of *Wilson's War* also cuts an unfamiliar figure, as a man with genuine strategic insight and finely honed political and diplomatic skills. This is a balanced and nuanced assessment of Wilson, a major contribution to the military and political historiography of Great Britain in the First World War. It takes its place among the essential books on the subject.

Gary Sheffield
Wantage & Wolverhampton, November 2019.

Introduction

Henry Hughes Wilson (1864-1922) remains one of the most controversial British generals of the Great War. A colourful character in life, he attracted admirers and detractors in equal measure; in death, his reputation was ruined by a biography based on his personal diaries. The Wilson of the historiography is, at best, a politician rather than a soldier, with 'politician' being a particularly dirty word. At worst, he is an ambitious intriguer whose rabid Francophilia worked in competition with and at times against British interests. At best, he was one of the few British soldiers of the period who appreciated the essential nature of the Anglo-French alliance, and who used his unique diplomatic skills to preserve and enhance it. This book is not a biography of Wilson. Rather it is a reassessment of his role in the development of British and allied strategy, with particular emphasis on the final 18 months of the conflict and its immediate aftermath when, at last, Wilson combined influence with power.

In the writing on the Great War Wilson too often appears as a one-dimensional figure, descriptions of his idiosyncratic character preferred to close analysis of his professional views and actions.[1] Many works interpret his of-the-moment comments in his private diary both as a reflection of his considered views and, by extension, evidence of his subsequent conduct. Whether this is a reasonable assumption is at the heart of this book. It aims to reassess elements of Wilson's Great War career, concentrating not on his interest in domestic politics, although this cannot be ignored, but on the execution of his military responsibilities. Particular attention is paid to his interest in and contribution to military strategy and higher level, or grand strategy.

Wilson began the war as Sub-Chief of Staff to the BEF's C-in-C Field Marshal Sir John French, and for much of 1915 was Principal British Liaison Officer with the French Army. He spent 1916 in the unfamiliar role of battlefield commander, as General Officer Commanding (GOC) IV Corps in a relatively quiet sector of the Western Front around Arras. An uneventful year was enlivened only by the embarrassing loss of a kilometre of front-line trench to a German attack.[2] The incident confirmed, if confirmation were needed, that whatever skills Wilson might have he did not excel in commanding large bodies of men. He spent much of 1917 in varied, unfulfilling roles until his fortunes finally changed in the autumn with the creation of the SWC.

---

1   The honourable exception is Keith Jeffery, *Field Marshal Sir Henry Wilson: A Political Soldier* (Oxford: Oxford University Press, 2008 [2006]) Despite this much more balanced assessment, the one-dimensional characterisation persists.

2   Edmonds, J.E., *Official History of the War: Military Operations France and Belgium, 1916, vol. 1* (London: Macmillan, 1932), pp. 210-226.

Prime Minister David Lloyd George turned to Wilson after failing to persuade Britain's leading generals to change their strategic focus. Wilson's approach to winning the war was, initially at least, much more to Lloyd George's taste. His proposal for an overarching body to consider and recommend allied strategic policy, as opposed to the ad hoc arrangements which had preceded it, found favour in both London and Paris. The Supreme War Council (SWC), Wilson's creation, led almost inevitably to the establishment of unity of command on the Western Front.

In his time Wilson was a divisive character, loved and detested in equal measure by his military peers and political acquaintances. To admirers he was intellectually gifted beyond the standards of the typical brass-hatted staff officer, refreshingly flippant and with a gift of the gab that meant he was able to hold his own with slippery politicians.[3] To his enemies he was a serpent-tongued gossip, a dangerous 'intriguer' who Janus-like could face either way dependent upon his audience.[4]

As with all characterisations, there is merit in both judgements. Wilson had a high opinion of his military abilities, one which bore only passing resemblance to his limited and unremarkable performance as a battlefield commander. He could laugh and joke with a colleague over lunch, only to fulminate about him in his diary that evening. Henry Wilson was unable to see an ankle without feeling an overwhelming urge to tap it. Relentlessly ambitious he sought the company of politicians as much as that of soldiers. This was resented by those military men who were either unwilling or unable to engage with untrustworthy 'frocks'. Yet Wilson was not alone amongst British army officers of his generation when it came to employment of the political dark arts. Where he differed is that he openly revelled in such behaviour. What his detractors saw as anathema, mixing political and military policy, his admirers saw as an asset. Before the war and on several occasions during it Wilson's greatest skill, his ability to cajole, convince and charm made an important contribution to allied relations. The focus of this study is the world in which Wilson was best employed, as a soldier-diplomat, whether as a senior liaison officer or as Britain's Permanent Military Representative (PMR) at the SWC in Versailles. Once he became the British government's principal military adviser, the Chief of the Imperial General Staff (CIGS) in early 1918, he played a pivotal role in bolstering the brittle Anglo-French alliance. During that fraught year, when the allies snatched victory from the jaws of defeat, his strategic vision was, for better or worse, an important influence in shaping Britain's place in the post-war world order. Once the war in the west was over, he was quick to realise the dangers strategic overstretch posed to the security of the British Empire.

There was no inevitability about Henry Wilson's rise to prominence. In December 1916 Lloyd George headed a shaky and problematic coalition government. Sir Douglas Haig as Commander-in-Chief (C-in-C) of the British Expeditionary Force (BEF) on the Western Front, and Sir William 'Wully' Robertson as CIGS, were popular with Unionist politicians, the

---

3   'Frocks and brasshats', a mixed metaphor alluding to the formal long-tailed frock coat worn by politicians in Parliament and the gold braid on a general's cap.

4   The Secretary to the War Cabinet Sir Maurice Hankey called Wilson an 'arch intriguer', Stephen W. Roskill, *Hankey: Man of Secrets, Vol. I, 1877–1918* (London: Collins, 1970), p. 238; Beaverbrook condemned him as 'a schemer and intriguer both', Lord Beaverbrook, *Politicians and the War: 1914–1916* (London: Oldbourne Book Co., 1960), p. 192.

public, and, for the most part, the Press.[5] Yet Wilson, Lloyd George's disruptor of this formidable partnership, was no politicians' cipher, a mere catalyst through which non-specialists got their way in steering Allied strategy. He had clear strategic views of his own, the result of important pre-war roles at the heart of the British Army's strategy-making system. First amongst these was his unshakable belief in the need to maintain the strongest possible links with Britain's principal ally, France. This conviction was developed in the years preceding the outbreak of war in 1914 and Wilson pursued it doggedly thereafter.

Wilson has suffered more opprobrium than most Great War British generals. In his case the brickbats were thrown not because he was viewed as a 'chateau general', one of the so-called donkeys leading lions to destruction in a 'futile' war. Instead his critics were, initially at least, colleagues and contemporaries. The focus of their criticism was not his talent for leading men, planning offensives or tactical doctrine, but his character. The British official historian of the Great War, Brigadier-General Sir James Edmonds expressed 'contempt and dislike' for Wilson.[6] Lloyd George, who bestowed on him both power and influence did so only, he wrote with the benefit of hindsight, because there was no obvious alternative. Wilson, said Lloyd George, was 'a shrewd politician'; a back-handed compliment from one of Britain's canniest Parliamentary pugilists.[7] Wilson's reputation was undone not by his actions, which were not unusual in the higher echelons of the British Army at the start of the 20th century, but by his writings. Like many of his class and education Wilson kept a journal for much of his adult life. In it he dashed off thoughts and impressions of the day's events. Had he not been assassinated by Irish Republicans in 1922 it is likely he would have joined in the 'battle of the memoirs' and used both the diaries and his extensive correspondence, especially that from his time as CIGS, to write his own epitaph.[8] As it was his reputation was left to the tender mercies of his friend and biographer Charles Callwell and his widow's naïveté.[9]

While the diaries are a goldmine for the historian, the publication of a selection from them in 1927 created an image of their author which has stood the test of time. The expressions of irritation, outrage, and abuse aimed at foe - and often friend - with which Wilson peppered his jottings ruined his reputation. Two years later, the Great War veteran Sir Andrew MacPhail demolished what remained of Wilson's character in what was effectively an extended review of Callwell's book.[10] For almost a century, the echo of late-night scribbled exclamations drowned out any opportunity for a more even-handed analysis. Sir Hubert Gough's biographer accurately described Wilson as 'an extraordinary man' who was 'imaginative, shrewd and articulate.' He also thought him 'lacking an original mind or depth of intellect.'[11] This latter claim is incorrect.

---

5   Haig was C-in-C from 19 December 1915 until the end of the war; Robertson was CIGS from 23 December 1915 to 18 February 1918.

6   Ian F.W. Beckett, (ed.), *The Memoirs of Sir James Edmonds* (Brighton: Tom Donovan Editions, 2013), p. xxiii.

7   David Lloyd George, *War Memoirs of David Lloyd George* (2 vols.), (London: Odhams, 1938), (Vol. II), pp. 1688, 1713.

8   Jeffery, *Wilson*, p. 290; Ian F.W. Beckett, *The Great War* (2nd ed.) (Harlow: Pearson Education, 2007), pp. 645-6.

9   Callwell, C.E., *Field-Marshal Sir Henry Wilson: His Life and Diaries* (2 Vols.) (London: Cassell, 1927).

10   Sir Andrew MacPhail, *Three Persons* (London: John Murray, 1929), pp. 17-153.

11   Anthony Farrar-Hockley, *Goughie: The Life of General Sir Hubert Gough CGB, GCMG, KCVO* (London: Hart-Davis, MacGibbon, 1975), p. 5.

In life Wilson had many admirers, both political and military. Lord Esher, an adviser on military matters to successive British Cabinets, thought him 'always loyal...If he is trusted he will run as straight as any thoroughbred.'[12] His charm and witty facetiousness made him good company. He also had many enemies who, no doubt correctly, mistrusted his love of 'intrigue', or in the modern idiom, 'office politics'. That said, Wilson was not alone in using connections, friendships and networks to further his career. He was, rather, 'the most politically adept member of the most politically aware generation of soldiers Britain had seen since the Civil War.'[13] Those wishing to thrive in any organisations have always had to form alliances, occasionally kowtow to authority, sometimes flatter to deceive. For almost a century Wilson was condemned not so much for what he did, as for what he wrote. His reputation had to wait until 2006 for Keith Jeffery's reassessment.[14] Focussing on Wilson the 'political soldier', it provided a much more even-handed analysis of his career. This book builds on this 'revisionist' view of Wilson, reviews his contribution to the entente cordiale, and aims to shed new light on his contribution to the strategic debate facing the Allies in the final 18 months of the Great War.

Wilson's detractors, both contemporaries and subsequent historians, made much of his love of 'intrigue', suggesting this was why he rose to become the government's principal military advisor. Wilson was a schemer, so the narrative goes, a lover of politicians whose ungentlemanly conniving paved the path to unmerited greatness. In fact, until the alignment of several other stars in the civil-military firmament, Wilson's Machiavellian 'talents' did little to advance his prospects. His pre-war career followed a similar path to other able contemporaries, culminating in Commandant of the British Army Staff College (1907-10) and then Director of Military Operations (DMO) at the War Office. While in the latter post, Britain's strategic reorientation towards partnership with France hardened, in opposition to a resurgent Germany. Wilson was not sole creator of this position, but his, 'drive, enthusiasm and complete conviction about the necessity to render effective land support to France were to provide the stimulus to move military strategy on from the period of consideration and of deciding between alternatives to that of detailed planning for action.'[15] His 'masterful blueprint' for the BEF's mobilisation worked like clockwork.[16] He had good reason to hope that when war came he would be appointed to a senior position, but fate intervened. On the eve of the conflict his reputation was severely damaged by his involvement in the toxic Curragh Incident. His behind the scenes encouragement of a cadre of officers who refused to coerce Unionists in the north of Ireland meant he fell afoul of Prime Minister H.H. Asquith. It severely hampered his advancement for at least three years. There was no inevitability about Wilson's rise to the post of CIGS.[17]

12   Esher to Derby, 29 December 1917, in Oliver, Viscount Esher (ed.), *Journals and Letters of Reginald Viscount Esher (vol. IV), 1916-1930* (London: Ivor Nicholson & Watson, 1938), p. 172.
13   Brock Millman, 'Henry Wilson's Mischief: Field Marshall [sic] Sir Henry Wilson's Rise to Power 1917-18,' *Canadian Journal of History*, vol. XXX, (December 1995), p. 467.
14   Jeffery, *Wilson*.
15   John Gooch, *The Plans of War: The General Staff and British Military Strategy c.1900 – 1914* (London: Routledge, 1974), p. 289.
16   Ian Beckett, Timothy Bowman and Mark Connelly, *The British Army and the First World War* (Cambridge: Cambridge University Press, 2017), p. 208.
17   For a detailed discussion of this event see Ian F.W. Beckett, *The Army and the Curragh Incident 1914* (London: Bodley Head for the Army Records Society, 1985).

The accession of Lloyd George to 10 Downing Street in December 1916 was fundamental to Wilson's advancement. Nonetheless, it took the Prime Minister six months before he turned to the clubbable Irishman for support. Lloyd George had always opposed what he saw as the unimaginatively wasteful strategy of large-scale attritional offensives on the Western Front. Wilson's apparent willingness to view the strategy embodied in the Haig-Robertson axis from a different perspective, presented him with an opportunity to force change. His chance came when, as the costly Third Ypres campaign was grinding to a close, Lloyd George asked his generals for their proposed strategy for 1918. Haig and Robertson could come up with nothing more imaginative than another large-scale offensive in Flanders. The frustrated Prime Minister, who had already been in discussions with Wilson, asked him and Haig's predecessor Field Marshal Lord French to propose an alternative. This was the turning point in Wilson's fortunes, and he grasped the opportunity. Unlike French, who criticised Haig and Robertson personally, Wilson concentrated on strategic priorities, critiqued his colleagues' proposals, and recommended a defensive posture in the west to await the arrival of the American Expeditionary Forces (AEF). Significantly for future Allied strategy however, he ruled out large scale campaigns in 'sideshow' theatres, something he knew was a favoured option of the Prime Minister. Wilson was no Lloyd George dupe. He was prepared to go against the strategic thinking of his fellow generals, but not to the point of refocussing Allied military priorities away from the Western Front to please his political master. As the most recent work on the British Army in the Great War has noted, in 1918 Wilson 'was no more biddable' than Robertson; their differences were ones of personality and detail rather than core principles.[18] Wilson's most significant achievement, in a seminal strategy paper of October 1917, was to press for a body to take responsibility for what he hoped would be joined-up inter-Allied strategic planning, what became the SWC at Versailles outside Paris.[19] His paper was, in effect, a job application for high office. It was also a bold gamble.

Haig and Robertson were resilient individuals who, despite some important differences on strategy, presented a united front when dealing with politicians. They saw Wilson, rightly, as a stalking horse for Lloyd George's opposition to another major offensive on the Western Front in 1918. When Wilson became Britain's military representative at the SWC it was not a foregone conclusion that he, or the new body he came to dominate, would survive let alone be successful. The Allies had 'spent three years, against a background of strategic rivalry and personal mistrust,' unable to develop an effective coordinating machinery.[20] Wilson had Lloyd George's backing, but Haig and Robertson had significant support in the country and at Court. Robertson dominated the Army Council, the body which effectively ran the British Army machine, and ensured it made life difficult for Wilson and his staff.[21] Despite the hurdles placed in his way, and thanks in part to initial apathy amongst Britain's partners, Wilson's strategic

---

18   Beckett et. al., *British Army*, pp. 49, 348.
19   TNA, CAB 27/8, WP 61, 'Present State of the War, future prospects and future action to be taken,' General Sir Henry Wilson to War Cabinet, 20 October 1917 (hereafter CAB 27/8, WP 61).
20   William Philpott, 'The Supreme War Council and the Allied War Effort, 1939-40', in Philippe Chassaigne, and Michael Dockrill, (eds.), *Anglo-French Relations 1898-1998: From Fashoda to Jospin* (Basingstoke: Palgrave, 2002), p. 109.
21   During the Great War the Army Council comprised military members, headed by the CIGS, the deputy CIGS (from December 1915), the Adjutant General, the QMG, Master General of Ordnance, Director General of Military Aeronautics (from February 1916). The civil members included the Secretary of State for War and his deputy, A.F. Becke, *History of the Great War Based on Official*

views dominated the business of the SWC between November 1917 and February 1918, when he became CIGS. It resulted in more than a dozen Joint Notes (JNs), policy documents covering a range of important, sometimes prosaic, subjects. Two, JN1 and JN12, put paid to planning for another major Allied offensive in the west in 1918. It also stymied Lloyd George's hopes for new large-scale offensives in the Middle East and elsewhere. The SWC model for inter-Allied cooperation was far from perfect, but it was considered effective enough to have been revived at the start of the Second World War in 1939.

Wilson's hand was strengthened when Georges Clemenceau became French Prime Minister at the end of 1917. He developed a nuanced relationship with the 'Tiger', one which helped preserve the Anglo-French alliance at a time of extreme stress. French resources were stretched to breaking point and Clemenceau, although a 'prickly ally', appreciated the need to nurture the alliance, as did his army's Chief of Staff (CoS) Ferdinand Foch.[22] Wilson took a similarly pragmatic view. Thus, just as in the first 18 months of the war, Wilson's skills as a soldier-diplomat came to the fore, acting as both lightning rod and catalyst between two mercurial Prime Ministers. This was particularly relevant in the seemingly endless dispute over the British taking over more of the French front. Wilson reminded the politicians of the importance of doing more to meet French demands but defended the British position at a time of acute manpower shortages. It was a difficult balancing act. As CIGS, he was horrified by the lack of men for the front and the determination of the government to prioritise naval and other sectors of the war economy at the expense of the army. Throughout the war he had criticised politicians for their failure, as he saw it, to deploy conscription energetically. Once at the War Office this was an abiding theme.

A logical but by no means inevitable concomitant of the creation of inter-Allied strategic planning, through the auspices of the SWC, was the establishment of Allied unity of command. For most of the war Wilson was no more an advocate of this model for strategy implementation than any other senior British soldier. Nonetheless, when the Allies were under greatest pressure following the shock of the German 1918 Spring Offensive, he was a key influence in Haig accepting Foch as Allied 'Generalissimo'.[23] Foch and Wilson had been friends for more than a decade. It meant that as CIGS Wilson could deploy his diplomatic skills to neutralise, or at least soften, French criticism of British efforts. Once again, however, Wilson was no Gallic puppet. His defence of the British interest led to several serious spats between the two. Had it not been for the underlying strength of their relationship the Anglo-French partnership might have foundered just when it was most needed.

After the signing of the Armistice, Wilson had an important role in the Peace Conference at Versailles, spending most of the first half of the year as the senior soldier in the British delegation. Within days of the guns falling silent on the Western Front he identified Britain's

---

Documents: Order of Battle of Divisions, Part 4, The Army Council, GHQs, Armies and Corps 1914-18 (London: HMSO, 1945), pp 2-3; *The War Office List* (London: HMSO, 1932).

22   Eliot A. Cohen, *Supreme Command: Soldiers, Statesmen and Leadership in Wartime* (London: Simon & Schuster, 2003 [2002]), p. 90.

23   Foch's title of 'Général en Chef des Armées Alliées' was agreed by Lloyd George on 14 April and formalised on 22 April 1918; he was appointed Marshal of France on 5 August 1918, Elizabeth Greenhalgh, *Foch in Command: The Forging of a First World War General* (Cambridge: Cambridge University Press, 2011), pp. 316, 406.

fundamental challenges. The empire was at its largest, covering a quarter of the globe, yet also vulnerable. British troops were stationed across the world, at huge cost to the public purse and with a war-weary population agitating to bring the boys home. For Wilson the politicians needed to prioritise Britain's interests and, in his opinion, concentrate on the regions and territories of greatest importance. These 'storm centres' included, inevitably, Ireland. His views clashed with those of his prime minister and other senior politicians – yet many of them were remarkably prescient. The issues echo a century on.

Structure

Diplomacy, influencing and downright politicking dominated Henry Wilson's military career; and that of many of his contemporaries. As a result this work begins with an examination of this phenomenon at a time of upheaval and change in both the British military, and British politics. Wilson was not unique in employing the dark arts of 'intrigue', merely the most overt practitioner in a generation of ambitious and talented officers. The next chapter analyses his role in the build-up to the Great War, with particular attention to the inter-service debate over the future role, size and deployment of a British Expeditionary Force to the continent of Europe. Chapter 3 considers the first 18 months of the war which saw Wilson performing a vital liaison function between mercurial British and French commanders. Wilson's unrewarding stint as IV Corps commander on the Western Front is discussed in Chapter 4, with particular attention paid to the impact the experience had on his relationship with Sir Douglas Haig. Wilson's far from inevitable rise to becoming the Prime Minister's favourite general (albeit a temporary state) is discussed next, with particular reference to the seminal strategy paper he produced in the autumn of 1917. Chapter 6 examines the establishment of the Supreme War Council at Versailles, while Chapter 7 addresses the perennial problem facing the allies throughout the war, and one to which Wilson believed he had the answer – manpower. The succeeding two chapters (8 and 9) concentrate on Wilson's strategic views, firstly as the government's unofficial military adviser at Versailles, and then as Chief of the Imperial General Staff in 1918. Wilson's impact on the establishment of unity of command on the Western Front is considered in detail, together with his impact on policies in other theatres. Chapter 9 also focuses on Henry Wilson's role in developing British military strategy for 1919. Although these were negated by the unexpectedly speedy defeat of the German army, the principles they contained directly influenced British post-war foreign policy. Wilson's early realisation that his country's economy could not sustain a global political hegemony is considered in Chapter 10.

Historiographical Outline

Considering Wilson's contribution to preparing the British Army for war against Germany, and his varied roles once it began, it is not surprising that there are few scholarly works on the strategic and command issues of the period in which his name does not feature. Very often, however, Wilson's notorious 'scheming' and penchant for 'mischief' colours the writing, effectively blurring the overall view of a soldier who at the time had at least as many loyal admirers as detractors.

Wilson has attracted surprisingly few modern biographers, but more than certain other key figures in the British military elite, such as Henry Rawlinson or Hubert Plumer. The most recent and by far the most scholarly examination of his life, by Keith Jeffery, was an exhaustive analysis of his often overt political activity, with particular reference to his lifelong interest in Irish Unionist politics.[24] Jeffery addressed key phases in Wilson's Great War career. A single chapter was devoted to his role as British PMR to the SWC, and as CIGS from February 1918 until the end of the war. The sub-title *A Political Soldier* summed up the work's primary focus. The result was an analysis of Wilson's prominent and developing role in Ireland's political tribulations. Wilson's relationship in the final two years of the war with Lloyd George was covered in some detail, particularly his role as stalking horse for the premier's wish to break the Haig-Robertson alliance. The book prioritised the political elements *vis a vis* the military elements of Wilson's career. This work aims to complement Jeffery's seminal study.

The impact of the first Wilson biography on his reputation has already been noted. Two others, dating from the 1960's, before many official archives were open to scholars, followed a similar line to Callwell, quoting extensively from Wilson's indiscreet diaries while offering only limited strategic context and analysis.[25] The fifth work on Wilson concentrated on his assassination and the political events leading up to it.[26] Brock Millman's article on Wilson's role in the creation of the SWC made a valuable contribution to the subject but omitted an analysis of Wilson's strategic influence once in a position of real power.[27]

The finest biography of Wilson, and the most recent, is that by Keith Jeffery. It addressed key phases in Wilson's Great War career. A single chapter was devoted to his role as British PMR to the SWC, and as CIGS from February 1918 until the end of the war. The sub-title *A Political Soldier* summed up the work's primary focus. The result is an analysis of Wilson's prominent and developing role in Ireland's political tribulations. Wilson's relationship in the final two years of the war with Lloyd George is covered in some detail, particularly his role as stalking horse for the premier's wish to break the Haig-Robertson alliance. The book has many strengths. Its weaknesses, if they are such, are centred on the priority given to the political elements *vis a vis* the military elements of Wilson's career. This work aims to complement Jeffery's seminal study.

According to Keith Jeffery, Callwell's 'official' biography painted a picture of a man who was an 'over-ambitious, self-serving monster, with such violent passions and prejudices as to appear at times actually unbalanced.'[28] There is no doubt that Callwell's work, which called extensively on Wilson's 41 manuscript diaries, has provided a handy if simplistic character portrait.[29] The book itself, while quoting liberally from the diaries, comprised a detailed résumé of Wilson's life. Often diary extracts appear to have been chosen as much for their colourful tone as for their value in illuminating and informing the accompanying narrative. Almost inevitably, considering the era in which he was writing, Callwell told his story from a personal angle with limited referencing of source material. While the book offended some of Wilson's former colleagues

---

24   Jeffery, *Wilson*.
25   Basil Collier, *Brasshat* (London: Secker & Warburg, 1961) and Bernard Ash, *The Lost Dictator: Field-Marshal Sir Henry Wilson* (London: Cassell, 1968).
26   Rex Taylor, *Assassination* (London: Hutchinson, 1961).
27   Millman, 'Wilson's Mischief', pp. 467-486.
28   Jeffery, *Wilson*, p. vii.
29   The diaries, now held at the Imperial War Museum (IWM), (HHW 1) cover the years 1893-1922: future citations are described as 'Wilson diary'; Jeffery, Keith, (ed.), *The Military Correspondence of Field Marshal Sir Henry Wilson: 1918-1922* (London: The Bodley Head for the Army Records Society, 1985), p. ix. Hereafter *MCHW*.

and friends, his biographer diplomatically removed many of the highly personal critiques with which his diary is peppered. Many appear here for the first time. Most importantly from the perspective of this study, Wilson's actions and responses to events were recorded with limited analysis of broader motivational context, or their effects.

Basil Collier wrote *Brasshat* before he had access to the wealth of material in the official archives. The narrative, while detailed, included little scrutiny of events and their causes and effects. An important limitation was the lack of historiographical referencing. Collier's was a sympathetic biography, too often coming down on the side of his subject when evidence pointed to the contrary. Field Marshal Lord Kitchener's accurate prediction that the war would be a long one, as opposed to Wilson's assessment that it would be short and bloody was dismissed as 'the uninstructed guess of a man who must differ from the majority at all costs, while Wilson's was a sound inference from reliable intelligence. It was only by unforeseeable chance that Wilson was wrong and Kitchener very nearly right.'[30] The other main Wilson biography also suffered from being too dependent upon Wilson's diary, unsupported by his correspondence and other primary source material. In *The Lost Dictator* Bernard Ash noted the risks involved: 'The diaries are highly intimate and highly personal and often represent Wilson's private views rather than his public intentions, and …because for the most part the entries were written in haste, following immediately upon occurrences, and therefore did not always represent his more considered thoughts.'[31] Despite the sagacity of this observation, the work sometimes construed much from little detail. Wilson's year as Principal British Liaison Officer with the French in 1915 was, according to Ash, the period during which he began considering the need for greater co-ordination between the Allied armies and, ultimately, the formation of the SWC. While the personal diaries support this suggestion, Ash went further and construed that the liaison role held 'the key to power in the military operations of the Western Front.' If the co-ordination of the Allied armies rested in him, Wilson could be more powerful than the BEF's C-in-C Sir John French or his French counterpart General Joseph Joffre: 'He could be a more powerful person than Asquith or Kitchener.'[32] As the current study will show, Wilson's role was important and influential, but it is far-fetched to suggest that it was as pivotal as Ash claimed. Equally, there is no specific reference in his diaries to indicate that Wilson, despite his tendency to hubris, viewed his position in 1915 so loftily. Ash further claimed that the SWC had such power that in late 1917 and early 1918 Wilson, with Foch controlling France's military representative General Maxime Weygand, 'were for all practical purposes in control of Allied military operations.'[33] Wilson might have wished it was so, but the claim is in stark contrast to the facts. Wilson had to coax and cajole and was often unsuccessful. The book's least convincing argument, however, was enshrined in its title. Wilson's uncompromising views on the future of Ireland meant that he was feted by, and had strong sympathies with, the Conservative and Unionist Party, and in 1922 eventually became one of its MPs, for the Ulster seat of North Down. His diary comments and his political views generally would undoubtedly be considered reactionary today, but they were not unusual in an Edwardian officer of his background. From these unguarded personal diary entries and remarks to friends and acquaintances, Ash speculated on a post-war world in

30   Collier, *Brasshat*, p. 198.
31   Ash, *Lost Dictator*, p. v.
32   Ibid., p. 181.
33   Ibid, p. 240.

which Wilson, had he lived, would have taken effortless control of his party, then the country, attempted a 'reconquest of Ireland, the subjugation of India, Egypt and other lands' accompanied at home by 'military confrontation with the forces of organised labour.'[34] This conclusion, which underpins the whole work, was best summed up by Keith Jeffery: 'Ash's fanciful prediction that Wilson might have become some sort of quasi-fascist leader, while it may well have been a useful device to sell his biography, is absurd.'[35]

The historiography of this period in the development of the British Army and the administrative structures that underpinned it is substantial, with Wilson given due credit for the efficient deployment of forces in August 1914.[36] Roy A. Prete concentrated on Wilson's pre-war role as DMO, working with the French on plans for the BEF's complement, mobilisation, initial location on the continent and its role on the left wing of the French Army.[37] Prete argued that while Wilson did much to reassure the French about his country's intentions if Germany attacked, planning was ultimately defective due to the British government's failure to make firm policy decisions. The result was that, 'The French Staff merely made demands and Wilson, on behalf of the British Staff, made every effort to comply.'[38] The details of what were good intentions and what were firm commitments was never ironed out prior to the outbreak of war. As a result, the French were disappointed when their expectations of British commitment were not always met, or at least not with the alacrity they expected. The British were equally dismayed that their efforts were rarely acknowledged. These contradictions were an abiding theme in Anglo-French relations throughout the war. As this book reveals, there were plenty of occasions when misunderstanding and frustration found Wilson smoothing frayed relations between British and French commanders.[39] Broader strategy and the role of the military vis-à-vis the state and its allies was of great interest to Wilson.[40] The soldier-diplomat was a role in which Wilson excelled, and one he played for much of the war. The historiography of inter-allied liaison work is extensive and focussed on the work of key individuals. Interestingly, the liaison work of arguably the most influential British officer, Wilson, has received limited attention until now.[41]

---

34   Ash, *Lost Dictator*, pp. 278-279.
35   Jeffery, *Wilson*, p. 295.
36   Brian Bond, *The Victorian Army and the Staff College 1854-1914* (London: Eyre Methuen, 1972) and Spencer Jones, *From Boer War to World War: Tactical Reform of the British Army 1899-1914* (Norman: University of Oklahoma Press, 2012).
37   Roy A. Prete, 'French Strategic Planning and the Deployment of the BEF in France in 1914', *Canadian Journal of History*, XXIV, April 1989, pp. 42-62 and idem., *Strategy and Command: the Anglo-French Coalition on the Western Front 1914* (London: McGill-Queen's University Press, 2009).
38   Ibid., p. 44.
39   Richard Holmes, *The Little Field Marshal: A Life of Sir John French*, (London: Jonathan Cape, 1981), pp. 208-209; Gary Sheffield and John Spencer, 'Soldiers and Politicians in Strife: The Case of Henry Wilson in 1915', in Peter Liddle (ed.), *Britain and the Widening War, 1915-1916: From Gallipoli to the Somme* (Barnsley: Pen & Sword, 2016), pp. 83-99.
40   S.R. Williamson Jr., The *Politics of Grand Strategy: Britain and France Prepare for War 1904-1914* (Cambridge, Massachusetts: Harvard University Press, 1969).
41   Works on inter-allied liaison include: Major-General Sir Edward Spears, *Liaison 1914: A Narrative of the Great Retreat* (London: Cassell, 1999 [1930]); idem, *Prelude to Victory*, (London: Cape, 1939); Max Egremont, *Under Two Flags: The Life of Major-General Sir Edward Spears* (London: Phoenix, 1998 [1997]); General [Victor J.M.] Huguet, *Britain and the War: A French Indictment* (London: Cassell,

The performance of the BEF has been much studied. For some historians, the 'Old Contemptibles' of 1914 were let down by their commanders. Tim Travers argued that senior officers brought an Edwardian culture to the battlefield, one at odds with the industrialised nature of modern conflict.[42] David French judged that the pre-war failure to define a formal alliance between Britain and France impacted negatively on the fighting efficiency of the Allied armies.[43] He paid particular attention to the British government's dilemma in favouring, as in previous conflicts, a 'limited war', contributing economically but keeping the human cost to a minimum, while over time being gradually pulled into a much deeper conflict by the inevitable demands of its main ally.[44] French questioned the 'Easterner-Westerner' distinction commonly applied to both politicians and senior soldiers as too simplistic. His companion volume, covering the period of Lloyd George's coalition government, continued the theme of characterising the 'East-West' debate as one concerned more with limiting casualties than simply territorial in nature.[45] French asserted that a 'pivotal' figure in favour of a Western Front-only policy was Wilson's predecessor as CIGS, Robertson. Wilson, he contended, believed that the war would be won in the west but that significant progress to that end might be achieved by additional campaigns elsewhere; a perspective that found favour with Lloyd George. In fact, once Wilson had both influence and power, he paid lip-service to the notion of offensives on multiple fronts, while doing little to enhance it.

The apparent ideological proximity between Wilson and the Prime Minister, and the events that stemmed from them, received extensive coverage in David Woodward's *Lloyd George and the Generals*.[46] Wilson ended 1916 effectively unemployed following his period as commander of IV Corps. The first half of 1917 saw him participate in a fruitless diplomatic mission to Tsarist Russia, followed by an uncomfortable role as Chief of the British Mission to the French Army. The latter posting was another in which Wilson's familiarity with the French language, the country's politics and its army were put to good use. Lloyd George created the role for Wilson to smooth British support for the planned spring campaign of France's new C-in-C Robert Nivelle. The appointment ended once the offensive failed to achieve its ambitious objectives and its architect was dismissed. According to Woodward, Wilson's career revived under Lloyd George for two main reasons. Firstly, they shared a similar temperament, in contrast to some of the more reserved senior British Army officers with whom the Prime Minister did business. Secondly, Lloyd George's preferred war policy disagreed profoundly with that advocated by his

1928); Charles Seymour, (ed.), *The Intimate Papers of Colonel House: Into the World War – April 1917-June 1918* (vol. 3) (London: Ernest Benn, 1928); Elizabeth Greenhalgh, (ed. and trans.), *Liaison: General Pierre des Vallieres at British General Headquarters, 1916-1917* (Stroud: The History Press for the Army Records Society, 2016) and Idem. (ed. and trans.), Lieutenant General Sir John Du Cane, KCB, *With Marshal Foch: A British General at Allied Supreme Headquarters April-November 1918* (Solihull: Helion & Company, 2018).

42 Tim Travers, *The Killing Ground: The British Army, the Western Front and the Emergence of Modern War 1900-1918* (London: Allen & Unwin, 1987).

43 David French, *British Strategy and War Aims: 1914-1916* (London: Allen & Unwin, 1986).

44 The classic work on the theory of limited military commitment is B. H. Liddell Hart, *The British Way in Warfare* (London: Faber & Faber, 1932).

45 David French, *The Strategy of the Lloyd George Coalition, 1916-1918* (Oxford: Clarendon Press at Oxford University Press, 1995).

46 David R. Woodward, *Lloyd George and the Generals* (Newark: University of Delaware Press, 1983).

two most senior military advisers, Haig and Robertson.[47] In other words Lloyd George, always searching for a less costly way of winning the war, needed an ally who not only apparently sympathised with his views but who was willing to see them to fruition. Wilson seemed the ideal candidate, yet as so often he flattered to deceive.

Most works concerned with the Supreme War Council have credited Wilson with being one of the principal figures in its creation, but details of the work he undertook, are limited. William Philpott noted its role in initiating a 'more dynamic management' of the coalition war effort.[48] Elizabeth Greenhalgh paid considerable attention to the formation of the SWC and the development of Foch's powers following his formal appointment as generalissimo in April 1918.[49] There are valuable insights into the creation and tensions in the functioning of the Versailles body, but it is ultimately dismissed as a 'talking shop'. The work reveals the author's scholarship of the French military and political scene during the Great War that is not always mirrored in evaluation of British protagonists. For example, the decision to replace Wilson as Britain's PMR to the SWC with Sir Henry Rawlinson is described as 'bizarre' but the probable result of Haig preferring to 'have one of his own men at Versailles.'[50] In fact, while Rawlinson was undoubtedly one of Haig's 'most important lieutenants', their relationship was nuanced.[51] In March 1915 Haig had saved Rawlinson's career after errors at the battle of Neuve Chapelle and as a result the junior officer was to some extent 'beholden' to the C-in-C.[52] Nonetheless, Rawlinson remained his own man. While Haig might have been content to see Rawlinson at Versailles, Wilson welcomed the appointment, the latter two having been friends since 1886.[53] Meighen McCrea's detailed study of the workings of the SWC downplays Wilson's role in its establishment and his direct influence on its strategy.[54] Jeffery acknowledged that the SWC 'completed much useful, mostly prosaic, work towards the promotion of an efficient and well-coordinated war effort.'[55] In fact, his role in steering the Council towards the contentious issue of allied strategic unity, and ultimately unity of command, was far from common place.

47   Woodward, *Lloyd George*, pp. 243-44.
48   William Philpott, 'Marshal Ferdinand Foch and Allied Victory' in Matthew Hughes & Matthew Seligmann, (eds.), *Leadership in Conflict 1914-1918* (Barnsley: Pen & Sword, 2000), p. 39.
49   Elizabeth Greenhalgh, *Victory Through Coalition: Britain and France during the First World War* (Cambridge: Cambridge University Press, 2005), p. 316.
50   Ibid., p. 179.
51   Gary Sheffield, *Command and Morale: The British Army on the Western Front, 1914-1918* (Barnsley: Pen & Sword, 2014), pp. 37-53, and Idem, *The Chief: Douglas Haig and the British Army* (London: Aurum Press, 2011), p. 110.
52   See also Robin Prior and Trevor Wilson, *Command on the Western Front: The Military Career of Sir Henry Rawlinson 1914-1918* (London: Blackwell, 1992), p. 72 and J.P. Harris, *Douglas Haig and the First World War* (Cambridge: Cambridge University Press, 2008), pp. 125-127.
53   Jeffery, *MCHW*, p. 2.
54   Meighen McCrae, *Coalition Strategy and the End of the First World War: The Supreme War Council and War Planning, 1917-1918* (Cambridge: CUP, 2019.
55   Jeffery, *MCHW*, p. 17.

1

Wilson and his 'Politics'

The image of Wilson which dominates the historiography of the Great War is that of a silver-tongued 'Svengali,' winding gullible men - politicians for the most part - around his little finger.[1] His historical reputation as a 'self-important, outspoken, ambitious political intriguer', is deserved.[2] Yet there was more to Henry Wilson than this. His ability to say what his masters wanted to hear, smiling to their faces while rubbishing many of them behind their backs in his diaries, has often been presented as somehow unique in the British army of the time. This, his critics have long suggested, was not the 'normal' conduct of an officer and a gentleman. Thus Wilson's 'untrustworthiness' stood out as exceptional, maverick behaviour. Such behaviour, it is implied, gave impetus to Wilson's career progression and, almost inevitably, appointment to the post of CIGS. Kitchener's biographer described Wilson as 'Arrogant, presumptuous, impatient, given to scheming…[his] intellectual gifts commended him to politicians and equally rendered him suspect to his colleagues and subordinates in the army.'[3] An early historian of the war noted, presumably euphemistically, that Wilson 'the most lucid, supple, and ambitious of British generals, of whom a military colleague cruelly said that he got into a state of sexual excitement whenever he saw a politician.'[4] This chapter discusses his network of friends, and foes, in order to illuminate why, until autumn 1917, the trajectory of Wilson's war-time career failed to live up to his pre-war expectations. It also considers how his fortunes changed once politicians who admired rather than decried his 'diplomatic' talents came to the fore.

The commonly accepted view of Wilson's character as exceptional is peculiar, considering the amount of space given over in the historiography to the overt 'politicking' that went on in the British Army of the late-Victorian and early Edwardian period and which continued into the Great War. It is unclear, therefore, why Wilson's love of gossip and ability to make friends

---

1   George H. Cassar, *Kitchener's War: British Strategy from 1914 to 1916* (Dulles, Virginia: Potomac Books, 2004), p. 81.

2   William Philpott, *Anglo-French Relations and Strategy on the Western Front, 1914-18* (London: Macmillan, 1996), p. 4.

3   George H. Cassar, *Kitchener: Architect of Victory* (London: William Kimber & Co, 1977), p. 229; see also Paul Guinn, *British Strategy and Politics: 1914 to 1918* (Oxford: Clarendon Press, 1965), p. 266, and John Grigg, *Lloyd George: War Leader: 1916-1918* (London: Faber & Faber, 2011 [2002]), pp. 286-287.

4   C.R.M.F. Cruttwell, *A History of the Great War 1914-1918* (Oxford: Clarendon Press, 1934), pp. 500-501; see also Sir Sam Fay, *The War Office at War* (London: Hutchinson, 1937), p. 100.

of politicians and other men of influence has been considered remarkable for so long. Haig, Hubert Gough, John French, Wully Robertson, all 'politicked' in one way or another before, during - and after - the war. Kitchener's 'capacity for intrigue', most notably against the Viceroy Lord Curzon while the former was C-in-C India was 'notorious'.[5] It would have been unusual had career officers not attempted to further or at least bolster their positions by pulling strings and using friendships to best advantage. As the management guru Charles Handy observed, all organisations comprise 'pressure groups and lobbies, cliques and cabals, rivalries and contests, clashes of personality and bonds of alliance. It would be odd if it were not so, and foolish of anyone to pretend that in some ideal world those differences would not exist.'[6] What was true when Handy was writing was true in the First World War. It remains so today.

Far from the pariah his post-war reputation would suggest he ought to have been, Wilson had many long-standing friendships with both fellow officers and politicians. Inevitably, under the pressure of the greatest military conflict Britain had ever faced, those alliances came under stress from time to time. Despite this, and significantly, the vast majority of these friendships survived the war. Indisputably he also had enemies; some of them very powerful. His love of gossip and displays of self-assurance sometimes bordering on arrogance meant he was not to everybody's taste. Nonetheless, if Wilson was as evidently duplicitous a character as his enemies suggested, it is difficult to understand why Winston Churchill, Foch, and Lord Milner all remained loyal to him in the post-war period, and to his memory after his death. The truth is that Wilson was extremely adept at playing the 'political' game, but so were many of his peers. As Hew Strachan noted, the Curragh Incident 'emphasised that the British army entered the First World War deeply politicised and well versed in the arts of political intrigue.'[7] This was so because most senior officers had a 'penchant for intrigue and lobbying,' in part a legacy of the organisation's imperial history and the resulting tension between centralising authority in London and the long-established and jealously guarded independence of the Indian Army. Wilson was the soldier 'who most obviously acted as the bridge between the politics of empire and the politics of integrated control.' Simply put, in an example of his familiar role as a interlocutor between opposing interests, Wilson was able to reconcile the near-autonomy of the old Victorian Army of Empire with a modern organisation founded on a clearly-defined partnership between politicians and soldiers. He performed a similar function for much of the Great War, this time between Britain and her often fractious allies. Schooled by Lord Roberts, he 'brought the in-fighting skills of his mentor to bear on the problems of grand strategy and coalition warfare.'[8] Significantly, and the historiography fails to give due emphasis to this point, Wilson was unable to apply these 'skills' to full effect until the last 18 months of the war. Only then, when politicians and soldiers who took a similar strategic view to his came to prominence, did Wilson achieve true power and influence.

5   Hew Strachan, *The Politics of the British Army* (Oxford: Oxford University Press, 1997) p. 126; see also Kenneth Rose, *Superior Person: a Portrait of Curzon and his Circle in late Victorian England* (London: Weidenfeld & Nicolson, 1969); Kitchener was C-in-C India 1902-9.
6   Charles Handy, *Understanding Organizations* (Fourth Edition) (London: Penguin 1993 [1976]), p. 291.
7   Strachan, *Politics*, p. 116.
8   Ibid., p. 124.

Military Networks

Along with his contemporaries, Wilson's network of friends and allies was built on the foundations of his early military service, interlocking circles of relationships which touched and often melded. The senior ranks of the British Army at the end of the nineteenth century were riven with factionalism.[9] Pre-eminent were the so-called 'rings' composed of acolytes of Lords Roberts and Wolseley.[10] Wilson was a member of Roberts's 'ring', serving as his private secretary in South Africa. These informal groupings acted as nurturing grounds for promising young officers who found their careers assisted by powerful mentors.[11] 'The Chief', as Wilson referred to Roberts, was adept at 'exploiting political contacts and the press to promote his military views and career.' This behaviour was a 'product of the entire nature of the British Army at the start of the twentieth century.' Roberts, like Wilson later, might have been 'an intriguer and a self-advertiser', but while he 'bent the unofficial rules a little further than his opponents and victims felt was comfortable, he neither broke them nor invented them.'[12]

Wilson and Roberts were ardent Unionists opposed to Home Rule for Ireland, where both had been born, and both had firm views on the essential nature of British imperialism.[13] Roberts was a leading figure in the National Service League which campaigned for compulsory military training on the continental model, a subject dear to Wilson's heart and one he took every opportunity to promote both before and during the Great War.[14] The League was closely aligned with Conservative and Unionist Party politicians, including their wartime leader Andrew Bonar Law, the MP and historian Leo Amery, and Milner. Interestingly, and further evidence of the range of overtly political views amongst officers at this time, French, Haig and Ian Hamilton all took a sceptical view of the practicalities of conscription in peacetime.[15] Roberts's control of service career opportunities meant that as C-in-C he often advanced, or 'did a job', for loyalists who had served with him.[16] Those who impressed 'Bobs' and benefitted from his support included French, Gough, Hamilton, Henry Rawlinson, Robertson, and Wilson.[17] By contrast Haig was a protégé of Sir Evelyn Wood, himself a one-time member of the Wolseley

9   For the most recent detailed discussion on the role of the army 'rings' see Ian F.W. Beckett, Ian F.W., *A British Profession of Arms: The Politics of Command in the Late Victorian Army* (Norman: University of Oklahoma Press, 2018), pp. 74-108.
10   Field Marshal Sir Garnet Wolseley (1833-1913), succeeded the Duke of Cambridge as Commander-in-Chief of the Forces in 1895; Field Marshal Lord Roberts V.C. (1832-1914) succeeded Wolseley in 1901. The post was abolished in 1904; see also Stephen Badsey, *Doctrine and Reform in the British Cavalry 1880-1918* (Aldershot: Ashgate, 2008), p. 35.
11   Badsey, *Doctrine*, p. 38.
12   Ibid., p. 119.
13   Strachan, *Politics*, p. 111.
14   The National Service League was established in 1902, and Roberts became its chairman in 1905; Gregory D. Phillips, *The Diehards: Aristocratic Society and Politics in Edwardian England* (Cambridge Massachusetts: Harvard University Press, 1979), pp. 97-102.
15   Strachan, *Politics*, p. 110.
16   Badsey, *Doctrine*, pp. 53 and 155; Timothy Bowman and Mark Connelly, *The Edwardian Army: Recruiting, Training and Deploying the British Army, 1902-1914* (Oxford: Oxford University Press, 2012), p. 35.
17   Ibid., pp. 156-8, Sheffield, *The Chief*, p. 24 and Jeffery, *Wilson*, p. 39.

clique.[18] Rawlinson, a close friend of Wilson and an acolyte of Roberts, had a 'difficult' nuanced relationship with Haig during the Great War.[19] One of Roberts's Aides-de-Camp (ADCs) in South Africa was Hereward Wake who Wilson chose in the autumn of 1917 as one of his staff in the SWC secretariat. Edward Stanley, another Conservative MP at the turn of the century, was Roberts's private secretary during his time in South Africa. In 1917, as Lord Derby, he succeeded Lloyd George as Secretary of State for War. All were to play key roles in the war and in Wilson's career. The officer corps of the British Army in the years before the Great War was a small world in which everybody knew each other. Barriers between groupings were porous and, thanks to the social background of most army officers, many knew politicians as well. Roberts died on a visit to the Western Front in November 1914 with Wilson at his bedside. He was an insignia-bearer at his old chief's funeral.[20]

Wilson's closest friend, and professional rival, in the British Army was Henry Rawlinson, or 'Rawly' as Wilson knew him. The pair served together in Burma in 1886 and became lifelong friends.[21] Almost exact contemporaries, and both originally members of 'smart' Greenjacket regiments, their career paths crossed often.[22] Both were intelligent, quick-witted and ambitious. In 1904 they upset Sir John French who believed they had stood in the way of one of his protégées:

> Now both those fellows did much harm in Roberts' time. They are very clever and were R[obert]'s special 'Pets'… these two young gentlemen must have their wings clipped. Their chance is in the weakness of others.[23]

Wilson followed Rawlinson, or 'Rawly' as he knew him, as Commandant of the Staff College at Camberley in 1907. They both favoured a broad curriculum which included encouraging officers to consider the political aspects of their duties along with the military, a novel and for the time controversial approach.[24] Wilson gave a lecture on the vexed question of conscription to the Staff College on 4 November 1909.[25] Where they differed was Wilson's career followed an entirely staff officer biased trajectory. Rawlinson pursued a staff route but also gained extensive combat command experience in South Africa and in the Great War. Haig's intelligence chief John Charteris, a Wilson critic, noted 'Rawlinson is a good fighting soldier…, which Wilson is not.'[26] Wilson succeeded Rawlinson in command of IV Corps in 1916 when the latter was elevated to

18   Sheffield, *The Chief*, pp. 25-6.
19   Gary Sheffield, 'Omdurman to Neuve Chapelle: Henry Rawlinson, Douglas Haig and the Making of an Uneasy Command Relationship, 1898-1915', pp. 37-51 in idem. *Command and Morale*.
20   Wilson diary, 14 and 19 November 1914.
21   Jeffery, *Wilson*, pp. 13, 19-20.
22   Wilson joined the Rifle Brigade in late 1884, while Rawlinson was in the King's Royal Rifle Corps; see Badsey, *Doctrine*, for a discussion of 'smart' regiments in the British Army, p. 7.
23   French to Esher, 8 September 1904, (original emphasis), in Holmes, *Little Field Marshal*, p. 127.
24   Bond, *Staff College*, pp. 263-6.
25   IWM, Wilson papers, HHW 33/3/22, notes of a lecture: 'Is Conscription Necessary?'; Wilson repeated the lecture on 11 July 1910.
26   Charteris diary, 24 April 1915, in John Charteris, *At GHQ* (London: Cassell, 1931), p. 87.

lead Fourth Army in the forthcoming Somme campaign.[27] Later, when the wheel of fortune had turned and he found himself CIGS, Wilson chose Rawly to succeed him as Britain's PMR at the SWC. In fact, once ensconced in the War Office, Wilson was more focussed on pursuing his own strategy than on the views of his erstwhile colleagues at Versailles. Rawlinson, although frustrated, was mollified when Wilson influenced his move from Versailles to the command of Fifth (soon to become Fourth) Army in March 1918 after Hubert Gough's removal.[28] They remained on good terms. Speculating in July on the future of General Sir William Birdwood, then commanding Fifth Army, Rawlinson told Wilson: 'Don't go and make him C-in-C in India! I want to go there myself after the war!'[29] Rawlinson, due no doubt in part to help from Wilson who as CIGS sat on the Army Council which influenced such matters, had his wish in 1920. Another valuable ally, particularly when he became CIGS, was his old friend General Sir John 'Jack' Cowans. He was Quartermaster General to the Forces (QMG) throughout the war and a contemporary of Wilson's in the Rifle Brigade.[30]

As in any professional body, progress in the British Army of the early twentieth century relied, at least in part, on personal connections. The rings of influence of the late-Victorian period were gradually replaced by less formal 'teams' or 'firms', groupings of officers brought together when the most senior obtained a new post. Rather than patronage based on family connections and money, shared experiences at the Staff College or in previous appointments were the key drivers.[31] Significantly, senior officers did not enjoy free rein to hand-pick their subordinates. Power of appointment lay with the government acting on the advice of the Army Council. Senior officers had to negotiate and lobby for those they wanted, with problematic success. Wilson's Great War career path was, by comparison with many of his peers, fragmentary. Instead of periods in command of units or departments, Wilson hopped from a quasi-staff/liaison role in 1914, to formal Anglo-French liaison in 1915 and then a corps command the following year. In 1917 he toured Russia, liaised again during the Nivelle offensive, was effectively unemployed, had a brief home command and finished the year establishing the British secretariat at the SWC. Unsurprisingly therefore, when he took on the latter role Wilson's 'team' of trusted lieutenants was an interesting one.

Most important was Sir Charles Sackville-West, known to Wilson as 'Tit Willow'.[32] He had been one of his directing staff at the Staff College and they became firm friends.[33] In 1910 when Wilson moved to the War Office as DMO, Tit Willow joined him.[34] He distinguished himself in brigade commands on the Western Front where he was wounded twice before Wilson overcame objections from Robertson and the Army Council and made him his CoS at Versailles.[35] As an example of the ubiquity of 'intriguing' between senior officers, once Wilson had moved to the

27 The most complete modern study of Rawlinson's career is Prior and Wilson, *Command on the Western Front*.
28 Sheffield, *Command and Morale*, p. 50.
29 IWM, Wilson papers, (HHW 2/13A/23), Rawlinson to Wilson, 8 July 1918.
30 Terry Dean, 'General Sir John Steven Cowans', *Stand To!*, 108, (2017), p. 26.
31 Travers, *Killing Ground*, pp. 6-10.
32 Sackville-West obituary, *The Times*, 9 May 1962.
33 Another loyal ally from this period, also a Staff College instructor, was Major-General Sir George 'Uncle' Harper.
34 Callwell, *Wilson*, (vol. I) pp. 68, 93.
35 Wilson diary, 3 November 1917.

War Office as CIGS, Sackville-West denounced his successor Rawlinson as a Haig loyalist. He portrayed him as a new Robertson plotting behind Wilson's back and supporting GHQ's offensive strategy: 'Versailles is to become an appanage [sic] or buffer between LG & DH & you are left out... What a pie.'[36] This was an incorrect and simplistic assessment of the complex Rawlinson-Haig relationship.[37] In any case, Wilson paid little attention to the criticism of his old friend and when Rawlinson moved on Wilson ensured that Sackville-West took the post. Illustrating the trust between them, Wilson consulted Sackville-West on the controversial subject of a suitable new title for Foch once he was in overall command of Allied forces in France. Wilson also sought assurance on the American PMR General Tasker H. Bliss's position on the future deployment of US forces.[38] Another loyalist Wilson had to fight the War Office to secure for Versailles was his long-standing ADC, Viscount Duncannon, an MP and one of the founders of the right-wing, pro-conscription National Party.[39] Wilson knew Duncannon as 'the Lord' and discussed a possible future in parliament with him in the summer of 1917.[40]

Wilson's fondness for mixing military life with the political found him another admirer in the shape of Leo Amery, another Unionist MP and an influential figure in the British war effort. Amery and Wilson became acquainted during the Boer War. When the former was commissioned to write *The Times* history of that conflict he cited Wilson as a particularly valuable source.[41] They met frequently during the Great War. In 1916 Amery hosted regular parties at his home when guests included Milner, the Ulster Unionist leader Sir Edward Carson, Geoffrey Robinson (later Geoffrey Dawson), editor of *The Times*, Lord Astor (proprietor of the *Observer*), and the writer and Unionist politician F.S. 'Fred' Oliver. Lloyd George, his Parliamentary Private Secretary (PPS) Philip Kerr, and Wilson when on leave from his duties as IV Corps commander, 'occasionally joined our discussions.'[42] Amery was an important figure in Wilson's team at Versailles in the winter of 1917-18.

Absent from Wilson's pre-war circle of friends was Haig, but absence of friendship should not be taken as evidence of discord. Haig was not known for his social skills and was unlikely to have been comfortable with Wilson's irreverent and often flippant style.[43] Launcelot Kiggell, a close friend of Haig's and his CoS with the BEF, believed Haig 'had a good deal to do' with Wilson receiving his CB [Commander of the Order of the Bath] in 1908.[44] The evidence suggests they got on well enough in the pre-war period, to the point of secretly conspiring on military strategy.[45] When Haig was CoS India he wrote to Wilson seeking the DMO's views on

---

36   IWM, Wilson papers, Sackville-West to Wilson, (HHW 2/12B/4), 5 March 1918, and Wilson diary, 24 March 1918; 'appanage' or 'apanage', originally a French word meaning 'A dependent territory or property; a dependency'.

37   Sheffield, *Command and Morale*, pp. 45-47; idem, *The Chief*, pp. 110, 168.

38   Wilson diary, 9, 10 April 1918.

39   Hon. Captain Vere Brabazon, later Earl of Bessborough (1880-1956); for a discussion of the short-lived National Party see William D. Rubinstein, 'Henry Page Croft and the National Party 1917-22, *Journal of Contemporary History*, vol. 9 (1), (1974), pp. 129–148, and Keith M. Wilson, 'National Party Spirits: Backing into the Future', in Hughes and Seligmann, *Leadership*, pp. 209-226.

40   Wilson, 'National Party', in Hughes and Seligmann (eds.), *Leadership*, p. 217.

41   Badsey, *Doctrine*, p. 148.

42   L.S. Amery, *My Political Life, Volume Two: War & Peace, 1914-1929* (London: Hutchinson, 1953), p. 81.

43   Sheffield, *The Chief*, pp. 12-13, 66.

44   Wilson papers, Kiggell to Wilson (2/69/35), 27 June 1908.

45   Jeffery, *MCHW*, p. 21.

the strategy of both Germany and the Ottoman Empire.[46] He also recruited Wilson's input and support for his abortive plans for the mobilisation of the Indian Army to Europe in the event of war.[47] It is hard to believe Haig would have shared such sensitive information with a man who, according to Haig's early biographer Alfred Duff Cooper, 'produced no impression but distrust in the mind of the cautious Scotsman.'[48] With his characteristic ability to spot a poison chalice, Haig declined to take sides overtly in the toxic Curragh affair which so undermined Wilson's credibility with Asquith; thus he avoided alienating either side.[49] They had very different roles once war broke out. Haig's combat commands were never threatened directly by Wilson's liaison work. Nonetheless, according to Charteris, in 1914 Haig believed Wilson to be 'a politician, and not a soldier, and "politician" with Douglas Haig is synonymous with crooked dealing and wrong sense of values.'[50] Haig's prominent role in the removal of Sir John French in 1915, and his abandonment of Robertson in early 1918 when both were fighting for their professional lives, illustrates how willing, and adept, he was at high level 'politics'.[51] The relationship reached its nadir in 1916 when a disillusioned Wilson blamed the C-in-C for his disappointing period as commander of IV Corps. By 1918 the relationship had coalesced into one of cautious tolerance, with occasional irritation shown by both sides. One of Haig's aristocratic friends claimed that he had considered Wilson 'an enemy' yet on the day of his assassination he had appeared in her rooms in full Field Marshal's uniform with 'tears rolling down his face.'[52] It is safe to conclude that the relationship was, at the very least, nuanced.

Wilson had a different relationship with Robertson, the man he would eventually replace as CIGS. Robertson succeeded Wilson as commandant at the Staff College in 1910. According to Sir James Edmonds, Wilson embarrassed Robertson, a poor man by army officer standards, by demanding that he pay for some items of furniture he had left in the commandant's quarters. The details of the story are unclear, but the two men were never close thereafter.[53] In terms of career progression and personality Wilson and Robertson were poles apart; it is hardly surprising that each looked askance at the other. One of Robertson's staunchest and most influential supporters while CIGS was a former Rifle Brigade officer and erstwhile friend of Wilson's, Charles à Court Repington. During the war he wielded great power and influence as war correspondent of *The Times* and in 1918 of the right-wing *Morning Post*. Unfortunately for Wilson, he and Repington had quarrelled in 1901 over a divorce case involving the latter who was forced to resign his

46   Wilson papers, Haig to Wilson, (2/70/3) 16 March, (2/70/4) 19 April, (2/70/6) 29 June, (2/70/7) 2 August 1911.
47   Ibid., (2/70/17) 7 September, (2/70/19) 9 November and (2/70/18) Hamilton Gordon to Wilson, 6 November 1911.
48   Alfred Duff Cooper, *Haig* (2 vols.), (London: Faber & Faber, 1935-6), (vol. I), p. 143.
49   Beckett, *The Curragh Incident 1914*, pp. 6-11; Sheffield, *The Chief*, pp. 62-65.
50   Charteris, *At GHQ*, p. 11.
51   Sheffield, *The Chief*, pp. 131, 264.
52   Elizabeth Burke Plunkett, Lady Fingall, *Seventy Years Young: Memories of Elizabeth Countess of Fingall* (Dublin: The Lilliput Press, 1991 [1937]), p. 173.
53   Jeffery, *Wilson*, p. 79; for variations on the nature of this disagreement, see also Strachan, *Politics*, p. 136; David R. Woodward, *The Military Correspondence of Field-Marshal Sir William Robertson, Chief of the Imperial General Staff, December 1915-February 1918* (London: Army Records Society, 1989), (hereafter *MCWR*), p. 346; Bond, *Victorian Army*, pp. 268-9.

commission.[54] Repington 'attached the blame for his dismissal entirely upon Henry Wilson thereby managing altogether to exculpate himself.'[55] He made Wilson's life difficult during the creation of the SWC and thereafter.[56] Repington was strongly in the Haig-Robertson camp and opposed Lloyd George's efforts to wrest control of strategy on the Western Front away from the War Office and GHQ. Another Wilson adversary was Sir Hubert Gough, who played a leading role in the Curragh Incident. He never forgave Wilson for failing to publicly support his position and as CIGS he was ultimately responsible for ordering Gough's dismissal after the disaster of the German Spring Offensive in 1918. Almost four decades on, Gough's animosity was unabated. He devoted a short chapter in his memoirs to Wilson who, he wrote, 'exercised a considerable and somewhat baleful influence on the conduct of the First World War. This was due to his own lack of sound strategical sense and his blind devotion to everything French, coupled with the glib and easy way with which he talked.'[57]

A particularly notable absentee from the Henry Wilson supporters club was King George V. The monarch cultivated the opinions of leading soldiers throughout the war, including Haig, whose wife Dorothy had been Maid of Honour to his mother, Queen Alexandra.[58] These connections reflected a long-held view amongst most regimental officers in the British Army that they 'saw their loyalty as being to the sovereign rather than the government.'[59] Robertson, French, Horace Smith-Dorrien, Hubert Gough and others kept the King informed of their activities and views. Interestingly, Wilson was not in this charmed circle and his interactions with his sovereign were even limited to formal occasions once he became CIGS.[60]

Political Networks

The course of the events discussed above is important in understanding Wilson's attitude, both to his fellow officers and, more importantly, politicians. Aware that Asquith was responsible for his failure to progress, Wilson naturally enough courted those politicians whose views on how the war ought to be fought, and on other key issues such as conscription and Irish Home Rule, coincided with his own. These included strongly pro-Unionist Tories such as Lords Curzon and Milner, together with the Liberal Winston Churchill and - fundamentally for his future career – Lloyd George. Although like Asquith a Liberal, Lloyd George struck Wilson as a much stronger potential war leader than the apparently blasé 'wait and see' Prime Minister.[61] Wilson

---

54   For a résumé of the Repington – Wilson quarrel see A.J.A. Morris, *Reporting the First World War: Charles Repington, The Times and the Great War* (Cambridge: Cambridge University Press, 2015), pp. 4-6; also, idem, (ed.), *The Letters of Lieutenant-Colonel Charles à Court Repington CMG: Military Correspondent of The Times, 1903-1918* (Stroud: Sutton Publishing for the Army Records Society, 1999), pp. 7-10 and Jeffery, *Wilson*, pp. 48-53.
55   Morris, *Letters*, p. 10.
56   Lieutenant-Colonel C. à Court Repington, *The First World War, 1914-1918* (2 Vols.) (London: Constable, 1920), (vol. II), p. 132.
57   Hubert Gough, *Soldiering On* (London: Arthur Barker Ltd, 1954), p. 171.
58   Sheffield, *The Chief*, pp. 57, 153-4.
59   Badsey, *Doctrine*, p. 50.
60   Ian F.W. Beckett, 'King George V and his Generals' in Hughes & Seligmann, *Leadership*, pp. 247-264.
61   Wilson to Amery, 17 September 1915, in John Barnes and David Nicholson, (eds.), *The Leo Amery Diaries, Vol. 1., 1896-1929* (London: Hutchinson, 1980), p. 124; for Asquith's style of government,

and Lloyd George, who became Secretary of State for War on 6 June 1916, saw each other from time to time during that year.[62] Of particular note was Wilson's assertion that while Britain would win the war he agreed with Lloyd George that more help ought to be given to Russia. In order to do this, he suggested, Haig ought to be 'told exactly how many men he was going to be given & when, & then he could calculate how many fronts he could attack on ... Lloyd George was clearly dissatisfied with Haig and also with Robertson, but did not, of course, discuss either of them directly.'[63] Wilson's apparent willingness to restrict the freedom of British action in the west in order to help an ally prosecute the war elsewhere would resonate in the Wilson-Lloyd George relationship for the rest of the conflict. As for the Welshman's antipathy towards Haig and Robertson, this soon became more overt.

Wilson was a dyed-in-the wool Unionist who cultivated like-minded politicians. Chief among them was Bonar Law, and Churchill, although a Liberal, was a life-long supporter and regarded Wilson as 'an officer of extraordinary vision and faith' even though, ironically enough, from time to time Wilson despaired of his friend's capriciousness.[64] Wilson was an established acquaintance of Lloyd George by the time the latter entered 10 Downing Street on 6 December 1916. Lloyd George's coalition administration was in fact 'a thoroughly Tory beast with an attenuated Liberal tail.'[65] Senior Unionists such as Bonar Law, Curzon and Milner wielded significant influence in the new government. The new prime minister needed allies, in both political and military circles.[66] In the latter he found slim pickings, thanks in part to 'a psychological gulf between civilian and service leaders.'[67] Wilson was one of the few senior British officers who in autumn 1917 was seemingly able and willing to help bridge the gap. Lloyd George's plan to subordinate his country's military strategy to the French, a cack-handed attempt at limiting British casualties, had backfired with catastrophic results for civil-military relations. Consequently, senior military figures distrusted him and 'the ultimate result of the prime minister's effort to reduce the army's leverage was to enhance it.'[68]

Following the Nivelle debacle, Haig was in a stronger position than ever, with his Conservative supporters ready to back him in a trial of strength with the Prime Minister. In Whitehall, the War Office was dominated by Robertson and his team. Lloyd George judged that instead of getting independent counsel from the government's principal military adviser he received little more than Haig's position from the uncritical Robertson. Wully avoided any suggestion of disagreement between himself and the C-in-C when interacting with politicians, but he was far from the Haig lackey Lloyd George believed him to be.[69] As a result, the Prime Minister sought alternative military pundits. For once Wilson was in the right place at the right time: 'In party

see George H. Cassar, *Asquith as War Leader* (London: Hambledon Press, 1994), pp. 31-34 and Roy Jenkins, *Asquith* (London: Collins, 1964), pp. 350-352.

62   Wilson diary 28 January, 13 August 1916.
63   Ibid., 13 November 1916.
64   Winston S. Churchill, *World Crisis* (single volume edition) (London: Thornton Butterworth, 1931), p. 49.
65   R.J.Q. Adams and Philip P. Poirier, *The Conscription Controversy in Britain, 1900-1918* (Columbus, Ohio: Ohio State University Press, 1987), p. 196.
66   Woodward, *Lloyd George*, pp. 133-137.
67   Grigg, *Lloyd George*, p. 3; Strachan, *Politics*, p. 135.
68   Ibid.
69   Woodward, *Robertson*, pp. 176-8.

political terms, his loyalties were very different from Lloyd George's, but so too were those of most of the Prime Minister's cabinet colleagues, and Lloyd George may have felt that Wilson's political credentials could buttress his position with the Conservatives on whom he depended.'[70] Unlike the tongue-tied Haig, Wilson was loquacious, irreverent and in some ways similar in character to Lloyd George. Both men wore their hearts on their sleeves, both had the 'gift of the gab', both revelled in the company of like-minded, apparently clever men. Lloyd George's ally, the newspaper proprietor Sir George (later Lord) Riddell noted that temperamentally 'Wilson was much better fitted than Robertson to get on with L[loyd] G[eorge]. W[ilson] had the happy knack, which suited LG, of interspersing serious business with jokes and badinage.'[71] In contrast to the dour and abrupt Robertson, Wilson listened, seemingly in thrall, to politicians - particularly those with power - and appeared as if he agreed with their every word. He 'was endued with the political mind and could and did talk the language of the politicians.'[72] Unlike Robertson, whose contemptuous dismissals of what he saw as political interference in military strategy infuriated the Prime Minister, Wilson reserved his abuse of the 'frocks' for his diary and letters to trusted friends.

Lloyd George had long been an admirer of Wilson's.[73] As Prime Minister he knew where to turn for alternative military advice. Even then, it was almost a year before Wilson attained real authority. Wilson's chance came in October when, with Third Ypres dragging on, he was called in to critique Haig's and Robertson's proposals for Allied strategy for 1918. Unsurprisingly he took the opportunity to make some suggestions of his own. This was a crucial point in Wilson's career, but the patronage of Lloyd George alone was unlikely to have been sufficient to propel him to the highest position in the British Army. Years of assiduous cultivation of political allies finally began to pay off. Most important of these was the support of Milner, whom Wilson had got to know when he became DMO at the War Office.[74] Both strong Unionists, they saw eye to eye more often than either did with the Prime Minister. One area of agreement was a determination that Britain's imperial ambitions would emerge from the war not only intact but enhanced. Lloyd George took a more nuanced approach to this point; he had no desire to see the British Empire founder but his wartime predilection for 'sideshows' was more concerned with victory over Germany by dint of defeat of her allies than further expansion of the 'Pax Britannica.'[75]

Milner was one of the Prime Minister's most important supporters and a member without portfolio, first of the War Cabinet, established on Lloyd George's accession to the premiership, and the smaller War Policy Committee set up to advise on future strategy in June 1917.[76] In Milner, Wilson had a 'friend and mentor' at the heart of government.[77] They participated in the

70   Strachan, *Politics*, p. 137.
71   Lord Riddell, diary 16 February 1918, in *Lord Riddell's War Diary 1914–1918* (London: Ivor Nicholson & Watson, 1933), p. 312.
72   Beaverbrook, *Politicians*, p. 192.
73   Jeffery, *Wilson*, p. 177.
74   Wilson diary, 17 and 21 June 1911.
75   Grigg, *Lloyd George*, p. 345.
76   The War Policy Committee first met on 11 June 1917, and consisted of Lloyd George, Curzon, Milner, and the South African, General Jan Smuts, with Hankey as secretary, French, *Lloyd George Coalition*, p. 101.
77   Adams and Poirier, *Conscription Controversy*, p. 219.

Allied delegation to Russia in early 1917, with Wilson as senior British military representative, and Milner supported his proposals for the SWC. They met four times while Wilson was writing his report for the War Cabinet in October and it is unlikely that the scheme could have succeeded without Milner's backing.[78] In addition, Milner and Amery were confidants, the younger man regarded Milner as 'my leader, as well as my best friend.'[79]

Another politician who Wilson considered a friend, if a critical one, was Bonar Law. As Chancellor of the Exchequer, Bonar Law was a permanent member of the War Cabinet and supported Wilson as CIGS. They met in 1912 when Wilson was DMO and Bonar Law Leader of the Opposition; they associated regularly thereafter.[80] In late 1915 Wilson was convinced that Asquith and his coalition government was not up to winning the war, in part because of Asquith's reluctance to enact full military conscription. Bonar Law's support was fundamental to Asquith remaining in power, but according to Wilson: 'It is impossible to conduct successful war if you base yourself on INDECISION. You can get nothing but indecision out of the PM *Quod est.*'[81] Bonar Law had supported Wilson's suggestion to put Anglo-French liaison on a more formal footing by creating a committee of six political and military representatives. Nonetheless, he had little truck with his friend's desire to remove the Prime Minister. Wilson had barely arrived on the Western Front as IV Corps commander before he was urging Bonar Law to 'get rid of Squiff'.[82] In March he denounced the 'ramshackle of a coalition' running the country, condemning Asquith as a man 'who has never gone to war, who has no intention, even now, of going to war, & who has no intention either of allowing anyone else to go to war.' He urged Bonar Law to withdraw his party from the coalition:

> You owe Squiff no loyalty, absolutely none. You saved him once when you joined him & a bad day's work it was – whereas you owe the whole of your loyalty to our country & you know as well as I do how shamefully, how disastrously Squiff has tried to govern us.[83]

Wilson, the so-called 'political soldier' still had much to learn in his dealings with the professionals. Telling them their job was something to avoid. Seemingly irritated by the back-handed compliment about loyalty, Bonar Law put Wilson in his place. Things were not as simple as he suggested. His arguments 'would do for an article in the *Daily Mail*' but were unrealistic. If the Unionists broke up the government there would have to be a general election, no party would achieve a majority, social and political unrest could result, and martial law might be necessary. Bonar Law believed that instead of unity the nation would be bitterly divided. His view was that:

---

78 Bodleian Library Oxford (hereafter BLO), Milner diary, 11, 12, 18, 19 October 1917; Wilson diary, 18, 19 October 1917.
79 Amery, *Political Life*, p. 91.
80 Wilson diary, 27 June 1912.
81 Parliamentary Archives (hereafter PA), Bonar Law papers, 52/1/65, Wilson to Bonar Law, 29 December 1915.
82 PA, Bonar Law Papers, 52/3/1, Wilson to Bonar Law, 1 February 1916.
83 Ibid., 52/4/29, Wilson to Bonar Law, 24 March 1916.

With all its disadvantages the best chance of winning the war is by a Government such as the present; and of course as long as I hold that view I shall not do anything to change it. Do not suppose that I don't fully realise that the other what I may call the ruthless-method may not be the best; but that must be a matter of opinion, and my judgement is against it.[84]

Wilson learned his lesson. Over the next 18 months his manner in dealing with the resolute and ruthless Lloyd George was much more deferential, less hectoring.

The French

Wilson's ability to develop and sustain alliances with British politicians was echoed in his relationships with members of the political-military establishment in France.[85] Britain and France had been entente partners since 1904, but few British officers had fostered close ties with colleagues across the Channel. Wilson was one who had. His work with Foch and others to plan Britain's role should Germany attack France had nurtured a climate of trust which was of great importance during the war.[86] Wilson's ability to keep the Anglo-French entente alive at times of great stress was his most significant contribution to Allied victory in 1918. Wilson's Francophilia was well known both before and during the war and appears prominently in the historiography of his career.[87] Thanks to a French governess, Wilson spoke the language well, although there are varying assessments as to his facility. Edward Spears, who undertook several Anglo-French liaison roles during the war and did speak French fluently, wrote that in 1914 Wilson 'did not speak French as well during this stage of the war as he did later.'[88] Peter Wright, who worked as an interpreter in the British Military Secretariat at the SWC and was another of Wilson's Staff College graduates observed:

> Though not good at French, he understood something far more difficult than their language, the free, violent, rhetorical modes of speech used by Latins, always baffling, usually shocking, and sometimes exasperating to grave contained, romantic northerners.[89]

Whatever the precise level of Wilson's fluency, he was more accomplished than most of his peers. When war broke out, Wilson knew the French Army well, the Franco-German frontier intimately, and had forged a number of alliances with military and political figures. Most important for the course of Anglo-French relations were his friendship with Foch, and his

---

84   PA, Bonar Law Papers, 53/6/68, Bonar Law to Wilson, 31 March 1916.
85   Huguet, *Britain and the War*, pp. 19-23; Gooch, *Plans of War*, pp. 119-124.
86   Williamson, *Grand Strategy*, pp. 89, 141, 223; Jeffery, *Wilson*, pp. 85-87.
87   Philpott, *Anglo-French Relations*, p. 4.
88   Spears, *Liaison*, n. p. 298.
89   Captain Peter E. Wright, *At the Supreme War Council* (New York & London: G.P. Putnam's Sons, The Knickerbocker Press, American Edition, 1921), pp. 41-2; Wright graduated from the Staff College in 1908.

acquaintanceship – it would be misinterpreting the relationship to describe them as friends - with the politician Georges Clemenceau.

In 1915 the relationship was put under considerable stress. With Wilson in his liaison role and Foch in command of the French Northern Army Group fighting beside the BEF, they co-operated to smooth over tensions between their respective C-in-Cs, French and Joffre.[90] This ability to pour oil on the troubled waters which often flowed between the allies should not be underestimated. Sir John French's relations with Joffre and his staff were notoriously poor. There were many occasions during 1915 when Wilson, often in concert with Foch, smoothed out the peaks and troughs in his chief's mercurial approach, to the benefit of both allies. This contribution was not, as some of Wilson's colleagues often suggested, an uncritical allegiance to the French position. In 1918 Wilson clashed often, and with great passion, with Foch and Clemenceau.[91] Nonetheless, Wilson had the ability to see issues from the French perspective and then strive to harmonise what sometimes appeared to be irreconcilable differences. In 1915 his long-standing relationship with Sir John helped in this regard. Familiarity with French colleagues allowed both sides to adopt a frankness which between other less well-acquainted individuals might have done irreparable damage. It should be stressed that Wilson never favoured the French position at the expense of the British. There is no evidence for Gough's assertion that Wilson had a 'blind devotion to everything French'.[92] He was, nonetheless, able to oil the wheels of communication at times of greatest inter-Allied friction. This was particularly true during his tenure at the SWC and then as CIGS when his loyalties were put to the test regularly. In his memoirs Foch paid testament to this diplomatic balancing act, noting his old friend's 'patriotic vigilance and far-sighted intelligence.'[93]

In Wilson's absence while commanding IV Corps in 1916, Anglo-French military relations rested for the most part with Sidney Clive, a junior officer with little command experience. By comparison, one of IV Corps staff officers, Brigadier-General General Staff (BGGS) Hugo de Pree, (a cousin of Haig's) recalled that Wilson and Foch 'used to be closeted together for hours, discussing, gossiping and chaffing. They used to exchange caps and in this get-up they would stride up and down the drawing room, laughing heartily and exchanging experiences.'[94] Wilson's relationship with other senior French generals was more problematic. He got on well with Joffre's successor Nivelle. In March 1917, during the controversy over Lloyd George's decision to put Haig and the BEF under French command, he returned to familiar ground when he was persuaded to accept the appointment of Britain's Chief Liaison Officer at *GQG*. This episode in Wilson's career is a case study in the tensions and jostling for power and authority which went on in the senior echelons of the Allied armies during the Great War. Thanks to Lloyd George's sleight of hand the French were once more in the ascendant in deciding Allied strategy, with the British C-in-C effectively under their command.[95] In order to reinforce Nivelle's authority their plan, initially, had been that Wilson would be tantamount to Chief of

90   Sheffield and Spencer, 'Soldiers in Strife', pp. 83-99.
91   See Chapter Five, 'Unity of Command'.
92   Gough, *Soldiering On*, p. 171.
93   Colonel T. Bentley Mott (trans.), *The Memoirs of Marshal Foch* (London: Heinemann, 1931), p. 141.
94   Callwell, *Wilson*, (vol. I), p. 282 and Huguet, *Britain and the War*, p. 129.
95   For an assessment of the Nivelle Offensive, which began on 16 April 1917, see Elizabeth Greenhalgh, *The French Army and the First World War* (Cambridge: Cambridge University Press, 2014), pp. 170-219.

Staff at *GQG* giving Nivelle's orders direct to Haig 'and the French intended to make sure that he would be a willing instrument in their hands.'[96] Clive, the British Head of Mission at *GQG*, was considered insufficiently senior by Nivelle. The new French C-in-C's rationale in requesting Wilson for this role, whatever its official title, merits reiteration in full as it sums up the French view of him and their determination to get him on board:

> I cannot dream of accepting the heavy task which has been entrusted to me in respect of the British Army unless I can have at my disposal a certain number of British staff officers speaking French well, familiar with our methods of work and capable, not only of serving as liaison officers, but also of foreseeing the problems of every kind which we shall have to settle together, and of studying their solution.
>
> The British General Officer who will be placed at the head of this Mission must have the necessary authority and experience to fill this rôle. That is why I have asked you to have General Wilson nominated to this post; he has both during and before the war done a great deal of work with the French General Staff and for every reason he seems to me to be absolutely qualified to perform these duties. I must be allowed to insist once more on his appointment.[97]

Haig resisted the appointment, unsurprisingly considering the hand he had already been dealt by Lloyd George. He finally accepted it when it was agreed that Wilson would report directly to him.[98] Wilson too was reluctant, his diary making clear that he would only accept the position if Haig asked him, and if he could resign if he considered the post untenable. Milner urged him to take the post 'because he did not think that any other man in the world could hold the two armies together.'[99] Wilson agreed after another meeting with Haig at which:

> I told him that within a month of my going to Beauvais [location of Nivelle's headquarters] any number of people would tell him that I was intriguing to put him out – that in point of fact I probably could put him out if I wished - and so I advised him not to have me but to keep Clive.[100]

Haig 'having concluded that it would be best to trust him' told Wilson he should take the role.[101] Edward Spears, then a junior British liaison officer with the French Army wrote: 'I dined with General Henry Wilson and his officers. He was in splendid form. He had a post that suited him admirably, great power and no responsibility, and he had around him an appreciative audience of particularly clever men.'[102] Wilson and Spears came to 'loathe each other', and thus the latter's judgements should be treated with caution.[103] Wilson's new posting, however agreeable, did not

---

96   Spears, *Prelude*, p. 144; Wilson diary, 5 February 1917.
97   Nivelle to Haig, 6 March 1917, in Spears, *Prelude*, Appendix XVI.
98   Jeffery, *Wilson*, p. 187-8.
99   Wilson diary, 12 March 1917.
100   Ibid., 13 March 1917.
101   Haig diary, 12 March 1917, in Gary Sheffield and John Bourne (eds.), *Douglas Haig: War Diaries and Letters 1914-1918* (London: Phoenix, 2006 [2005]), pp. 274-5; Wilson diary, 13 March 1917.
102   Spears diary, 22 March 1917, in *Prelude*, p. 276
103   Egremont, *Two Flags*, p. 11.

last long. The failure of Nivelle's offensive and his subsequent downfall also resulted in Wilson's removal. In May, Spears was promoted to the British Mission in Paris, responsible for liaison between the British and French governments. Pétain succeeded Nivelle, and on 17 May told Spears that he wanted Wilson, whom he did not trust, out of his headquarters by the time he arrived: 'Wilson, Pétain said, was an intriguer: a supporter of the ousted Nivelle, too close to Foch and therefore no friend of his.'[104] Three weeks later Wilson was back in London looking for a job.

Wilson's relationship with Clemenceau was more complex. They were never friends, but they developed a level of mutual respect once Clemenceau became French Prime Minister on 19 November 1917, while Wilson was establishing himself at Versailles. Clemenceau was at first opposed to the establishment of the SWC. He favoured a more direct form of unity of command for Allied forces in the west headed by a French general. Nonetheless, Wilson's mix of charm and intellect won over the 'Tiger' who saw him as easier to deal with than his colleagues Robertson and Haig.[105] Wilson's diary reveals that Clemenceau had a distinctive style for getting his way. Several times in the last year of the war Wilson was treated to an outburst of irritation and often anger, usually directed at British generals or the British government's alleged failure to devote sufficient men, materiel and/or fighting spirit to the war. Wilson then had to mollify Clemenceau, reassure him of Britain's fidelity as an ally and sometimes intercede with Haig on his behalf. Even allowing for the old statesman's canny histrionics, Wilson's diplomatic skills usually succeeded in soothing Clemenceau's mood before matters got out of hand and damaged the alliance irretrievably.

Wilson's fondness for gossip and 'intrigue' was not unusual in the officer corps of the British Army at the beginning of the 20th Century. Plenty of his peers also involved themselves in politicking in order to enhance their careers, promote their strategic views, and influence military policy. Where Wilson did stand out was his overt familiarity with politicians, a profession viewed with open cynicism by many of his military colleagues. Wilson's contemporaries understood the need to swim with the political tide but usually did so while metaphorically holding their noses. Wilson, instead, cultivated politicians and debated with them on military policy, including conscription, and on his interest in Irish politics. Such openness harmed rather than enhanced Wilson's professional fortunes, especially his role in the Curragh Incident. In the next three years Wilson failed to achieve the recognition he felt he deserved following a promising pre-war career. It was only in 1917, when politicians in Britain who saw Wilson's potential were in the ascendant, that his stalled trajectory took flight once more. A similar change in the civil-military leadership in France enhanced his influence and he was able to finally develop his desire for formalisation of Anglo-French strategic planning and decision-making.

---

104 Egremont, *Two Flags*, p. 55; Pétain was appointed C-in-C of the French Army on 10 May 1917, with Foch as his CoS.
105 David S. Newhall, *Clemenceau at War* (Lewiston, New York: Edwin Mellen Press, 1991), p. 392.

2

Pre-War Planning

From the beginning Henry Wilson's career was as much dependent upon his relationship with powerful men as it was with his own military talents. In this respect, as we have already seen, he was far from unusual in the British Army of the late Victorian and Edwardian period. 'Jobbery', where like-mindedness was often - though not always - seen as an acceptable alternative to talent, was rife. Wilson, fleet of mind and wit, together with his enthusiasm for conscription won him the invaluable patronage of Lord Roberts. While many of his contemporaries found similar backing from influential figures, Wilson cast his net wider than most. After a distinguished term as Commandant of the Army Staff College at Camberley (1907-1910) he secured the position of Director of Military Operations (DMO) at the War Office. It was a crucial period in the development of British military strategy and one in which Wilson played a key role. One authority characterised Wilson as the first DMO to display the 'tenets of the General Staff mind as it was understood in Germany.'[1] In the seven years leading up to the outbreak of war Wilson, almost single-handedly, nurtured the nascent Anglo-French Entente into a fully-fledged alliance of mutual assistance. In so doing he developed life-long friendships with a number of leading British public figures. Equally importantly, and here Wilson differed from most of his fellow officers, he initiated and sustained close relationships with French officers, most importantly with Ferdinand Foch.

Like many of his military colleagues, Wilson was convinced that Britain faced an existential threat from Germany. Unlike many members of the British Army and Royal Navy, he was convinced that only close co-operation with France could save Europe from the German menace. Many of Wilson's contemporaries labelled him a 'Francophile'. Although accurate the term was not intended to be complimentary. Wilson reserved particular admiration for the French Army. He was convinced it was essential for military planners in London to work as closely as possible with their counterparts in Paris. He was not the only senior British soldier to support Anglo-French cooperation, but the pre-war period gave him unique opportunities to do so.

During his time at the Staff College and then as DMO Wilson devoted at least half a dozen vacations to touring the Franco-Belgian frontier. The trips took in the battlefields of the Franco-Prussian War (1870-71), the network of fortresses the French maintained to prevent a repeat of

---

1   Gooch, *Plans of War*, p. 289.

that defeat and other strategically important locations down to the Swiss border.[2] In addition he observed French military manoeuvres and regularly visited Foch. As a result, he gained a detailed insight into the nature of the terrain, lines of communication and obstacles which would face a German army whose aggression Wilson saw as 'inevitable'.[3] He was convinced that Germany was committed to war with France and determined that Britain should be ready to offer immediate support.[4] Wilson was not alone amongst his fellow soldiers in this conviction but his role as DMO gave him unique insight into Britain's lack of preparedness.[5] Sitting at the heart of the British military system he had access to the latest intelligence, and clearly saw it as his mission to wake the British political establishment from what he saw as its complacent slumber. As early as 1905, following the tense 'First Moroccan Crisis' between Germany and France over hegemony in north Africa, one of Wilson's predecessors as DMO, James Grierson, had begun discussions with the French military attaché in London Colonel Victor Huguet.[6] Grierson also conducted a war game 'during a France-German war in which Germany violates Belgian territory and Great Britain assists Belgium to oppose this violation.'[7] The game proposed a British force of up to 50,000 men to support the Belgians, but acknowledged this would take up to one month to assemble and embark on the Continent. More ominously Grierson noted the 'reforms' taking place in the British army which 'cannot therefore be considered to be quite "at its best".'[8]

The French military attaché, whose memoir entitled *Britain and the War: A French Indictment* makes clear where his sympathies lay, was frustrated by the 'inadequate' steps taken by France's new ally. When Wilson took up his post at the War Office in August 1910 he was determined to build on the work of his predecessors and develop a workable and practical plan for early British assistance to France and neutral Belgium.[9] For Huguet, Wilson's appointment was a re-setting of the relationship: 'From that moment, thanks to his own impetuous force, the work started again with a certainty, a speed and a spirit of decision which it had never had before.'[10] Wilson's friendship with Foch began in 1909 when Wilson was Commandant of the Staff College and he visited his opposite number at the *Ecole Supérieure de Guerre*. Foch owed his position as Commandant at the *Ecole* to Joseph Joffre who in 1911 had become chief of the French army staff, and therefore commander-in-chief. Both doubted France's Russian ally's

2   Jeffery, *Wilson*, pp. 74-5 and 106. Wilson's diary records visits in May and August 1908, August and December 1909, April 1910, February and October 1911, and in February 1912.
3   Esher, *Kitchener* p. 84
4   The Entente Cordiale, a treaty of rapprochement between Britain and France after centuries of mutual antagonism was signed in April 1904. Essentially it offered mutual diplomatic support in the face of growing German ambitions. For a detailed discussion of this period see Williamson, *Politics of Grand Strategy*, pp. 7-13.
5   Jeffery, *Wilson*, pp. 92-4; see also Williamson, *Politics of Grand Strategy* pp. 172-182.
6   Greenhalgh, *Victory through Coalition*, Huguet, *Britain and the War*, pp. 4-5.
7   TNA WO 33/364: 'Strategic War Game,' Director of Military Operations, General Staff, 24 Jan. 1905, p. 4.
8   Ibid. p. 81. The reforms Grierson was referring to where those proposed by the so-called Esher Committee and implemented by the new Secretary of State for War Lord Haldane. For a detailed discussion of these reforms, which included the creation of an Army General Staff, see Gooch, *Plans of War*, pp. 32-61.
9   Jeffery, *Wilson*, p. 86.
10   Huguet, *Britain and the War*, p. 21.

ability to intervene swiftly and effectively in any war with Germany and Foch set out to improve his country's relationship with the British. In Wilson he found a like-minded officer.[11] Foch and Wilson agreed on the threat Germany posed to peace in Europe.[12] Between December 1909 and May 1914, they met at least 11 times, with Wilson making seven trips to France in 1913 alone.[13] When war came this familiarity meant that 'they were able to communicate honestly with each other.'[14] Such frankness stood them in good stead throughout the conflict.[15]

In mid-October 1910 Wilson attended the wedding of Foch's daughter.[16] Foch had just returned from Russia where he had been a guest of Tsar Nicholas II and observed the Imperial Army's annual manoeuvres. He had come away convinced that Germany was doing all it could to avoid antagonising Russia in order to concentrate its efforts in any forthcoming conflict on France. He had also reached the conclusion that Russian mobilisation would be a long and drawn out affair and would have little impact on France's fortunes in the early stages of a war. It was important therefore to ensure Britain was prepared to offer the French as much support as possible.[17] His friend's observations rattled Wilson who lambasted failings he had discovered in British preparedness for an expeditionary force. Instead of making 'proper arrangements' the War Office seemed content with 'a lot of time spent in writing beautiful but useless minutes. I'll break this somehow.'[18] His opportunity came the following year when the Second Moroccan Crisis, also known as the Agadir Crisis, in July 1911 sent another chill down the corridors of Whitehall and military planners scurrying to dust off plans on how to respond. Franco-German tensions subsided as quickly as they had risen, but few believed the respite would last. As a result Wilson's superior, the CIGS Sir William Nicholson, instructed him to prepare a report on 'the Continental problem'.[19] It followed a meeting Wilson had with the Secretary of State for War Lord Haldane and the Foreign Secretary Lord Grey. After 'a long and ineffectual talk' about a potential British response to Germany going to war with France, Wilson made three chief points: 'First, that we must join the French. Second, that we must mobilise the same day as the French. Third, that we must send the whole six divisions. These were agreed to but with no great heartiness.'[20]

'Old Nick', as he was sometimes disparagingly referred to by Wilson, gave the report legitimacy by putting his name to the first section. Despite Nicholson's initials, the tone and style suggests that he had either become so convinced of his DMO's case that he began to sound like him or, more likely, Wilson did the drafting. Either way, the General Staff argument assumed that if Britain remained neutral Germany would 'in all probability' defeat France and that Belgium and Holland might be annexed. Although Russia was expected to come in alongside France her slow pace of mobilisation would make no material difference to German success. In the

11 Greenhalgh, *Foch*, pp. 9-10.
12 Wilson diary, 2, 3 December 1909.
13 Ibid., *passim*.
14 Greenhalgh, *Foch*, pp.10, 81.
15 Huguet, *Britain and the War*, p. 129.
16 Wilson diary, 12 October 1910.
17 Greenhalgh, *Foch*, p. 10.
18 Wilson diary, 13 and 27 October 1910.
19 TNA CAB 38/19/47: 'The Military aspect of the Continental problem', Memorandum by the General Staff, 15 August 1911.
20 Wilson diary, 9 Aug. 1911 (original emphasis)

long-run this 'single-handed war' would 'prove fatal to this country.' If, alternatively, Britain became an active ally of France, Anglo-French sea power could dominate German supply lines, damage German morale and, over time, wear down the German economy.[21] Intervention by a small British expeditionary force could play a significant role, but only if it came into action at the same time as the French and Germans. Any delay in mobilisation while the French fought alone would negate the value of British support: 'We ought to be able to mobilize as soon as the French and Germans, and put our whole available strength of 6 divisions, 1 cavalry division, and army troops into the field so as to be present at the opening actions...'[22]

Henry Wilson, as already noted, had an intimate knowledge of the Franco-German frontier. His personal recce tours, intelligence reports and additional material discussed during his frequent meetings with Foch added veracity to his argument His report explained how the heavily defended French forts at Épinal, Verdun and elsewhere made large stretches of the border problematic for invading forces. A limited number of suitable through roads would constrain the invaders to 31 divisions in the opening phase of the war. By the evening of the fifteenth day, however, German strength would have risen to 84 divisions, thus the importance of British forces arriving on the battlefield promptly. While the hour of mobilisation was a matter for the Secretary of State for War, Haldane 'should be fully aware of the difference it will make to the course of the campaign whether we mobilize early or late. It is scarcely too much to say that the difference may be that of victory or defeat.'[23] Wilson summed up as follows:

> A war between Germany and France alone would almost certainly end in disaster to France, even should Russia try to help her ally.
>
> A war between Germany on the one hand and France and England on the other, with Russia of course playing her part, might, I think, end in the defeat of Germany provided three things are done:
>
> First - Our mobilization must be ordered the same day as France.
>
> Second - The whole six divisions, cavalry division, and army troops complete must be sent at once, all details having been worked out beforehand.
>
> Third - Arrangement must be made to enable the expeditionary force to maintain its effective throughout the war, and if possible other formations from home, from India, or from the dominions should be brought to the theatre of operations as rapidly as possible.[24]

The result of this study was the infamous meeting of the Committee of Imperial Defence (CID) of 23 August 1911.[25] This meeting, chaired by the Prime Minister, exposed Wilson's verbal dexterity and grasp of his brief as DMO to the most senior political figures of the day, some of whom would make his career in the years to come. Alongside Asquith the audience included David Lloyd George, the Chancellor of the Exchequer, Grey, the Foreign Secretary, the Home

---

21   TNA CAB 38/19/47: 15 Aug. 1911, pp. 1-2.
22   Ibid., p. 2.
23   Ibid., p. 5.
24   Ibid., 15 August 1911, p. 6.
25   TNA CAB 38/19/49: Committee of Imperial Defence (CID), Minutes of 114th Meeting, 23 August 1911.

Secretary Winston Churchill, and Haldane from the War Office. Nicholson and Wilson were joined by Sir John French, then Inspector General of the Forces, to present the General Staff position. The 'Senior Service', which had also been asked to produce a paper on the issue, was represented by the First Lord of the Admiralty, the political head of the Royal Navy, Reginald McKenna, the First Sea Lord Admiral Sir Arthur Wilson, and Rear-Admiral Alexander Bethell, Director of Naval Intelligence.

This meeting was the first significant example of the silver-tongued Henry Wilson, only a temporary Brigadier-General at this time, using his brilliant diplomatic and rhetorical skills to persuade a group of experienced and naturally sceptical politicians of the rightness of his cause. By contrast, the apparent incompetence of his naval adversaries served to enhance his argument. Wilson used maps and the tables in his initial report to make the General Staff case that early British intervention alongside the French was essential. He demonstrated how even a small British expeditionary force might swing events in favour of the defenders in the early days of the campaign. More important, he argued, was the effect on both German and French morale if Britain stood side by side with the latter from the start. Wilson had the facts of his argument at his fingertips, and when questioned was able to call on his wide personal knowledge of the Franco-German frontier. His positive relationship with Foch and his familiarity with the planning of the French General Staff also impressed.

In response to the General Staff's original paper the Admiralty had produced a two-page denunciation which perceived the army's role as entirely subservient to the needs of the navy.[26] As far as Sir Arthur Wilson was concerned, the army's role ought to be to support the navy in its primary effort of destroying the enemy fleet and blockading its coastline. Under this plan military forces would be used to storm shore batteries, radio signalling stations and the like in defence of the fleet and to protect the British Isles from enemy raids. Landing an expeditionary force in France would negate this function. If a British force landed on French soil, it noted presciently, 'it cannot be withdrawn without great damage to our pride and national honour, and the tendency will be to make increasing sacrifices in men and material to support it.'[27] The First Sea Lord stressed the challenges of a British force working successfully with the French army and the constraints of French logistical infrastructure:

> If the proposed landing of the Expeditionary Force gave any hope of ensuring the final victory to France, and of marching in triumph to Berlin, it might be considered worthwhile to forgo the cooperation of the Army with the Navy and to accept the increased responsibility of the latter for the defence of the coast, but even the advocates of the scheme do not pretend that that is the case.[28]

Forearmed, Henry Wilson described his namesake's assessment as 'one of the most childish papers I have ever read.'[29] When the meeting opened the admiral and his political master McKenna illustrated the dysfunctional nature of British strategic planning in the run up to the

---

26   TNA CAB 38/19/48: 'The Military Aspect of the Continental Problem: Remarks by the Admiralty,' 21 August 1911.
27   Ibid., p. 1.
28   Ibid., p. 2.
29   Wilson diary, 21 August 1911.

Great War. Sir Arthur Wilson dismissed the General Staff request for an assurance that the proposed expeditionary force of six divisions, plus a cavalry division, could be transported across the English Channel in the earliest stages of a future war. The navy could 'spare no men, no officers and no ships' to assist the army. The whole naval force would be deployed containing the enemy in the North Sea. McKenna, who claimed to be unaware of the Staff plans, emphasised that the Naval Transportation Department would be unable to help in any way for at least a week after the outbreak of war – the period Wilson and his colleagues saw as fundamental to the effectiveness of any British intervention. An evidently amazed Nicholson said discussions had been going on between the General Staff and the Royal Navy's Directors of Transport and Naval Intelligence since 1909. He thought these issues had been resolved. Sir Arthur Wilson also pleaded ignorance of the army scheme, saying he had heard something of the kind had been 'mooted' but it had been abandoned. This was too much for the Prime Minister. Asquith said that since 1908 the General Staff had been emphatic about the need to mobilise and deploy its forces immediately on the outbreak of war. He was 'at a loss to understand why it should be supposed that the Fleet would not be mobilising at the same time.'[30]

With the naval team in the doldrums Henry Wilson spent the rest of the morning presenting the General Staff's proposals for the rapid mobilisation and deployment of the Expeditionary Force to France. Questioned on points of fact and of interpretation by Lloyd George, Grey, Churchill, McKenna and Haldane, Wilson had ready answers, with great command of detail. Maurice Hankey, who attended as Naval Assistant Secretary, noted that 'from that time onward there was never any doubt what would be the Grand Strategy in the event of our being drawn into a war.' Although unconvinced by the 'witty and debonair' DMO's arguments, he acknowledged that henceforth it was clear that the expeditionary force would indeed be sent to France, and promptly.[31]

When the First Sea Lord's turn came, he outlined the Admiralty's main objections to the General Staff plan. Firstly, he feared 'panic' among the civilian population if the entire army was dispatched to the continent on the outbreak of war; this would circumscribe naval operations at a crucial point. Secondly, he was concerned that the absence of regular troops in Britain would make the country vulnerable to small enemy raids, again impacting naval operations. Finally, if the Expeditionary Force was deployed, there would be no trained troops available to help the Royal Navy carry out its war plans. The fact that the first objection was clearly a matter for political rather than military judgement seems to have escaped his attention. As for the navy's own plans, it has been suggested that the Admiral's incompetent presentation, contrasted with Henry Wilson's brilliance as a lecturer, resulted in victory for the General Staff. While this must have been part of the reason, a closer look at the Admiralty's strategy is revealing. Naval planners seem to have been stuck in a nineteenth century mindset. The idea in principle was uncontroversial, a close blockade of the whole of the north German coastline with the expectation of a decisive sea battle should the German fleet decide to emerge from its home ports. Where the scheme ran into criticism from both the soldiers and the majority of the politicians at the meeting was the notion that in order for the blockade to be effective the British needed to attack, neutralise and occupy enemy forts and communications centres in

30   TNA CAB 38/19/49.
31   Lord Hankey, *The Supreme Command*, 2 Vols. (London: George Allen & Unwin, 1961). (Vol. I) pp. 81-82.

both the North Sea and on the German coast. Sir Arthur proposed using marines to take the island of Heligoland and using units of 'highly mobile' British Regular troops to secure other important objectives. These included the island of Wangeroog which commanded the entrance to the strategically vital rivers Weser and Jade. The coastal stronghold of Schillighorn would have to be taken, as would the port of Busüm at the mouth of the Kiel Canal. Admiral Wilson even suggested taking the port of Wilhelmshaven, the primary base of the German High Seas Fleet.[32] A least one division of regular troops would be required to take these objectives, according to naval planners, plus artillery to defend them against German counter-attacks. The whole exercise, it was estimated, could detain up to 10 German divisions which would otherwise be used in the invasion of France.

Even the formal and staid minutes of the CID reveal the amazement of the admiral's audience. Hankey described the navy's plan as 'having been cocked up [sic] in the dinner hour.'[33] Nicholson, the CIGS, denounced the proposals as 'madness'. With no guarantee of night time protection, small detachments would be easily overwhelmed. While 'this class of operation possibly had some value a century ago, when land communications were indifferent...now, when they were excellent, they were doomed to failure.' Naval confidence that the fleet could knock out shore fortifications and protect landing forces was 'overrated'. It was difficult enough for trained field artillery to support troops and the ships would 'find it difficult to discriminate even between friend and foe.' Considering the desperate difficulties faced by the Royal Navy when it attempted to take out coastal fortifications in order to force the Dardanelles in early 1915, 'Old Nick's' observations were remarkably foresighted. Churchill was equally sceptical, dismissing the admiralty's suggestion to besiege Wilhelmshaven as 'surely out of the question'. Sir Archibald 'Archie' Murray, then Director of Military Training, was summoned to assure the meeting that if the bulk of the regular army was deployed to France, the Territorial Force was more than capable of dealing with potential German raids.

Henry Wilson's proposals were far from perfect, but the confusing and inconsistent presentation of the admiralty alternative combined with Sir Arthur's poor performance, meant the General Staff argument won the day.[34] Recent scholarship has argued that Sir Arthur Wilson's argument was, rather than reflective of reactionary myopia, progressive strategic thinking.[35] Convincing though this argument is, at the time the admiral's audience viewed it in an entirely negative light.

Thereafter, Britain's already established policy that it would go to France's aid in the event of a German attack morphed into an understanding that the help would be immediate. Churchill, who had further discussions with the DMO over the next fortnight, wrote that from then on the War Office began planning for the deployment of the Expeditionary Force in earnest, right down to where the mobilised soldiers would drink their coffee.[36] While Henry Wilson's career

32   TNA CAB 38/19/49, p. 12 and *passim*.
33   Hankey, *Supreme Command* (Vol. I) p. 81. This phrase has been described as a typographical error; Hankey intended to describe the plan as 'cooked up'; David Gethin Morgan-Owen, 'Cooked up in the Dinner Hour? Sir Arthur Wilson's Plan Reconsidered', *English Historical Review*, Vol. CXXX, (545), pp. 865-906; p. 855.
34   Jeffery, *Wilson*, p. 97.
35   Morgan-Owen, 'Cooked up in the Dinner Hour?', *passim*.
36   Wilson diary, 28 August 1911; Churchill, *World Crisis*, p. 62.

flourished as a result of the 'profound impression' he had made at the 23 August meeting, that of his namesake was holed below the waterline.[37] An undoubtedly brave man, Sir Arthur Wilson had won the Victoria Cross in 1884 for holding off Mahdist rebels with his sword and then his fists. A brilliant naval tactician, he was ill-suited to the political cut and thrust required of a First Sea Lord.[38] He had been adamantly opposed to Haldane's wish to establish a Naval War Staff, along the lines of the Army's General Staff. The CID meeting demonstrated to the Prime Minister the desperate need for a body to develop and co-ordinate naval strategy. As a result McKenna, who loyally supported Sir Arthur, was forced to swap his post as Lord of the Admiralty for the Home Office with Churchill. The latter had long coveted the Admiralty role, and after the ill-fated CID meeting complained that the Royal Navy's leadership was 'cocksure, insouciant and apathetic.'[39] One of Churchill's first actions on taking up his post at the Admiralty was to sack Admiral Sir Arthur Wilson VC. Soon after he established a Naval War Staff.[40] The events of the summer of 1911 confirmed 'irrevocably' Britain's 'Continental Commitment' in support of France, advanced the planning for the Expeditionary Force, and 'powerfully' established Wilson's reputation with leading politicians, particularly Lloyd George and Churchill.[41]

Over the next two years the organisation for the Expeditionary Force speeded up. Wilson implemented British policy with an enthusiasm it had not enjoyed before; he did not create it. Churchill at the Admiralty ensured a much more joined up army and navy approach to planning.[42] Wilson continued his diplomatic duties, visiting France regularly and liaising with both soldiers and politicians. Foch, Joffre and his deputy General Noël de Curières de Castlenau often hosted Wilson on these visits, seven of which he made in 1913 alone. The familiarity with key figures in the French army that he developed during this period were to be invaluable in the coming conflict. While Wilson's liaison skills were bearing fruit with Britain's allies, and his organisational talents bringing order and vitality to the army's planning for intervention in the event of war, a political storm clouds was about to break in his homeland.

The consequences of the so-called 'Curragh Incident', were far reaching for the British civil-military partnership. They were also highly damaging for Wilson's burgeoning career. In 1912, Prime Minister H.H. Asquith's Liberal government, reliant on the votes of Irish Parliamentary Party MPs to stay in power, introduced a bill to grant Home Rule to Ireland. This proposal of a limited form of devolved government met with such fierce opposition from Ulster Unionists that Ireland was on the brink of civil war by the beginning of 1914. The events of this crisis have received an extensive airing in the historiography and need not be repeated in detail here.[43] In short form, in March 1914 a group of 60 Anglo-Irish army officers of 3rd Cavalry Brigade stationed at the Curragh camp outside Dublin threatened to resign their commissions rather than lead their troops north to coerce Ulster into accepting Home Rule.[44] The brigade's CO

37   Hankey, *Supreme Command*, (vol. I) p. 80.
38   Andrew Lambert, *ODNB*, 2004.
39   Churchill to Lloyd George, 14 September 1911 cited in Roswell, *Hankey*, p. 102.
40   Hankey, *Supreme Command* (vol. I) p. 83.
41   Jeffery, *Wilson*, p. 92.
42   Collier, *Brasshat*, pp. 118-9.
43   See esp. Beckett, *The Curragh Incident*; Jeffery, *Wilson*, pp. 121-6; Strachan, *Politics*, pp. 112-17 and *passim*.
44   Sheffield and Spencer, 'Soldiers and Politicians', p. 85.

Hubert Gough went to London and demanded and received assurances that the government would not order the army to use coercion. Those giving the assurances, the CIGS Sir John French, the Adjutant General Sir John Spencer Ewart and the Secretary of State for War J.E.B. Seely, had acted beyond their remit, contradictory to government policy, and were forced to resign. Asquith immediately repudiated the agreement, but the issue had destabilised the government's position and embarrassed the Prime Minister. Henry Wilson was a key figure in the affair. A die-hard Unionist, he had been a cheerleader for Gough and his fellow officers and had lobbied French in their support. At the height of the crisis Wilson had dinner with Lord Milner, another ardent Unionist, and discussed the issue 'for hours' Two days later he confided the latest details of his meetings with Sir John French and others to Bonar Law.[45]

Hubert Gough and his brother Johnnie, who was also embroiled in the incident, took the view that once the issue blew up Wilson took cover leaving them and others to face the flak. Johnnie, another Rifle Brigade officer, had been on good terms with Wilson before this affair. He, Rawlinson and Wilson played golf together on Boxing Day 1913.[46] After the Curragh the Goughs' relationship with Wilson was strained, with Johnnie apparently never speaking to Wilson again.[47] In his bitter memoir Hubert Gough accused Wilson of encouraging the revolt 'to refuse any concessions by Mr Asquith's Government, while he never emerged from the background.'[48] The criticism is not unreasonable. Wilson had encouraged others in their threats of resignation, yet failed to do make a similar commitment himself, even though he considered how he might have done so.[49] He also encouraged Sir John French to resign, lobbying the views of officers at the Staff College in support.[50] 'Squiff' as Wilson contemptuously called the Prime Minister in his diaries and correspondence, believed him to be the true ringleader of this nadir in civil-military relations, dismissing Field Marshal Lord Roberts, another key participant, as 'in a dangerous condition of senile frenzy.'[51] According to Asquith, Wilson was at one time or another 'a poisonous mischief-maker', a 'clever ruffian', and 'that serpent'.[52] It was Wilson, therefore, and not the other prime-movers Hubert and Johnnie Gough, who was blackballed for his role in the 'Incident'. Wilson's critics thought the judgement fair and overdue reward for his meddling directly in political affairs.

In the days that followed he had meetings with a number of leading Unionist politicians and other sympathisers in which he gloated over the damage which had been done to Asquith and his government. Gloating might have given Wilson short-term satisfaction, but the consequences for him were long-lasting. The result was that Wilson spent the years 1914-17 in a series of what to him were largely unrewarding roles. From the perspective of Britain's war effort, the results were more mixed.

45   Wilson diary, 19 and 21 March 1914.
46   Ibid., 26 December 1913.
47   Farrar-Hockley, *Goughie*, p. 102
48   Gough, *Soldiering On*, p. 172; Farrar-Hockley, *Goughie*, p. 106.
49   Wilson diary, 21 March 1914.
50   Ibid, 28 and 29 March 1914.
51   Asquith to Venetia Stanley, 21 March 1914, in Michael & Eleanor Brock, (eds.), *H.H. Asquith: Letters to Venetia Stanley* (Oxford: Oxford University Press, 1982), pp. 58-9.
52   Ibid., 6 November 1918, p. 311, 20 December 1914, p. 333, 28 December 1914, p. 342.

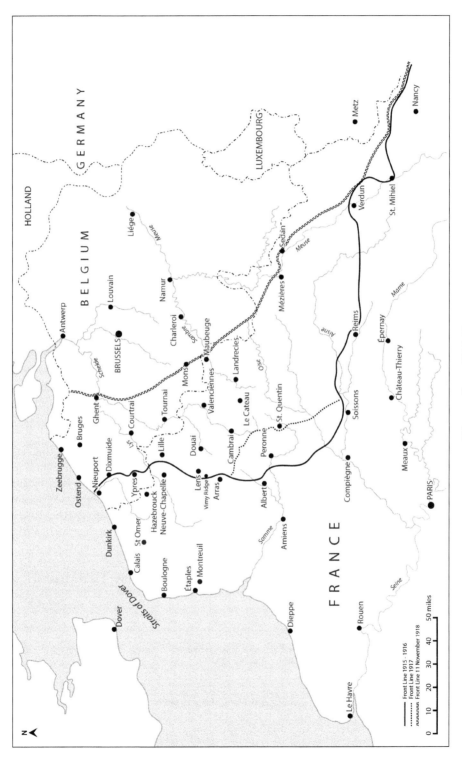

Western Front 1915-18.

3

The First Eighteen Months[1]

As DMO Wilson had planned meticulously for the immediate dispatch of the BEF to fight alongside the much bigger French Army as soon as war was declared. When put to the test in early August 1914 the scheme went like clockwork. When the senior command of the BEF was confirmed, with Sir John French as C-in-C, Wilson was appointed to the new and incongruous position of 'Sub-Chief of Staff' to Archibald Murray.[2] The appointment involved considerable wrangling, with Wilson clearly disappointed that his ambition to be CoS had been stymied. He was convinced Asquith was behind the decision. This seems highly likely, although there is no primary evidence of the fact.[3] French was a friend and something of a mentor. He too had served under Roberts when the latter became C-in-C in South Africa. French was 12 years older than Wilson, and his diary references, even negative ones, were often couched in the affectionate terms reserved for an elder sibling.[4] Wilson, like many of French's fellow officers, admired his bravery but was often frustrated, sometimes irritated, by his mercurial temper and mood swings. Nonetheless, they developed a close association in the decade before the war.[5]

Murray's performance during the retreat from Mons in late August was disappointing, at one point he broke down under the pressure. Over time Sir John's confidence in him waned while his opinion of more self-assured Henry Wilson grew. The unfortunate Murray was, according to a recent monograph, 'an able, honourable, dedicated man who was in the wrong job, with the wrong commander, in the wrong place, at the wrong time.[6] According to another authority the ambitious and self-serving Wilson deliberately undermined his superior. Several of Wilson's colleagues from his time as DMO formed the nucleus of the staff of the Operations section at GHQ. This partisan group looked to Wilson rather than Murray for guidance, something that wore down the latter's authority. Thus Wilson gained undue influence over Field Marshal French

---

1   This chapter is based upon Gary Sheffield and John Spencer, 'Soldiers and Politicians in Strife' in Liddle, (ed.), *Britain and a Widening War,* at pp. 83-99.
2   Jeffery, *Wilson,* pp.132-133.
3   Wilson diary, 30 July 1914.
4   The best biography of French is Holmes, *Little Field Marshal;* see also Cassar, *Tragedy.*
5   Badsey, *Doctrine,* p. 199.
6   John Bourne, 'Major General Sir Archibald Murray', in Spencer Jones (ed.), *Stemming the Tide: Officers and Leadership in the British Expeditionary Force 1914,* (Solihull: Helion & Company, 2013), pp.68-9.

to the detriment of the BEF.[7] While accepting that Murray was undermined by Wilson, a recent essay has argued convincingly that there is little evidence of Wilson's 'influence' resulting in Sir John changing policy in response to his advice.[8]

When it became clear at the end of 1914 that Murray was not up to the demands of the role of French's CoS, Wilson hoped his moment had arrived.[9] This time there is no doubt that Asquith vetoed his appointment, which went instead to Robertson.[10] Wilson recorded that he and Robertson discussed which of them might get Murray's job but neither felt they would be able to work with Sir John 'the chance of a lifetime & two men in a car both refusing it.'[11] Robertson, who had acquitted himself well as QMG, finally took the post and brought administrative order where Murray had presided over chaos, impressing Sir John and visitors alike with his administrative efficiency.[12] Importantly for their future relationship Wilson had to make do with the much less prestigious job of the BEF's Principal Liaison Officer at French Army Headquarters, the *Grand Quartier General* (GQG). He clearly felt cheated by Asquith and bemoaned the loss of a job he had 'worked for and dreamt of for many years.'[13] As a consolation prize, he was promoted to (temporary) Lieutenant-General and wrote, somewhat self-deludingly, that the new role made him 'much bigger and more powerful than before.'[14] For his part, Robertson was aware that he had not been French's first choice.[15]

In early 1915 relations between the French and British military high commands were, as might be expected in coalition warfare, fragile and sometimes strained. French losses in the first five months of the war had been enormous[16]. Although British forces on the Western Front were increasing, with elements of Kitchener's 'New Armies' expected by the summer, France thought her ally could and should do more. Britain's senior soldiers sometimes struggled to hide their irritation with what they considered to be unreasonable French expectations. Unfortunately for both countries Sir John French was a difficult character who found it easier to fall out with friends than to adapt to fighting as junior member of a coalition in an industrialised war.[17] The appointment of the Francophile Wilson to smooth the rocky road of Entente relations was, in this respect, inspired. It was the formalisation of a function he had carried out unofficially in

7   Nikolas Gardner, *Trial by Fire: Command and the British Expeditionary Force in 1914* (Westport, CT: Praeger, 2004), pp. 5-7.
8   Brian Curragh, 'Henry Wilson's War', in Spencer Jones (ed.), *Stemming the Tide: Officers and Leadership in the British Expeditionary Force 1914* (Solihull: Helion & Company, 2013), p. 87.
9   J.M. Bourne, *Britain and the Great War 1914-1918* (London: Edward Arnold, 1989), p. 27.
10   Wilson diary, 9 January 1915.
11   Ibid., 17 January 1915.
12   Churchill Archives Centre (hereafter CAC), Hankey Papers, (HNKY 4/7), Esher to Hankey, March 1915 (precise date obscured by hole punch in original notepaper).
13   Wilson diary, 30 January 1915.
14   Ibid., 31 December 1915.
15   Field Marshal Sir William Robertson, *From Private to Field-Marshal* (London: Constable, 1921), p. 218.
16   French casualties for 1914 have been estimated at 300,000 killed, 600,000 wounded, missing or captured: Alistair Horne, *The Price of Glory: Verdun 1916* (London: Penguin, 1993 [1962]), p.19. British casualties for the same period were 89,864 killed, wounded, missing or captured. Sir J.E. Edmonds, *Official History of the War: Military Operations France and Belgium 1914*, Vol. II, (London: Macmillan,1925), p. 469.
17   Holmes, *Little Field Marshal*.

the early months of the war 'smoothing out differences between the headquarters as they arose.' Much less credible is the suggestion by one of Wilson's contemporaries that he was now so influential that he was 'virtually [British] Commander-in-Chief under Joffre.'[18] While it was not the job he wanted, Wilson nonetheless held the post for almost the whole of 1915, a year of costly disappointments for the Allies. His talent for diplomacy was put to the test regularly.

Callwell's assessment was that even before this appointment Wilson had been combining his Sub-Chief role with that of 'principal intermediary between GHQ and GQG':

> Wilson was so essentially a persona grata at French GQG and amongst French superior commanders in general, that he possessed altogether exceptional qualifications for filling the post of principal liaison officer between Sir John's headquarters and Chantilly [Joffre's HQ]. That, in view of the relations existing between the leaders and the General Staffs of the two allied hosts, such liaison work needed to be in skilled and tactful hands had been plainly demonstrated during the previous months.[19]

On taking up the new position the French C-in-C Joffre told him he was 'the best known and best beloved officer to the French Army'.[20] As the '"political dimension" became increasingly significant in the wider prosecution of the war, so too did the value of his talents'.[21]

'Wully' Robertson quickly brought administrative rigour to the CoS function. Lord Esher wrote that the C-in-C liked Robertson's methods: 'French gives his general instructions. Robertson comes in with a few questions on half a sheet of note paper. They are answered, and everything goes forward'.[22] Wilson was therefore free to concentrate on improving relations between the British and French commanders and their staffs; a much-needed function. The French had a negative opinion of their ally, he noted, because 'of our want of enterprise… this hostility must be stopped.'[23] Conveniently, in 1915 Foch the French colleague with whom Wilson had the closest relationship, was commander of the French Northern Army Group, fighting alongside the BEF. Their established friendship meant 'they were able to communicate honestly with each other.'[24] Such frankness stood them in good stead throughout 1915. As an example of the trust Wilson engendered, soon after taking up his new post he was permitted a tour along whole of their line from Amiens to the Swiss border: 'No other officer in any army, not even a Russian, has been allowed to go down the French line except me.'[25]

In his biography Callwell portrayed Wilson as a kind of unofficial Chief of Staff, a rival to Robertson 'unhampered by responsibility, whose relations with Sir John were especially close and cordial' and who in 1914 'had actually been more in Sir John's confidence than any member

18   Lieutenant-Commander Wedgwood, 'Report on visit to France and Belgium, 8 October 1915, cited in William Philpott, *Anglo-French Relations and Strategy on the Western Front, 1914-18* (London: Macmillan, 1996). p. 96.
19   Ibid., (Vol. I), p. 204.
20   Callwell, *Wilson* (Vol. I), pp. 203-4.
21   Jeffery, *Wilson*, p.144.
22   CAC, Hankey Papers, (HNKY 4/7), Esher to Hankey, March 1915.
23   Wilson diary, 2 February 1915.
24   Elizabeth Greenhalgh, *Foch in Command: The Forging of a First World War General* (Cambridge: Cambridge University Press, 2011), pp.10,81.
25   Wilson to Lady Wilson, 21 January 1915, quoted in Callwell, *Wilson* (Vol. I), p. 203.

of the Head-quarters Staff.'[26] This image of Wilson as Svengali to an impressionable chief has persisted in the historiography. Those who encountered him were often disarmed by his easy charm and carried away by his rhetoric. Douglas Haig's intelligence chief John Charteris wrote of an early encounter:

> At GHQ itself things are very unsatisfactory. Sir J. French seems altogether in Wilson's pocket. Wilson lives with French, and Robertson in another mess altogether. I came out in the same boat as Wilson on Thursday and we talked all the way across – rather he talked and I listened. He is an extraordinarily amusing and interesting conversationalist. I can easily understand how he fascinates those who do not know him well. But it all leads nowhere.[27]

Wilson certainly talked, but it appears that Johnnie French ignored the advice as often as he took it up. All too often he complained in his diary that his chief went his own way. He had access, but the BEF's commander was too independent a character to dance to the ministrations of others. There is no doubt that Sir John French, like so many others, enjoyed Wilson's company and preferred it to that of the dour ex-ranker Robertson. In April 1915 he invited Wilson to join him in his mess.[28] In his memoirs Robertson, who was excluded and ate with his own team, made light of the snub, but it must have rankled and meant that as time went on and Sir John's star dimmed Robertson was one of those happy to see him go.[29] In fact, Wilson's influence with the French, especially Foch and to some extent Joffre, was far more important.

The year 1915 was dominated by a series of large and costly French offensives in support of which the BEF fought four battles of their own, Neuve Chapelle (10-13 March), Aubers Ridge (9-10 May), Festubert (15-25 May) and Loos (25 September-16 October). In addition, the allies took a mauling at the Second Battle of Ypres in the last week of April. Each of these encounters to a greater or lesser extent exposed the BEF's shortcomings in both manpower and materiel, particularly heavy artillery and high explosive shells. In the words of the Official Historian, shortages of all kinds meant that French and his commanders 'never had the means to conduct defence or undertake offence with reasonable confidence.'[30] Wilson concerned himself directly with the tensions surrounding these actions, shuttling between the BEF's headquarters at St Omer and Joffre's at Chantilly and acting as unofficial translator for the two C-in-Cs during their occasional meetings to discuss forthcoming operations.

The events leading up to the Battle of Neuve Chapelle provide a good illustration of the type of work Wilson did in 1915, and its often frustrating and disappointing outcome. Mutual distrust between French and Joffre meant that apart from agreeing on the primacy of the Western Front their relationship was bad.[31] On 19 February, with Wilson fresh into the liaison role, Joffre

---

26 Callwell, *Wilson*, p.205.
27 Charteris, *At GHQ*, 24 April 1915, p. 87.
28 Jeffery, *Wilson*, p. 147.
29 Robertson, *Private to Field-Marshal*, p. 222 and Charteris, *GHQ*, p. 87; Robertson's predecessor Archie Murray had suffered similar treatment, once again in favour of Wilson. See Bourne, 'Murray', p. 65.
30 Sir J. E. Edmonds & Captain G.C. Wynne, *Official History of the War: Military Operations France and Belgium, 1915*, Vol. I (London: Macmillan, 1927), p. 3.
31 Greenhalgh, *Foch*, p. 100.

asked for the BEF to take over additional line by relieving Foch's IX Corps near Ypres.[32] This had been agreed in principle the previous month and the French needed the men for an offensive against the Vimy heights around Arras. The attack was planned for March and the British intended a supporting offensive further north in the area of La Bassée. Wilson was sympathetic to the principle of taking on more line, but dismissed the extent of the proposal, and that it should be completed by the end of February, as 'impossible'.[33] Ever sensitive to perceived slights, Sir John appeared to have been as much offended by the tone of the French request as its content and made clear he would not comply, citing lack of troops. Wilson condemned Joffre's letter as 'a stupid one, inaccurate in some important details and rather hectoring in tone'.[34] Nonetheless, it wouldn't do to refuse to help 'in the face of the reinforcements, giving a total of 36 Batt[alion]s, exclusive of the Canadians who have just finished arriving.'[35] He met Foch on succeeding days in an effort to find a solution but Sir John was adamant that he would do nothing to relieve the French until 1 April, at the earliest.[36] Anxious to avoid a major rift in Anglo-French relations Wilson and Foch worked to intercede between their respective C-in-Cs:

> I asked Foch as a personal favour to me to write to Joffre at once…begging Joffre not to be angry, but to write a private line (through me) to Sir John, saying how disappointed he was, and begging him to reconsider and to help if he could, as success at Arras depended upon it. Foch promised to do this at once.[37]

The note had no effect and on 27 February French was told the regular 29th Division he was expecting to come to France would instead go to the Dardanelles for the upcoming Gallipoli campaign.[38] Sir John's response was that not only would he not take over the IX Corps trenches but that he now also wanted the French to relieve some of his cavalry units. Wilson broke the bad news to Foch and drafted an explanation for Joffre to the effect that Lord Kitchener, unaware that the 29th Division was earmarked to relieve French forces massing for a major offensive, had decided to send them elsewhere. Understandably exasperated, Wilson wrote in his diary: 'I cannot do any more, and this is our last chance. Sir John has not told Kitchener about the projected attacks, beyond the vaguest outlines, so it is possible that when Kitchener realises all this he may change.'[39] Sir John's failure to communicate with Kitchener would blight British policy throughout 1915.[40]

In fact, all that changed was that Joffre, unmoved by Wilson's creative attempt to explain away Sir John's obduracy, postponed his proposed Arras offensive, citing the BEF's failure to

---

32   Holmes, *Little Field Marshal*, p. 269.
33   Wilson diary, 20 February 1915.
34   Ibid., 21 February 1915.
35   Ibid., 20 February 1915.
36   Ibid., 21, 22 February 1915.
37   Ibid., 22 February 1915.
38   Edmonds & Wynne, *Military Operations France and Belgium 1915* (Vol. I), p. 72.
39   Wilson diary, 28 February 1915.
40   John Spencer, 'Friends Dis-United: Johnnie French, Wully Robertson and "K of K" in Spencer Jones (ed.), *Courage Without Glory: The British Army on the Western Front 1915* (Solihull: Helion & Company, 2013).

relieve his forces.[41] As a result, the British attack, originally intended as a supporting effort, went ahead on 10 March. The Battle of Neuve Chapelle began positively but quickly ran out of steam thanks to limited artillery and a shortage of reserves.[42] Foch provided some artillery support but was constrained in what he could do because 'Joffre had been so angered by Sir John's refusal to relieve the French that he gave strict orders that Foch should not undertake any action around Arras.'[43] As the battle was coming to an end, Foch offered eight batteries of heavy guns and wanted to know where to send them: 'Sir John would not tell him anything, said he wanted to keep his moves and Haig's secret. As far as I can judge, our fight at Neuve Chapelle is finished. We have neither infantry nor gun ammunition to go on with it. This is a disappointing business.'[44]

In the coming weeks Wilson worked with some success to mend relations with the French, as ever using Foch as both sounding board and, when necessary, intermediary, with Joffre. Foch likewise used his friendship with Wilson to at least remain on reasonable terms with Sir John French.[45] Wilson's diplomatic skills came to fore again when the French C-in-C told him that he intended writing to his British counterpart and to tell him bluntly that the BEF was doing far too little to help. Knowing only too well Sir John's likely reaction to such a tone, Wilson persuaded Joffre to 'look at the picture in a different way'. By listing the many trials and tribulations facing French: 'I got Joffre round to quite a different frame of mind. I told him to give us orders, but without appearing to do so, not to refer to our numbers or dispositions but to refer to Sir John's loyalty and to leave the rest to his good heart – and me.'[46] Thanks to Wilson's undoubted diplomatic skills, while he was in post relations between the two Allies never again reached the nadir of February-March 1915; a noteworthy achievement in itself.

As if the challenges posed by their German adversaries were not enough, things were made worse for the BEF by the often-dysfunctional relationships between its senior commanders and their political masters. Sir John French's relationship with Field Marshal Lord Kitchener got off to an infamously poor start in 1914 and went from bad to worse the following year.[47] Wilson succeeded in crossing swords with 'K of K' before the Expeditionary Force even left for France, over a meeting he had had with the French liaison officer Colonel Huguet. Wilson condemned Kitchener as a 'd[amned] fool' in his diary and the two were on unfriendly terms thereafter.[48] It meant that Wilson was in no position to pour balm on the fractious relationship between Kitchener and French, although their relationship did improve marginally as the year progressed.[49] This debilitating feud reached its climax in May, with the so-called shells scandal which embarrassed both Kitchener and Asquith, hastening the end of Britain's last Liberal government.[50]

41   Edmonds & Wynne, *Military Operations 1915* (Vol. I), p. 73; Holmes, *Little Field Marshal*, p. 270.
42   Ibid., pp. 74-156.
43   Greenhalgh, *Foch*, p. 102.
44   Wilson diary, 13 March 1915.
45   Greenhalgh, *Foch*, pp. 106-9.
46   Wilson diary, 23 March 1915.
47   Holmes, *Little Field Marshal*, esp. pp. 231-5.
48   Wilson diary, 7 August 1914.
49   Callwell, *Wilson* (Vol. I), p. 161.
50   Holmes, *Little Field Marshal*, pp. 287-9; see also Peter Fraser, 'The British "Shells Scandal" of 1915', *Canadian Journal of History*, 28 (1983), pp. 69-86.

In the summer the French and British began discussions for another offensive. Wilson recognised the need for the BEF to play its full part and told Robertson: 'One thing was clear – if the French were left under the impression that a serious attack was going to be made, and then it was not made, it would lead to serious trouble.' He repeated his concerns to Sir John, stressing the need to inform the French of his intentions, and that 'a serious attack was essential…I rubbed in the danger of failing the French'.[51] The result was the Battle of Loos which began on 25 September in support of a much larger French offensive to the south.[52] Insufficient artillery support meant Haig, who was commanding the British forces, was forced to use gas in the hope of clearing the German trenches. The tactic failed and the British, despite some early localised success, suffered heavy losses. Haig blamed the failure on the handling of the reserve force, laying responsibility with the C-in-C. Four days before the offensive Wilson wrote presciently:

> Apparently Haig thinks he will catch them 'quiet' at 5am and does not want to disturb them! The fact is that Haig is unfit to 'mount an attack'.. He has failed every time and this is crowning folly. Having based his attack on gas he is not able to see the difference if he can't use it.[53]

On 29 September he summed up the situation thus:

> Haig claims if he had had command of these [reserves] a day or two before he would have pushed in … and smashed the line. Rawly evidently thinks so.[54] I imagine Robertson says so and thinks so and I think he is working all he can to get rid of Sir J. and put in Haig. My own opinion is that Haig's attack was a muddle[d] business, that he was to a great extent depending on gas and XI Corps which was Sir John's Reserve which he had no right to depend on, and that Sir J. ought to have made this clear to him.[55]

Wilson's antipathy towards Asquith grew throughout 1915 with Wilson regularly condemning 'Squiff' in both diary and private correspondence. At the heart of his criticism was the shortage of men and material for the Western Front. Wilson believed the reasons were the failure to bring in conscription, something Wilson considered as evidence of Asquith's refusal to treat the war seriously, and the government's diversion of resources to other theatres. He was not alone in opposing the Gallipoli campaign, condemning it as 'madness' and adding that 'Winston [Churchill] ought to be and must be *dégomme* for this'.[56] The failed landings at Suvla Bay in August 1915 proved the Gallipoli campaign was 'a vile and dangerous mess'. He was even more opposed to the Allied campaign in Macedonia and was clear who he thought responsible for

---

51   Wilson diary, 15 August 1915.
52   For the full story of the battle see Nick Lloyd, *Loos 1915* (Stroud: History Press, 2008).
53   Wilson diary, 21 September 1915.
54   Rawlinson commanded IV Corps at Loos.
55   Wilson diary, 29 September 1915.
56   Ibid., 7 April; *dégomme*: to be dismissed.

both 'sideshows': 'It is an awful thing for a great country to be governed, at a time of crisis, by knaves and fools, and these only of the second order.'[57]

As the year progressed, Wilson's diary and correspondence became increasingly critical of the inconsistent and essentially *ad hoc* nature of Allied policymaking. He witnessed first-hand the misunderstandings, disagreements and self-interested initiatives of the French and British high commands, and the lack of political direction at home. If the politicians could not provide clarity and structure, he believed, soldiers such as he needed to come up with some answers. In October he sent the first of a series of letters to the Andrew Bonar Law proposing the establishment of a 'Committee of Six' to co-ordinate Anglo-French strategy. It would comprise the two countries' foreign ministers, war ministers and C-in-Cs and neither government would embark on 'any enterprise' without this group being consulted:

> I don't want to be in the least alarmist but I do want to impress on you the fact that we are running into serious difficulties and difficulties which can and <u>must</u> be avoided if we want to win this war...We have now reached the point when neither country is going to be so lenient to the other's faults, and it is a very short distance from where we now stand to the point where both countries will be positively on the watch for each other's mistakes. Therefore I am uneasy and if my solution is not acceptable let some other be discovered, but I beg you to be under no illusion about the dangers that lie ahead of us, or about the disasters that are sure to come if we are content to drift.[58]

Despite his lobbying, neither politicians nor soldiers had the will or wherewithal to take up Wilson's idea.[59] He would have to wait another two years for the creation of the SWC with himself as its leading light before structured strategic policymaking came into being.

Reviewing Wilson's role in the early part of the war it is clear that he had both access to and influence over Sir John French, but that influence should not be overestimated. William Robertson was a resilient and efficient CoS who gained authority as Sir John's declined. Wilson was increasingly anxious about Wully's rise. In a jibe about Wilson's apparent Francophilia: 'Robertson blurted out that he thought I ought to be at Chantilly! [Joffre's HQ] That's it. R.[obertson] told me this morning that K. had told him that he was going to recast the Gen Staff at W[ar] O[ffice] as they did not know their business but he did not know who to move in as C[I]GS.'[60]

Wilson hoped that the post would be his, but it was not to be, as he predicted on 2 December: 'Esher now in favour of Robertson succeeding Murray. I seem to have dropped out of his picture! How amusing these fellows are.'[61] French's failures as C-in-C cost him his command when in the latter half of 1915 Haig, Robertson and to some extent Wilson, turned against

---

57   Wilson diary, 11 September and 10 October 1915.

58   PA, Bonar Law papers, (BL 51/4/310), 27 October 1915, Wilson to Bonar Law, see also (BL 51/5/34), 19 October 1915, Wilson to Bonar Law, (BL 52/1/10 and BL 117/1/27), 3 December 1915, Wilson to Bonar Law

59   William Philpott, 'Squaring the Circle: The Higher Co-Ordination of the Entente in the Winter of 1915-16', *English Historical Review*, 458 (114), (September 1999), pp. 875-898.

60   Wilson diary, 24 September 1915.

61   Ibid., 2 December 1915.

him; his overt politicking had damaged his cause.[62] At the end of the year Sir Douglas Haig replaced a discredited French as C-in-C and Wully Robertson became CIGS. Wilson accepted the consolation prize of command of IV Corps; his final diary entry for 1915 observed:

> I part from 1915 with no regret. To me, personally, it has been an unkind year, commencing with the offer by Sir John of C[hief of]G[eneral]S[taff] and [which] Squiff refused to allow, finishing with Robertson getting CIGS which at one time it looked as though I was certain to get, whether when Murray got it, or later, before Robertson got it. So long as we keep that cynical callous blackguard Asquith as PM we have a serious chance of losing the war. Wars <u>cannot</u> be won by INDECISION.[63]

That the Alliance survived the stresses of 1915 is at least in part due to Wilson's efforts and his excellent relations with the French in a difficult year. Unfortunately for him, not all his colleagues recognised or appreciated his efforts. Douglas Haig bemoaned Sir John French's inability to work closely with Joffre and appeared unconvinced that Wilson the diplomat was a satisfactory substitute.[64]

Arguably his greatest failure was his inability to persuade the Allied commanders and the politicians in London and Paris that much closer liaison, planning and ultimately unity of action were essential elements in achieving victory. For that he had to wait until the close of 1917 when he at last found an audience able to do more than simply applaud and encourage from the sidelines.

---

62 John Spencer, 'Friends Disunited: Johnnie French, Wully Robertson and "K. of K." in 1915', pp. 80-102 in Spencer Jones, (ed.), *Courage Without Glory: The British Army on the Western Front 1915* (Solihull: Helion & Company, 2015).

63 Wilson diary, 31 December 1915.

64 Haig diary, 17 October 1915, Sheffield & Bourne, *Haig Diaries*, p. 166.

4

Combat Command

For Henry Wilson, 1915 had been a disappointing year. At its close, instead of becoming the government's principal military adviser as he had hoped, he found himself shuffled off to command IV Corps which was deployed in a quiet sector of the Western Front south west of Béthune. It soon moved further south to the area close to the strategically important Vimy Ridge and the neighbouring city of Arras. A century later it is hard to see why Wilson thought he would become CIGS at this point. He and his main rival Robertson both lacked combat command experience, but the latter had served competently under Sir John French and appeared a logical choice to succeed Sir Archie Murray.[1] With Asquith still in Downing Street, albeit at the head of a coalition government, it was hardly likely that 'Squiff' would go out of his way to reward an officer who had loudly criticised him and his administration with such a senior position.[2] Maurice Hankey, the indispensable and ubiquitous Whitehall bureaucrat, believed the 'mistrust' Wilson had awakened during the Curragh Incident continued to haunt Wilson's career.[3]

Haig became C-in-C of the BEF and Rawlinson expected to be promoted to command First Army. It must have been particularly galling for Wilson to find himself being touted to replace his old friend and professional rival Rawly at IV Corps. Rawlinson supported the appointment, but Wilson admitted to his diary that: 'I would rather not be under Rawly & I hear they are going to make a XIV Corps with the Ulster Divn. in it down in the 3rd Army under Allenby & I would rather have that.' Two days later Rawlinson visited Wilson at GHQ in St Omer to tell him he was certain he would be offered a corps. He asked Rawlinson to intercede with Haig for the new XIV Corps, citing his personal interest in the Ulster Division, but the die was already cast.[4] In an illustration of the political influences on the British army at this time, both Bonar Law and Kitchener went out of their way to urge Wilson to accept a corps command.[5] He took over IV Corps on 22 December 1915 but his anxiety about becoming a Rawly subordinate was

---

1   Archibald Murray had replaced Sir James Wolfe Murray as CIGS in September 1915; Jeffery, *Wilson*, p. 151.
2   Asquith's coalition ministry was formed on 25 May 1915, and brought several senior Conservatives, plus one Labour member into the Cabinet.
3   Hankey, *Supreme Command* (Vol. II), p. 445.
4   Wilson diary, 13 and 15 December 1915.
5   Ibid., 16 and 17 December 1915.

unfounded. The latter took command of the newly formed Fourth Army. Sir Charles Monro, a general Haig trusted, took over First Army and became Wilson's direct superior.[6]

As far as winning the war was concerned, Wilson's time leading IV Corps was uneventful. The most notable episode, although far from an uncommon one in the annals of the fighting on the Western Front, was the loss of a section of trench to a German attack. Wilson, as the man in charge, carried the can and suffered the associated embarrassment. Most important for this study is the impact the incident had on Wilson's view of Haig as Commander-in-Chief and their subsequent relationship. It is also important for what it reveals about Wilson's reputation for gossip, intrigue, and Francophilia.

Although Wilson had only ever commanded to company level, his diary entries reveal a work pattern similar to that adopted by the majority of corps commanders on the Western Front in the Great War. Andy Simpson's study of the war diaries of a number of such officers, including Wilson, concluded that they recorded six main categories of activity, namely: attending inspections, parades and demonstrations; meetings with subordinates and superiors, including operational planning; fighting battles; meals with others and entertaining; exercise, and being on leave or under-employed.[7] Wilson, whether under the guidance of his experienced BGGSs, or by applying simple common sense, understood the need to not only visit the troops under his command but to also meet their officers and tour their trenches, dug-outs and first aid posts.[8] He was no armchair general, regularly recording visits and unit inspections involving walking several miles along wet and inhospitable trenches. At least three times his diary recorded coming under shell fire while touring his corps's positions. On 9 May 'Coming back through Hersin[-Coupigny 10km south of Béthune] I nearly got caught by a shell & had to turn the car backwards to get out of the way.' The following month, while visiting trenches near Cabaret Rouge, close to Vimy Ridge, he was 'slightly shelled', and in August near Berthouval Wood he 'got shelled at once, some coming quite near.'[9] He often dined with his fellow corps commanders and took every opportunity to visit his divisional COs and hosted them and their subordinates at his headquarters.[10] This was a time consuming yet vital task; during Wilson's tenure at IV Corps 27 divisions moved through it, 18 of them spending less than a month under his command. It was a frustration all corps commanders faced. GHQ would allocate units as strategy demanded with the officer on the spot having little if any influence over, or even warning of, the changes. On taking command Wilson was, predictably enough given his rabidly Unionist political affiliations, unimpressed with the 16th (Irish) Division, a predominantly nationalist unit. Inspecting the men of the 8th Dublin Fusiliers and 9th Munsters he decided

6   In January 1916 First Army was composed of III, XI, I and IV Corps.
7   Andy Simpson, *Directing Operations: British Corps Command on the Western Front 1914-18* (Stroud: Spellmount, 2006), p. 184. I am grateful to Dr Simpson for allowing me access to his unpublished data on Wilson's day-to-day activities while GOC IV Corps; the data was gathered from Wilson's diaries.
8   Ibid., p. 186; Wilson's BGGS were Brigadier-General Archie Montgomery (to 4 February 1916) and then Brigadier-General Hugo De Pree who served in the role until March 1918. Both were highly professional and widely experienced staff officers
9   Wilson diary, 9 May, 5 June and 13 August 1916.
10   When Wilson took over IV Corps on 22 December 1915 it was headquartered at Labuissière south west of Béthune and comprised 1st, 15th (Scottish), 16th (Irish) and 47th (1/2nd London) Divisions. In March the Corps line moved slightly south and Wilson established his HQ in the chateau in the village of Ranchicourt [now known as Rebreauve – Ranchicourt] to the west of Lens.

'at least 50%' were 'quite useless, old, whisky sodden militiamen.'[11] Presciently, the new CO thought the 47th (1/2nd London) Division looked 'weak'.[12] This unit would land Wilson in bad odour with his superiors in May. By contrast, less than a fortnight later he inspected the 15th (Scottish) Division at the end of a three-day exercise and concluded they were 'looking hard and well. A fine Division.'[13] Much to his chagrin the 15th was transferred in March.

Wilson's reputation as an incorrigible gossip is borne out by the numerous references in his diary for 1916 to meetings with politicians and other men of importance. Charles Callwell included many of these references in his biography of Wilson; proof-positive that even at the front he was unable to resist 'intriguing'. In fact, the situation is more nuanced. There is no doubt that he mixed the collegiate networking common to any effective military leader in a combat zone with socialising with politicians and other men of importance. However, this was par for the course for army and corps commanders who received frequent visitors allocated to them by GHQ.[14] Lieutenant-General Sir Aylmer Hunter-Weston, who commanded VIII Corps from 1916 until the end of the war, received numerous high-profile visitors both from England and from France and Belgium, as did Wilson's predecessor at IV Corps, Rawlinson.[15] Wilson, therefore, was unexceptional in welcoming powerful and influential civilians to his headquarters. February 1916, for example was a busy month. First he hosted Dr John Crozier, the Lord Primate of All Ireland, and the island's most senior Anglican.[16] No sooner had the distinguished prelate left than Lord Newton, the Paymaster-General came for a three day visit.[17] Although an ardent Tory, Newton was trusted by Asquith and stood in for the Secretary of State for War in the Lords when Kitchener was unavailable. The day Newton left, Lord Curzon, another Conservative grandee and Lord Privy Seal in the first coalition administration 'called in for tea.' Old habits die hard. Where Wilson undoubtedly differed from the majority of his fellow officers was in his willingness to comment freely on matters of partisan politics. Curzon, who had been staying with Haig at GHQ, was 'attacked' by Wilson about the 'sideshow' campaigns and 'about not filling up out divisions out here. He admitted he had been quite wrong about Gallipoli.'[18] His criticism, which centred around Curzon's support for the disastrous Dardanelles Campaign, does not seem to have harmed relations between them. Curzon continued to be a strong supporter of Wilson, particularly in 1917 when Lloyd George's War Cabinet, after much debate, appointed him to the post of Chief Liaison Officer to the French Army.[19]

Considering Wilson's well-deserved reputation for 'intrigue', and his insatiable appetite for political gossip it would be surprising had he put aside a lifetime of chatter merely because he was in command of 70,000 men. Prime Minister Asquith may have consigned Wilson to the dreary battle-shattered countryside of Artois to keep him from stirring the political pot in London.[20]

11   Wilson diary, 28 December 1915.
12   Ibid., 3 January 1916.
13   Ibid., 7 January 1916.
14   Simpson, *Directing Operations*, p. 201.
15   Ibid., pp. 201-6.
16   Wilson diary, 1 February 1916. It was not uncommon for senior establishment figures to visit the Western Front on 'fact-finding' tours.
17   Ibid., 1-5 February 1916.
18   Ibid., 5 February 1916.
19   Jeffery, *Wilson*, p. 189.
20   Ibid., pp. 152-3.

If so he had achieved the lesser of two evils, not silenced him completely. Wilson conferred diligently with colleagues, visited unit training schools and inspected Royal Flying Corps bases. He gave numerous instructive and often entertaining talks to junior officers and lobbied for more artillery and more ammunition. But he also continued his campaign for conscription, especially in Ireland, and for the removal of 'Squiff's' government. He grumbled about British strategy behind the backs of his chief, not only with London-based armchair strategists but with French generals. Significantly enough, this activity intensified after May 1916.

Operation Schleswig Holstein, 21-22 May 1916

This action, a successful German assault on a precarious length of the IV Corps front line was important for several reasons. In itself it threw IV Corps off a useful stretch of raised ground close to Vimy Ridge, claiming 2,475 British casualties and negating some valuable mining operations. For Wilson it was an embarrassing and career-hindering blow, with significant consequences for his future relationship with Sir Douglas Haig. The facts of the incident are straightforward. At 5.30pm on 21 May 80 German batteries opened fire on 1,800m of British line south of the hamlets of Souchez and Givenchy en Gohelle, in the vicinity of the topographical feature known as Zouave Valley.[21] By early the next day, despite ferocious hand-to-hand fighting, the Germans had established themselves in the British first and support line positions. They had achieved their principle objective of halting costly and extensive British mining operations. Wilson immediately set to work devising a counter-attack to recover the lost ground but after intervention from Monro commanding First Army, and ultimately Haig himself, the action was called off.[22] Predictably enough, Wilson got the blame for this setback. Haig, who was in the midst of planning for the upcoming Somme offensive, complained to Monro that: 'The IV Corps was the most efficient one in the Army when Sir H. Wilson took over the Command. Since then it had much decreased in military value. He (Monro) must go into the matter at once and get things right without delay.'[23] Haig's transcript diary, which he amended later includes the additional sentence: 'Monro criticised Sir H. Wilson very severely. There is no doubt that he has failed as a Commander in the field.'[24]

Reviewing the facts, this seems a rather harsh judgement. On 9 May Monro went on leave and Wilson assumed temporary command of First Army, balancing this responsibility with changes to the deployment of his own corps. On 19 May IV Corps' right flank was moved slightly to the south, taking over the section of front where the attack took place. That evening he wrote: 'Bungo [Sir Julian Byng, CO XVII Corps] to lunch & tells me that the part he hands over tonight to me is a beastly bit, overlooked by craters which he cannot get at & very heavily minenwerfed by a 200lb shell.' Wilson resolved to ask George 'Billy' Barrow, Monro's ADC,

21   Jack Sheldon, *The German Army on Vimy Ridge 1914-1917* (Barnsley: Pen & Sword 2008 [2013]), p. 152. Modern battlefield tourists have an excellent view of the area from the Commonwealth War Grave Commission Cabaret Rouge and Zouave Valley cemeteries.
22   National Library of Scotland, Field Marshal Sir Douglas Haig (manuscript) diaries, (Acc. 3155/96-97), 22-24 May 1916, hereafter Haig (manuscript) diary.
23   Haig (manuscript) diary, 27 May 1916.
24   Haig diary, 27 May 1916, with additional sentence from the typescript version, cited in Sheffield & Bourne, *Haig Diaries*, pp. 188-9.

for a large extra allowance of ammunition to tackle the problem.[25] The next day was a busy one. He took Barrow to the northern section of his corps area near Houdain to watch 99th Brigade (2nd Division) practice 'a capital trench attack'. Next, he found himself having lunch with the Archbishop of Canterbury, Randall Davidson who was fresh from a visit to GHQ, and Bishop L.H. Gwynne, deputy chaplain-general to the forces.[26] Wilson then chaperoned the Archbishop to the heights of the Notre Dame de Lorette to watch German heavy guns being shelled. The cleric was, noted Wilson, 'greatly pleased with himself.' The final sentence in the diary for this day concluded ominously: 'I took over another bit of line last night from Bungo. A horrid bit.'[27] On Sunday 21 May Wilson and his ADC Duncannon were touring the lines near Cabaret Rouge when they ran into the German preliminary bombardment: 'After waiting some time & finding it [the bombardment] increased I turned for home. The Boch was shelling everywhere. At the batteries around us, along Cabaret Rouge[,] in the Zouave Valley, on our front lines, on Souchez, Carency, Ablain[-Saint-Nazaire], Lorette, Servin[s], Bouvigny[-Boyeffles], Hersin[-Coupigny] etc. <u>Very</u> heavy.'[28] The official historian recorded that 'The whole front area was soon enveloped in a cloud of smoke and dust, so that the British artillery never really knew when the assault was delivered; and confusion was rendered worse by bursts of lachrymatory shell.' It is estimated that 70,000 shells were poured into this small section of front over a four hour bombardment.[29] In reply, the British artillery was uncoordinated and there was 'little doubt that tactical surprise had been achieved,' with most of the fire coming down on the British reserve and support trenches, isolating the front-line defenders.[30] At 7.45pm the German guns lifted and the German infantry poured forward.

In the months leading up to the attack of 21 May Haig, anxious to distract German attention and resources from his upcoming major offensive on the Somme, had wanted to give the impression of an imminent assault on the Arras front. As a result, the British undertook an extensive raiding campaign against the Germans on the high ground, together with active mining activities.[31] The costs were high. In the five weeks leading up to Operation Schleswig Holstein the British 25th Division in the Berthonval sector where the attack took place, lost 70 officers and 1,200 other ranks.[32] On 15 May the British took German ground after detonating five mines known as the 'Crosbie Craters'. Initially the Germans did nothing to regain them, except heavy night bombardments. According to the Official Historian, 'The Germans … had come to the conclusion that being worsted underground, the only way to restore the situation was to capture the mine shafts by an attack above ground.' They 'proceeded systematically with

25 Wilson diary, 19 May 1916.
26 Gwynne was the brother of H.A. Gwynne, editor of the right-wing *Morning Post* and a close friend a supporter of Wilson.
27 Wilson diary, 20 May 1916.
28 Ibid., 21 May 1916.
29 Sir J.E. Edmonds, *Official History of the War: Military Operations France and Belgium 1916,* Vol. 1 (London: Macmillan, 1932), p. 217.
30 Sheldon, *Vimy Ridge*, p. 153.
31 Ibid., pp. 149-151; Edmonds, p. 212
32 Edmonds, *Military Operations France and Belgium 1916* (Vol. I), p. 213; 'Schleswig Holstein' was the German designation of one of the craters, identified on British maps as 'Broadmarsh', they hoped to capture during the operation.

trench mortars to obliterate the British line, gradually destroying the defences on the ridge.'[33] Unsurprisingly, British frontline officers believed an attack was imminent. However, because no signs of preparation had been seen from the air and intelligence reports said the Germans had neither sufficient men nor guns for an attack, GHQ decided to remove five divisions from First, Second and Third Armies in order to strengthen the Fourth Army as a general reserve for the Somme. It is hard to understand why Haig's staff was so sanguine. As Edmonds observed, in the four weeks leading up to the German assault bad weather and poor visibility meant that RFC aerial reconnaissance missions were restricted to just 10 days, with several of those producing little useful information.[34] Nonetheless, the reorganisation went ahead leading to a change in Army, corps and divisional commands and garrisons in the Berthonval sector, the exact spot on the front where the enemy intended to attack on the night of 19-20 May. 'It brought with it the inevitable disturbance of the Signal and other arrangements for obtaining information and ensuring co-operation: brigades of field artillery of the 47th (London) and 25th Divisions…were actually changing when attack occurred.'[35] As if this disruption was not bad enough, Wilson was standing in for Monro, and 47th Division, the unit which took the brunt of the German assault, was under the temporary command of an officer deputising for his superior who was also on leave.

The Germans had invested significant resources and planned their attack down to the last detail; this was no raid. When the British took over the area from the French in March 1916 it was considered a quiet sector. The French trenches were described by incoming troops as 'merely shell holes joined up' and 'a line of detached posts, accommodated in grouse butts.'[36] The Official History recorded that:

> There were few good communication trenches: most were unfit for use, all were undrained and utterly unsanitary. Dead bodies, months old, still lay unburied, and a vast amount of debris and rubbish covered the whole area. The wire, where any existed, was 'thin and weak', or 'in bad condition'; the positions for machine guns were 'very poor'… To sum up, the ground might be sufficiently organised for the launching of an offensive but offered only precarious tenure as a defensive line.[37]

British tactics in this sector were far more aggressive than those of their French predecessors. This approach meant that any attempts to strengthen the defences were subject to nightly destruction by an alert and increasingly unnerved enemy. Consequently, 'there was practically no wire covering the front line, very little of a support line, and no shelters of any kind in the detached posts.'[38] The statistics are remarkable. Over six nights the Germans moved 9,000 loads of ammunition and equipment, including 3,000 rolls of barbed wire and 28,000 hand grenades.[39] It was hardly surprising therefore that when the Germans attacked, following an

33   Edmonds, *Military Operations France and Belgium 1916* (Vol. I), p. 214
34   Ibid., p. 214.
35   Ibid., p. 215.
36   Ibid., p. 211.
37   Ibid., p. 212.
38   Ibid., p. 216.
39   Sheldon, *Vimy Ridge*, p. 151.

extended and ferocious heavy artillery bombardment totalling around 70,000 shells, with 80 four gun batteries each firing 200 shells, they succeeded in throwing the British out of their flimsy defences. The Official History claimed that once the bombardment lifted the enemy 'had little more to do than take possession of the 140th Brigade [47th Division] sector.'[40] In fact, there was extensive close quarter fighting. The British fought hard in the support trenches and, apparently believing their enemy would take no prisoners, fought to the last.[41]

Wilson, almost inevitably considering the fog of battle and the ferocity of the attack, was at first slow to recognise the magnitude of the situation. After sheltering from the initial bombardment, he and Duncannon visited Brigadier-General Gerald James Cuthbert, who was commanding 47th Division in place of Major-General Charles St Leger Barter. Cuthbert had been CO of 140th Brigade since November 1914, knew the unit well and although he decided to move up '2 or 3 Batt[alion]s … thinks he is well able to cope with the situation.' Wilson established that Cuthbert had plenty of ammunition and while he offered more infantry and more guns 'he did not want either.' It being a Sunday, Wilson then attended church parade but at 6.30pm he ordered one brigade of 2nd Division which was resting to the rear to stand by to move at one hour's notice. At 10pm 'owing to contradictory but unsatisfactory reports that we had lost trenches etc' he ordered this brigade forward and put another on stand-by. Wilson went to bed at 1.30am, by which time the situation had become clearer: 'We, (47th Division, 140th Brigade) had lost about 1,200 yards of front of the trenches [sic] we took over from Bungo on Saturday (yesterday morning) & had fallen back about 300-600 yards.' He ordered additional units forward and asked First Army for additional heavy guns and for 'strong aeroplane support' and 'arranged in my own mind that I would retake tonight (22nd) if the various local counter attacks were not successful. It is a nasty little knock. Our casualties seem to be about 1,200-1,500.'[42]

Wilson ordered a counter-attack for the evening of 23 May 1916 but confusion amongst the commanders, combined with fierce resistance from the enemy, meant the action failed to make any headway. 99th Brigade was one of two deployed for the counter-attack. Christopher Stone described it as 'a pretty bad time' and a 'wasted effort' in which his unit sustained 100 casualties.[43] Predictably enough Wilson applied the age-old law of cascade management, a gravitational phenomenon which states that at times of misfortune recrimination and blame invariably flows downhill. He commenced an inquiry into the failure of the counter-attack and felt that the two commanders responsible ought to be court martialled.[44] He kicked upwards as well, grumbling unconvincingly that Monro's 'interference' in curtailing the counter-attack was all that stood between it and success.

On the face of it, Wilson did all that would have been expected of a corps commander in similar circumstances. When the situation became clear he ordered a counter-attack which, with hindsight and bearing in mind the investment the Germans had placed in their original

---

40   Edmonds, *Military Operations France and Belgium 1916* (Vol. I), p. 217.
41   Sheldon, *Vimy Ridge*, p. 153.
42   Wilson diary, 21 May 1916.
43   Gary Sheffield, (ed.), *From Vimy Ridge to the Rhine: The Great War Letters of Christopher Stone DSO MC* (Ramsbury, Marlborough: Crowood Press, 1989), pp. 52-3; Edmonds, *Military Operations France and Belgium 1916* (Vol. I), p. 221.
44   Wilson diary, 25 May 1916. In the event, neither officer faced official sanction.

assault, was under-resourced. This failed and he and his staff set to work planning a larger scale operation to regain the lost front line and support trenches. More experienced hands, particularly Monro, the First Army commander, doubted the chances of success. Once GHQ became involved Haig was far too preoccupied with planning for the Somme to distract effort and resources to dislodge the enemy from a section of ground in a peripheral sector of his front and vetoed any large-scale response. As one veteran observed, the careers of corps and army commanders in the Great War often depended as much upon the fates as upon sound judgement.[45] On 21 May 1916 Wilson certainly found himself in the wrong place at the wrong time.

While an interesting diversion into the lot of an army commander on the Western Front, from the perspective of this study the real significance of this event is how its aftermath coloured Wilson's views of his colleagues, and particular his opinion of Sir Douglas Haig.

Characteristically Wilson took the aftermath of Operation Schleswig Holstein hard and personally. He baulked at criticism from Monro, and the implication that those at the top believed he was at fault. On 27 May, after Haig had hosted a meeting of Army commanders, Monro called on Wilson and 'he was loud in his abuse of poor Hugo [de Pree, Wilson's BGGS and deputy] but I really could not agree.'[46] In the almost incestuous relationship which existed between senior officers in the British Army it did not always do for one brother officer of such senior rank to directly criticise another, but as Haig's diary shows Wilson was right to see Monro's admonishment as being aimed at him. Worse still, Haig had been informed by Charteris that Wilson's officers were:

> Downhearted and spoke of the British climbing to victory on the backs of the French: that Gen H. Wilson spoke of the French as even better fighters than the British, and that the Germans were better than ours. All this seems to spring from Gen Wilson's attitude on the subject of the French. Gen Monro is to look carefully into the matter and take action if necessary.[47]

Haig had long been suspicious of what he considered to be Wilson's overly close relationship with the French. In early 1915, when it became clear that Murray was to be replaced as CoS Haig had been told by Repington, *The Times* correspondent, that: 'Henry Wilson has got Huguet (the head of the French Mission) to get Joffre and the French Govt to ask that H.W. should be appointed C.G.S. instead of Sir A. Murray! Such an intrigue greatly astonished me.'[48] As has already been discussed, Repington was a sworn enemy of Wilson, but whether the allegation was true or not it is clear Haig believed Wilson to be capable of such a tactic. Wilson composed a robust response to Monro's dressing down but had two more uncomfortable meetings with his CO. On 5 June the latter summoned Wilson to his HQ and 'rather straffed me about spending too much ammunition & about the failure of the attack on the 23rd, but I was able to show him

45   Sir Henry Karslake in conversation with Basil Liddell Hart, 26 November 1936, cited in Jeffery, *Wilson*, p. 167.
46   Wilson diary, 27 May 1918.
47   NLS, Haig (manuscript) diary, 28 May 1915. Haig amended the transcript version to blame Wilson's 'inexperience as a commander' and 'his infatuation with the French': cited in Jeffery, *Wilson*, p. 165.
48   NLS, Haig (manuscript) diary, 22 January 1915.

good reasons for everything.'[49] However much he might have wanted to convince himself that he was in the right, Wilson developed an almost obsessional conviction that GHQ and Haig in particular, were set to sabotage his career.

Until mid-1916 Wilson's diary entries concerning the C-in-C are limited, and largely neutral. In March he noted that: 'After lunch Haig and Kigg [Launcelot Kiggell, Haig's CoS] came in for 1/4 of an hour. Not seen Haig for 3 mo[nth]s: since I became a Corps Comm[ande]r. He was civil and nice, but, as usual, I never can get inside his head.'[50] Not exactly a positive comment, but hardly evidence of deep animosity and distrust. After the 'nasty little knock' at Berthonval the temperature in the relationship went from cool to frosty, at least from the perspective of the junior officer. From late May onwards, Wilson's diary is replete with uncompromising criticism of Haig, his staff and GHQ strategy in general. Late night scribblings of discontent are one thing, sharing animosity and doubt with others is a different matter altogether. If only a percentage of the conversations he documented in his journal are accurate, Wilson can be judged to have been disloyal to his chief. His jottings relate conversations with military colleagues in which they shared gossip and grumbles about their superiors, particularly Haig and his staff. So far, so unremarkable, although it is almost inevitable that some of these criticisms eventually reached Haig's ears. More damaging to his reputation was the criticism of Haig that Wilson shared with senior politicians and other influential civilians and which in a serving senior officer were entirely inappropriate. His interlocutors would have been long familiar with his denunciation of politicians such as Asquith, but his raging about Haig's alleged inadequacies was breaking new ground.

Even worse was the condemnation of both Haig and British strategy which Wilson tolerated, and effectively encouraged, from senior French figures including Foch and the French C-in-C Joffre. In June, thanks to an introduction from the newspaper editor Leo Maxse, a long-time friend, Wilson met the leading French politician Georges Clemenceau who had 'come down from Paris to see me.' Like Wilson, Clemenceau was opinionated, critical of his own government's conduct of the war, and convinced that he was surrounded by incompetents. 'The Tiger' was a politician with military pretensions and Wilson was a corps commander in the field who far too often behaved like a politician, free with his opinions and careless of the consequences. Clemenceau was a leading member of the French Senate and a thorn in the side of the government of Aristide Briand. He told Wilson he intended getting rid of Joffre who he accused of taking no precautions to protect Verdun from the German offensive which had begun in February:

> When Joffre is moved out he thinks the choice lies with Castelnau, Foch & Petain. He, personally, favours Foch & so do I, telling him I knew all three & Foch was the most brilliant by far, Castelnau the best staff officer & Petain a fine dogged fighter but without Foch's drive & wide outlook.

Having promoted the fortunes of his friend Foch, Wilson went on to lambast allied plans for the forthcoming Somme offensive:

49   Wilson diary, 30 May and 5 June 1916.
50   Ibid., 18 March 1916.

He [Clemenceau] was as insistent as me that we should not attack prematurely...and that it was mad to do so. There was no hope of breaking through unless we had unlimited amm[unitio]n which we have <u>not</u> got & were prepared to face a loss of 250,000 which we are not. He said Foch continued to be as hostile to attacking as me & it was all Joffre & the politicians.

Clemenceau concluded by telling Wilson that 'Haig did not like me because of my loyalty to Johnnie French!'[51] A few days later Wilson went to see Foch who was recovering from a serious road accident. The latter told his friend that he had little confidence that the 'big push', in which he would command the French armies straddling the Somme on the BEF's right flank, would achieve its aims. The commander of the French Northern Army Group complained that: 'He never sees Haig who never takes the slightest notice of him & did not even call on him after his accident. He is a little mistrustful of Rawly who, he thinks, is afraid of Haig, & keeps one eye on him & only one on the Boches.'[52] Wilson continued to have his doubts about the planned offensive and less than 48 hours before the attack was launched on 1 July, Billy Barrow told him that the British barrage had not knocked out sufficient machine guns: 'He said Haig never told them anything, nor did Kigg ... I can't help thinking that Haig is completely out of touch with the Army, & as he won't allow Kigg to come & see us poor Kigg is absolutely ignorant.'[53]

Five days into the offensive Wilson met Foch to laud the French effort on the British right as 'the finest attack performance of the war.' Seemingly unphased by the fact that before coming to IV Corps he had commanded nothing more than a company; Wilson was clear where the fault lay:

Now most, if not all, of this comes from our inability to 'mount' an attack. Haig is incapable of 'mounting' an attack. As I have often written before, he is a good stout hearted <u>defensive</u> soldier with <u>no</u> imagination, & very little brains & very little sympathy therefore really quite a poor class soldier judged by any high standard.

Foch related a falling out between Joffre and Haig at the latter's Advanced Headquarters at the Chateau du Valvion in Beauquesnes, north east of Albert. According to Foch, rather than attacking again in the Thiepval sector Haig said he intended exploiting his success further south:

This infuriated Joffre who simply went for Haig & as Foch said it was quite 'brutal'. Haig said he was not speaking as one gentleman to another and old Joffre said he would have no further dealings with Haig over this matter & that Haig must work it out with Foch. So now we have Haig asking Foch to lunch to-day (Foch said he could not go as he had important work ie me!) & Foch agreeing to lunch tomorrow. And after all these months when Haig has studiously ignored Foch – markedly so – he has now to work with him.[54]

51   Wilson diary, 11 June 1916; original emphasis.
52   Ibid., 22 June 1916.
53   Ibid., 29 June 1916.
54   Ibid., 5 July 1916.

Haig recorded that Joffre 'exploded in a fit of rage.' He felt that afterwards the French general seemed 'ashamed' of his outburst and 'All present at the interview felt ashamed of Joffre... However I have gained an advantage through keeping calm!'[55] If this was the case, it did not last long. By the time Foch visited Wilson his opinion of Haig was that 'he is stupid & has no stomach for fighting, & both he & Joffre have formed a very poor opinion of him.' Wilson thought this 'unfortunate, & not quite fair.'[56] Unfair it might have been, but the fact that he felt it appropriate to discuss his C-in-C's alleged failings with a senior officer from an allied army illustrates why so many of his colleagues distrusted Wilson.

An abiding characteristic of Wilson's diary entries is his ability to look both ways at the same time, something his critics often cited in his public persona. The flexibility of imagination to evaluate both sides of an argument can be an advantage, and at certain key stages in the Great War Wilson was able to deploy this skill successfully. In mid-1916 however, frustration and an abiding sense of injustice addled his judgement. Less than a fortnight before the attack Haig told his cousin and Wilson's BGGS, Hugo de Pree, that 'our attacks were coming off now to help the French at Verdun.'[57] Two days later he described French irritation at the British 'doing nothing' as 'entirely natural'. On 5 July, the day Foch lambasted Haig's strategy, Wilson correctly identified one of the several reasons for the disappointing and costly British performance on the first day of the Somme 'viz not nearly sufficient concentration of fire before Inf. attack.' An officer normally so sensitive to the demands of statecraft ought to have realised that Haig's offensive options were limited by both time and resource. Yet, according to Wilson, Haig's offensive was 'very badly planned' and he and Rawlinson would have to face the consequences.[58] Henry Wilson liked having his cake and eating it.

The next time Wilson saw Foch and Joffre the French C-in-C said he had not seen Haig since their 'row' and that he had no intention of seeing him as 'he says Haig "embêtes" him.'[59] Towards the end of July Lord Esher, with whom Wilson always enjoyed a good gossip, told him that the French were now happy with British strategy: 'I threw a fly over him about the relations between Haig & Joffre but he did not rise although I gathered Haig had told him.' Esher was a well-connected freelance busybody who enjoyed power and influence while eschewing any form of responsibility. Having attempted, unsuccessfully, to stir the pot for Haig with someone he knew was likely to repeat his opinions, Wilson then claimed surprise that Haig might view him in a less than positive light, 'Esher gave me to understand that Haig is still hostile to me; how curious. He is suspicious of me & in a sort of a way afraid of me.'[60]

Haig was right to be suspicious of Wilson, but a few days later he illustrated that he certainly was not afraid. In early August General Monro was ordered eastwards as C-in-C India. Monro was reluctant to go and suggested to Haig that Sir Richard Haking take what he hoped would

55   NLS, Haig (manuscript) diary, 3 July 1916.
56   Wilson diary, 5 July 1916.
57   Ibid., 18 June 1916. Later in the year Wilson, ignoring the fact that Haig and de Pree were related, chose to feel snubbed that the C-in-C invited de Pree to lunch without him; Wilson diary, 24 October 1916. See also Gary Sheffield, *In Haig's Shadow: Brigadier-General Hugo de Pree and the First World War* (London: Greenhill Books, 2019).
58   Ibid., 20 June, 5 and 7 July 1916.
59   Ibid., 12 July 1916; *embêter*, French, to annoy.
60   Ibid., 27 July 1916.

be temporary command of First Army.[61] Haking had become GOC of the newly formed XI Corps in September 1915, just in time for two of his inexperienced and tired divisions to suffer a severe beating at the Battle of Loos. Despite this setback, and further costly failure at the Battle of Fromelles on 19 July 1916, Haking retained Haig's confidence.[62] 'If this is so it only shows how hopelessly out of touch GHQ is with what we all think of Haking,' wrote Wilson, doubting the appointment was temporary. He had some grounds to be disappointed. Although he had far more command experience than Wilson, Haking had not performed well at XI Corps and was 'junior' in terms of army seniority.[63] Monro had evidently told Wilson that he had recommended him as his successor 'but Haig would not have that at any price! He evidently has no opinion of me – nor I of him!'[64] He also railed against Wully Robertson who, as CIGS, he presumed had had a hand in the decision. In fact despite his grumblings, Wilson and Haking appear to have worked together reasonably well, co-operating effectively in preparing for a diversionary assault on Vimy Ridge which Haig initially scheduled for September.

As for the Commander-in-Chief, in Wilson's eyes Haig could do nothing right. His diary for the second half of August is replete with invective. Told by Haking that Haig wanted the intended assault on Vimy Ridge brought forward, 'I said I could not do it with even a moderate chance of success. Of course I could lose 5000 to 7000 men any day Haig liked but I could not take & keep the Vimy trenches before the 1 Sept.' Haig had a 'muddle mind' and was 'simply unintelligible, & a d___ stupid man.'[65] Hubert Scott, a friend of both Wilson and Duncannon, repeated the assertion that Monro had proposed Wilson to command First Army, citing his seniority: 'Haig said that Haking should have the appointment, & as I was senior to Haking, my corps could be transferred to the 3rd Army & I would come under the "Bull" So Haig doesn't like me, nor I him!' The same source told Duncannon that neither Haig nor Haking were friends of Wilson's and that Haig had wanted to send him home after the May setback 'but Monro would not stand it.'[66] Wilson heard much the same later from his friend the Conservative MP Arthur Lee.[67] In fact, regardless of Haig's support, Haking was indeed only a temporary CO. The War Council opposed his promotion and Robertson put forward four names, including Wilson and Horne.[68] Robertson, who Wilson had wrongly believed had been involved in Haking's appointment, noted that Wilson had the ability to do the job, but left the decision to Haig.[69] Horne, like Haking, was a Haig protégée and was confirmed in the post on 30 September 1916.[70] Disappointed, Wilson saw the decision as yet another black mark against

61   NLS, Haig (manuscript) diary, 3 August 1916; Greenhalgh, *Foch*, p. 171.
62   Andy Simpson, 'Sir Richard Haking', *ODNB*.
63   Henry Wilson was appointed Lieutenant-General on 19 February 1915; Richard Haking attained the same rank on 4 September 1915.
64   Wilson diary, 5 and 6 August 1916.
65   Ibid., 16 and 18 August 1916.
66   Ibid., 20 August 1916; 'the Bull' was General Edmund Allenby, at this time GOC Third Army.
67   Ibid., 13 September 1916.
68   Simon Robbins, 'Henry Horne' in Ian F. W. Beckett & Stephen J. Corvi, (eds.), *Haig's Generals*, (Barnsley: Pen & Sword, 2009 [2006]), p. 101.
69   Liddell Hart Centre for Military Archives (hereafter LHCMA), Robertson papers (7/6/67), Robertson to Haig, 10 August 1916.
70   Don Farr, *The Silent General: Horne of the First Army* (Solihull: Helion & Company, 2009 [2007], p. 135.

Haig: 'So that stupid Haig has been beat over Haking & I think both Haking (& I!) have cause for grievance.'[71]

Despite much careful planning, the date for Wilson's proposed assault on Vimy Ridge was put back several times as IV Corp's unit strength was slowly denuded to bolster the forces slogging it out on the Somme. It came to nothing and yet some of the work undertaken by Wilson and his staff was useful in the planning for the Battle of Arras the following year. Amidst this disappointment, Wilson continued to record the comments of some colleagues who were also apparently disgruntled with GHQ, but he also shared his misgivings with politicians, including Lord Derby. The newly appointed Under-Secretary of State for War had visited GHQ and Wilson wanted to know about Haig's relations with the French 'which I hear are not very good, & I don't wonder for he is an ill-mannered and under-bred man.'[72]

As this study shows, at key stages in the Great War Henry Wilson's strategic vision and easy relationship with certain leading French soldiers and politicians helped oil the wheels of diplomacy and diffused tensions between fractious allies. In the latter half of 1916, embittered and disappointed, Wilson's conversations with his Gallic chums too often verged on disloyalty and malice. It did not enhance his career prospects, nor his relationship with his colleagues. GHQ's suspicions were aired when Haking, as acting Army commander, questioned Wilson's plans for a lunch with Foch:

> Haking asked me if I knew that GHQ did not approve of my going to see Foch. I said I did not, nor could I think that GHQ would insult both Foch & me in that way. So Haking said he had no objection if I was not afraid for my own sake… What a rather jealous suspicious frame of mind for Haig to adopt not liking me to visit my old friend Foch.[73]

Although unwilling to formally object to the visit, Haking was right to be suspicious. Foch told Wilson 'all his secrets,' and of his (and Joffre's) profound dissatisfaction with Haig. The French officer regretted his inability to talk openly with the British C-in-C and there was no one on the GHQ staff:

> Senior enough to go between them, as I used in the old days to work between Sir John & Foch seeing Foch … & possessing Foch's entire confidence & also Sir John's. Foch is worried about the present state of affairs. He sees Haig occasionally, but he might as well not see him at all; he sees Rawly more but he doesn't trust Rawly a yard.

Foch asked for Wilson to return to his old liaison role but realised 'this was impossible with Haig.' At the same meeting Foch told him that he had seen Clemenceau's opposite number as War Minister, Lloyd George, who had apparently criticised Haig while praising Wilson.[74] Even allowing for a degree of hubris, it is possible to see more than a grain of truth in this diary entry.

71   Wilson diary, 21 August 1916.
72   Ibid., 5 September 1916.
73   Ibid., 10 September 1916.
74   Ibid., 12 September 1916.

As Wilson railed against Haig he developed a short-lived rapprochement with his old sparring partner Robertson. While visiting the front the CIGS grumbled about his political masters and speculated prophetically that Lloyd George, now Secretary of State for War, would 'make a lot of trouble'. Wilson, no doubt primed by Foch, counselled Wully that soon the French would ask the British to take on more of the front line and that it was important to maintain positive relations. A week later Wilson entertained the newspaper editor H.A. Gwynne. He told him that when Monro was posted to India Robertson had written to Haig strongly urging him to appoint Wilson to First Army: 'This was good of R[obertson].' Gwynne was an old friend of Wilson's and in the pre-war period a strong supporter of Lord Roberts. According to Wilson's diary the newspaperman thought Haig 'stupid' and at risk of losing his command.[75] It is difficult to imagine any other senior British officer having such a conversation with the editor of a right-wing anti-government newspaper while the British Army was engaged in the biggest offensive in its history to date. Lloyd George also put in an appearance at the Chateau de Ranchicourt, taken there by Lee in an 'act of friendship' to Wilson. According to his diary, Wilson played a straight bat when questioned about the current British performance. He explained that the troops and artillery were 'new to the game' and the army had grown from six divisions to 60. However, the Prime Minister-in-waiting was 'evidently dissatisfied with the whole thing.' Considering his negative attitude at this time it is tempting to assume Wilson might have voiced his criticism of Haig's command. However, he and Lloyd George were not particularly well acquainted at this point. Foch had met the Welshman two days earlier and had already warned of his likely questions, to which he had also given neutral responses. Nonetheless Lloyd George was 'very nice' to Wilson.[76] Perhaps he had identified a potential ally in the army ranks. Foch told Haig about Lloyd George's questions: 'Unless I had been told of this conversation personally by Gen. Foch I would not have believed that a British minister could have been so ungentlemanly as to go to a foreigner and put such questions regarding his subordinates.'[77]

An alienated Wilson returned to London on leave in October and his diary appointments comprise a list of influential figures critical of Asquith's coalition government. Edward Carson, Lord Milner and Andrew Bonar Law were all treated to Wilson's views on the conduct of the war and the failings of the 'Squiff' government. He also met up with F.S. 'Fred' Oliver, the imperialist writer and businessman, Lord Derby and Arthur Lee. The latter told him that Lloyd George favoured him but Sir Richard Butler, the Deputy CGS at GHQ 'was hostile to me.'[78] The Wilsons' wedding anniversary was marked by a breakfast visit from Leo Maxse, editor of another right wing journal the *National Review*, followed by Sir Clive Wigram, the King's deputy private secretary, who was apparently 'much upset' about him not getting the First Army position.[79] Expressions of surprise from a courtier were of little value to a man without the royal connections of Haig and Robertson.

75   Wilson diary, 20, 28 and 29 September 1916.
76   Ibid., 12 and 13 September 1916.
77   NLS, Haig (manuscript) diary, 17 September 1916.
78   Butler was removed from GHQ in February 1918, one of the victims of the Wilson-Lloyd George clear out of Haig loyalists. He spent the remainder of the war in the consolation prize role of GOC III and XIX Corps.
79   Wilson diary, 1-9 October 1916 inclusive.

The second half of 1916 was the nadir of Henry Wilson's military career. His hopes of leading a significant offensive had faded, his corps gradually dissipated as divisions came and went. Overlooked, twice, for promotion to army commander and seeing 'so many enemies out here,' including the C-in-C. At one point he was tempted to resign and enter the House of Commons. Sir Arthur Steel-Maitland, the chairman of the Conservative and Unionist Party, offered to give him a seat in the House of Commons 'anytime', but he was unable to afford the reduced income.[80] By the end of the year he was disillusioned and resentful, with little prospect of advancement. A year later he was the British government's favoured military strategist.

80   Wilson diary, 20, 21 and 22 August 1916.

5

Zero to Hero

In early 1917 Wilson found himself in the role of senior British liaison officer at *GQG*. Wilson and Nivelle got on well, despite some misgivings in the War Office. Nivelle's April offensive failed to achieve its objectives and he was replaced by General Philippe Pétain who distrusted Wilson, considering him too close to Nivelle, and had him sent home.[1] Wilson was put on half-pay, during which time he threatened to get into 'mischief' if he failed to find appropriate employment.[2] He spent the summer considering a parliamentary career but generated little enthusiasm, either personally or amongst his political friends.[3]

Effectively out of work Wilson, in Amery's opinion 'much the most active brain in the Army' had 'nothing to do except think and talk, both gifts in which he excelled.' It meant that, once ensconced as head of Eastern Command, a post he took up on 1 September 1917:

> For the first time in the war he was in a position to see it from a wider perspective than that of the Western Front and, for the first time, headquarters in London gave him the opportunity for continuous intercourse with Lloyd George, Milner and the rest of the War Cabinet, as well as with an old confederate like myself.[4]

This proximity to political power led directly to the Prime Minister ordering him, and Lord French, to submit their views on future British Strategy to a frustrated and directionless War Cabinet. The paper Wilson submitted on 20 October 1917 has received limited attention in the historiography.[5] For one authority it was the product of Wilson's tireless pursuit of self-interest.[6] Another saw it as the latest weapon in Lloyd George's equally tireless campaign to wrest control of the war from Haig and Robertson, with Wilson little more than a dupe, albeit a willing one.[7] This chapter considers the development of Wilson's thinking by analysing the paper in detail for the first time, and aims to set it in its broader strategic context. While Wilson might have seen

---

1   Wilson diary, 31 May 1917; see also Egremont, *Under Two Flags*, p. 55.
2   Millman, 'Wilson's Mischief', pp. 467-486
3   Jeffery, *Wilson*, pp. 196-8.
4   Amery, *Political Life*, pp. 124-5.
5   TNA CAB 27/8: WP 61.
6   Brock Millman, *Pessimism and British War Policy: 1916-1918* (London: Frank Cass, 2001), pp. 155-170.
7   Woodward, *Lloyd George and the Generals*, esp. pp. 210-11.

opportunities for personal advancement, his report deliberately steered clear of overt criticism of colleagues. He told Lord Esher that he 'had avoided saying a word...that could offend D.[ouglas] H.[aig] and hoped their relationship would be cordial.'[8] Instead the report was a closely argued critique on the course of the war, and of the events and decisions Wilson believed had brought Britain and her allies to the current impasse on the Western Front. Rather than an exercise in political point-scoring, the paper should be seen as a formal statement of Wilson's long-held strategic views. Had the paper been merely an exercise in criticism of past performance, it is doubtful his career would have gained the momentum it did. Unlike Lord French who was also consulted, and allowed personal invective to intrude on what was an otherwise detailed review, Wilson adhered to the War Cabinet's request for a study of 'the present state of the war, the future prospects, and the future action to be taken'. His response shaped the characteristics not only of British strategy, but that of her main allies, for the rest of the war. It paved the way for his appointment as Britain's PMR at the SWC and confirmed his position as Lloyd George's favoured professional adviser on war policy. Whether he intended it or not, it also served as Wilson's informal application for the post of the government's principal military advisor, the CIGS.

The Papers

Wilson and French were asked to produce their 'appreciations' by the War Cabinet on 11 October 1917.[9] That afternoon they were at work in Lord French's office at Horse Guards, Wilson sitting at Wellington's desk.[10] They conferred throughout the writing period; the two papers, although different in style, were products of extensive collusion.[11] The context for the Cabinet's request was the receipt of status reports from Haig and Robertson. Haig's, requested on 25 September, reviewed the military situation on the Western Front. It offered the C-in-C's views of the British role if Russia dropped out of the war 'having regard to the weakened state of France and Italy'.[12] Robertson submitted two reports, as requested at a meeting of the War Policy Committee on 5 October. His principal document, in response to Lloyd George's concerns about the costly battles on the Western Front, was an assessment of the prospects for a major offensive in Palestine; specifically, an advance north from the present line at Gaza-Beersheba. His second paper examined such a campaign in detail.[13] There was also a supporting report from the First Sea Lord, Admiral Sir John Jellicoe, on prospects for moving troops to the Middle East to undertake an offensive of this kind[14] Wilson's analysis, while it took an holistic view of

---

8   CAC, Esher journal, (ESHR 2/20), 4 November 1917.
9   TNA CAB 23/13/21: War Cabinet, 11 October 1917.
10   Wilson diary, 11 October 1917.
11   Wilson's diary records him working alongside or discussing his paper with French on 11, 12, 14, 15, 16 and 17 October 1917, by which time he had begun sharing them with his political allies, Wilson diary, 11-20 October 1917.
12   TNA CAB 27/8: GT 2243, Haig to Robertson, 8 October 1917, (hereafter CAB 27/8: GT 2243).
13   TNA CAB 24/28/42: GT 2242, 'Future Military Policy', and 'Occupation of Jaffa-Jerusalem Line', CIGS to War Cabinet, 9 October 1917.
14   TNA CAB 27/8, WP 54: 'Question of reinforcing the army in Palestine,' and 'Effect on Imports into the United Kingdom of proposed transfer of troops from France to Egypt,' First Sea Lord to War Cabinet, 9 October 1917.

the war thus far, addressed the key elements in both papers.[15] His report was closely argued and impersonal, in stark contrast to Lord French's more discursive invective-ridden assault on two of the British Army's most senior soldiers.[16]

The request for their strategic advice surprised neither Wilson nor French. At a War Cabinet meeting the day before, 'the view was clearly expressed' that Haig's report 'did not provide a convincing argument that we could inflict a decisive military defeat on Germany on the Western Front next year' even if Russia remained an effective participant.[17] As a result, the Prime Minister recalled that at the start of the war, when 'equally grave decisions' had to be taken, his predecessor had called a 'War Council' to hear the views of a range of military experts. That had not happened because of lack of confidence in the commanders, he said. Wilson and French would be invited to offer their views, regardless of possible objections:

> In reply to a suggestion that the Chief of the Imperial General Staff might resent this procedure, the Prime Minister pointed out that neither General Sir Charles Douglas, then Chief of the Imperial General Staff, nor Field Marshal Lord French, the Commander-in-Chief Designate of the British Expeditionary Force had resented the War Council held in August 1914, and he himself would undertake to explain the matter fully to General Robertson.[18]

Lloyd George's mendacity did not fool Esher who noted that the 1914 meeting 'was called because no confidence was felt that Sir C. Douglas or Sir John French were capable of giving military advice upon such grave issues'.[19] Wilson and French dined with Lloyd George who had 'told Robertson that it is no slight on him but that the patient after a three year course of treatment not being yet cured he thinks it advisable to call in another couple of specialists!'[20] Whatever Lloyd George told Robertson, the latter was not mollified. Hankey noted that Robertson had told Derby he was considering resignation. Curzon had warned him that if the CIGS was forced out he would 'probably' resign, as would Cabinet members Lord Robert Cecil, Carson, the Foreign Secretary Arthur Balfour, and Derby.[21] The whole process caused an exasperated Esher to ask: 'Is this Government or Anarchy?'[22]

At the War Cabinet meeting the following day, aware of Curzon's threat, Lloyd George justified his actions by referring to the 'Council of War' of August 1914. He did so 'impartially and judiciously' and was 'quite at his best, handling Robertson (who was as sulky as a bear with a sore head) quite admirably'.[23] He said that in the light of the papers from Haig, the CIGS and

15   TNA CAB 27/8: WP 61.
16   TNA CAB 27/8, WP 60: 'Present State of the War, future prospects, and future action,' Field Marshal the Lord French to War Cabinet, 20 October 1917, (hereafter CAB 27/8, WP 60).
17   TNA CAB 23/13/20: War Cabinet, 10 October 1917.
18   Ibid.
19   CAC, Esher papers, ESHR4, VII (1917), Esher journal, 17 October 1917, original emphasis.
20   Wilson diary, 10 October 1917. Lloyd George was fond of this medical metaphor, using it first at a meeting of the War Policy Committee, TNA CAB WP 27/6: 9 October 1917 (misdated 11 October).
21   CAC, Hankey diary, HNKY 1/3, 10 October 1917, and CAC, Esher journal, 15 October 1917.
22   Ibid., 17 October 1917.
23   Ibid.

the Admiralty he believed there were four 'alternative policies' facing Britain. In short, these were:

1. Concentration of 'the whole of our forces on the Western front' with all other theatres treated as not only subordinate but with forces sufficient for 'safety on the defensive'. This, Lloyd George said, was Haig's recommendation.
2. Concentrate mainly on the Western Front but maintain active operations in other theatres, such as Mesopotamia and Palestine, in the hope that by 'rough handling' the Turks might be induced to 'come to terms'.
3. Lloyd George ascribed the third option to the French C-in-C Pétain. This comprised of limited attacks while concentrating on economic warfare until Russia recovered and the USA could supply enough men to ensure superiority.
4. Option four was described by the Prime Minister as 'knocking the props from under Germany'. The underlying basis was to counter the loss of Russia by depriving Germany of her allies, 'with a view to an eventual great concentration against an isolated Germany. This might be achieved by a combination of military and diplomatic operations against Turkey.' First it would be necessary to deliver a major military blow against them.[24]

Lloyd George said 'a turning point in the war' had been reached. Wilson set to work only to be interrupted that afternoon by Milner who told him and French that 'relations between L.G. and Robertson are impossible. Faults on both sides and mutual dislike. L.G. often unfair and Robertson often special pleading of gross and offensive type.'[25]

Haig's Paper

This was influenced by the apparent ineffectiveness of Britain's main allies, and the progress of the Third Battle of Ypres. It was produced during the Battle of Broodseinde, at a time when the offensive was still considered, by the C-in-C at least, to be going the BEF's way.[26] Haig's confidence is clear from his diary, which in the week before the submission of his report referred at least five times to the positive progress the BEF was making.[27] Unsurprisingly, the conclusion of his report was to urge further operations on the Western Front in 1918, building on what he believed were the successes of 1917. In the coming year the main weight of the fighting would fall to the British. While he knew the Prime Minister believed there might be alternatives to concentrating on the Western Front, he wanted to stick to the policy of devoting effort and resources to defeating Germany in the west. Haig, somewhat unconvincingly, said he had examined and 'carefully considered' the other options but there was not one of them 'which

24 TNA CAB 23/13/21: War Cabinet, 11 October 1917, pp. 7-8.
25 Wilson diary, 11 October 1917.
26 Nick Lloyd, *Passchendaele: A New History* (London: Viking, 2017), pp. 212-3; Battle of Broodseinde, 4-8 October 1917.
27 NLS, Haig (manuscript) diary, 5 and 7 October 1917.

offers any prospect of defeating the German armies, and until we defeat those armies I see no prospect of gaining the peace we seek'.[28]

According to Wilson, Lloyd George condemned both Haig and Robertson as:

> [P]ig-headed stupid and narrow-visioned. Haig has submitted, what LG called, a 'preposterous' paper which sets out to prove that the west front is the only front. LG says that, in fact, on Haig's own showing the Western front is a hopeless front. Allenby has apparently said that he needs 2 to 1 to beat the Turks and therefore it would follow that it was no use sending troops out there. Haig claims that even if the Boches are reinforced by 32 Divisions from Russia he can still beat them although inferior in men and guns.[29]

By this stage of the war the C-in-C's positive outlook was viewed by some senior politicians with more than a degree of cynicism, with his head of intelligence John Charteris fielding much of the criticism. Haig's optimism failed to convince Esher. It was 'too long and too discursive; but it is elevated in tone, and very sanguine about prospects on this Front. I did not care much for it.'[30] Haig's 'sanguine' approach to the threats facing his front coloured British strategy into the spring of 1918. According to Wilson, Derby agreed with him that Haig's staff was 'rotten and that all his forecasts are wrong, and that Robertson endorses them. But Derby is a weak creature... he cursed Charteris heartily which amused me.'[31] Derby had turned against GHQ's head of intelligence in February 1917 for his overly optimistic appraisals, telling Lloyd George that Haig had been 'badly let down by Charteris'.[32] Esher said Charteris was considered a '"national danger" by all the Army Commanders, and goes by the name of the "U-Boat."'[33] Charteris's card was marked, although it would take the rest of the year to dislodge him.

Robertson's Paper

Robertson's submission received a similarly critical reception. It took a familiar, strongly pro-Western Front position, with gloomy predictions for the prospects of expanded operations in Palestine. An offensive towards Jerusalem, even if successful, entailed extending the British front from 30 to 50 miles in width. He predicted at least three costly battles against strong Turkish resistance leading to 'little result beyond the moral advantages which we may gain'.[34] Worse, he calculated that the British force of seven infantry and three cavalry divisions would need reinforcing by three infantry divisions with two more in relief.[35] This, Robertson claimed,

28   TNA CAB 27/8: GT 2243, p. 2.
29   Wilson diary, 10 October 1917.
30   CAC, Esher papers, Esher Journal, 2/20, 15 October 1917, original emphasis.
31   Wilson diary, 16 October 1917.
32   Lloyd George papers, LG-F14-4-21, quoted in Sheffield, *The Chief*, pp. 204; see also p. 258; for a more balanced critique of Charteris's role see Jim Beach, *Haig's Intelligence: GHQ and the German Army, 1916-1918* (Cambridge: Cambridge University Press, 2015 [2013]), esp. pp. 48-56.
33   CAC, Esher journal, 16 October 1917.
34   TNA CAB 24/28/42: GT 2242, 'Occupation of Jaffa-Jerusalem Line,' CIGS to War Cabinet, 9 October 1917, pp. 1, 3 and 7.
35   Ibid., pp. 4-5.

meant that 'Turkish territory will become, for an indefinite period, the decisive theatre and the West front must meanwhile be delegated to secondary importance.'[36] He warned of 'disastrous' consequences if the government insisted on major offensives on two fronts; expecting success from concentrated action in the Middle East would be a 'more dangerous' gamble than usual.[37] The estimate of forces required for a push to Jerusalem increased when General Sir Edmund Allenby, C-in-C Egyptian Expeditionary Force (EEF), reported that he would, in fact, need 14 infantry divisions and another six in relief, a demand one authority described as 'one of the most absurd appreciations every presented to a British government.'[38]

As a consummate politician Lloyd George was particularly exercised when the Royal Navy estimated it needed 100 ships to transport six divisions from France to the Middle East, with them arriving no sooner than the third week of February 1918. This would mean that 'the whole of the traffic in the Mediterranean' would be 'seriously interfered with', with severe impacts on supplies of coal and wheat to Italy which was already struggling to resist the Central Powers.[39] As for the consequences at home, diverting transports from trans-Atlantic convoys would reduce British imports by up to 1.2 million tons from November 1917 to December 1918.[40] It is hardly surprising that he sought new advice from individuals he knew had a less than sympathetic relationship with the War Office – GHQ alliance.

Wilson's Paper

Wilson's Paper was as much concerned with the civil-military interface as with pure military strategy. In Wilson's view, Britain's war policy thus far had been reactive rather than proactive. Britain had 'tried to adapt ourselves to the ever-changing, ever-increasing demands, but, generally speaking, following on German leads rather than taking a line of our own. As examples we have Gallipoli, Salonica [sic], the defence of the Suez Canal and Kut.' A review was required because in three years Britain had moved 'from being the most "contemptible" to being the most formidable' of Germany's enemies.[41] Russia was effectively lost as an ally, to be replaced by the USA which might be of significant value in 'the somewhat distant and problematical future.'[42] Wilson was not, unlike Haig, convinced that the time was right or the resources available to strike a decisive blow in the west. Haig had said he was 'confident that if the course I have recommended be adopted whole-heartedly we shall gain far more than a limited success in the field next year.'[43] Wilson disagreed. It was 'no use throwing "decisive numbers at the decisive

36   TNA CAB 24/28/42: GT 2242, 'Future Military Policy,' CIGS to War Cabinet, 9 October 1917, p 1.
37   Ibid., pp. 1-2.
38   There is evidence Robertson and Allenby colluded on this evaluation, Woodward, *Lloyd George*, p. 206; TNA CAB 27/8: WP 52, Allenby to CIGS, 10 October 1917.
39   TNA CAB 27/8: WP 54, 'Question of reinforcing the army in Palestine,' First Sea Lord to War Cabinet, 9 October 1917, pp 1 and 3.
40   TNA CAB 27/8: WP 54, 'Effect on Imports into the United Kingdom of proposed transfer of troops from France to Egypt,' First Sea Lord to War Cabinet, 9 October 1917, p. 2.
41   TNA CAB 27/8: WP 61, p. 3.
42   Ibid., pp. 3-4.
43   TNA CAB 27/8: GT 2243, pp. 13-14.

time at the decisive place" at my head if the decisive numbers do not exist, if the decisive hour has not struck or if the decisive plan is ill-chosen.[44]

For Wilson, timing was crucial. The autumn of 1917 saw discussion amongst politicians and public about the prospects for a negotiated peace. In September, the Germans had made indirect overtures to the French and British governments hinting at a compromise in which Germany seemed 'willing to accept defeat in the West for compensations in the East'.[45] British politicians were concerned that a war-weary France might sue for peace. Esher set the tone for those who might be prepared to consider a compromise. He told Robertson that awaiting the Americans seemed to be the favoured French policy and 'what a policy!':

> The sooner our excellent rulers make Peace the better. Why not accept the terms offered by Germany? They are more favourable than we are likely to obtain this day twelvemonth…as matters stand, no unbiased mind can resist the conclusion that while we have bested the Germans in the West, they have won, hands down, on the Eastern Front.[46]

He told Haig that it was 'amazing' that Lloyd George and some of his colleagues could 'not see that their sole chance of making a favourable peace is to balance the tremendous successes of Germany on the Eastern Front by equally striking ones on the Western.'[47] Esher was known for his pessimism. In December 1916, he had given Wilson the impression that he did not think Britain could win the war.[48] Nonetheless, Russia's inability to fight added to fears that the Allies might be forced to seek a compromise.[49] It has been argued that British grand strategy from mid-1916 until the end of the war was characterised by a general feeling of 'pessimism' amounting to defeatism. Some of Britain's political and military leaders were focussed on concluding the war on acceptable terms, in contrast to their public utterances epitomised by Lloyd George's commitment to total victory thanks to a 'knockout blow' on the Western Front.[50] Wilson was more positive. He remained opposed to a compromise peace and was confident that, with changes to strategic decision-making, Britain could emerge from the war with her empire and prestige intact. He told the War Cabinet that if a compromise was forced upon Britain:

> It is incontestable that the German position is better to-day with all the gains I have mentioned above (vis-à-vis terms of peace) than it would be had they not gained Turkey as Allies, had they not effectively occupied all the Balkans, Roumania [sic], Poland

44   TNA CAB 27/8: WP 61, p. 4.
45   David R. Woodward, 'David Lloyd George, a negotiated peace with Germany, and the Kulhmann Peace Kite of September 1917', *Canadian Journal of History*, March 1971, Vol. VI (1), p. 86.
46   CAC, Esher papers, Esher to Robertson, 22 October 1917.
47   Ibid., Esher to Haig, 23 October 1917.
48   Wilson diary, 1 December 1916.
49   For the War Cabinet discussion on the German peace overtures of Autumn 1917, see TNA CAB 23/16/2, War Cabinet, 24 September 1917 (Hankey, handwritten draft).
50   Millman, *Pessimism*, and idem, 'A Counsel of Despair: British Strategy and War Aims, 1917-18', *Journal of Contemporary History*, 2 (36), (2001), pp. 252-4.

and part or Russia; had they in fact, during the last two years, restricted themselves to attempting a final decision, as we have done in the main theatre, i.e. the West.[51]

Wilson said was making these points now, not because the West 'is not the decisive front – because it is', but because the final decision could only be reached when the decisive numbers were applied at the decisive place 'and the place and the time are not yet, and the Germans are trying their best that they never shall be'.[52]

He summarised his views in a section headed 'the Future' and asked if it were possible for the allies, 'now that we are only three instead of four – for the moment I do not count America', to 'enlarge our view' and draw up plans so that 'when the decisive moment arrives we can produce the decisive numbers at the decisive place?'[53] According to Wilson there were three, not necessarily mutually exclusive, routes towards this objective:

i.   By eliminating some of the smaller of our enemies and thus releasing all the troops and material we now have in such secondary theatres – and incidentally setting free a large amount of tonnage.
ii.   By recruiting the necessary number of men, and placing them in the field where and when required.
iii. By an enormous and overwhelming increase in guns, munitions, aeroplanes, tanks and all engines of war.

Regardless of which course(s) the War Cabinet chose, and this was the principal theme throughout, it was 'essential that a much closer and more effective co-operation' should be established between the Allies.[54]

The next section of this chapter considers these potential routes.

Theatres of War

Haig's assessment of the state of the war and prospects for 1918 was clear. While allowing for the possibility of 'local' successes against Turkey or Austria-Hungary, distracting effort elsewhere would weaken the British position on the Western Front. The BEF would have to go on the defensive, with the negative impact that would have on French morale. If Britain rejected large-scale offensives in France and Flanders in 1918 there was no likelihood of either France or Italy launching their own. As for the nascent American forces, they would 'not be capable of achieving any important results alone by offensive action next year'.[55] Therefore, 'success on the Western front is the only real alternative to an unsatisfactory peace'.[56] At this point, in his personal copy of Haig's report, Wilson wrote: 'This is true but what is under consideration is

---

51   TNA CAB 27/8: WP 61, pp. 5-6.
52   Ibid., p. 6.
53   Ibid., p. 7.
54   TNA CAB 27/8: WP 61, p. 8.
55   Ibid., GT 2243, p. 3.
56   Ibid., p. 3.

whether such a success would not be made easier if Turkey (& Bulgaria) were knocked.'[57] For Haig: 'The question for decision therefore, is whether the allies are capable of overcoming the Germans on the Western front even though Russia should be unable to take an active part in the war next year.'[58] Wilson disagreed and wrote in the margin: 'No. This is only part of the question'.[59]

Despite knowing that the Prime Minister harboured hopes of winning important victories in other theatres, Haig urged that 'we must take risks elsewhere and cut down our commitments in all other theatres to the minimum necessary to protect really vital interests'. Britain should adopt a similar approach to its Allies and stand back from assisting them directly. It was not in the Allied interest for 'the only really effective offensive army which will exist next year' to throw away 'what is a good prospect and practically the only prospect of a real victory by disseminating its forces…Great Britain has not the means to maintain more than one offensive.'[60]

Robertson agreed. Even if successful in Palestine 'the military effect would be of no value to us'.[61] It was 'very desirable' to reduce the number of Britain's enemies, but since Russia's collapse he did not see an extensive offensive campaign in Palestine 'as a sound military measure'. In his view 'the right military course to pursue is to act on the defensive in Palestine and the east generally and continue to seek a decision in the West'.[62] Throughout the war Robertson consistently opposed any large-scale offensives that would hamper Britain's effort in the west. In 1915, he condemned the forthcoming Gallipoli offensive as a 'ridiculous farce'.[63] Once he became CIGS he was, from time to time, prepared to consider actions away from France and Flanders to exploit perceived enemy weaknesses or to boost morale at home. He would not, however, subjugate the BEF's needs for those of armies to other theatres.[64]

In response Wilson reiterated his strategic belief in the primacy of the Western Front. On this point at least, he emphasised, he was in step with his colleagues:

> I have always been (even years before the war broke out) and I shall always remain, an ardent 'Westerner', for the simple reason that it is along the west front that the bulk of the forces of our principal enemy is disposed and the death-grapple must be engaged in at the time and place and in the manner best suited to our cause.[65]

Britain, he said, had been unable to consider the 'decisive maxim' (major offensives with the potential for strategically important results) until Spring 1916. The Battle of the Somme had been 'one of the steps we are treading to a final decision'. Since then 'we have had several attempts at a final decision, or shall we call them steps towards a final decision, notably at Arras, Messines, Ypres, Chemin-des-Dames, Champagne and Verdun, but the final decision has not

57   IWM, Wilson papers, 3/13/16, 'Notes on Sir D. Haig's Memo of 8 Oct 1917'.
58   TNA CAB 27/8: GT 2243, pp. 3-4.
59   Wilson papers, 3/13/16.
60   TNA CAB 27/8: GT 2243, p. 11.
61   TNA CAB 24/28/42: GT 2242, 'Future Military Policy,' CIGS to War Cabinet, 9 October 1917, p. 3.
62   Ibid., p. 4.
63   LHCMA, Robertson papers, (7/2/15), Robertson to Callwell, 19 March 1915.
64   See esp. Woodward, *Robertson*, pp. 114-123 and 157-168.
65   TNA CAB 27/8: WP 61, p. 4.

yet been reached.'[66] For Wilson, Britain's single-mindedness on the Western Front meant potential opportunities had been missed elsewhere:

> In no other theatre than along the Western front has any serious attempt been made by us during the last twenty months to reach a decision in that theatre ...We have been unwavering and unwearying in our hopes and in our actions to gain a final decision by a series of actions each of which we hoped would have given us that decision, but which, as events proved, were only steps in [sic] the ladder leading to the final decision.[67]

Wilson questioned Haig's and Robertson's continuing optimism for decisive results in the west in 1918: 'We seem to be as confident of success when Russia and Romania have collapsed and France is temporarily weakened as we were when all these three countries were capable of heavy offensive actions.'[68] Conversely, Germany, having failed to win in the west in 1914, had turned eastwards and had 'succeeded in the Balkans, in Romania and now in Russia.' Germany's plan had been to gain territory and supplies 'and put himself in the position to mass a much larger number of troops in the decisive theatre (i.e. in the West) when the time for the death-grapple came.'[69]

Although Lloyd George had long favoured 'knocking away the props',[70] Wilson believed opportunities 'to "knock out" some of our smaller antagonists', had disappeared.[71] As far as Austria-Hungary was concerned the matter was 'too complex' and 'eminently fitted' for a decision by a 'Superior Council'.[72] Bulgaria could not be tackled until Turkey had been taken out of the war. As for Turkey, the Allies had missed the boat. Wilson had, he said, been a long-time advocate of 'getting Turkey out of the war.' In a rare criticism in this document of his military colleagues Wilson went on:

> I cannot help thinking that, had we taken a somewhat broader and longer view of different theatres and made a juster [sic] appreciation of the moment for the decisive action, we could, and we ought to, have detached Turkey, and with her probably Bulgaria. But this is in the past, and the question here is – can we do so in the future.[73]

The answer, he concluded, was 'no'. This was a significant change of heart. Less than three weeks earlier Wilson had told Rawlinson that he favoured sending '10 or 12 D[i]vs to Egypt to make sure of beating the Turks this winter [and] bringing them back to France for the summer offensive of 1918...H.W. is for concentrating on the Turk this winter.'[74] At a meeting with Lord French and the Prime Minister, the latter had been 'mad to knock out the Turk in the winter'

---

66   TNA CAB 27/8: WP 61, p. 5.
67   Ibid.
68   Ibid.
69   Ibid., p.5
70   Lloyd George had been a supporter of seeking alternative theatres to the Western Front since early 1915, see Woodward, *Lloyd George*, pp. 28-9.
71   TNA CAB 27/8: WP 61, p. 8.
72   Ibid.
73   Ibid., p.8.
74   CAC, Papers of Sir Henry Rawlinson, Rawlinson Journal, RWLN 1/9, 2 October 1917.

and a similarly enthusiastic Wilson had 'expressed the strong belief that if a really good scheme was thoroughly well worked out, we could chase the Turks out of Palestine and very likely knock them completely out <u>during the mud months,</u> without in any way interfering with Haig's operations next Spring and Summer'.[75]   Once required to provide an authoritative assessment, and demonstrating a mix of both opportunism and pragmatism, Wilson changed his mind. On the day the War Cabinet asked for his views, and in the light of Robertson's and Jellicoe's negative reports, Wilson discussed the issue with the French CoS, Foch. Predictably enough the French general thought it 'late for Syria [Palestine] and we must spend the winter in making guns, arms etc.'[76] By the following day he had concluded that 'we are late to plan and carry out an attack on the Turks this winter' and thus 'this confines us to Europe'.[77] Having garnered the facts, and heard the opposition of his friend and mentor Foch, Wilson came 'very reluctantly, to the conclusion that we are too late'.[78] It was a notable conclusion, bearing in mind the Prime Minister's abiding interest in other theatres. Wilson explained that a successful offensive against Turkey in either Palestine or Mesopotamia would have had to have been carried out during the 'mud-months' in France, a period spanning 1 November and 30 April, when weather in the region was 'admirably suited for campaigning. We are too late now – in the middle of October – to make plans for the coming winter, and we are too late for other reasons also.'[79] Robertson's study had claimed two German divisions were available to reinforce the Turks and, if it became clear Britain intended a major offensive, more would be sent.[80] Wilson agreed. The Germans had second guessed the British and had 'taken a much firmer grip of the Turk, they have massed a large force in a central position, they have accumulated munitions and stores and vastly improved the communications in the Asiatic theatre.'[81] There was also the perennial problem of a shortage of troops. Agreeing with Haig and Robertson, Wilson advised that there would be insufficient manpower to send the necessary force to campaign in the Middle East and to remain effective in the west.[82] Thirdly, he reiterated the Admiralty view that 'dwindling tonnage and difficulties of escort would make the transportation, upkeep and return of the necessary force impossible'.[83] Wilson then sounded the death-knell for future large-scale adventures against Ottoman Turkey:

> For all these reasons, but not because the West is the decisive theatre in the winter, I am clearly of opinion that it is impossible to send an expedition against the Turks this winter *and wrong to send an expedition next spring or summer.*[84]

75   Wilson diary, 5 October 1917 (original emphasis).
76   Ibid., 11 October 1917.
77   Ibid., 12 October 1917
78   TNA CAB 27/8: WP 61, pp. 8-9.
79   Ibid., p. 9.
80   TNA CAB 27/8: GT 2242, 'Occupation of Jaffa – Jerusalem Line,' CIGS to War Cabinet, 9 October 1917, p. 4.
81   TNA CAB 27/8: WP 61, p. 9.
82   Ibid.
83   Ibid.
84   Ibid., author's italics.

Thereafter, though Lloyd George returned to the point often, the War Cabinet's appetite for major offensives away from the Western Front, on the premise that of themselves they would bring about Germany's defeat, waned. Wilson continued to pay lip-service to the notion, but at Versailles and later as CIGS, he ensured the BEF's manpower would not be denuded at the expense of major offensives elsewhere. In future, initiatives beyond France and Flanders would be motivated by the defence and extension of Britain's imperial interests rather than as potential war-winning operations. As result they would be limited, pragmatic and always subservient to operations in the west.

Manpower and Resources

Wilson argued that Britain and her Allies would not be ready for a major offensive in the west in 1918. As already discussed, he had been a long-time and prominent advocate of conscription, including conscription for Ireland, and was in step with his military colleagues who believed the government could and should do more to provide men for the war.[85] However, Haig and Wilson disagreed on a crucial point. Haig believed that with concerted effort the BEF could conduct a major offensive in 1918. Wilson did not. According to Haig, Germany had so far brought few divisions to the Western Front from the Eastern. Evidence, he believed, that Germany 'does not expect any immediate total collapse in Russia'.[86] Wilson noted in his copy of Haig's report: 'This may be so but it may equally be taken as affording truth that Germany is not really frightened by our present attack?' The marginalia records that Wilson's discussions with the DMI Macdonogh, 'make clear that the Boch [sic] can draw, easily, on the Russian front'.[87] Wilson was wrong. The recent fighting during the Third Battle of Ypres had pushed the Germans to the limits of their endurance.[88] According to Haig, of the 147 German divisions on his front, 135 had been driven from their positions or withdrawn 'broken by their losses' since 1 April 1917, 'many of them twice and some three times…I quote this as proof of what our armies are capable of.'[89] Wilson did not question the statistics but instead asked: 'How many English and French divisions have been roughly handled in the same period?'[90] Haig insisted that in the light of such favourable circumstances it should be:

> Beyond question that our offensive must be pursued as long as possible. I have every hope of being able to continue it for several weeks still and of gaining results which will add very greatly to the enemy's losses in men and moral[e] and place us in a far better position to resume an offensive in the spring. Amongst other advantages, we shall end this year's campaign with practically all the observation points originally held by the enemy in our possession – a very important consideration.[91]

---

85   Jeffery, *Wilson*, esp., pp. 196-7 and 222-3.
86   TNA CAB 27/8: GT 2243, p. 4.
87   Wilson papers, 3/13/16, 'Notes on Sir D. Haig's Memo of 8 Oct 1917'.
88   Lloyd, *Passchendaele*, pp. 217-8, 292.
89   TNA CAB 27/8: GT 2243, p. 4.
90   Wilson papers, 3/13/16.
91   TNA CAB 27/8: GT 2243, p. 5.

The capture of the Bourlon Ridge would allow British artillery to bring down accurate fire on the Hindenburg Line, and on the important railhead at Cambrai.[92] Haig was confident of entering the 1918 campaigning season 'with excellent prospects of decisive success if we throw into the scale wholeheartedly the full weight of the Empire's strength and if Russia can maintain on her front even the number of German divisions now there'. He added: 'Future developments in Russia are so uncertain that in considering our future plans we cannot ignore the possibility that she may be able to do at least as much.'[93] Wilson was sceptical, noting 'the assumption about Russia is a large one'.[94] Nonetheless, as Haig conceded, the Prime Minister had asked the C-in-C for his proposed policy in the event of Russian capitulation. If this happened, Haig believed, Germany would have to keep 59 divisions in the east to monitor Russian activity and to supervise her allies in the region. Haig thought Germany could only divert 32 divisions to the west, bringing the complement to 179 divisions. By 1 April 1918, these would be faced by 176 Allied divisions, comprising 62 British divisions 'if our forces in France remain as they are', 100 French, 12 American and 2 Portuguese.[95] He conceded that at 'first sight such a force would appear to be insufficient to justify the hope of a successful offensive on this front next year', but 19 of the German divisions were of 'poor quality, only fit for defensives on quiet fronts'.[96] Wilson asked 'what of the Belgian, the Portuguese, the Americans and some French'.[97] Haig claimed German losses were being largely replaced by 'quite inferior material' and that by May or June 1918 'the German reserves will be exhausted.'[98] Alongside this statement Wilson wrote: 'What of the French and British Reserves.'[99] As for troop numbers, Haig calculated that the Allies would be up to 30% stronger thanks to the greater number of battalions, and of men in battalions, in British, American and Portuguese divisions.[100] Wilson made a note to check this claim with the DMI and subsequently wrote in his copy 'Macdonogh agrees.'[101] Wilson challenged the assertion that the 100 French divisions Haig calculated on having available in 1918 could be considered as 'fully equivalent' to the same number of German divisions facing them, writing: 'This is not the present state of affairs.'[102] He was right to be sceptical. Between 1 November 1917 and March 1918, the Germans moved 48 divisions from east to west (with two going in the opposite direction), and eight more from Italy to the Western Front. On 21 March, the first day of *Operation Michael*, the start of the German Spring Offensives, there were 191 German divisions on the Western Front, 22 more than Haig had predicted.[103]

Thus, Haig was 'confident that the British Armies in France, assisted by the French and American Armies, will be quite capable of carrying through a sustained and successful offensive

92   Sheffield, *The Chief*, p. 253.
93   TNA CAB 27/8: GT 2243, p. 6.
94   Wilson papers, 3/13/16.
95   TNA CAB 27/8: GT 2243, p. 7.
96   Ibid.
97   Wilson papers, 3/13/16.
98   TNA CAB 27/8: GT 2243, p. 7.
99   Wilson Papers, 3/13/16.
100 TNA CAB 27/8: GT 2243, pp. 7-8.
101 Wilson papers, 3/13/16.
102 TNA CAB 27/8: GT 2243, p. 8, and Wilson papers, 3/13/16.
103 David T. Zabecki, *The German 1918 Offensives: A Case Study in the Operational Level of War* (Oxford: Routledge, 2006), pp. 89-90.

next year,' but only if certain conditions were met. Diverting troops would put this 'successful offensive' at risk, he warned. All the 62 British divisions currently in France would be needed, at full establishment, with new drafts trained by early spring. Moreover, 'further drafts to replace wastage in next year's offensive should be trained and sent to France in time to take their place in the ranks when required'.[104] Wilson's note on his copy of the Haig paper noted that Macready, the Adjutant General, and Sir Auckland Geddes, the Director of National Service, 'profess this is impossible'.[105] French demands for the BEF to take over more line had to be resisted to allow troops to recover, take leave and be trained. This would be 'both justifiable and wise', particularly as the French armies were unlikely to consent to major offensives in the foreseeable future, 'since the British armies alone can be made capable of a great offensive effort it is beyond argument that everything should be done by our allies as well as ourselves to enable that effort to be made as strong as possible.'[106] Correctly predicting French opposition, Haig argued that the best test of commitment was not the length of line held, but the numbers of enemy divisions faced, and the role of the armies concerned in the offensive he wanted to launch next spring. Therefore the British had to 'refuse to take over more line and to adhere resolutely to that refusal, even to the point of answering threats by threats if necessary'.[107] Clearly bemused, Wilson wrote 'Whew!' against this sentence.[108]

Having consulted Macdonogh on Haig's manpower assumptions, Wilson concluded that Britain could not recruit 'a sufficient number of men to overwhelm the enemy by numbers', at least not until the USA was able to 'transport very large forces and maintain them in the field, and this will certainly not be the case in 1918'.[109] None of Britain's main European allies was in a position to assist. Unlike Haig, whose paper still held out some hope that the Russians would continue as a viable force, Wilson considered them relevant only for the numbers of German troops which would be diverted to the west when they collapsed. Early in 1917 Wilson had undertaken an inspection tour of Russia, and although his initial impressions of the Tsarist forces had been positive, he became less sanguine once he returned to London.[110] By the autumn he was convinced the end was near. He calculated, like Haig, that once Russia withdrew from the war, something he considered imminent, Germany would be able to divert between 20 and 40 divisions to the west.[111] As for the Italians, their own commanders felt it unlikely they could maintain their present numbers into 1918.[112] Worse still, the French army was already declining and would soon be forced to reduce its number of divisions.[113]

Wilson then turned to the British position. In his personal copy of Haig's report, annotated in his own hand, he highlighted the C-in-C's assumptions about both recruitment and 'wastage' and noted he would check them with Macdonogh, the DMI. Although a long-standing ally of Robertson, Macdonogh also worked amicably with Wilson and briefed him at least twice

104 TNA CAB 27/8: GT 2243, p. 8.
105 Wilson papers, 3/13/16.
106 TNA CAB 27/8: GT 2243, p. 9.
107 Ibid., p. 10.
108 Wilson papers, 3/13/16.
109 TNA CAB 27/8: WP 61, p. 10.
110 Wilson diary, 10, 14 February 1917.
111 TNA CAB 27/8: WP 61, p. 11.
112 Ibid, p. 10.
113 Ibid.

during the writing of his report.[114] As a result, Wilson told the War Cabinet that the British were 'roughly speaking' in the following position:

> If the Infantry in France is filled up to establishment now – we are at this moment some 50,000 to 60,000 Infantry under establishment – and if we take, in the coming 12 months, a punishment equal to that which we have taken in the last 12 months, then the present deficit of 50,000 to 60,000 will be turned into a deficit of anything from 100,000 to 200,000.

In the 12 months from October 1918 the situation would be even worse 'with nothing in Reserve to make good wastage except the boys who become matured and returned Expeditionary Force men', that is, those who had been wounded and returned to the ranks.[115]

The German position, he argued, was more positive. Against a growing British shortfall, and not taking into account the potential for up to 40 additional divisions currently facing the Russians, Wilson calculated Germany had an extra 100,000 men available for the front line in field depots. In Germany, Macdonogh reported, there were another 620,000 fit men. To this could be added an estimated half a million young men from the '1920 Class' of recruits. This came to a potential 1.2 million available for drafting in Germany in the coming 12 months.[116] This was twice the figure Haig's paper had predicted.[117] In fact, while at the beginning of 1918 there were 1.1 million men fit for field service employed in German war industries, it was not thought practical to put them in uniform. The next 'class' of new recruits, totalling 637,000 men, higher than Macdonogh's estimate, would not be ready until the autumn of 1918.[118] In reality, GHQ's estimate of the German manpower situation was more accurate than that of the General Staff at the War Office. At the time, however, distrust in London of the assessments of GHQ's intelligence operation meant Haig's pronouncements were received with scepticism.[119] In the light of such contradictory predictions it is not surprising that Wilson concluded this section with the assessment that 'until the Americans can be got over in sufficient force we cannot hope to beat the enemy by force of numbers'.[120] The manpower challenge continued to dominate British strategy for the rest of the war.

Superior Direction

Having undermined the optimistic predictions of Haig and Robertson, Wilson's argument moved to its denouement. In his report Haig had taken a dim view of inter-Allied control of war strategy. Referring to the failed Nivelle Offensive of April 1917, when he and his army had been placed under French orders, he recommended that in future, Britain should:

---

114 Wilson diary, 12, 16 October 1917.
115 TNA CAB 27/8: WP 61, p. 10.
116 Zabecki, *German Offensives*, pp. 89-93.
117 CAB 27/8, GT 2243, p. 5.
118 Zabecki, *German Offensives*, pp. 89-93.
119 Beach, *Haig's Intelligence*, pp. 256-259.
120 TNA CAB 27/8: WP 61, p. 11.

Insist on occupying the predominant positions in the Councils of the Allies to which our strength entitles us. More than once already we have subordinated our judgement to that of our allies with highly unsatisfactory results. We cannot afford to make such mistakes again, and whatever they may threaten [,] our allies cannot afford to quarrel with us. [121]

Robertson believed 'the principle of "unity of command" and "one front" must be cautiously applied. In theory it is attractive, in practice it has not been encouraging.' Like Haig he reminded the War Cabinet that it was 'responsible for the Nivelle era and its consequences'. As far as Robertson was concerned, Allied co-operation had seen Britain and France obliged to send 150 heavy guns to Italy, and another 550 to Russia. 'All are lost to us,' he said.[122] Despite these guns, diverted from Flanders, the Italians had cancelled a promised offensive and decided to adopt a 'more passive attitude' on their front. General Luigi Cadorna, the Italian Army's commander, thought this *volte-face* 'would not prejudice Allied operations elsewhere'.[123] In the light of these developments Robertson was dismissive of Britain's allies' willingness to fight. In his view, the French had also 'failed us badly this year' and 'must be made to fight'. Therefore:

As far as 'unity of command' is concerned, we should endeavour to acquire for ourselves the control of operations next year on the West front, as we are entitled to do by our successes this year, the efficiency and spirit of our Armies, and the stability of our Government as compared with that of practically all our European Allies.[124]

As a long-term advocate of closer Allied co-operation, Wilson disagreed. Lloyd George had discussed the notion of a form of superior direction with him in August and suggested a trio of senior officers to review Robertson's recommendations. Wilson had counselled against this as unfair to Robertson, but maintained the view that an inter-Allied body, including senior political representatives, was required.[125] While writing his policy paper, Wilson met the French Minister of Propaganda, Henri Franklin-Bouillon, and pressed on him 'the necessity of the Superior Organisation which I think essential to the prosecution of the war and he was much taken with it and said he would discuss it with L.G. this afternoon.'[126] The next day Wilson had lunch at the Ritz with Lloyd George, Franklin-Bouillon, the French Prime Minister Paul Painlevé 'and another minister (with a snub nose).' The French delegation was in London to urge Britain to take over more French line, and to discuss Middle East strategy and recent German peace overtures.[127] Wilson took the opportunity to lobby support for his idea:

121 For the placing of Haig under French orders and the subsequent Nivelle Offensive see esp. Sheffield, *The Chief*, pp. 204-222, and French, *Strategy* pp. 52-61; TNA CAB 27/8: WP 61, p. 12.
122 TNA CAB 24/28/42: GT 2242, 'Future Military Policy', CIGS to War Cabinet, 9 October 1917, pp. 6-7.
123 TNA CAB 23/4/12: War Cabinet, 24 September 1917.
124 TNA CAB 24/28/42: GT 2242, 'Future Military Policy', CIGS to War Cabinet, 9 October 1917, pp. 6.
125 Wilson diary, 23 August 1917.
126 Ibid., 12 October 1917.
127 TNA CAB 23/13/20: War Cabinet Minutes, 10 October 1917 and CAC, Esher journal, 15 October 1917.

All were insistent on my going back to Paris [as head of liaison] but, as I told them, unless the Superior War Cabinet is started there is no place for me. At the lunch I drew a graphic for the snub-nose of this organisation (on the back of his menu) which he made me sign, and Painlevé, who was sitting on my left insisted on my drawing a similar graphic for him and signing it.[128]

In his report Wilson avoided the implication that 'superior direction' of the war would inevitably mean 'unity of command' at the military level, offering assurances to the soldiers about their future status *vis-a-vis* such an organisation. There seems little doubt, however, that this was his ultimate expectation.[129] After dining with Lloyd George and French on 17 October he wrote:

It became very clear to me tonight that L.G. means to get Robertson out *and* means to curb the powers of the CinC in the field. This is what I have been advising the last 2 ½ years & this is what the whole of my paper is directed to. Not to getting R.[obertson] put out but to forming an [sic] Superior Direction over all the CGSs and CinCs.[130]

In 1915 Wilson had written to Bonar Law advocating a 'Committee of Six', made up of the British and French C-in-Cs, Foreign Secretaries and War Secretaries, to adjudicate on joint strategic plans.[131] In August 1917, while 'unemployed' on half-pay, Wilson revived the idea and discussed it twice with the Prime Minister.[132] Little wonder then that in his final report he advised that it was at the political-military interface where fundamental change was required. He told his War Cabinet audience that he did not believe the current state of affairs was the fault of the senior generals.[133] Instead, he implied, responsibility lay with them, and other Allied leaders, because: 'The superior direction of this war has, in my opinion been gravely at fault from the very commencement – in fact, it is inside the truth to say that there has never been any superior direction at all.'[134] At first reading this might have appeared a career-limiting conclusion, especially for a soldier so experienced in the dark arts of political intrigue. In fact, Wilson was in no peril. He and Lloyd George had discussed the subject several times; the Prime Minister was not going to be surprised by Wilson's conclusions.[135] Joffre, while in command of the French armies, had tried: 'With poor results indeed but still he tried, to assume and exercise a kind of benevolent control over all the Allies, but his position was not sufficiently exalted his

128   Wilson diary, 13 October 1917; Hankey, diary, 13 October 1917, cited in Hankey, *Supreme Command* (Vol. II), p. 712.
129   As Chapter Eight illustrates, the definition of the concept of 'unity of command' differed over the course of the war, and between soldiers and statesmen.
130   Wilson diary, 17 October 1917.
131   PA, Bonar Law papers, Wilson to Bonar Law, (BL 51/4/31 and BL 52/1/10), 27 October and 3 December 1915.
132   Wilson diary, 16 and 23 August 1917, and Riddell, *War Diary*, 14 August 1917, p. 265.
133   'This tendency to narrowness of vision is not due, it seems to me, to any fault of our military Chiefs but to another cause which I shall refer to later,' TNA CAB 27/8: WP 61, p 7.
134   Ibid., pp. 11-12.
135   Wilson met Lloyd George and discussed this and related issues on 5, 10, 13 and 17 October 1917, Wilson diary.

powers were not sufficiently great to admit of success.'[136] Since then the Allies had tried 'many expedients but always with most disappointing, sometimes even with disastrous results.' Thus:

> We have had frequent meetings of Ministers, constant conversations between Chiefs of the Staffs, deliberations of Commanders-in-Chiefs, Mass [sic] meetings of all these high officials in London, in Paris, in Rome. We have tried the experiment of placing one Commander-in-Chief under the orders of another, and all these endeavours have failed to attain any real concerted and co-ordinated effort in diplomacy, in strategy, in fighting or in the production of war material.[137]

For Wilson, the failure of Britain and France and more recently Italy to address the issue of co-ordinated control had resulted in fragmented and self-seeking strategies:

> Curiously enough, our constant thought of a decision in the West – a frame of mind amounting almost to an obsession – has led us to consider only that part of the Western front which is held by ourselves, and partly because of this and partly from other causes the tendency for the whole line from Nieuport to Trieste to be cut up into three sections – British, French, Italian – has become more and more accentuated.[138]

This was noticeable in the latest status reports from Haig and Robertson 'although the latter very wisely remarks that "the British Army alone cannot with the war. Our allies must be made to fight".'[139]

Inter-Allied co-ordination was also vital to improve the production of war materiel. Wilson asked if the Allies could increase output so that 'we shall be able to overwhelm the enemy?'[140] He believed they could, but on two conditions:

a. That there is absolute co-ordination between the four countries of England, France and Italy and in future America.
b. That the whole of our united energies are concentrated on this one work, and that the date of the attempt to reach a 'final decision' is made subordinate to the completion of this great effort. [141]

In other words, in Wilson's strategic analysis, Allied co-operation and co-ordination was fundamental if victory was to be snatched from the jaws of defeat. Without decisive action, the prospects for this essential co-working were gloomy:

> It seems to me that there is less concerted action now in our strategy and in our various plans than at any time since the war began. I do not wish to exaggerate, but human

136 TNA CAB 27/8: WP 61, p. 12.
137 Ibid., p. 12.
138 Ibid., p. 6.
139 Ibid., pp. 6-7.
140 Ibid., p. 11.
141 Ibid., original emphasis.

nature being what it is and our Commanders-in-Chiefs and Chiefs of Staff being what they are – all men of strong and decided views, all men whose whole energies are devoted to their own fronts and their own national concerns – we get as a natural and inevitable result a war conducted not as a whole but as a war on sections of the whole.[142]

Consequently, there was 'a war on the British front', one on the French and one on the Italian 'and the stronger and the better the various Chiefs the more isolated and detached the plans'.[143]

This was the core of Wilson's strategic argument. 'All this confusion, overlapping and loss of collective effort' was inevitable and 'the better the sectional Commanders-in-Chiefs are, the more loyal and responsive the Chiefs of the Home Staffs, the more we see the whole of the national effort restricted to the national fronts.' Lack of concerted, effective, oversight was 'undoubtedly prolonging the war to an unnecessary and even to a dangerous extent.'[144] He summed up thus: 'The net results seems to me to be that we take short views instead of long views, we look for decisions today instead of laying our plans for tomorrow and as [con]sequence we have constant change of plans, with growing and increasing irritation and inefficiency.'[145] The time had come for the establishment of 'an intelligent, effective and powerful superior direction'.[146] This would result from the creation of a small 'War Cabinet of the Allies informed and above all entrusted with such power that opinion on all the larger issues of the war will carry weight of conviction and be accepted by each of the Allies as final.'[147] Deploying all his political subtlety, Wilson reassured the politicians that there was 'no question' of overruling national Cabinets since the 'Supreme War Cabinet, or Superior Direction as I have called it' would represent them. He also attempted, unsuccessfully, to reassure the generals that there was not 'the least danger of any interference with the soldiers in the field, since the Chiefs of the Staff in each country will remain as today'.[148] This new body would look beyond the narrow confines of sectional fronts and treat the line of battle 'from Nieuport to Mesopotamia as one line, and it would allot to each of the Allies the part which it would play'. According to Wilson, if such a body had been in place a year or two earlier it would have arbitrated on whether the Allies should have sought a 'final decision' on the Western Front 'or whether the time for such an attempt should be postponed until a favourable decision had been reached in some of the minor theatres, thus enabling a larger force to be concentrated at a later date for the death-grapple in the West'.[149]

Wilson's grand vision was that his 'Superior Direction' would define the 'broad line of action' for the next one or two years and decide 'when and under what conditions and in which part of the main theatre the final decision should be attempted and reached'.[150] With this body in place the 'vexed question' of taking over more line from the French could be addressed. Thanks to the current state of strategic decision making, without agreed plans for the future, this was impossible. If Wilson's mechanism was adopted it would be 'quite easy' to solve 'when the broad

142 TNA CAB 27/8: WP 61, p. 12.
143 Ibid.
144 Ibid., p. 13.
145 Ibid.
146 Ibid.
147 Ibid.
148 Ibid., p 14.
149 Ibid.
150 Ibid.

lines of next year's campaign have been arranged'. It would lay out broad policies for a joint air campaign and adjust war material manufacture accordingly. In short this body would take over the 'Superior Direction' of the war 'a thing that has not yet been done, and for the lack of which we have suffered so grievously in the past and without which we shall, so certainly, suffer even more in the future'.[151] Without such a body each ally would continue to concentrate on 'his own war, each thus drifting further and further from his neighbour, while all the time the enemy, under one governing authority, will be able to concentrate and to defeat each of the local efforts.' As for the naysayers:

> I may be told that, excellent as such an idea is in theory, it is wholly impossible in practice; that we are already overloaded with machinery; that if we cannot come to decisions under the present conditions, then we certainly cannot under any others; that there are no men fitted by knowledge, temperament or position to fill the new posts, and so on and so on. My answer would be very simple. I admit the difficulties, but I deny the impossibilities. Further, we have tried every other conceivable variant and always with the same unsatisfactory result – in short, if we cannot make up our minds to catch a hold of the situation as a whole and really direct and command the main issue of this war, we are gambling with the future in a manner we have no right to do, and we are in fact running a very serious chance of losing the war by stalemate.
>
> We (the Allies) hold all the cards in our hands – men, munitions, guns, aeroplanes, food, money and the High Seas – there remains only the question of how to play them and when to play them, and my absolute conviction is that there is no other way than by the creation of a Superior Direction.[152]

French's Papers

Field Marshal Lord French's paper has received limited critical attention in the historiography. It has been largely passed over, dismissed as partisan and invective-ridden and by implication of little merit. Haig described it as 'a poor production' and 'evidently the outcome of a jealous and disappointed mind'.[153] It is true that it was more personal in tone than Wilson's, and critical of both Haig and Robertson, but this does not justify it being overlooked. In fact, study reveals a clarity of argument which, while more strident in tone than the usual public discourse of senior military figures of the time, in several ways echoed Wilson's own line of argument. Historians have noted that French's paper, as originally submitted to Hankey, required editing by the Cabinet Secretary and Wilson before it was considered suitable for War Cabinet consumption.[154] Until now, French's first draft and his final submission have not been compared in detail, but doing so casts new light on the febrile strategic debate going on in the British leadership at the time.

Wilson delivered the finished reports to Hankey. According to the latter's diary, the papers should have gone in the first instance to Robertson as CIGS, a fact Hankey had failed to record

---

151   TNA CAB 27/8: WP 61, p. 15.
152   Ibid.
153   NLS, Haig (manuscript) diary, 31 October 1917.
154   See esp. Roskill, *Hankey*, p. 446, Jeffery; *Wilson*, p. 206 and Holmes, *Little Field Marshal*, p. 332.

in the relevant minutes. Presumably nervous of Wully's reaction, French objected, the wily Lloyd George refused to rule on the matter and the documents went first to the Cabinet Secretary. Eventually Hankey passed them to Derby:

> The whole subject is so thorny, and Robertson is in so prickly a state that I did not wish to make any mistake in procedure... The reports confirmed my worst anticipations. They both recommended a central council including a staff of generals, in Paris, to be independent of the national General Staffs. This, alone, is enough to drive Robertson into resignation. They both condemned the continuation of the Flanders offensive, next year, which is the course what Robertson and Haig recommend. In addition, Lord French's report hits out hard at Robertson and Haig whose views were challenged in principle and in detail.

Hankey then added, but perhaps understandably omitted from his memoirs:

> Incidentally I may remark that the whole thing is a clever plot on Ll G's part. Earlier in the year at Litchfield he sounded them both [Wilson and French] and ascertained this was their view, no doubt playing on their ambition and known jealousy and dislike of Robertson, by letting them see that he agreed, accompanying this no doubt with a good deal of suggestions. Then he lets Haig go on, and even encourages him to do so, knowing that the bad weather was preventing a big result, in order to strengthen the argument. Then he guilelessly proposes the War Council, knowing perfectly well that the jury is a packed one, which will only report in one direction. By these means he fortifies himself with apparently unbiased military opinion in the great struggle with Robertson and Haig, which he knows he cannot face without it.[155]

Wilson saw Derby on 24 October: 'He told me he had not yet shown our papers (Johnnie's and mine) to Robertson. He said Johnnie's was too personal and mine too unanswerable and if they were shown to Haig and Robertson there would be a hell of a row which might mean resignation of Haig, R. and himself!'[156] At this point the Prime Minister ordered French to tone down his paper.[157]

French's biographer ascribed his combative mood not only to his animosity towards both Robertson and Haig, whom he blamed for his removal as C-in-C, but also to his 'increasingly gloomy outlook on the war in general'.[158] Unlike Wilson's diplomatic approach, his report overtly echoed the criticisms the Prime Minister recently deployed against his C-in-C and CIGS when they met on 5 October:

> L.G. said Robertson simply 'thwarted' him in every scheme... I asked L.G. about a superior organisation & he said of course that was the best plan but the French (and

155 CAC, Hankey diary, HNKY 1/3, 20 October 1917 and Hankey, *Supreme Command*, (vol. II), pp. 714-715.
156 Wilson diary, 24 October 1917.
157 CAC, Hankey diary, 24 October 1917.
158 Holmes, *Little Field Marshal*, p. 332.

Italian) governments were absolutely rotten – in fact there were no governments – & so it was impossible to get such an organisation started; & therefore he was reverting to his former idea of calling me in to examine Robertson's plans. Johnnie fulminated against R.[obertson], & L.G. agreed but said that R had got so much of the Press (M.[orning] Post, Northcliffe, Leo Maxse etc) & Asquith that it was a difficult question to remove him… Johnnie said he felt very hopeless about the whole thing, for although L.G. <u>knew</u> that Robertson was not big enough for the post yet he funked kicking him out… the fact is that L.G. is profoundly dis-satisfied (as he was on Aug 23rd) but does not know what to do, or how to get rid of Robertson. I saw no animus against Haig.[159]

The main thrust of Haig's proposal, according to French, was for the War Cabinet to accept that Britain could be successful on the Western Front in 1918, and that it would be so. Conviction would carry the day, regardless of the realities on the ground. Such a belief had obtained since 1 July 1916 and the results were clear. Haig had assured the Cabinet, the public and his troops 'that he could break the enemy's line in such a manner as to pour large bodies of cavalry through the gap he had made and compel a great German defeat.' Despite bringing 'masses' of cavalry 'up to points close to the trenches, at considerable loss in men and horses, in this expectation' this had not happened. Wilson struck the accusatory words 'at considerable loss in men and horses' from the original draft.[160] French admired Haig's 'magnificent efforts' but 'the results so far obtained have not only fallen far below expectations, amounting almost to promises, of the Commander-in-Chief, but have in fact brought us but little nearer to any effective decision.' Haig was now asking the War Cabinet 'to accept his assurance that he can overthrow the enemy in the field and compass the German defeat next year. But such appeals [at this point Wilson struck out the words "for confidence and trust in his judgement" from French's draft][161] have been made on many previous occasions, with the results to which I have referred.'[162]

French was also unconvinced by Haig's suggestion that decisive action on the Western Front had a positive impact in the countries of the Middle East where Britain's imperial interests lay. Inserting a self-congratulatory reference, he said he imagined that:

India and the East took more interest in the capture of Baghdad than all the battles on the Western front after the first definite set-back of Germany in September 1914, which was a thing they could understand…fighting battles on the Western front to impress the East, or even to impress the German people, is not a good military reason.[163]

As for comparative manpower numbers, he asked 'on what basis' Haig could claim that 132 German divisions had been severely weakened by recent action. British units had also suffered

159 Wilson diary, 5 October 1917.
160 IWM, French papers, JDPF 7/7, draft of Lord French's paper on the 'Present State of the War, future prospects, and future action,' 20 October 1917, (in its final version CAB 27/8, WP 60), (amendments to the original in Wilson's handwriting), p. 12.
161 Ibid., p. 12.
162 TNA CAB 27/8: WP 60, pp. 11-12.
163 Ibid., p. 4.

set-backs, and had not 'many, if not all, of them gone on again and succeeded?'[164] French critiqued GHQ's assessment of Germans losses between 1 October 1917 and the end of the year. These had been put at 720,000, he said, 'surely this is too much to hope for!'[165] Having reviewed the figures with both Macdonogh and Macready he did not believe Haig was justified in suggesting the Allies would have a numerical advantage on the Western Front in 1918: 'The arguments used are the same as those brought forward early in 1916, and that these have not been borne out ['falsified' in the original draft] by the actual test of battle between July 1st 1916 and October 1917.'[166] Furthermore, there was no evidence to show that the 132 German divisions had been 'broken by their losses' and the forecast for the enemy's 'wastage' by the start of 1918 were 'inaccurate' and the conclusions arrived at 'unwarranted'.[167]

French questioned GHQ's assertion that during Third Ypres the Germans had suffered 50 percent more casualties than the British. Macdonogh had told him that the Germans had not issued any casualty figures since July: 'In view of the fact that we have almost invariably been attacking, I find it very difficult to believe that our enemy's losses have not been greatly overrated.'[168] French had initially written 'greatly exaggerated', but Wilson inserted a milder verb.[169] He concluded that he did not believe Haig had 'inflicted any greater loss upon the enemy than he has suffered himself'.[170] His report showed that British casualties for the period 1 July 1916 to 9 April 1917 were 'nearly' 53,103 per month; casualties in the succeeding period [the period which included the Battles of Arras and the ongoing Third Ypres] were 'nearly' 83,318 per month. These figures were 'certainly a surprise to me in view of frequent reports that our casualties during 1917 were "increasingly light"'.[171] Since the start of the Somme battle Haig's armies had incurred more than one million casualties and recovered 200 square miles of French and Belgian territory. A high price for small gain, French implied, considering the Germans still occupied 13,500 square miles of France and Flanders.[172]

French said he entertained 'very grave doubts as to whether we have not been playing the German game throughout the whole of our operations in the last year and a half.' In a paragraph which must have been music to the ears of Lloyd George he added:

> It is quite open to question whether they have not deliberately led us on to the capture of ground which is, in the long run, of little military importance to them, and which they know they never want to keep, even if they could. It is by no means unlikely that their object throughout has been to hold on to the Western side, and to do so in such a manner as to invite our attack and impose enormous casualties upon us, with a minimum loss to themselves.[173]

---

164 TNA CAB 27/8: WP 60, pp. 4-5; in fact, Haig's paper said 135 divisions had been weakened. TNA CAB 27/8: GT 2243, p. 4.
165 Ibid., p. 6.
166 IWM, French papers, JDPF 7/7, p. 7.
167 TNA CAB 27/8: WP 60, p. 7.
168 Ibid., p. 8.
169 IWM, French papers, JDPF 7/7, p. 8.
170 TNA CAB 27/8: WP 60, p. 18.
171 Ibid., p. 10.
172 Ibid., p. 12.
173 Ibid., p. 14.

In sum, the amendments Wilson made to French's critique of Haig's work were significant but limited, and for the most part involved substituting intemperate words with more sensitive ones. This was not the wholesale rewrite the historiography suggests.

French took a stronger line with Robertson's paper, condemning it as 'chiefly a form of special pleading in favour of continuing the offensive in the West.'[174] Wilson rewrote the sentence so that it described Robertson's paper as one 'devoted to advocating to a continuance of' the Ypres offensive.[175] French questioned the CIGS' warning against 'gambles' in the Middle East. He opposed another offensive in the west as 'much more of a "gamble" than anything we have undertaken in the war.' This method had been tried already with 'enormous loss and produced comparatively little result.'[176] Robertson said he had considered an offensive in the east for months, ultimately rejecting the idea.[177] French said he believed such a strategy 'offered such favourable chances and possibilities as should have induced the General Staff to bring it up for discussion by the War Cabinet at a time when it would have been possible to consider it.'[178] In the draft, the sentence continued 'namely, some three months ago'; Wilson also crossed this out.[179]

French took Robertson to task for his criticism of the Nivelle Offensive as 'somewhat severe' and 'misleading'. Nivelle had captured important military features and made 'as long if not longer advance than we have yet accomplished in the Ypres area'. According to French 'A feeling of resentment against our French Allies is somewhat apparent in the mind of the Chief of the Imperial General Staff,' and 'I cannot help regarding these remarks as somewhat severe.'[180] Wilson's diplomatic pen was employed once again to strike out French's addition of the words 'and without justification'.[181] Robertson's conviction that the Allies could 'beat the Germans every time we fight them' and inflict heavier losses was, according to French 'not altogether consistent with the facts'.[182] Wilson toned this down, replacing these words with 'somewhat optimistic'.[183] French believed that Haig's confidence in himself and his troops had 'somewhat warped his judgement'. Moreover, the General Staff had failed in its primary responsibility of putting all the C-in-C's assumptions to 'the most crucial test.' In other words, Robertson had acquiesced in the face of Haig's enthusiastic self-confidence 'without question or demur'. French claimed that 'statements from the front have not been tested as to their accuracy'. [184] As if this slur on Robertson's professionalism was not enough, French claimed that: 'Wild statements have been allowed to pass unchallenged. They have apparently been blindly accepted.' Wilson crossed this out.[185] French concluded this section with praise for the 'splendid work' of the Army

174 IWM, French papers, JDPF 7/7, p. 17.
175 TNA CAB 27/8: WP 60, p. 17.
176 Ibid., p. 16.
177 TNA CAB 27/8: GT 2242, 'Future Military Policy', CIGS to War Cabinet, 9 October 1917, p. 4.
178 TNA CAB 27/8: WP 60, p. 16.
179 IWM, French papers, JDPF 7/7, p. 16.
180 TNA CAB 27/8: WP 60, pp. 17.
181 IWM, French papers, JDPF 7/7, p. 17.
182 TNA CAB 27/8: GT 2242, 9 October 1917, p. 3 and French papers, JDPF 7/7, p. 18.
183 TNA CAB 27/8: WP 60, pp. 18.
184 Ibid., pp. 19-20.
185 IWM, French papers, JDPF 7/7, pp. 19-20.

but which had 'led to no strategic result, and our limited resources in man-power will not allow us to reach a strategic end by tactical slogging alone.'[186]

Predictably enough French rejected the first two of Lloyd George's strategic options - total or partial concentration on the Western Front. A successful offensive capable of breaking down the enemy's morale was impossible unless and until sufficient American forces arrived to make a significant difference, something he did not expect until 1919. British strength was 'being gradually sapped by the enemy in indecisive attacks which attain inadequate results and entail undue loss'.[187] As for option four, an offensive in the Middle East, French took a similar view to Wilson. He liked the idea in principle, but the window of opportunity had closed.[188] As a result, only option 3 was appropriate, the 'Pétain policy' of standing on the defensive until the Allies could recover and align themselves with a sufficiently large American force. This would mean the BEF would have to take over more French line, but he expected a compromise could be agreed. French backed Wilson's recommendation for a 'Superior War Council' to 'appreciate the general situation and to formulate plans'.[189]

In the autumn of 1917 Wilson finally found himself in a position where politicians, led by the Prime Minister, wanted to hear his views. This was a novel situation; for most of the war to this point his interaction with his political friends can be summed up as much talk, full of fury, but signifying very little. Lloyd George needed a senior soldier prepared to look critically at how Britain's military leadership was fighting the war. Wilson was under-employed, in London and desperate to play his part. Haig and Robertson, the leading advocates of British policy on the Western Front appeared devoid of ideas and for 1918 had little to offer strategically than more of the same. Wilson was in the right place at the right time, but he was no dupe. His seminal document offered the politicians an opportunity to regain control of military strategy, and an overarching inter-Allied body tasked with making key decisions had been a Wilson ambition for at least two years. The result was the creation of the SWC at Versailles. For both Lloyd George and Wilson its establishment was not the end of the process for revising Allied military strategy, but the beginning.

---

186 TNA CAB 27/8: WP 60, p. 21.
187 Ibid., pp. 22-23.
188 Ibid., p. 23.
189 Ibid., pp. 25-26.

General Sir Henry Wilson at Versailles, January 1918. (*L'Illustration*, 21 February 1918)

Field Marshal Frederick Roberts, 1st Earl Roberts, Wilson's mentor.

Marechal Ferdinand Foch, old friend of Wilson, yet often spiky adversary as Allied Generalissimo in 1918.

General Sir Charles Callwell (hands in pockets) with Russian officers at Sarikamish 1916. His 1927 biography ruined Wilson's reputation. (Callwell, *Experiences of a Dugout, 1914-1918*)

Earl of Bessborough, Viscount Duncannon ('the Lord'), Wilson's ADC.

General Sir Charles Monro, GOC First Army during Wilson's lacklustre command of IV Corps.

General Hugo De Pree, Sir Douglas Haig's cousin and Wilson's BGGS whilst in command of IV Corps during 1916. (Image courtesy of Lady Janet Glover)

Chateau Ranchicourt. (Author)

Zouave Valley: Scene of 'Operation Schleswig Holstein', the German assault of 21-22 May 1916. (Author)

German infantryman sits amongst debris in a ruined British trench following the assault of 21-22 May 1916.

Andrew Bonar Law, Unionist Party leader
and friend of Wilson.

Maurice Hankey, the ultimate Cabinet
mandarin.

General Sir William Robertson, working class, stolid, and the complete antithesis of Wilson.

General Sir Henry Rawlinson, Wilson's life-long friend and occasional rival.

General Sir George Tom Molesworth Bridges, soldier-diplomat and long-time ally of Wilson.

Wilson and the British military secretariat at the Supreme War Council, Versailles, winter 1917-18. Front row: Leopold Amery (first on left), Hereward Wake (second left), Sir Charles Sackville-West (third left), Henry Hughes Wilson (centre), far right, Brigadier-General Frederick Sykes. (Image courtesy of Dr Michael LoCicero)

6

Supreme War Council

The SWC, the direct result of Wilson's strategy paper, was officially constituted at a meeting of Allied leaders in Rapallo, Italy, on 7 November 1917. The location was significant. The politicians had gathered to discuss additional support for Italy in the face of a major offensive by the Central Powers. Disaster was only averted after Caporetto by the diversion of French and British troops from the Western Front.[1] Minds were finally focussed on the essential need for more formal allied co-operation.[2] Wilson was appointed as Britain's Permanent Military Representative (PMR) to work with his Allied opposite numbers in what was effectively an inter-Allied general staff. Lloyd George, having successfully sought military advice from outside the War Office, was determined to formalise the principle. He and Wilson had secured French support for some form of superior direction of war strategy, a long-held priority for the latter.

In fact, Wilson and his Prime Minister did not have things all their own way. Robertson and the War Office machine conducted a rearguard action to stymie the influence of the PMRs, and by extension the Council itself. Lloyd George's main purpose in establishing the SWC was to weaken the stranglehold he felt his generals, specifically Robertson and Haig, held over British war strategy by ultimately removing either man, or both.[3] Robertson took a sinister view of the Prime Minister's motives. Referring to the recent overthrow of the moderate 'Provisional' government in Russia by revolutionary Bolsheviks, he condemned Wilson's secretariat at Versailles as 'the new Soviet.'[4] Hankey's biographer took a different view. While there was 'an element of truth' in Robertson's fears 'it is equally certain that it was not the Prime Minister's only, or indeed his main purpose – which was, quite simply, to establish a centralised and coordinated system of strategic direction.'[5] While this is an overly-generous interpretation of Lloyd George's motives, this chapter argues that it could fairly be applied to those of Wilson. His diary entries for 1917 contain references to his belief in the need for a move from independent national commands towards a more coordinated and co-operative Allied

---

1   Caporetto (11th Battle of the Isonzo), 24 October-19 November 1917; one of the Italian army's greatest defeats.
2   McCrae, *Coalition Strategy*, p. 97.
3   See, for example, Woodward, *Lloyd George*, p. 221; idem, *Robertson*, p. 191; French, *Strategy*, p. 164.
4   LHCMA, Robertson papers, Robertson to Haig, (7/7/66), 15 November 1917; Orlando Figes, *A People's Tragedy: The Russian Revolution* (London: Bodley Head, 2017 [1996]), pp. 191, 484-6.
5   Roskill, *Hankey*, p. 454.

strategy; one the British might shape and eventually dominate. It was a year in which, uniquely for such a senior British soldier, he was able to review the workings of the French, Russian and Italian armies at close quarters. While the downfall of Haig and Robertson might have been Lloyd George's ultimate aim, there is no evidence in Wilson's diary for this year, nor in his correspondence, of a desire to see Haig removed. In fact, Wilson supported Haig's retention as C-in-C, only reluctantly concluding that he be replaced in mid-1918. As for Robertson, Wilson was critical of his strategic judgement and appears to have concluded that, as his authority as PMR grew, Wully's would decline. At that point, professional criticism evolved into personal animosity, but Wilson's priority remained that of establishing 'superior control' of war policy.

Wilson attempted to formalise this 'superior control' by using the SWC to take hold of the strategic debate. Despite initial setbacks in three months Wilson and his colleagues produced 14 'Joint Notes', or position papers, covering a range of strategic issues with several more soon after.[6] While some of the more contentious of these documents have received attention in the historiography, the range of the subjects deserves further study, illustrating as they do Wilson's breadth of view.[7] In addition, the SWC secretariat during Wilson's tenure and its aftermath, produced a range of other policy documents which illuminate key aspects of British strategic thinking. Greenhalgh dismissed the Council as 'nothing more than a sounding board or talking shop.'[8] This study favours Jeffery's description of the creation of the SWC as 'an extremely important advance in the co-ordination of Allied policy- and decision-making.'[9] The Joint Notes (JNs) produced while he was PMR, and the majority of those produced once he had moved to the War Office reflected Wilson's long-held strategic views, many of which received their first official scrutiny in his paper of 20 October 1917.[10] JNs 1 and 12 built on this and ended Haig's hopes for another offensive in Flanders in 1918.

Creation of the SWC

The day after Wilson drew his outline for an inter-Allied council on the back of a Ritz Hotel menu card, his admiring Gallic audience of the French Premier Painlevé, Propaganda Minister Franklin-Bouillon and Foch, visited Lloyd George. He floated the notion of supplementing meetings of heads of Allied governments by 'the establishment of a Permanent Staff of military officers who would study the war as a whole and give the several governments their views as to the strategy which should be adopted.' The 'defect of the system hitherto pursued had been that each General was interested mainly in his own front.' As a result, when C-in-Cs met they 'did not draw up a plan in which the war was treated as a whole but they each approved each other's plans…This, however, was not a real co-operation such as was needed to ensure victory.'[11] Hankey was 'horrified' by Lloyd George's suggestion, 'I had no time to warn the PM that

---

6   Wilson started work at Versailles on 19 November 1917 and became CIGS on 18 February 1918; Wilson diary, November 1917-February 1918.
7   See esp. Jeffery, *Wilson*, pp. 211-113, and French, *Strategy*, pp. 189-90.
8   Greenhalgh, *Victory Through Coalition*, p. 174.
9   Jeffery, *Wilson*, p. 216.
10   TNA CAB 27/8: WP 61.
11   TNA CAB 28/2: War Cabinet, IC (Allied Conferences), Volume II, IC 28, 'Secretary's notes of a conversation at Chequers Court', 14 October 1917.

in Robertson's bruised and suspicious frame of mind' he would see the move as a proposal to 'upset his authority and may resign. When I warned him of this afterwards he was astounded, and hardly credited it! Why is he so blind, sometimes?'[12] Whether Lloyd George was blind or not, and it seems highly unlikely that he was, Franklin-Bouillon welcomed the suggestion and thought 'the Staff ought to be constituted this very week.'[13] The Prime Minister had obtained the French support he needed a week before Wilson and French submitted their policy papers. One of the unresolved questions was for the BEF to take over 100 kilometres of front from the French. Thus, Wilson and Lloyd George secured French support for the SWC by making a significant extension of the British front dependent on an assessment by the body they were proposing to establish. For the present Lloyd George stressed the negative impact an extension would have on British effectiveness and morale, and suggested Haig and Pétain conferred on options.[14]

Wilson had been busy promoting his 'big idea' amongst his friends and supporters. Before submitting his policy paper, he had tried to convince his ally Lord Milner that his proposed inter-Allied staff was the mechanism for curbing the obsession the politicians felt some generals had for large-scale and costly offensives in the west.[15] Milner 'seemed as determined as L.G. to stop any more of these attempts at final decisions by Haig and he was just as dissatisfied with Robertson, and he is no longer afraid that if Robertson resigned the Government would fall. He was all for "the fellow going and be hanged to him".'[16] The two met again the next day once Milner had read both papers:

'At last' he said, 'the tyranny is over' and he was looking forward to the end of the 'reign of terror'! It seems to me there will be a holy row over all this, and of course the frock coats will quote Johnnie and me against Haig and Robertson. We must avoid this as much as possible. It is the system and machinery I am aiming at and not the man.[17]

With the benefit of hindsight vis-à-vis Robertson this seems a particularly disingenuous remark, but Wilson's diary for the period, while critical of his military policy displays little outright personal animus towards the CIGS. That changed once it became clear Robertson and his supporters would not easily accept the new policy machinery. On 23 October, the diehard Tory *Morning Post* carried a leader 'about Cabinet interfering with Haig and Robertson.' Wilson, suspecting Robertson was behind the report, told the editor H.A. Gwynne that:

I thought he was barking up the wrong tree, that L.G. had - so far not interfered with Robertson - that, in my opinion the machinery was at fault and until we got a superior

12 CAC, Hankey diary, HNKY 1/3, 14 October 1917.
13 TNA CAB 28/2: IC 28, 14 October 1917.
14 Ibid.
15 A.M. Gollin, *Proconsul in Politics: A Study of Lord Milner in Opposition and in Power* (New York: Macmillan, 1964), pp. 454-5.
16 Wilson diary,18 October 1917.
17 Ibid., 19 October 1917.

body we should never have unified action, and so on … We will see in the next few days whether I made any impression.[18]

A few days later Wilson saw Milner again. He was 'in one of his pessimistic moods…He saw insurmountable difficulties to my proposal for a Superior Direction! He said that I was the only possible soldier to put there but great difficulties in that! … Milner did not know what L.G. proposed to do [regarding Wilson's future strategy paper].'[19] Milner was not only pessimistic about Wilson's prospects. Two days earlier Austro-German forces began their major offensive at Caporetto, 'the most disastrous reverse suffered by Italy in the First World War.'[20] Robertson and then Wilson were shuttled off to Italy to assess the damage and advise on an Allied response. The set-back strengthened Wilson's hand in his argument for coordinated strategic planning. On 27 October, he recorded that the French had decided to send four divisions to Italy, the British would play second-fiddle by sending only two: 'So again we are governed by Haig and R[obertson]. If anything was needed to prove the necessity of my "Superior Direction" we have it here.'[21]

On 30 October Lloyd George warned the Cabinet that Painlevé was again demanding the British to take over more line. Before a decision could be taken, he wanted a review of options for 1918. Lloyd George felt 'we were being out-manoeuvred and beaten by an enemy who was inferior in material and personnel…every year the enemy succeeded in ending up [sic] his campaign with a great success.'[22] The setbacks in Italy were 'due to the fact that the [strategic] situation was never considered as a whole. The Conferences we had with our Allies, which had lately increased in number, were not really Conferences. They were only meetings of people with preconceived ideas who desired to find a formula which would reconcile them.' He therefore felt that Wilson's advice for an 'Inter-Allied Staff' was 'sound.' Its functions would not be to give orders:

> No government could concede the right to issue orders, but their duties would be to examine the military situation of the Allies … No one was thinking out the whole plan as though he were responsible for the whole battle-front of the Allies. In order to achieve success the War ought to be conducted as though there were one man sitting in the centre with equal responsibility for all fronts.[23]

Lloyd George outlined the structure and function of what was soon to become the permanent military staff of the SWC, and that of the Council itself. What was needed was 'for the first time, a real Inter-Allied General Staff, to examine the situation as a whole and to advise, without divesting the Government or General Staffs of their responsibility.' Stressing the body's

---

18   Wilson diary., 23 October 1917.
19   Ibid., 26 October 1917.
20   George H. Cassar, *The Forgotten Front: The British Campaign in Italy, 1917-1918* (London: Hambledon Press, 1998), p. 65.
21   Wilson diary, 27 October 1917.
22   TNA CAB 23/13/27: War Cabinet, 30 October 1917, (draft), p1.
23   Ibid., p. 2; for the ineffectiveness of inter-Allied co-operation in 1917 see McCrae, *Coalition Strategy*, pp. 8, 25 and *passim*.

advisory status, he said it would receive plans from the Allied commands and then 'suggest' what action should be taken:

> It was essential that this Inter-Allied General Staff should be an entirely independent body, not consisting of representatives of the National General Staffs, as in that case each representative would simply fight for the views of his own General Staff.[24]

The Cabinet debate centred on the role and powers of the permanent 'Inter-Allied General Staff' which 'would make a continuous study of the Allied War plans, just as the General Staff of the War Office made a continuous study of our own military plans.' The draft minutes recorded, 'It was pointed out that this was a change which might, to some extent, diminish the authority of the Chief of the Imperial General Staff, but it was suggested that in practice it would not do so very materially.' This sentence was later crossed out by the cautious Hankey, along with a subsequent one concerning the sensitivities of Robertson and his War Office colleagues:

> Some doubts were expressed as to whether ~~the scheme could be carried out without friction with the present Military Advisers of the Government, and as to whether in practical working this scheme would not involve great friction, and as to whether~~ the new machinery would, in fact, cure the evils mentioned by the Prime Minister.[25]

A key question for the new body would be 'the nature of the offensives for next year, and whether the main effort of the Allies was to be made in 1918 or 1919.'[26] It was agreed that the Prime Minister would write to his French counterpart proposing the establishment of the SWC. Such a body was essential because after three years of war 'the German Government is still militarily triumphant.' Furthermore:

> As compared with the enemy the fundamental weakness of the Allies is that the direction of their military operations lacks real unity...There has never been an Allied body which had the knowledge of the resources of all the Allies, which could prepare a single co-ordinated plan for utilising those resources in the most decisive manner taking into account the political, and diplomatic, as well as the military weaknesses of the Central Powers.

As for taking over more French line, there was no point in discussing this until the campaign for 1918 was agreed and this was 'exactly the sort of question which would be referred to the Allied Council.' [27] Wilson saw Leo Amery and 'pushed into him the absolute necessity of a Superior Direction which if properly handled would give us a dominating influence in <u>all</u> plans. He came to see me before dinner to tell me he had seen Milner and he thought Milner was now convinced

---

24   TNA CAB 23/13/27: War Cabinet, 30 October 1917, (draft), pp. 2-3.
25   Ibid., original deletion as indicated, pp. 4-5.
26   Ibid., p. 5.
27   TNA CAB 23/13/27: Appendix to War Cabinet minutes, 30 October 1917, (draft), 'Letter from Lloyd George to M Painlevé.'

of the necessity.' That evening he recruited Winston Churchill, then Minister of Munitions, to his cause:

> Had a long chat with Winston. He is enthusiastically in favour of my paper and has written a whole paper – which he sent me – on the par[agraph] in my paper where I urge the enormous increase in materiel – guns, aeroplanes, tanks, railways etc. … Winston is quite clear that we must have a Superior Direction. He tells me that LG thinks this also but is afraid to take the plunge because of the opposition of Haig, Robertson <u>and</u> Asquith. I told Winston that I did not for a moment think that Squiff would take up the challenge for one moment if LG put his case properly, for neither Haig nor Robertson would have a leg to stand on. …I quoted also my example of the different strategies – ours and the Boches:
>
> 1.   We take Bullecourt, they take Romania
> 2.   We take Messines, they take Russia
> 3.   We <u>don't</u> take Pachendaal [sic], they take Italy[28]

This was one of Wilson's favourite lines of argument, the one which had, he told Esher, persuaded Lloyd George to back his new scheme.[29] Lloyd George and Painlevé agreed to set up the SWC, with the issue of the BEF taking over more line to await advice from the PMRs.[30] The War Cabinet agreed a constitution for the SWC and the terms under which Britain's PMR would work. It is hard to disagree with the conclusion that the Prime Minister had 'cleverly' manoeuvred Major-General Sir Frederick Maurice, Robertson's DMO, into this invidious task while Wully was visiting the Italian front.[31] Article 4 of the draft said the PMRs would receive proposals for future plans from their general staffs and 'in consultation' would then produce a 'coordinated statement of those plans together with proposals for the combined action of the Allies.' The next sentence confirmed Wilson's future as a driving force in British strategic planning: 'Should the plans received from the Chiefs of General Staffs not be, in the opinion of the military representatives, the best for ensuring such combined action it will be within their functions to suggest other proposals.'[32] In an illustration of how closely the two were working together Lloyd George had shown Wilson the draft the night before:

> He [the PMR] is not to be <u>on</u> the council because Robertson is not on the War Cabinet. All plans to be submitted to him by CIGS, and he has the power to alter, or even to make fresh plans without reference to the CIGS. I asked this particularly for it was in a formal note in Maurice's handwriting at the dictation of L.G! The Mil[itary] Member can call for any and all information, and on the whole I was satisfied with the proposals.[33]

---

28   Wilson diary, 30 October 1917, (original emphasis).
29   CAC, Esher journal, (ESHR 2/20), 4 November 1917.
30   TNA CAB 23/13/28: War Cabinet, 31 October 1917.
31   Woodward, *Lloyd George*, p. 213.
32   TNA CAB 23/4/36: War Cabinet, minutes and Appendix III, 1 November 1917.
33   Wilson diary, 31 October 1917; CAC, Hankey diary, HNKY 1/3, 31 October, 1 November 1917.

When the War Cabinet met on 2 November 1917, Lieutenant-General Wilson was formally confirmed as the British representative on the 'Permanent Inter-Allied Advisory General Staff' of the 'Supreme Inter-Allied Council' (the working title of the SWC). He was to hold the temporary rank of General and Derby, as Secretary of State for War, was instructed to help Wilson set up his staff.[34] The insertion of the word 'Advisory' into the title of this new 'General Staff' served as a fig leaf to Lloyd George's assertion that the initiative did not erode the authority of the Robertson-dominated Imperial General Staff at the War Office. At the previous two War Cabinet meetings, Derby had tried to stymie progress, firstly by asking for more time for the military leadership to consider the issue and then by asserting that the Maurice 'constitution' had been drawn up at short notice and that 'in the circumstances it would not represent considered military opinion. It was for discussion only.'[35] Derby eventually bowed to the inevitable and 'expressed his approval' of Wilson's appointment.[36] Wilson recorded in his diary: 'I went then to see Derby who is in the devil of a funk of what Robertson will say, and he (Derby) thinks he may have to resign.'[37]

Wilson pressed home his belief that current strategy, comprising large-scale offensives on the Western Front, carried out by national armies with minimal Allied co-operation, would not bring victory. After seeing Derby, he met Haig's Chief of Staff Kiggell: 'He pleaded that in another 8 days D.[ouglas] H.[aig] could take enough of the Paschendaal [sic] Ridge to make himself secure for the winter and that this operation ought not to be stopped.' Kiggell, enunciating GHQ's anxiety over manpower and in an oblique reference to the upcoming Battle of Cambrai, confided that Haig:

> Had another secret operation in view which promised most satisfactory results provided no more troops were sent to Italy. Kigg. said the Boches had skinned the whole front in a manner they had never done before and that therefore this was a great chance. I could not help saying that if this was so ie the skinning, then all our attacks had had a very disappointing result as they had not saved Russia nor Italy nor prevented the Boches weakening the front in face of us! Kigg. found this difficult to answer.[38]

In the historiography, Robertson at this stage in the war is painted as a hapless, even helpless, victim of the cunning and mendacious Lloyd George, ably assisted by the wily Wilson. According to Woodward: 'Lloyd George marched under the banner of unity of command, but his primary objective was to diminish Robertson's influence over future British strategy.'[39] While this is clearly the case, the CIGS, with some support from Haig, fought a rearguard action aimed if not at derailing the SWC, certainly limiting the powers of the PMRs. Robertson received the terms of reference for the new organisation while touring the Italian front.[40] He asked Haig what he

---

34 TNA CAB 23/4/37: War Cabinet, 2 November 1917.
35 TNA CAB, 23/13/27 and 23/13/28: War Cabinet, 30 October and 31 October 1917.
36 TNA CAB 23/4/37: War Cabinet, 2 November 1917.
37 Wilson diary, 2 November 1917; Derby regularly threatened to resign, but never did. See Dutton, *Paris 1918*, p. xxii and *passim*.
38 Ibid.
39 Woodward, *MCWR*, p. 245.
40 LHCMA, Robertson papers, 'Foreign Office telegrams to Robertson', (4/8/2-3), November 1917.

thought of 'the new Allied Council System & of our representative. It has all happened in my absence, & I think Derby has let the Army down badly, as I shall tell him.'[41] Lloyd George asked Haig for his views of the SWC:

> I told him that the proposal had been considered for three years and each time had been rejected as unworkable. I gave several reasons why I thought it could not work, and that it would add to our difficulties having such a body. The PM then said that the two Governments had decided to form it; so I said, there is no need to say any more then![42]

Haig's willingness to accept the rulings of his political masters, regardless of his personal views, was one reason why he prospered both before and during the war, especially at times when his position was under critical scrutiny. Robertson would not stay silent. He thought the government was wrong and that its actions would lead to confusion about where military authority lay, leading to defeat. When the Allied leaders met at Rapallo, Robertson submitted an amended version of Lloyd George's scheme which Wilson had accepted on 1 November. Article 4, the crucial paragraph which gave Wilson and his colleagues power to over-rule the General Staffs, had been reworded, and toned down, by Lloyd George:

> (4) The general war plans drawn up by the competent Military Authorities of the Allied countries are submitted to the Supreme War Council which, under the high authority of the Governments, ensures their concordance. If the plans submitted to the Supreme War Council do not appear to them to be the best for ensuring combined action, it will be within their functions to recommend other proposals.[43]

Although the wording was more diplomatic than in Maurice's original, Robertson was not mollified. He submitted an alternative, striking out the second sentence and replacing it with: 'and submits if needed any necessary changes.'[44] This minor alteration made little difference to the overall tenor of the clause, and the Prime Minister accepted it.[45] Henceforth the plans of the General Staffs would have to be submitted to the SWC (and thus its PMRs) for approval and/or amendment. Robertson 'persisted in his opposition to the last', Hankey wrote in his memoirs. 'During the meeting at which the scheme was being examined in detail he got up rather ostentatiously and walked out of the room, stopping on the way out in order to ask me to record the fact that he had withdrawn, a request with which I complied.'[46] Hankey's biographer

---

41   Haig to Robertson, 4 November 1917, in *MCWR*, p. 251.
42   NLS, Haig (manuscript diary), 4 November 1917.
43   LHCMA, Robertson Papers, 'Scheme of Organisation of an Inter-Allied War Committee (Amended draft proposed by Mr. Lloyd George),' (4/8/5), 4 November 1917.
44   TNA CAB 21/91: War Cabinet, Formation of Supreme War Council, 'Scheme of Organisation of an Inter-Allied War Committee (Amended draft proposed by Mr Lloyd George, and amended by R 42, from the Chief of the Imperial General Staff') 7 November 1917.
45   Ibid.
46   Hankey, *Supreme Command* (Vol. II), p. 721; TNA CAB 28/2, War Cabinet, IC (Allied Conferences), Volume II, IC 30c, '*Procès-verbal* of a Conference of the British, French and Italian Governments, held at the "New Casino Hotel", Rapallo,' 7 November 1917.

believed that: 'After such a display of intransigence, not to say public bad manners, it is surprising that Lloyd George did not dismiss Robertson on the spot.'[47] While Hankey thought the incident so worthy of note that he included it in his memoirs four decades later, he made no note of it in his diary at the time. Most relevantly for this study, Wilson himself, although present for the whole meeting, made no reference to it in his own diary. The omission is hard to understand if, as some sources have suggested, Wilson and Robertson were so personally at odds. A likely explanation is that Hankey, never a fan of Robertson, simply repeated a similar story included in Lloyd George's unreliable war memoirs.[48] Whatever the facts of the incident, Wilson was more concerned with the new body's structures and procedures than personal arguments with the notoriously prickly Robertson. These would come later.

In the meantime, Lloyd George had achieved a major victory. When Robertson was appointed CIGS in December 1915 he ensured that his powers were much greater than those of his predecessors.[49] The three previous occupants of the post had found themselves over-ruled, over-looked, and over-shadowed by the Secretary of State for War, Lord Kitchener. By the time of Robertson's appointment Kitchener's conduct of the war, in political and military circles if not in the public mind, had been discredited. In addition, Robertson was a much more robust character than his predecessors.[50] The result had been that from then on the government received military advice directly from the CIGS, and that Robertson issued orders to the Army, albeit under the Secretary of State's authority.[51] This latter point took on great significance as the war progressed and was greatly resented by Lloyd George when he was War Secretary. The SWC structure weakened Robertson's influence and Lloyd George ensured that when Wilson finally replaced Wully as CIGS the power was rescinded and returned to the political head of the military.[52]

The French favoured Paris as home for the embryonic SWC, but Wilson was 'entirely opposed' because it was too big to allow the staffs to confer easily.[53] 'We had a conference from 10am to 1.30 trying to draft a paper bringing the Supreme Council into being …Another meeting at 5'o'[clock] when the Supreme Council sat for the first time and gave Foch and me our orders. It was also decided to have our HQ at Versailles.'[54] The orders were for the two generals to set off immediately to the Italian Front to 'advise as to the amount and nature of the assistance to

47   Roskill, *Hankey*, p. 454.
48   Lloyd George, *Memoirs* (Vol. II), pp. 1440-1.
49   For a full discussion of Robertson's 'bargain' with Kitchener over extended powers, see John Spencer, 'The Puppetmaster: Sir William Robertson as CIGS in 1916', in Spencer Jones (ed.), *At All Costs: The British Army on the Western Front 1916* (Solihull: Helion & Company, 2018), pp. 53-70.
50   For Kitchener's domination of the General Staff at the War Office see George H. Cassar, *The Tragedy of Sir John French* (Newark, Delaware: University of Delaware Press, 1985), pp. 85-6.
51   David R. Woodward, *Field Marshal Sir William Robertson: Chief of the Imperial General Staff in the Great War* (Westport, Connecticut: Praeger, 1998), p. 24.
52   The familiar narrative of Wilson's appointment to the position of the government's principal military advisor is best told in Woodward, *Robertson*, pp. 187-201.
53   TNA CAB 28/2: War Cabinet, IC (Allied Conferences), Volume II, IC 30c and 30d, '*Procès-Verbal*', Rapallo,' 7 November 1917.
54   Wilson diary, 7 November 1917.

be given by the British and French governments, and as to the manner in which it should be applied.'[55]

Robertson's Reaguard

While Wilson was away, Robertson and the military members of the Army Council got to work undermining the SWC, or more specifically its Staff. Robertson was aware of Lloyd George's antipathy towards him and his strategic priorities. Put starkly, the Prime Minister's 'primary motive was to wrest strategic control of the war from Robertson.'[56] When he accepted the post of CIGS at the end of 1915 Robertson had insisted that he should give advice to the government directly, not via the then Secretary of State for War, the beleaguered Kitchener. 'Our Bargain', as Wully called it, bestowed powers on Robertson as CIGS which were 'unprecedented in British history.'[57] Lloyd George resented the arrangement when he succeeded Kitchener in mid-1916, and the issue lay at the heart of the tension between the two when he became Prime Minister.[58] Therefore, Robertson's principal, and understandable, argument against the role of the PMR was the risk that politicians would receive mixed and potentially contradictory advice; Robertson's opinion and Wilson's opinion. In this spirit Major-General Sir Thomas Furse, Master General of Ordnance (MGO), submitted a memorandum to the Army Council condemning the proposals as 'unpractical and dangerous to the best interests of the Allies.'[59] For the government to receive the best advice the General Staff needed to be in close, detailed and 'hourly' contact with the numerous ministries of government, and military departments. To suppose that the PMR could do so from Versailles was 'chimerical' and 'the inevitable result of the scheme will be that the Prime Minister of this country will have two official military advisers belonging to our army, the Army Council in the person of the CIGS and our Permanent Military Representative on the Supreme War Council.' Friction between the two would 'inevitably be mirrored in the relations between their respective staffs and will spread throughout the Army.' He concluded:

> It is in a crisis such as this that the Army looks to us, the Members of the Army Council, to watch over their interest and the interests of the country and we shall fail in our duty to the army and the country if we do not protest immediately and persistently against the formation of a Supreme War Council on the lines agreed upon at Rapallo.[60]

The Army Council informed the War Cabinet it 'presumed that the technical advice given by the British Military Representative will be given on behalf of the Army Council, and that he

55   TNA CAB 21/91: War Cabinet, Formation of Supreme War Council, 'Draft terms of reference to the Allied Military Council', 7 November 1917.
56   Woodward, *MCWR*, p. 245.
57   Woodward, *Robertson*, p. 25.
58   LHCMA, Robertson papers, memorandum from Robertson to Kitchener (4/3/27), 5 December 1915; a slightly revised version appears in Robertson, *Private to Field-Marshal*, pp. 239-243.
59   LHCMA, Robertson papers, Memorandum: 'The Scheme of Organisation of a Supreme War Council', Major-General W.T. Furse, Master General of Ordnance, (4/8/8), 11 November 1917.
60   Ibid., (4/8/8), 11 November 1917.

will be subject to the authority of, and receive his instructions from, the Army Council.'[61] The following day Macready, the AG, weighed in, informing Derby that the details as to Wilson's powers and responsibilities were so slight that 'I can only draw upon my imagination to visualise that officer's functions.'[62] Condemning the proposals as 'nebulous' and 'half-baked' Macready reminded Derby that as a soldier Wilson must be appointed by the Army Council and receive orders from a branch of his department: 'In the event of the technical advice given by him to the Supreme War Council being at variance with the expressed views of the Army Council, it is legally in their power, so long as he is a soldier, to remove him from his post.' Macready, so recently a supporter of Wilson, insisted that his understanding of the new system was that the PMR would only act in an advisory capacity providing information supplied by the Army Council. If the Representative was to have greater powers then the CIGS should have the role and 'in the event of him exceeding his powers there could be no question as to how to deal with the situation.'[63]

Derby asked Robertson for his opinion. The CIGS said he was in general agreement with the MGO but that instead of an Inter-Allied Staff, 'a misnomer without an Inter-Allied C-in-C', he would establish a Military Secretariat for the SWC. This would co-ordinate information from the various Allied forces, point up contradictions and lack of co-ordination, and prepare agenda:

> Beyond this all military advice to the Supreme Council should remain in the hands of the responsible military advisers of the respective Governments. Dual advice can only lead to delay, friction, weakening of responsibility and lack of confidence amongst the troops.[64]

The War Cabinet had no immediate answer and deputed members Smuts and Carson to seek advice from the Attorney and Solicitor Generals.[65] Their reply, not at all what Lloyd George wanted to hear, recognised the Army Council as the 'Supreme Military Authority', and that as Wilson was a British Army officer he was subject to their authority. The draft continued, 'the Army Council are entitled to issue instructions to him, in connection with his work on the Supreme War Council, so far as the military forces of the Crown are affected.'[66] This latter sentence was crossed out by Hankey, who thought the Army Council's paper 'absurd', and it was omitted from the final version.[67] This recognised the Army Council's legal authority over Wilson but pointed out that the new procedures had been drawn up:

61   TNA WO 163/22: Army Council, Minutes and Précis, Proceedings of the Army Council, 12 November 1917.
62   LHCMA, Robertson papers, Adjutant General to Secretary of State, (4/8/10), 13 November 1917.
63   Ibid.
64   LHCMA, Robertson papers, Robertson to Secretary of State for War, (4/8/11), 15 November 1917.
65   TNA CAB 21/91: War Cabinet, Formation of Supreme War Council, 'Minutes of the War Cabinet', 14 November 1917.
66   TNA CAB 21/91: War Cabinet, Formation of Supreme War Council, 'Relations between Army Council and British Military Representative: Draft reply to the Army Council', 15 November 1917.
67   CAC, Hankey diary, 14 November 1917.

[T]o meet the requirements of an exceptionally grave situation. They [the War Cabinet] realise that the success of the new scheme, will depend largely upon the cordial co-operation and goodwill of the Army Council, on which they count.

The War Cabinet desire to express their wish that, in developing the work of the Supreme War Council, it should be understood that the British Permanent Military Representative will have unfettered discretion as to the advice he offers.[68]

Lloyd George had acknowledged the Army Council's authority but appealed to their sense of duty, insisting on Wilson's independence. The Army Council were not to be bought off by smooth political language and responded that they felt it 'their duty to point out the great danger that may arise from the powers proposed' for the PMR. It would create 'duality of military counsel' leading to delay which could 'imperil the successful prosecution of military operations.' The best way of minimising such dangers would be for the CIGS to attend SWC meetings. It was essential that Wilson should not tender any advice to the SWC 'without first informing the Army Council of the nature of that advice.'[69] In response, Hankey prepared a eulogistic note for Lloyd George, making a virtue of Wilson's Francophilia, which stated it would be difficult to find any officer 'more peculiarly suited' to the new role than Wilson: 'Very few British Officers of any rank have the same intimate knowledge of any sympathy with the French Army.'[70] Under pressure from both the Army Council and Derby, Lloyd George agreed that Robertson could attend SWC meetings, but sidestepped further discussion about Wilson's obligations by saying it was too early to be prescriptive.[71] The War Cabinet noted the Army Council's 'desire to co-operate cordially' in the work of the SWC 'with a view to better co-ordination of effort' and felt assured the new machinery could be made to work 'in spite of the difficulties referred to by the Army Council.'[72]

Creating the SWC

Unlike their Allies, the British lost no time setting up their new secretariat. Hankey 'determined that it must be linked up with the War Cabinet Secretariat'; in other words, he, and ultimately the Prime Minister, would control the functions of the British PMR's office.[73] On 2 November Wilson told Sackville-West that he would be going with him to Versailles as CoS.[74] He also wanted his Aide-de-Camp (ADC), Duncannon. He organised his staff 'in the same way I did my old MO Office viz: one branch to be Allies and one branch to be the Enemy.'[75] Hankey

---

68   TNA CAB 23/4/50: War Cabinet, 16 November 1917.
69   LHCMA, Robertson Papers, 'Proceedings (Draft) of the Army Council: response to War Cabinet', (4/8/12), 19 November 1917.
70   PA, Hankey to Lloyd George, Lloyd George papers, (F/23/1/27), 16 November 1917.
71   Woodward, *Lloyd George*, p. 227.
72   TNA CAB 21/91: War Cabinet, Formation of Supreme War Council, 'Minutes of the War Cabinet', 29 November 1917.
73   Hankey, *Supreme Command* (Vol. II), p. 718.
74   Wilson diary, 2 November 1917.
75   Ibid., 3 November 1917; SWC History, pp. 13-15.

helped Wilson assemble his team while they travelled to the conference at Rapallo.[76] Hankey ensured that two of his men, Amery and Lieutenant-Colonel Lancelot Storr were attached to the secretariat. Both worked under Hankey as Assistant Secretaries to the War Cabinet where, Amery claimed, 'we were to be at the disposal of its members and at the same time free, as a kind of informal "brains trust", to submit our ideas on all subjects for our chiefs.'[77]

Amery continued to report to Hankey, the Cabinet Secretary but, never one to downplay his own role, considered himself to be the 'personal representative of Lloyd George and Milner, and liaison officer with the War Cabinet.'[78] Despite Cabinet support, his appointment was held up temporarily by Robertson and Derby.[79] Amery played an important role at the SWC and authored several detailed, and often wordy, strategy reports, especially on Britain's post-war imperial future. These reflected not only his own views, but also those of Wilson, and of Milner whom he saw regularly. This trio did much to lay the foundations of British strategic policy in 1918. Milner was a strong voice in the War Cabinet. His authority was underpinned by Amery's intellectual diligence. Wilson provided eloquence, and a military vision more to Lloyd George's taste than that of Haig and Robertson. Amery was a linguist and scholar whose papers provided the intellectual heft for Wilson's strategic arguments. Wilson was alive to Amery's failings and once noted: "He is much too academic and much more in the mood of arranging what would happen after the war than arranging how to win the war. All this displeases me."[80] Amery was, nonetheless, a useful and influential ally.

Once at Versailles, Wilson assembled other loyalists to his operations team. This was common practice. When Robertson was promoted to the post of CIGS in late 1915 he took with him from France Edward M. Perceval as his CoS. Perceval soon moved to command a division and Wully replaced him with Robert Whigham. Both had been instructors under Robertson at the Staff College. Another Camberley colleague, Freddie Maurice, moved from GHQ to the War Office as Robertson's DMO. The new CIGS also ensured that 'most of the junior officers' in his various departments had trained under him at the Staff College and were both 'capable and loyal' to their chief.[81] In 1914, when Wilson was appointed the BEF's Sub-Chief of Staff,' almost the entire operations section consisted of his former subordinates at the War Office.'[82] Three years later at Versailles Wilson established three teams, under Sackville-West as CoS. They were tasked with viewing strategy from the following perspectives: Allied or 'A' Branch, Enemy or 'E' Branch and Man-Power and Munitions (Allied and Enemy) or 'M' Branch.[83]

76   CAC, Hankey diary, 5 November 1917; the diary entry for this date included a simple 'family tree' diagram with Wilson at the top and branches showing 'Allies' and 'Enemies' together with 'F.[oreign] O.[ffice]' and 'Liaisons.'

77   Amery, *Political Life*, p. 91; the other Political Secretary was Colonel Sir Mark Sykes, Conservative MP and author of the 1916 Sykes-Picot Agreement in which the Allies agreed to the post-war partition of the Ottoman Empire, see Lawrence James, *Dictionary of National Biography* (online edition) <http://www.oxforddnb.com/view/article/36393?docPos=1> (accessed 16 January 2017).

78   Amery, *Political Life*, p. 129.

79   Wilson diary, 19, 26 November 1917.

80   Ibid., 6 July 1917.

81   Robertson, *Private to Field-Marshal*, pp. 221-2.

82   Nikolas Gardner, 'Command in Crisis: The British Expeditionary Force and the Forest of Mormal, August 1914', *War & Society*, Vol. 16 (2), (October 1998), p. 17.

83   TNA CAB 25/127, 'Historical record of the Supreme War Council of the Allied and Associated Nations from its inception on November 7, 1917, to November 12, 1918, the day after the signature

Wilson picked the officers who headed each branch. Brigadier-Generals Herbert 'Bertie' Studd and Sir Hereward Wake headed, respectively, 'A' and 'E' Branches, and Frederick 'Freddie' Sykes headed 'M' Branch.[84] Studd had been a student of Rawlinson at the Staff College and served at the War Office while Wilson was DMO.[85] Wake was at the Staff College under Wilson as commandant, graduating in 1908.[86] They served together in South Africa, and as a staff officer at GHQ in 1914 Wake joined Wilson at Lord Roberts's deathbed.[87] Sykes was another Staff College graduate of Wilson's. He served at the War Office while Wilson was DMO, where he 'made some valuable contacts', working with George Macdonogh, the future Director of Military Intelligence (DMI) and later Adjutant-General (AG). Sykes was one of the leading proponents of air power before and during the war. Wilson 'supported Sykes's flying ambitions, but he was more interested in his abilities and value as an intelligence officer.'[88] Two months after Wilson became CIGS, Sykes was promoted to Major-General and appointed Chief of the Air Staff.[89] Wilson and Sykes continued to work closely, in an effort to improve co-operation between Army and Air Force. Wilson recruited other Staff College graduates from his time at Camberley, notably Lieutenant-Colonels R. Riley (graduated 1907), Alfred Ollivant (1908), and Archibald Wavell (1910).[90] Another beneficiary of Wilson's promotion was Sir Percy Radcliffe. He had served in Wilson's pre-War Operations directorate and succeeded Freddie Maurice as DMO in April 1918.[91]

The War Office did what it could to stymie the establishment of Wilson's Versailles secretariat. Sackville-West 'told me of the way the WO is blocking things, Eddie Derby terrified, Wully sulky, Maurice hostile. All this will have to be straightened out.'[92] Esher urged Hankey to send Milner to support Wilson 'for heavens [sic] sake don't weaken in the face of opposition or we are done here...Now that the PM has embarked upon this Allied G[eneral] S[taff] (whether wisely or not) he must go through with it to the bitter end with extreme boldness.'[93] Matters came to a head when, faced with further disagreements over his staff, Wilson saw Derby, who was:

> [T]errified of Robertson. He said I could not have Tit Willow because 'it was not considered he was any good', and I could not have Duncannon because of the National Party...so I got cross and said, 'very well then LG can't have me.'

of the Armistice with Germany, together with a note as to its role and work subsequent to that date,' hereafter SWC History, undated, but believed to have been compiled in late 1919.

84   Wilson diary, 3 November 1917; SWC History.

85   Paul Harris, *The Men Who Planned the War: A Study of the Staff of the British Army on the Western Front, 1914-1918* (Farnham: Ashgate, 2016), Appendix 12, pp. 223-246. I am grateful to Dr Harris for additional information on this point.

86   Ibid.

87   Wilson diary, 14 November 1914.

88   Eric Ash, *Sir Frederick Sykes and the Air Revolution – 1912-1918* (London: Frank Cass, 1999), p. 22; see also Sir Frederick Sykes, *From Many Angles: An Autobiography* (London: Harrap, 1943 [1942]).

89   *Frederick Sykes*, Robert Blake *ODNB*.

90   SWC History.

91   Maurice, *Maurice Case*, p. 19.

92   Wilson diary, 19 November 1917.

93   CAC, Esher papers, Esher to Hankey, 15 November 1917.

This startled poor Eddie and he did not know what to say and I am not sure that he is not more frightened of me than of Robertson.[94]

The argument simmered: 'I went to see Derby and of course he withdrew his objections to Tit Willow but he still stuck out about Duncannon! Silly ass.' Bonar Law, ostensibly an ally of Wilson's, was also against the appointment but Derby gave in eventually.[95] The dispute over this seemingly minor matter, and delays in providing the wherewithal to establish his secretariat, caused friction between Wilson and the War Office. From this point on Wilson's criticism of Robertson in his diary became more personal. There was further evidence of War Office pettiness when Derby refused to allow Amery to travel to France to an SWC meeting and insisted Duncannon wear plain clothes at Versailles because he was a civilian. Derby, wrote Wilson, was 'a fool.'[96] By the next day the gloves were off:

> Long talk in the train with Milner and LG. Milner is furious with Derby for his stupid obstruction about my promotion [to full General] about Duncannon and about Amery and Milner says he won't stand it. It is quite clear to me that Robertson and his gang mean to obstruct all they can. Well we shall have a fight.[97]

Wilson in Italy

The first formal session of the SWC instructed Wilson and Foch to report on the state of the Italian Front and recommend future policy.[98] They were given complete authority to move the six Allied divisions already in Italy, or on their way, to wherever they could be useful.[99] Wilson left for Italy the next day and was back ready to start work at Versailles on 19 November.[100] The 10 days he spent as the British Army's roving adviser on military policy are relevant as much for what they reveal of him as a diplomat as a strategist. An abiding theme of this work is that in comparison with his peers, Wilson stood out as a soldier able to quickly gain the confidence of senior officers and politicians, British and Allied. While in Italy, Wilson and Foch met almost daily and seemed in general agreement about the disposal of their relative units, and those of their hapless ally.[101] For the most part Wilson appeared to defer to Foch, indisputably the more experienced field commander. Foch told Wilson and Robertson that he believed the defending forces ought to make a stand on the River Piave, the last natural barrier before Venice and the

94 Wilson diary, 21 November 1917. Derby relented in December.
95 Ibid., 22, 23 and 24 November 1917.
96 Ibid., 26 November 1917.
97 Ibid., 27 November 1917.
98 TNA CAB 28/3: War Cabinet, IC (Allied Conferences), Vol. III, IC 30d, '*Procès-verbal* of a Conference of the British, French and Italian Governments, held at the "New Casino Hotel", Rapallo, First Session of Supreme War Council,' 7 November 1917.
99 Ibid., Four (later increased to six) French divisions began arriving in Italy on 31 October with two British (later four) the following day; they were all in country by 25 November, Sir J.E. Edmonds & H.R. Davies, *Official History of the War: Military Operations Italy 1915-1919* (London: HMSO, 1949), p. xxvii.
100 Wilson left the Italian front for France on 17 November 1917, Wilson diary.
101 Ibid., 10, 11, 12, 13 and 15 November 1917.

Adriatic. Robertson agreed but was 'much more pessimistic' that the river barrier could be held; Wilson shared the same view for the next week.[102]

All agreed that the key issue was that of command. Foch wanted the Italian commander General Luigi Cadorna replacing, as did Lloyd George who held the 'overbearing' Italian in 'utter contempt.'[103] Cadorna was dismissed, at Lloyd George's insistence, at the Rapallo meeting and at Hankey's suggestion nominated as the Italian representative on the SWC: 'I fancy that this suggestion had the double effect of tiding the Italians round a difficult corner and rendering Ll[oyd] G[eorge]'s scheme of a Supreme War Council more acceptable to them.'[104] As for command of the British forces, Wilson's persuasive skills were put to the test on the journey to Rapallo. On 3 November, Maurice wrote to Robertson: 'Latest development is that Prime Minister[,] anxious to ensure British Supremacy in Italy[,] is going to try to persuade Haig to take supreme command there, and if he accepts will try to force this on French and Italians.'[105] It is unclear where this notion originated; at the War Cabinet meeting the previous day, Rawlinson had been discussed as a possible candidate.[106] Whatever its source, Maurice also mentioned the idea to Wilson as the British delegation left for Italy:

> This of course is fantastic and I told LG so on the destroyer, and that the best we could do would be to get the English and French under one commander who ought to be an Englishman (Plumer for example) and who by his knowledge and character would practically command the broken Italians also.[107]

In an illustration of Wilson's influence with the Prime Minister, his proposal was accepted and on 6 November Wilson 'got Robertson to wire for Plumer to come down at once, and take up the command - I hope - of both French and English.'[108] Wilson's motivation for proposing Plumer is open to conjecture, but the result was that his old friend Rawly, who had spent most of 1917 kicking his heels, took command of Plumer's Second Army in Flanders.[109] While Rawlinson was delighted with the appointment,[110] Wilson's suggestion was not welcomed by Haig, who was ordered to send two more of his divisions to Italy, making a total of four. 'Was ever an Army commander and his staff sent off to another theatre of war in the middle of a battle?', he asked. Unaware that the Plumer idea had originated with Wilson and not Lloyd George, he condemned politicians as 'very ignorant and troublesome people!!'[111] The loss of at least four divisions from his front to Italy caused Haig to protest to Robertson that 'nothing should be done to stop our offensive next spring.'[112] It was to no avail.

102 Wilson diary., 5 November 1917.
103 Cassar, *Forgotten Front*, p. 81.
104 CAC, Hankey diary, 7 November 1917.
105 Woodward, *MCWR*, Maurice to Robertson (via Delmé-Radcliffe), 3 November 1917, p. 250.
106 TNA CAB, 24/4/37: War Cabinet, 2 November 1917, (original emphasis).
107 Wilson diary, 3 November 1917. General Sir Herbert Plumer was commanding Second Army in Flanders.
108 Ibid., 6 November 1917.
109 CAC, Rawlinson papers, War journal, 8 November 1917.
110 Prior and Wilson, *Rawlinson*, pp. 272-3.
111 NLS, Haig (manuscript), diary, 7 November 1917.
112 Ibid., 10 November 1917.

In Italy Wilson, exhibiting his flexible belief in the notion of unity of command, pressed for Plumer to be given overall command of the Allies, but it came to nothing. He attempted to over-rule Cadorna's orders for the withdrawal of the Italian First and Fourth Armies from strategically important high ground 'though not attacked and no sign of the enemy...this seems idiotic.'[113] With Cadorna relieved and his successor General Armando Diaz not yet in place Wilson and Foch were powerless to intervene. The next day they met Diaz who accepted Wilson's advice and countermanded Cadorna's orders.[114] A 'long and heated discussion' over placement of the French forces, which brought out the worst in the 'characteristically brusque and dogmatic' Foch were only brought to an amicable conclusion by 'the intervention of the charming and smooth-talking Wilson.'[115] Nonetheless, Wilson remained pessimistic about the prospects for holding the enemy: 'The loss of Venice means the loss of the Adriatic and a serious threat therefore to Salonica and Egypt, but I am afraid this is coming.'[116] A day later, confident of his authority, and perceiving Diaz as a compliant ally, he wrote and asked him to prepare rearward lines along the River Brenta: 'Diaz thanked me for my letter and would see to the rearward lines at once.'[117] As Jeffery has argued: 'Wilson at times operated as if he had executive command of Italian forces.' He often adopted a similar approach, or at least an assumption that he was first amongst equals, while British PMR to the SWC.

Wilson at the SWC

Wilson arrived in Paris on 19 November. Before he left Italy, he had told Foch that 'I was anxious to get off to Versailles as soon as I could so as to get on with next year's plans, and he said he was equally anxious.' Two days later Foch's CoS, General Maxime Weygand, informed Wilson that his government had decided that as Foch was commander of the French troops in Italy he had to remain until the crisis was over.[118] As soon as he arrived in Paris, Wilson saw Clemenceau, who had become Prime Minister three days earlier. 'Clemenceau told [me] he had ordered Foch to remain in Italy for the present – a stupid thing to do as I told him, for the Superior Council has many important things to deal with <u>at once</u>.'[119] The incident is an example, even allowing for a degree of hubris, of Wilson's ready access and easy manner with both French politicians and soldiers, unique amongst senior British military officers at the time. The next day he called on the President of the Republic, Raymond Poincaré, who was 'most friendly and all in favour of the Supreme Council. I told him to recall Foch and he rather agreed.'[120] Despite these positive remarks, the matter of Foch and the identity of the French PMR rumbled on until the Second Session of the SWC when Weygand was confirmed in the role.[121] Weygand was rightly seen as a cypher for Foch, but the effect of French prevarication was that Wilson and his team

113 Wilson diary, 8 November 1917.
114 Ibid., 9 November 1917.
115 Edmonds & Davies, *Military Operations Italy 1915-1918*, p. 92; Cassar, *Forgotten Front*, p. 87.
116 Wilson diary, 9 November 1917.
117 Ibid., 10 November 1917.
118 Ibid., 13, 16 and 19 November 1917.
119 Ibid., 19 November 1917, original emphasis.
120 Ibid., 20 November 1917.
121 TNA CAB 28/3: War Cabinet, IC (Allied Conferences), Volume III, IC 36 (SWC), '*Procès-Verbal* of the Second Session of Supreme War Council,' 1 December 1917.

got to work immediately. From the date of Wilson's return to France on 19 November 1917, to his appointment as CIGS on 18 February 1918, the Inter-Allied Staff of the SWC produced 15 Joint Notes on a broad range of strategic and military policy issues. Nine more, set in train during Wilson's time as PMR, followed over the next two months. From its inception to the Armistice in November 1918 the SWC staff produced 40 Joint Notes.[122]

The Joint Notes

This section examines the work of the SWC and its staff while Wilson was British PMR and argues that his strategic views dominated proceedings. Three of the Joint Notes produced during Wilson's period at Versailles (numbers 1, 12 and 14) feature to a greater or lesser extent in key texts in the historiography, but the remainder have not been analysed in detail, with little consideration of their broader impact. The Notes are considered thematically; as a body of work they covered three main policy areas:

- Allied strategy in 1918, with specific reference to the Western Front
- Policy in relation to theatres away from the Western Front
- An inter-Allied approach to the tools (especially aircraft and tanks) and infrastructure of war (i.e. supply, transportation and communications)

JN12 made proposals for the 1918 Allied Campaign for the Western Front and beyond and JN 14 concerned the creation of an Allied General Reserve for the Western Front, with an Executive War Board (EWB) to control it. Their recommendations, and the controversies they engendered, led directly to departure of Robertson as CIGS with Wilson as his replacement. As a result, these Joint Notes are discussed in Chapter Eight, devoted to Unity of Command.

Western Front: Joint Notes 1, 2 & 10

Joint Note No. 1, 'Military Policy', 13 December 1917[123]

This report, essentially a shopping list of subjects the SWC's PMRs intended to consider, set the agenda for Allied policy priorities in 1918 and illustrates how Wilson used his negotiating skills with the inter-Allied Staff and his fellow PMRs to achieve his own strategic priorities. In early December, Wilson complained that while he and his men were 'busy in the office all day' there was 'no sign at all' of the French, Italian or American staffs.[124] Wilson's strategy paper of October had begun the process of formally questioning the current military orthodoxy and favoured a defensive posture until adequate resources were available.[125] Once in a position of influence, if not authority, he was able to develop these themes.

---

122 A full list of the Joint Notes is in TNA CAB 25/127: SWC History, pp. 65-6.
123 Copies of the first 14 Joint Notes are at TNA WO 158/57: 'Supreme War Council: Joint Notes.'
124 Wilson diary, 2 and 3 December 1917.
125 TNA CAB 27/8: WP 61.

The context of Joint Note 1 was the imminent armistice on the Russian front, 'the present position with regard to Man-power in the Allied countries, and the necessity imposed of finding men for production of Munitions, the replacement of tonnage, and increase of domestic food production.'[126] At a meeting of the PMRs on 8 December Wilson:

> [P]assed round some notes I had made on the necessity for producing - as our first paper - recommendations that the whole line from N Sea to Adriatic and Salonica should assume the Defensive and develop all means of Defence, rest troops, form Reserves, develop rail communications, develop material, manpower, etc, and I said I wanted this matter considered and a paper written as soon as possible.[127]

Wilson's staff prepared a draft and Weygand submitted a version which was 'slightly different.' In an illustration of Wilson's influence over this group, he and Cadorna accepted Weygand's contribution 'subject to any slight alteration General Wilson might wish to introduce later.'[128] Although he appeared to be making progress, Wilson's travails with the War Office continued. The Army Council repeated its insistence that Wilson send his recommendations to them first:

> Another bid by the Army Council to keep a hold of me by an order to submit first to them any advice I was going to give to the Supreme Council. I wrote at once to Hankey enclosing a copy of the order and pointing out that I (Wilson) did not advise the Supreme Council but I was only one of four and that all our advice was collective and therefore could not be sent to the WO of any one country. This is a stumper for that old fool Robertson who is not playing the game.[129]

In direct defiance of his military colleagues Wilson, who had already told Lloyd George he would send his reports only to him, persuaded his fellow PMRs to agree that their first report should go to their respective Prime Ministers 'and to no one else.'[130] It recommended that 'a definite and coordinated system of defence from the North Sea to the Adriatic must be adopted by the Allies.' This would be achieved by a review of existing defensive arrangements and, in the expectation of a German offensive in 1918, the construction of 'further and successive defensive lines to check an advance by the enemy.'[131] JN1 did not rule out 'minor forms of active defence' necessary for maintaining the offensive spirit of troops:

> Furthermore the policy of a strong defensive not only does not preclude, but actually prepares for any offensive measures in any theatre of war as may be decided upon for

---

126 Russian and German forces agreed an armistice on 15 December 1917; TNA WO 158/57: 'Supreme War Council: Joint Notes', Joint Note 1, 13 December 1917, p. 1.
127 Wilson diary, 8 December 1917, (original emphasis).
128 TNA CAB 25/120: 'Supreme War Council: Papers and Minutes,' Minutes of a meeting of the Military Representatives, 12 December 1917.
129 Wilson diary 8 December 1917; Wilson papers, (HHW 2/6/2), Wilson to Hankey, 9 December 1917.
130 Ibid., 22 November and 11 December 1917.
131 TNA WO 158/57: Joint Note 1, 13 December 1917, p. 1.

1918 when the present political situation in Russia, and the military situation in Italy are more clearly defined.[132]

The PMRs recommended a defensive posture in the Balkans but acknowledged a major enemy attack leading to 'a systematic and pre-arranged retirement' from the existing front was possible. Significantly for future events, Wilson and his colleagues also mooted the need for a 'mobile reserve' and called for men to be rested and trained to serve in it.[133]

The note raised another abiding theme of the SWC, the need for improvements to, and closer integration of, rail and sea communications, particularly in respect of the Italian front, and in the event of a German attack through Switzerland.[134] On the same co-operative theme it recommended 'co-ordinated development to the utmost' for the manufacture of war materials, together with a 'study of the possibilities of a coordinated Air offensive on the largest possible scale.'[135] In summary, JN1 advocated a strategy of strong defence in the west and in the Balkans, while forces were marshalled and material stockpiled for an offensive. Future notes addressed these issues in more detail.

Joint Note No. 2, 'Increase in the number of divisions in the Belgian Army', 20 December 1917[136]

The second session of the SWC met at Versailles for its first substantive meeting on 1 December 1917. Diminishing manpower resources had plagued both the British and French armies in 1917. In his opening address, written by Hankey,[137] Clemenceau said sending troops to Italy was 'a considerable drain on the strength of the Anglo-French forces on the Western front, and correspondingly weakens their power of offence and defence.'[138] The war had become 'largely one of exhaustion.' It was essential to make better use of the Belgian Army 'which so far had been doing very little except issuing communiqués.' The Council asked the PMR to advise.[139]

The issue of Belgian military strategy had been a sore point for both the British and French since the beginning of trench warfare. The Belgians never formally declared war on Germany and since the autumn of 1914 its six divisions had sat on the defensive on inundated land adjacent to the River Yser 'as secure as any force along the Western front, for the next four years.'[140] The Belgian King, Albert, who commanded his country's forces, refused to participate in what

---

132 TNA WO 158/57: Joint Note 1, 13 December 1917, p. 2.
133 Ibid.
134 TNA WO 158/57: Joint Note 1, 13 December 1917; the French had long been concerned about a surprise German offensive through Switzerland. Nivelle told Wilson he feared an attack involving 30 divisions, Wilson diary, 9 December 1917.
135 Ibid., 13 December 1917, p. 3.
136 TNA WO 158/57: Joint Note 2, 20 December 1917.
137 Hankey, *Supreme Command* (Vol. II), p. 732.
138 TNA CAB 28/3: War Cabinet, IC (Allied Conferences), Vol. III, IC 36 (SWC), '*Procès-Verbal* of the Second Session of Supreme War Council,' 1 December 1917.
139 Ibid.
140 William Philpott, 'Britain, France and the Belgian Army' in Brian Bond et. al., '*Look to Your Front': Studies in the First World War by the British Commission for Military History* (Staplehurst: Spellmount, 1999), p. 122.

he considered to be costly and ineffective offensives and maintained an abiding suspicion of the expansionist motives of Britain and France. At the end of 1914 Wilson had asked Tom Bridges, GHQ's liaison officer with the Belgian Army, to propose that the country's divisions be incorporated into the British forces in Flanders. King Albert refused.[141] Both France and Britain attempted to amalgamate Belgian units with their own, with similar results.[142] By the end of 1917, at a time of acute manpower shortages, Britain and France were running out of patience with their 'obstreperous ally' and expected her to do more.[143]

In fact, the Belgian General Staff had already considered reorganising its army, which since 1913 had comprised six divisions, each of 18 battalions (a total of 108 battalions), by increasing its complement of artillery. The PMRs decided that this would create 'very cumbrous' divisions.[144] The French, who would provide the guns, produced a scheme increasing the six divisions to nine, each of nine battalions (a total of 81 battalions). The remaining 27 battalions would be used to create the newly equipped artillery units.[145] The British Staff supported the plan, Studd noting the 'many disadvantages in having a Belgian division which differs so widely from that of the British or French.'[146] At Wilson's insistence the Joint Note made clear that the provision of additional artillery 'must be conditional on an increase in the offensive or defensive activity of the Belgian Army, according to circumstances and governed by the general plan for the employment of the armies of the entente.'[147] In other words, it was a quid pro quo; guns in exchange for active engagement with the enemy. The efficient working of the Inter-Allied staff, especially on non-contentious issues, is illustrated by the fact that these proposals were formally approved at the Third Session of the SWC at the end of January 1918, by which time they had already been put into effect.[148]

Joint Note 10, 'Extension of the British Front', 10 January 1918[149]

The length of trench held by the BEF and the French had been a bone of contention since the outbreak of hostilities. In the first 18 months of the war Britain had been the junior partner with a small but growing army. Following enormous losses in the first two years, the French wanted the British to take over more of the front from them. Britain argued, especially from mid-1917, that it was doing more than its share of offensive fighting. Further, the Flanders sector straddling the Franco-Belgian border, although short in comparison with the line held by the French, was strategically vital, and vulnerable, because of its proximity to the Channel

141 Wilson diary, 27 December 1914 and 2 January 1915.
142 Greenhalgh, *Victory Through Coalition*, p. 22.
143 Philpott, 'Britain, France and the Belgian Army', p. 124.
144 TNA WO 158/57: Joint Note 2, 20 December 1917.
145 TNA CAB 25/47: Supreme War Council, 'Reorganisation of Belgian Army, papers submitted by General Weygand', December 1917.
146 Ibid. Note attached to file by Brigadier-General Studd, 14 December 1917.
147 TNA WO 158/57: Joint Note 2, 20 December 1917 and TNA CAB 25/120, Supreme War Council: Papers and Minutes, 'Minutes of a meeting of the Military Representatives,' 17 December 1917.
148 TNA CAB 28/3: War Cabinet, IC (Allied Conferences), Volume III, IC 39 (a) to 44 (a) (SWC), 'Resolutions passed at the Third Session of Supreme War Council, January to February 1918'. (The SWC met from 31 January to 2 February 1918).
149 TNA WO 158/57: Joint Note 10, 10 January 1918.

ports. Wilson's advice to the Cabinet in October 1917 had been that no decisions should be taken until Allied strategy for 1918 had been settled. His prominent role in the deliberations of late 1917 and early 1918 illustrates his powers of persuasion, levels of access and, ultimately in this case, their limits. Because the issue of extending the British front was entirely dependent on manpower, the deliberations over JN 10 will be discussed in the next chapter.

Strategy in Other Theatres: Joint Notes 3, 4, 5 & 6

Joint Note 3, 'Reinforcements to Italian Front', 21 December 1917 and Joint Note 6, 'The Italian Problem', 25 December 1917[150]

By the time the PMRs met, the crisis on the Italian front had been averted and the line stabilised. JN3 acknowledged the pressures on the Western front following the 'total collapse of Russia.' There had been no new developments in Italy, therefore no additional reinforcements would be spared. The PMRs agreed that the British and French General Staffs should reinforce the Italians 'at the most dangerous points' with all the artillery they had in theatre.[151] The related JN6 took a similar line, repeated the agreed Allied policy on standing on the defensive and urged the Italians to continue building defence in depth, especially around Venice. Due to manpower problems the Italians were urged 'with all despatch' to push on with the reorganisation and retraining of their army to facilitate the withdrawal of all or part of the Anglo-French [forces] in Italy at the earliest possible date.'[152] Wilson's 11-day sojourn in Italy in November inevitably influenced his contribution to JN3 and 6 and his creative approach to British strategy away from France and Flanders ensured it retained priority at the War Office. As CIGS during the German Spring Offensives of 1918 he attempted to finally impose British control over the Italian Army in response to what he feared was an inevitable attack.[153]

Joint Note 4, 'The Balkan Problem', 23 December 1917[154]

This note represented a clear example of 'joined-up' Allied strategic thinking of a kind not seen before the SWC was created. Although the Third Session of the SWC on 1 February merely asked for additional details, thanks to the work of Wilson and his team, its findings had already been accepted as Allied policy on the ground. JN4 recommended the abandonment of the important Greek port city of Salonika (modern Thessaloniki) if it was attacked by overwhelming forces. This, Wilson successfully argued, was better than the loss of the whole of mainland Greece.[155] Since 1916 an Allied force of French, British, Serbian, Greek, Italian and Russian divisions had been under the unified command of French General Maurice Sarrail. The operation reflected

150 TNA WO 158/57: Joint Note 3, 21 December 1917, and Joint Note 6, 25 December 1917.
151 Ibid.
152 TNA WO 158/57: Joint Note 6, 25 December 1917.
153 Cassar, *Forgotten Front*, pp. 136-150.
154 TNA WO 158/57: Joint Note 4, 23 December 1917.
155 Ibid.

French imperial interests, with Britain a sceptical participant.[156] Clemenceau's call at the Second Session of the SWC on 1 December for the PMRs' advice on strategy resulted in Wilson taking the initiative. He conducted a 'war game' and submitted a draft report which introduced the prospect of withdrawal 'in the event of a powerful attack.'[157] Amery produced a typically detailed study.[158] It calculated that following the enemy's occupation of much of Romania, with its strategically valuable rail network, the Allies' 23 divisions in Greek Macedonia could soon be facing 45 of the enemy. The mixed composition of the Allied force was exacerbated by internal political issues. The Serbian Army, 'which in actual fighting value may be regarded as superior to any of the other Allied contingents' had suffered terribly from continuous fighting and 'not too considerate or sympathetic treatment' from its officers. Large-scale desertions could not be ruled out, Amery warned. As for the three 'weak' Greek divisions 'though they do not want to fight at all, would probably just as soon fight against the Allies as for them.'[159] In the event of a major offensive, the Allies had three options: keep control of the environs and strategically important port of Salonika but lose the remainder of the Greek mainland (sometimes referred to as 'Old Greece'); abandon Salonika to retain Greece, but suffer the consequences for Allied prestige; or defend Salonika for as long as possible while strengthening the defence of the Greek mainland.[160] The paper favoured the third option, with the proviso that Salonika itself might have to be given up eventually.

Wilson rehearsed the findings in Amery's paper when he met Sarrail's successor General Adolphe Guillaumat:

> I told him I thought his first duty was to make love to the Servians [sic] and put a Servian on his staff, that Sarrail had treated the Servians very badly with result that if we retired from Monastir it was quite possible that the Servians would leave us … It was quite clear that he had not considered the problem at all … he did not impress me.[161]

The French still felt it possible to hold both Salonika and protect Greece.[162] It was hardly surprising, therefore, that they reacted badly when Wilson gave his recommendations about Italy and Salonika to his colleagues: 'This brought Weygand flying to my room to say the Italians <u>must</u> stand etc. etc. He got quite excited and said he would never agree to my notes. Quite amusing. …When Weygand left me he posted off to see Foch!'[163] The French ultimately accepted Wilson's

156 McCrae, *Coalition Strategy*, pp. 27-34.
157 TNA CAB 25/120/11: Supreme War Council: Papers and Minutes, 'Draft by Sir Henry Wilson of a Joint Note which it is suggested should be submitted by the Permanent Military Representatives to the Supreme War Council,' 10 December 1917.
158 TNA CAB 25/120/14: Supreme War Council: Papers and Minutes, 'Notes on the Military Situation in the Balkans,' 12 December 1917.
159 Ibid., pp. 4-5.
160 Ibid., p. 9.
161 Monastir, now known as Bitola in the modern Republic of North Macedonia, was a strategically important city on the Salonika front. Wilson diary, 12 December 1917.
162 Ibid., 13 December 1917.
163 Ibid., 21 December 1917.

analysis. On 30 December Guillaumat read out his orders, signed by Clemenceau and Foch, to Lieutenant-General Sir George Milne, the commander of the British forces:

> In these it was laid down that the Allied Armies under his command would be based not only upon Salonika but upon the whole of Greece…in the event of a retreat, it was more important to cover Old Greece than to retain Salonika.[164]

Joint Note 5, 'The situation in Russia,' 24 December 1917[165]

When Russia signed an armistice with Germany in mid-December 1917, despite the fact that the prospect had been clear for some months, the Allies had no agreed strategy. As a result, Wilson and his fellow PMRs had a blank canvas. His team produced several policy papers and the resulting JN5 was their outline of the challenges facing the Allies. The War Cabinet had asked whether the PMRs believed anti-Bolshevik forces in Southern Russia, and the Romanian army, could resist Bolshevik forces 'assisted and controlled by the Germans.'[166] The Representatives restricted their Note to the consequences if the Bolsheviks were left unhindered:

1. Wheat from Odessa and oil from Batoum (Batumi in modern-day Georgia) would be appropriated by the Central Powers, negating the Allied blockades of neutral Holland and Scandinavia. Germany could supply wheat to Switzerland, in place of supplies from the US, and 'would be able to force the Swiss to concede a free passage to their armies' into Italy.
2. Even if Southern Russia was lost it was important for the Allies to retain key naval bases on the Black Sea, including Batoum, Trebizond (modern Trabzon) and Novorissisk (Novorissysk).
3. The Allies should help Romania by establishing relationships with the Ukraine and 'the Cossack countries to secure supplies.'

The advisors were of the opinion that 'all national groups who are determined to continue the war must be supported by all means in our power.' They realised such resistance could not be sustained indefinitely unless the Allies found alternative supply routes.[167] Allied divisions over strategy towards Russia and its neighbouring territories would persist long after the Great War in the west ended.

---

164 Cyril Falls, *Official History: Military Operations: Macedonia*, Vol. II (London: HMSO1935), p. 49.
165 TNA WO 158/57: Joint Note 5, 24 December 1917.
166 Ibid.
167 Ibid.

Coordination of the 'Tools of War': Joint Notes 7, 8, 9 & 13

Logistics: Joint Note 8 ('Transportation'), 8 January 1918,[168] *and Joint Note 13 ('Supply'), 25 January 1918*[169]

By 1917 the British Army had mastered the art of logistics, supplying the troops in the field with the tools they needed to fight an industrialised war.[170] France had done the same. What the Allies had not done was establish mechanisms for sharing these hard-learned lessons and combining activities to mutual advantage. What was in place, and for the most part worked well, was a port and railway infrastructure which ensured men and supplies reached the front lines, but which for the most part operated independently. One of the raisons d'etre of the SWC was to ensure better co-operation between France, Britain and Italy. The growing presence of an increasingly important US partner made this even more urgent.

Transportation

The PMRs said Inter-Allied transportation should be placed urgently on a 'definitely coordinated basis.' They recommended a 'small strong Inter-Allied Expert Committee' reporting to the SWC. This would assess current systems, future projects and possibilities and make recommendations on 'their co-ordination on the most efficient lines.' The initial priorities were:

1. Co-ordination and improvement of railways behind the British, French and Italian fronts 'and the machinery necessary for their employment as one system.
2. Rail and shipping facilities in Greece to serve as alternative lines of defence to those already in place.
3. A railway scheme to help in the defeat of Turkey in Palestine.
4. Identification of sites on the enemy communications system 'where the maximum effect could be obtained by aeroplane attack.'[171]

As with the other Joint Notes in this section, the common sense and non-controversial nature of the proposal meant that the Third Session of the SWC approved it on 1 February 1918, a decision which 'reflected the crucial importance of transportation in the way the war was fought.'[172] Common sense it might have been, but without the SWC and Wilson's strategic overview it is problematic whether or not such co-operation would have been achieved. The Inter-Allied Transportation Council began work in late March, and, alongside other achievements,

---

168 TNA WO 158/57: Joint Note 8, 8 January 1918.
169 TNA WO 158/57: Joint Note 13, 25 January 1918.
170 See Ian Malcolm Brown, *British Logistics on the Western Front 1914-1919* (Westport, Connecticut & London: Praeger, 1998).
171 TNA WO 158/57: Joint Note 8, 9 January 1918.
172 Greenhalgh, *Victory Through Coalition*, p. 18. See also, McCrae, *Coalition Strategy*, p. 25.

'improved the lines of communication, especially those with Italy, and brought about better use of various Inter-Allied rolling stock.'[173]

Supply

Again, the Joint Note proposed an expert committee to co-ordinate Allied supply systems, identify areas of need and speed up organisational structures. This expert committee met simultaneously and alongside the Transportation body.[174]

Joint Notes 7 ('Aviation'), and Joint Note 9 ('Tanks'), 8 January 1918[175]

As with the previous two notes, Inter-Allied Expert Committees were set up. The priorities of the aviation body were to establish the minimum requirements of the national air forces on each front, the creation of Inter-Allied strategic air formations and their deployment, to plan 'systematic and scientific obliteration of areas in enemy territory vital to his munition supply', and the use of air power in the Eastern Mediterranean to disrupt Turkish military operations.[176] Wilson had bemoaned the state of Allied aviation strategy in December. No country, except possibly the French, he said, 'had any programme that was real' and recommended Lord Rothermere, who had just taken over the new British Air Ministry, should come to Versailles to 'explain his views.'[177] The Inter-Allied Aviation Committee met first on 9 May 1918 and 'studied and unified' the future programme of Inter-Allied aviation. In addition, it led to the creation of an 'Inter-Allied long-distance bombing force, the British nucleus of which contributed in the course of its …operations to the partial and total destruction of lines of communication', hampering the supply of food and munitions.[178] Wilson promoted this body at Versailles and as CIGS. One of his deputies at the SWC, Brigadier-General Freddie Sykes became Chief of the Air Staff in April 1918. Wilson supported Sykes' appointment and the two worked closely together for the rest of the war.[179]

JN9, setting up the Inter-Allied Tank Committee, illustrated the absence of coordinated thinking on use of the new weapon. The knowledge gap was to be filled by a review of needs for the proper deployment of tanks on each front, the 'speedy' creation of Inter-Allied reserve formations, and suggestions for the immediate creation of Inter-Allied anti-tank measures.[180] Despite the explicit call for haste, it first met on 6 May. The SWC history credited the initiative with improving co-operation around tank design, promoting best practice, and establishing an Allied school of instruction. It also claimed the body speeded production by hastening the construction of the Inter-Allied tank factory at Chateuroux. This enterprise, set up under an

---

173   TNA CAB 25/127: SWC History, p. 12 and CAB 125/110, 'Inter-Allied Transportation Council (Organisation and Functions).'
174   TNA WO 158/57: Joint Note 13, 25 January 1918.
175   TNA WO 158/57: Joint Notes 7 and 9, 8 January 1918.
176   TNA WO 158/57: Joint Note 7, 8 January 1918.
177   TNA CAB 25/120/17: SWC, British Secretariat, Minutes and Papers, PMR meeting, 8 December 1918.
178   TNA CAB 125/26: SWC History, p. 11.
179   Ash, *Sykes*.
180   TNA WO 158/57, Joint Note 9 'Tanks', 8 January 1918.

Anglo-American agreement, has been described as 'one of the most far-sighted and enterprising bits of industrial co-operation in the whole war.'[181] In fact, the project was beset with difficulties. Churchill, at the Ministry of Munitions, complained in August 1918 that labour problems meant that the factory was not finished, despite the materials being available for the tanks themselves. The factory was eventually completed and met its production targets for 1919.[182]

Wilson's seminal strategy paper of October 1917 led directly to the establishment of the SWC the following month, but there was no guarantee that it would serve any useful purpose. Despite recent setbacks on the Western Front the Haig-Robertson alliance retained powerful friends in government, at Court and in the Press. Allied enthusiasm for the Council was lukewarm, particularly in France whose new Prime Minister had not been involved in its creation. Wilson and his team were encouraged by the Prime Minister and Milner but faced a rearguard action from the CIGS and the Army Council, and the Secretary of State for War. Wilson had a challenge if the new body was to make a difference. Wilson's energy in galvanising an able team ensured British ideas dominated the work of the inter-Allied Staff and fed directly through to the decisions of the politicians on the War Council. Rather than a 'talking shop', it ensured that for the first time the Allies considered strategy co-operatively and thoroughly and presented their conclusions to a formal gathering of statesmen. The German Spring Offensives of 1918 superseded several of the Joint Notes produced by Wilson and his colleagues, perhaps explaining why the majority of them have received limited critical attention. Conversely, those concerned with future Allied military policy on the Western Front formalised the approach Wilson had outlined in October; no new offensive in Flanders in 1918 while the Allies regrouped and awaited the arrival of the Americans. The issue of the length of the British line, so long a thorn in the side of Anglo-French relations, had at its root the even more controversial issue of manpower resources. The next chapter considers Wilson's contribution to this vexed question.

181 J.P. Harris, *Men, Ideas and Tanks: British Military Thought: 1903-1939* (Manchester: Manchester University Press, 1995), p. 136.
182 Martin Gilbert, *Churchill and America* (New York: Simon & Schuster, 2008), p. 81.

7

Manpower Crisis

In 1918 the British army on the Western Front was 'able to prosecute a "rich man's war", possibly for the only time in its history.'[1] This alludes to the successful focussing of Britain's economic and manufacturing resources on the production of war material. When it came to that other fundamental resource, manpower, the country was in dire straits. Wilson summed up the problem: 'It is clear to me that L.G. [Lloyd George] is getting into a beastly mess about manpower, about Ireland and about taking over the lines, and if he is not careful he will be swamped by this.'[2] The BEF's manpower reservoir was draining faster than it was being topped up. France, on its knees after three and a half years of war, was pushing Britain to take over miles of trench line. The Allies much-vaunted saviour, the USA, had been disappointingly slow to provide the troops the entente powers had been relying on to meet the needs of another year of war.[3] As Britain's PMR at the SWC, and from February 1918 as CIGS, one of Wilson's greatest challenges was balancing the pressing needs of the army with the realities of coalition warfare, and a political establishment weary of the war and the toll it was taking on the population.

Manpower dominated British policy making throughout the Great War. By mid-1917 it had taken centre stage – a position it maintained until the end of the conflict. For the British Army's commanders, there were never enough men, particularly for the Western Front. For the politicians, the soldiers' insatiable demands for troops had to be balanced against a long list of pressures at home, with the production of war material at the top. By autumn 1917 Wilson had a unique perspective on the challenges facing Britain's political and military leadership. He had begun the year with an inspection tour of the Eastern Front and come away dismayed at the state of the Russian Army. This was followed by his second stint as senior British liaison officer with the French army, where he saw the morale-sapping failure of the Nivelle Offensive and its aftermath.[4] In November he had toured the front in north-east Italy following the Caporetto debacle.[5] As British PMR at Versailles, Wilson helped frame Anglo-French responses to the manpower challenge.

1   J.M. Bourne, *Who's Who in World War I* (London: Routledge, 2001), p. 176.
2   Wilson diary, 21 January 1918.
3   Sheffield, *Forgotten Victory*, p. 235.
4   The Nivelle Offensive, also known as the Second Battle of the Aisne, began on 16 April 1917.
5   Caporetto began on 24 October 1917.

Wilson had supported compulsory national service on the continental model for years. When his mentor Lord Roberts became president of the National Service League in 1905, Wilson drafted his speeches.[6] In late 1917 Wilson believed there were still men to be found if only the government had the will to make unpopular decisions. He advocated a more vigorous application of subscription in Britain, and its introduction to the island of Ireland. The latter was highly controversial but Wilson, usually so politically aware, was particularly tin-eared when it came to the politics of his homeland. If the government only grasped the nettle, he believed, British arms would both bolster French resolve and ensure Britain dominated the peace. As early as September 1915, he had lobbied Lord Bertie, Britain's ambassador in Paris, in favour of compulsion across the British Isles. Robertson, then the BEF's CoS, had told Bertie he was 'doubtful if conscription was necessary or advisable. The d____ old coward and skunk,' wrote Wilson of Wully.[7] In time soldiers, including Robertson, and statesmen, came over to the view that compulsory conscription was the only answer to the demands of modern industrialised warfare, yet Ireland remained an exception.[8] What divided opinion was the nature of such a policy, its parameters and scope. Wilson believed military conscription was essential, plus compulsory national service for essential industries on the homefront.

The challenge of manpower was a complex web of interdependent pressures and often contradictory priorities. In late 1917 Britain's military situation was in a parlous state. The two major campaigns of the year, Arras and Third Ypres, together with the Battle of Cambrai, had resulted in enormous casualties.[9] As a result of these setbacks, the War Office and GHQ's power over formulating strategy was diminishing in favour of Wilson and the SWC. Although this body grew in influence, it did not exercise executive authority. Lloyd George might have enhanced his control over his generals, but he had not tamed them. The PMRs offered advice, as a group; they could neither issue orders nor countermand those of the commanders in the field.[10] It was up to the heads of government to decide whether to accept the advice given. Wilson offered plenty of welcome advice to his Prime Minister. Lloyd George sought decisive victory over Germany but favoured a policy of 'active defence' in the west while the entente awaited the arrival of the Americans. By accepting Wilson's strategy for 1918 the Prime Minister also accepted that successes in other theatres would be a bonus, not the priority.[11]

When Wilson took up his post at the SWC, in November 1917, it was apparent that the American Expeditionary Force (AEF) were unlikely be in place in strategically significant numbers until 1919. The capitulation of Russia in late 1917 meant the inevitable transfer of large

---

6   Ian F.W. Beckett 'The Nation in Arms' in Ian F.W. Beckett & Keith Simpson (eds.), *A Nation in Arms: A Social Study of the British Army in the First World War* (London: Tom Donovan, 1990 [1985]), p. 4; Jeffery, *Wilson*, pp. 76, 108-9; in 1913, Wilson, French and Kiggell submitted a General Staff paper supporting some form of conscription, Wilson diary, 12 April 1913.

7   Wilson diary, 19 September 1915.

8   Milner urged the Asquith government to adopt conscription in early 1915, P.A. Lockwood, 'Milner's entry into the War Cabinet: December 1916', *The Historical Journal*, vol. VII (1), (1964), p. 212; Gollin, *Proconsul in Politics*, pp. 238-9.

9   The BEF suffered 759,000 casualties (killed, missing, wounded and prisoners) in 1917. See War Office, *Statistics of the Military Effort of the British Empire during the Great War 1914-1920* (London: HMSO, 1922), p. 361.

10   TNA CAB 28/3: War Cabinet, IC (Allied Conferences), Volume III, IC 30d (SWC).

11   TNA CAB 27/8: WP 61, 20 October 1917.

numbers of enemy troops to the west and a likely German offensive in the first half of 1918. Facing this threat was a British force in need of rest, training and reinforcement. The situation was complicated by the SWC's decision in January 1918 to create an allied 'General Reserve', something both British and French C-in-Cs resisted. Wilson found himself at the heart of this civil-military conundrum, one which grew in intensity once he became CIGS. During the final 12 months of the war Wilson had real power for the first time, but with it came responsibility. This chapter reassesses how he responded to that challenge.

British Manpower Challenges

Nearly a month before the Third Ypres campaign ended, Britain's politicians were given a stark warning of the size of the military manpower problem. In the autumn of 1917, in response to the generals' continuing demands for troops, and the government's failure to develop a coherent manpower policy, the Ministry of National Service was created, headed by Sir Auckland Geddes.[12] He was required 'somehow to utilise better – given the powers provided him by the State – what human resources were left to his care'. On 13 October 1917, he submitted to the War Cabinet a 'shocking' document.[13] 'The whole country' was 'close to the limit of its human resources'. He assumed a 'wastage' total for the period 1 October 1917 to 30 September 1918 of 800,000 men across all theatres; in line with losses of the previous 12 months. 'Combing out' men from essential industries might produce 270,000, with another 150,000 if conscription was imposed on Ireland, or if the upper age limit for compulsory service in Britain was increased from 41 to 50. In other words, even with radical changes to recruiting rules, only about half the predicted losses could be made up in the coming year.[14] The challenge to find men fit enough for front-line service was made worse by the poor state of health of many recruits.[15] This paper fell on Lloyd George's desk two days after he had ordered Wilson and Lord French to consider Britain's strategic options for 1918. Little wonder then that the Prime Minister resisted GHQ's enthusiasm for another major offensive on the Western Front in the coming year. Wilson's alternative strategy, a defensive posture, with the possibility of limited operations elsewhere, was supported by Churchill, Minister of Munitions.[16] He recommended that recruitment to the military be kept low with 'all our available labour, especially our skilled labour, being employed on shipbuilding, artillery and aeroplanes.'[17] At the SWC Wilson oversaw the creation of several policy studies into the manufacture of military materiel, particularly aircraft, tanks and heavy

---

12   For a detailed review of the various abortive attempts to establish a coherent manpower policy before autumn 1917 see Adams & Poirier, *Conscription Controversy* and Keith Grieves, *The Politics of Manpower* (Manchester: Manchester University Press, 1988).

13   Adams & Poirier, *Conscription Controversy*, p. 213.

14   TNA CAB 24/28/95: 'Recruiting Position: the Problem and Prospect', Memorandum to the War Cabinet by the Minister of National Service, 13 October 1917.

15   R.J. Clarke, '"Fit to Fight?" How the physical condition of the conscripts contributed to the manpower crisis of 1917-18,' *Journal of the Society for Army Historical Research*, Vol. 94 (370), Autumn 2016, pp. 225-224.

16   CAB 27/8, WP 61, p. 8.

17   TNA CAB 24/30/36: 'Munitions Possibilities of 1918', memorandum to the War Cabinet, 21 October 1917.

artillery. It was evident that there were insufficient men to supply both the military and the war economy.

At the end of 1917 the War Office and the Army Council, and GHQ, faced an uphill task persuading the Prime Minister of the need for yet more men for the Western Front. With Wilson at Versailles Lloyd George had a soldier he could communicate with on friendly terms; one who appeared to be sympathetic to at least some of his strategic views.[18] Wilson was acutely aware of the manpower crisis. In October 1917, while compiling his 'State Paper' for the War Cabinet, Macdonogh, the DMI, gave him the 'startling' casualty lists:

> Since July 1st 1916 up to Oct 10th last [,] Haig has lost 900,000 men in killed and missing[,]...it appears that our average monthly wastage in France is 50,000 and an optimistic estimate of intake is 30,000[,] though 25,000 will probably be more the mark. This shows a monthly deficit of 20,000 – 25,000. So that a year hence …we shall be 240,000 – 300,000 men deficient.[19]

The War Office casualty report for the period 1 January to 30 November 1917 showed 753,147 men killed, wounded, missing or taken prisoner, with 690,218 of those in France and Flanders.[20] Rather than helping Haig and Robertson's case for more men, the statistics served to harden the War Cabinet's resolve to take control of manpower priorities. On the way to the Rapallo Conference, Lloyd George told Wilson that:

> Haig really did talk the most awful nonsense about his front, said he was getting on splendidly that he would have done more if more men and guns had been sent to him - this infuriated LG - that no other front mattered and so on and so on. LG also let himself go about Robertson's pig-headedness and narrowness of vision, and said he was going to expose, on Friday in his speech in Paris, all our gross strategical blunders![21]

By late 1917 Lloyd George and his colleagues viewed the assessments of Robertson and Haig with great scepticism. The case for 'business as usual' was weakened by a series of conflicting and contradictory reports from the military leadership. The Prime Minister confided in Wilson that he was 'determined to stop this "butchering" on the West front and I am clear that as we cannot hope to walk over the Boches by dint of numbers we must develop their means.'[22] Derby told the War Cabinet that 'without a great legislative or administrative effort' to obtain men, the British would be '40 per cent below their present establishment' by the end of March 1918. 'Very grave reports' had been received from Haig and there was no longer any question of Britain deciding what next year's military policy would be 'as that will be decided by the

18   French, *Strategy*, p. 164; Woodward, *Lloyd George*, p. 221.
19   Wilson diary, 16 October 1917.
20   TNA CAB 24/34/66: War Cabinet, 'Casualties in the Expeditionary Forces, 1 January to November 1917'.
21   Wilson diary, 5 November 1917; in fact, Lloyd George made his controversial speech about the SWC and the need for greater Allied co-operation in Paris on 12 November, *The Times*, 13 November 1917, pp. 7-8; French, *Strategy*, p. 165.
22   Wilson diary, 27 November 1917.

Germans'. The BEF was 100,000 men below its proper strength and 'so far from there being any question of our breaking through the Germans, it was a question of whether we could prevent the Germans breaking through us.'[23] Wilson's reaction was that: 'It really is intolerable that one day he [Haig] should ask for 45,000 men before March 31st and the next day say he must reduce by 15 Divisions.'[24] Considering the fact that just a month earlier, in October, the C-in-C had been proposing a major British offensive in 1918, Hankey thought his concerns were:

> Absolutely inconsistent with Haig's continued reports of bad German moral[e]... War Office figures and statements are utterly unreliable, and their facts are twisted to support their arguments. If they want men they make out that they can hardly hold the line ... If they want to do an offensive they make out that the enemy is exhausted and demoralised and that they [the British] have lots of men.[25]

Hankey's dismay was understandable. The previous day, GHQ had issued a manpower assessment for the Western Front which showed 168.5 Allied divisions (excluding those in Italy or on their way there) facing 150 German divisions.[26] In response to Haig's plea, the government established a 'Cabinet Committee on Man-Power'.[27] Its conclusions placed the army at the bottom of the list of manpower priorities for 1918. Matters were made worse for Haig when Macdonogh somehow estimated that on the Western Front the French and British had '1,200,000 more men in the field than the Germans'. Even if the enemy transferred all his troops from the east they would still be in a minority and thus: 'In these circumstances the Prime Minister was unable to understand the rather alarmist tone as to the situation which had recently been exhibited.'[28] Macready, the AG, told Wilson that the result had been 'three days of Armageddon' at the Man-Power Committee:

> This, and the fact that GHQ France, in October wrote a Memorandum... saying in effect that the Germans were worn out and could only bring a limited number of Divisions over from the Russian front, has naturally given the civilians the impression that we so outnumber the Boche that the need for men is not urgent.
>   Macready assumed that Charteris had written the report and noted the figures included 'people like Belgians, Portuguese, and Italians, none of whom would stand up against the Boche.'[29]

Hankey summed up the political mood: 'Russia practically out of the war; Italy very much under the weather after [her] defeat; France unreliable; the USA not nearly ready; our own man-power much exhausted by the senseless hammerings of the last three years; and great demands for

23   TNA CAB 24/4/67: War Cabinet, 6 December 1917.
24   Wilson diary, 29 November 1917.
25   Hankey diary, 6 December 1917, in Roskill, *Hankey*, p. 469.
26   TNA CAB 24/34/70: 'Strength of Allied and Enemy Forces on 5 December 1917: Western Front', report to War Cabinet, 5 December 1917; the report showed manpower numbers as 1,596,400 Allied troops opposed by 1,177,700 Germans.
27   TNA CAB 24/4/67; Beckett et. al., *British Army*, pp. 348-9.
28   TNA CAB 24/4/67.
29   Wilson papers, (2/2A/1), Macready to Wilson, 13 December 1917.

labour ...'[30] In this climate it is unsurprising that the findings of the Man-Power Committee 'represented a wholesale defeat for the War Office and a victory for Lloyd George'.[31] It gave manpower priority to the Royal and Merchant navies, essential as these were in sustaining Britain during what was expected to be a year of retrenchment; it was also vital to be able to transport both men and equipment from the US to make a decisive difference in 1919. The army came last, after shipbuilding, aircraft, tank and food production. It would receive just 100,000 'Category A' men in the year, rather than the 600,000 the War Office estimated was needed. The report recommended that front-line divisions be reduced, from 12 battalions (plus one Pioneer battalion), to nine battalions (plus one Pioneer battalion).[32] Haig and Robertson had feared this policy, which had already been carried out by the German and French armies, since early in the year.[33] In December 1917 Foch and Weygand tried to persuade Wilson and Milner of the merits of such a change as an alternative to reducing the number of operational British divisions on the Western Front: 'He [Foch] wants the defence made secure before studying plans of offence. He wants our divisions turned into 9 Batt[alion]s also the Belgian and the Italians.' The British Secretariat at Versailles came out marginally in favour of the change.[34] Wilson discussed the suggestion with Kiggell, who was 'absolutely opposed' and said that Haig would 'rather abolish 15 Div[ision]s altogether than keep his 62 at 9 Batt[alion]s. I thought Kigg's arguments were wholly unconvincing.'[35] Wilson's unwillingness to jump instantly to the French tune disappointed Foch who reportedly told Spears that: 'General Wilson was not as good as he had thought he was, and required a great deal of close support and help; were it not for General Weygand Versailles would be in a bad way.'[36] Resigned to the reduction, Wilson told Lloyd George that if 'our man-power conditions – and I understand this is the case - make it necessary either to abolish Divisions or change from 12 to 9 then I would not hesitate for a minute but would change to 9'.[37]

Macready tipped off Wilson that the implications of Man-Power Committee's conclusions made:

> Dreadful reading, and amounts to this, that we must reduce our 56 Div[ision]s from 12 to 9 Batt[alion]s; that in July we shall have to reduce from 56 [divisions] to 44, and next winter from 44 to 30. This is simply damnable.

30 Hankey diary, 16 December 1917, in Roskill, *Hankey*, p. 470.
31 French, *Strategy*, p. 185.
32 TNA CAB 24/4/36: 'Final Revise of the Draft Report on Man-Power', 1 March 1918, with covering note by Hankey, 2 April 1918; (the initial draft report was completed on 9 January 1918); minutes of the meetings of the Cabinet Committee on Man-Power are at TNA CAB 27/14. See also Simon Justice, 'Vanishing Battalions: The Nature, Impact and Implications of British Infantry Reorganization prior to the German Spring Offensives of 1918' in Michael LoCicero, Ross Mahoney & Stuart Mitchell, (eds.), *A Military Transformed?: Adaptation and Innovation in the British Military, 1792-1945* (Solihull: Helion & Company, 2014), pp. 157-173.
33 LHCMA, Robertson papers, Robertson to Haig, (7/7/5), 13 February 1917.
34 TNA CAB 25/120/7: SWC, British Secretariat Minutes and Papers, 'Organisation of a Division with 9 Battalions instead of 13', 7 December 1918.
35 Wilson diary, 6 December 1917.
36 TNA WO 106/407: (LSO. 177), Spears to Maurice, 22 December 1917.
37 PA, Lloyd George papers, (47/7/5), Wilson to Lloyd George, 23 December 1917 (original emphasis).

I wrote Milner a long letter in which I told him that <u>if</u> these figures are true then we must do one of two things:

a. get more men

b. make peace now

Personally I rejected (b) as being cowardly and fatal in every way at least until we were strained to breaking point, but I saw no difficulty in (a) which mean <u>real</u> conscription in England <u>and</u> in Ireland, neither of which things have any terror for me compared with Peace. But I confess all this frightens me, and if Macready's figures prove true and if LG won't take drastic action then <u>I</u> will.[38]

It is unclear what the final sentence meant; there is no reference to any such 'drastic action' in subsequent diary entries, and the most likely explanation is that (as was his wont) Wilson was letting off steam in private. At this time Wilson and his Versailles team were conducting a 'war game', with discouraging conclusions. More men were needed and action was required. This would:

mean something much more drastic than what we have done, as yet, in England and of course it will mean Ireland...Our war game here has shown us that we can look forward with an easy mind if we have 56 Div[ision]s each of 9 Batt[alion]s and 1 Pioneer Batt[alion] but the war game also shows that a reduction from 56 to 44 would be a terrible gamble and a further reduction to 30 would bring us certain disaster.[39]

He was so concerned that the next day he sent Amery to London.[40] The mission backfired when Hankey accused Wilson's emissary of going behind his back to the Prime Minister. These were fraught times, and Wilson's tendency for dramatic interventions sometimes landed him in hot water.[41] As discussed earlier, Amery was a much more independent figure than either Hankey or Wilson gave credit for. After himself, his greatest loyalty was to Milner.

The response of the Army Council to the Committee's recommendations confirmed Wilson's fears. Dominated by Derby and Robertson, it noted 'with grave concern' that only 100,000 Category A men were going to be allocated to the Army, as opposed to the 615,000 estimated to be needed to keep up to strength. A defensive policy was likely to be as costly as an offensive one. The Army Council thought reducing battalion strength to nine per division was 'very undesirable'. They pointed out that the French had adopted a similar policy only because of lack of men. The Council appeared to have overlooked the fact that this was exactly why the Committee was making a similar recommendation. They also opposed the creation of a 'mobile reserve' for lack of men and calculated that the army, in all theatres, would be 264,000 below establishment by 1 January 1919. The 52 divisions in France in 1917 would be reduced to 42, with five of them currently in Italy, leaving 37 on the Western Front – a reduction of 25% on a year earlier. The Army Council believed the Committee had 'failed to realise the perilous situation' regarding

---

38   Wilson diary, 4 January 1918, (original emphasis).
39   IWM, Wilson papers, (2/11/6), Wilson to Milner, 4 January 1918.
40   Wilson diary, 5 January 1918.
41   Hankey diary, 9 January 1918, in Roskill, *Hankey*, p. 479; Amery diary, 9-10 January 1918, in Barnes and Nicholson (eds.), *Amery Diaries* (Vol. I), pp. 198-9.

drafts. There was 'every prospect of heavy fighting on the Western front from February onwards' and even if they withstood the initial assault, forces might become so exhausted that they would be 'incapable of continuing the struggle'. Accepting the recommendations would amount to 'taking an unnecessarily grave risk of losing the war and sacrificing to no purpose the British Army on the Western front.'[42] Nonetheless, accepting the inevitable, the next day (10 January 1918) the War Office ordered Haig to reduce his British (but not Dominion) divisions to nine battalions.[43] A situation Derby had long feared had come to pass. It appeared, he had said the previous June, as if the army was provided with men 'only after all other needs of the Nation have been cared for' and had warned that the strength of the army would 'continue rapidly to diminish, and, so far as military operations are concerned, our chances of winning the war will be correspondingly reduced.'[44]

Ironically, Haig himself put paid to any lingering doubts the politicians might have had about the military's demands for more troops at a War Cabinet meeting two days before the draft report of the Man-Power Committee. Robertson reported that there were 28 more German divisions on the Western Front than a year earlier, thanks to relocations from the east. The enemy was reorganising and now had 'the character of an offensive force'.[45] Carson asked Haig whether 'it would be possible for the Germans to break through our lines in France in the near future.' The C-in-C said he had 'every confidence that the British Army would hold its own, as it had always done in the past'.[46] Haig was given the opportunity to clarify when Bonar Law, a 'friend' of the soldiers, asked: 'If you were a German Commander, would you think there was sufficient chance of a smashing offensive to justify incurring the losses which would be entailed?' Haig said he thought attacks of limited scope were 'more probable' than one on a large scale which would be 'very costly'. The German manpower situation 'did not seem very satisfactory', but the Allies must, nonetheless, 'expect to be seriously attacked'. He was making preparations and while likely to lose ground 'he felt confident of holding his front provided his Divisions were maintained at proper strength.'[47] This was exactly the kind of answer the politicians wanted to hear. While it makes sense to blame the Field Marshal's 'inarticulacy' for the blunder, this performance was a particularly sustained example of the malady.[48] Robertson, who witnessed the presentation was horrified and immediately sent Haig a note urging him to clarify his remarks. 'For months past', Wully observed:

we have been trying to get more men for the Army. The Cabinet find difficulty in getting the men and therefore make every excuse for not providing them...For a long time past they have been trying to persuade me to say that the Germans may not attack us this year. Unfortunately you gave as your opinion this morning that they would not do so, and I noticed, as also did Lord Derby, that they jumped at the statement.

42   TNA CAB 24/38/66: 'Memorandum by the Military Members of the Army Council on the draft Report of the War Cabinet Committee on Man-Power', 9 January 1918.
43   French, *Strategy*, p. 186.
44   TNA CAB 24/15/66: 'The Position and Prospects of Recruiting', Derby to War Cabinet, 7 June 1917.
45   TNA CAB 23/5/8: War Cabinet, 7 January 1918.
46   Ibid.
47   Ibid.
48   Sheffield, *The Chief*, p. 260.

Robertson's note ended with the handwritten explanation that Carson's questions had been designed to give Haig the opportunity to 'rub in' the message about the need to keep the BEF up to establishment: 'Of course you do not quite understand these fellows as well as I do.'[49] In fairness to Haig, he made several references to the effect that it was essential to maintain his forces and predicted monthly losses of 100,000 in the event of a German offensive.[50] Despite submitting a note of clarification, in which he stressed the need to keep the BEF up to strength, the damage had been done.[51] Haig compounded matters the next day when at a lunch at 10 Downing Street he told Lloyd George and Derby that he doubted the Germans would attempt a breakthrough; such an attempt would be 'a gambler's throw'.[52] Wilson learned of the incident from Robertson who was a 'good deal flustered'. The CIGS informed him that the manpower report had allocated only 100,000 men for 1918, 'this of course would settle the war.' Robertson was visiting the front and appeared to have mis-remembered the totality of Haig's message: 'He said that the politicians were taking increasing charge in military affairs and he called Haig a fool because on Mon[day] last Haig had told the War Cabinet that he could hold the line and never insisted on the necessity of being supported with men. Haig really is incurably stupid.'[53] Wilson was further dismayed by the C-in-C's Dispatch for the campaigns of 1917 which included the claim: 'In the operations of Arras, Messines, Lens and Ypres as many as 131 German divisions have been engaged and defeated by less than half that number of British divisions.' Haig added another sentence, weakening the impact of his warnings about the increasing German threat: 'The addition of strength which the enemy has obtained, or may yet obtain, from events in Russia and Italy has already been largely discounted, and the ultimate destruction of the enemy's field force has been brought appreciably nearer.'[54] 'What a lie!' Wilson wrote in his diary.[55]

Ireland

The 1918 German Spring Offensive, which began on 21 March, brought the manpower issues discussed here into sharp focus. The BEF's shortage of troops was exposed as casualties mounted, the recent attempts to formalise Anglo-French co-operation remained to a large extent ad hoc, and the AEF was green and not ready to help in the defence of the British line. The War Cabinet met almost daily with Wilson, now in the post of CIGS having succeeded Robertson in February, in attendance. The desperate need for manpower led the government to finally adopt a policy

49   LHCMA, Robertson papers, Robertson to Haig, (7/7/77), January 1918.
50   In his diary for this date, Haig noted that 'In my opinion, the best defence would be to continue our offensive in Flanders, because we would then retain the initiative and attract the German Reserves against us', NLS, Haig (manuscript) diary, 7 January 1918. He did not make this point at the War Cabinet meeting
51   TNA CAB 24/38/69: Haig to CIGS, 8 January 1918; Robertson later wrote that when Lloyd George saw Haig's note he 'tossed it aside with the remark that is was entirely inconsistent with what Sir Douglas had said verbally', Field Marshal Sir William Robertson, *Soldiers and Statesmen* (London: Cassell, 1926), p. 324.
52   NLS, Haig (manuscript) diary, 9 January 1918, and Beckett et. al., *British Army*, p. 350.
53   Wilson diary, 9 January 1918.
54   'The Campaigns of 1917' in J.H. Boraston, (ed.), *Sir Douglas Haig's Despatches (December 1915-April 1919)* (London: J.M. Dent, 1919) p. 135.
55   Wilson diary, 9 January 1918.

it had avoided, and which Wilson had doggedly advocated since the war began: compulsory military conscription for Ireland. Geddes had estimated that there might be a manpower pool of 150,000 available in Ireland. Nonetheless he had rejected conscription as unworkable in view of 'the great political difficulties involved and the meagre results to be anticipated' in conscripting a reluctant population.[56] Predictably enough Wilson disagreed.[57] Unbowed by Geddes's recommendation, on 31 January he 'had a serious talk with LG about Ireland and his theory is that if we put conscription on Ireland, not only would we have trouble in Ireland but we would have trouble with the English Unions, with the Colonies and with America, and therefore this was out of the question.'[58] Wilson's chance came with the desperation engendered by the German offensive. His inability to see the evident risks associated with such a policy is a notable departure for one normally so politically astute. Ireland was 'a political blind-spot' for Wilson.[59]

On 23 March he spent five hours with Lloyd George: 'I insisted on the importance of taking a long, broad view of the future, of conscription of everyone up to 50, and, of course, on Ireland. I think I did good, and Winston [Churchill] helped like a man…Milner disappointing.'[60] Geddes was urged to tap 'such new sources as still remain' because the situation 'might afford exceptional opportunity for overcoming difficulties that had hitherto proved insurmountable.'[61] The next day Milner's view had changed; he was now 'nearly as strong as I was for the necessity of *levée en masse* in England & Ireland which could be carried out with real conscription.' Over dinner with the Prime Minister and Churchill: 'Winston backed me up when I pressed Lloyd George hard to really conscript this country & Ireland…I want Lloyd George to summon Parliament, conscript up to 50 years of age, & include Ireland. I am not sure he sees the gravity of the situation yet.' [62] The government's dilemma has been summed up thus: 'Unless the British army could be provided with manpower to rebuild the shattered divisions, the BEF would cease to exist. In these circumstances the War Cabinet took the most contentious decision of the war; they extended compulsory military service to Ireland.'[63] On 25 March, a 'wildly optimistic' Johnnie French, a fellow Irishman, said he strongly believed that if troops in Ireland were augmented 'to maintain order' it would be possible to carry out a recruitment policy.[64] The War Cabinet met twice on 27 March, the day after Foch had been appointed 'Generalissimo' at Doullens. Wilson outlined the parlous state of the BEF. There were signs the Germans were preparing another attack and were just 25km from the important rail junction at Amiens. The British Fifth Army 'could no longer be regarded as a fighting unit,' and had been placed under the French who were sending reinforcements. Wilson said there were 193 German divisions on the Western Front; 70 had been involved in the recent fighting with an estimated 31 in reserve.

56 TNA CAB 24/4/36: 'Final Revise of the Draft Report on Man-Power', 1 March 1918, (paras. 62-64).
57 Jeffery, *Wilson*, p. 197.
58 Wilson diary, 31 January 1918.
59 Jeffery, *Wilson*, p. 197.
60 Wilson diary, 23 March 1918.
61 TNA CAB 23/5/63: War Cabinet, 23 March 1918.
62 Wilson diary, 24 March 1918.
63 Adrian Gregory, '"You might as well recruit Germans": British public opinion and the decision to conscript the Irish in 1918', in Adrian Gregory & Senia Pašeta, *Ireland and the Great War: 'A War to Unite Us All'?* (Manchester: Manchester University Press, 2002) p. 113.
64 Ibid., p. 117; TNA CAB 25/5/64: War Cabinet minutes, 25 March 1918.

To make matters worse, the AEF C-in-C General John Pershing had refused a plea from Rawlinson (now Britain's PMR) to put American battalions into British divisions. It was agreed that Lloyd George, to make Pershing reconsider, would send a 'strongly worded' telegram 'with a view to ultimate publication' to US President Woodrow Wilson.[65] It made no difference.

The meeting then heard from the government's senior representatives in Ireland. The C-in-C Ireland, Lieutenant-General Sir Bryan Mahon, was in favour of the *principle* of conscription but predicted 'considerable trouble' if implemented. Brigadier-General Sir Joseph Byrne, head of the Royal Irish Constabulary, was in no doubt that compulsory military service 'would be a mistake' and predicted riots. The most vehement opposition came from Ireland's most senior political officer, the Unionist MP and Chief Secretary for Ireland, Henry E. Duke, who expressed grave doubts. The Cabinet, having discussed further relaxation of age limits to extend recruitment in the rest of Britain, faced a profound dilemma. How could it exempt Ireland yet bear down still harder on the rest of the country?[66] At the day's second meeting, Duke was adamant that conscription would unite Catholics and Protestants against the government and 'we might almost as well recruit Germans.'[67] Despite the opposition of three key government-appointed figures who, arguably, knew the current political climate in Ireland better than Wilson, French and Derby, the Cabinet decided to go ahead and impose conscription.[68] Gregory has argued that the government had little expectation of recruiting large numbers of Irishmen but acted to avoid charges of treating one part of Britain differently.[69] This work, while acknowledging the strength of this position, argues that Wilson also played an important role. Since November he had seen the Prime Minister and/or Milner, the most influential Unionist in the government, almost daily. His diary contains numerous references to speaking to both men, and others, about the 'need' to conscript Ireland. Having been instrumental in Wilson's appointment as CIGS, the Prime Minister backed his principal military adviser. In the event, while the legislation was enacted, conscription was never actually imposed on Ireland; once the spring crisis had passed the notion was quietly shelved, much to Wilson's disgust.[70]

Taking Over French Line

One of the most intractable problems Wilson faced at Versailles concerned the extension of the British line to relieve the hard-pressed French. The issue had been on the Allies' agenda since early 1915.[71] Lloyd George had effectively kicked the issue into the long grass on 7 November 1917 at the inaugural meeting of the SWC, by insisting that a joined-up Allied strategic plan for 1918 had to be agreed first. French pressure increased when Clemenceau became Prime Minister nine days later. Wilson was heavily involved in trying to find a solution acceptable to both allies. For much of the winter he acted as a conduit for British policy and a lightning rod

65   TNA CAB 25/5/66: War Cabinet, 27 March 1918.
66   Ibid.
67   Ibid.
68   The Military Service Act (No. 2) became law in April 1918; as well as extending conscription to Ireland it removed a number of other exemptions and increased the age limit of recruits to 50.
69   Gregory, 'You might as well Recruit Germans', p. 114.
70   Wilson diary, 21 June 1918.
71   Callwell, *Wilson*, (vol. II), p. 44.

against French impatience. His friendship with Foch, and his more nuanced relationship with Clemenceau, helped preserve fragile Anglo-French relations during a crucial period, and both merit further discussion.

Whilst Chief of British Mission to the French Army in 1917, Wilson had wanted to ensure Britain did all it could to bolster France's commitment to the war.[72] The failure of Nivelle's offensive saw him replaced in mid-May as C-in-C by Pétain.[73] Wilson recorded the 'disquieting' news that an attack, in support of the imminent British offensive against the Messines Ridge south of Ypres, had been cancelled 'because the moral[e] of the French troops is such that it cannot be carried out…if the French continue to feel the strain like this, we must expect them to ask us to take over some more line.'[74] Macdonogh reported 'serious trouble, practically amounting to mutiny, in a number of French regiments… It was hoped that this disaffection would be set right in five or six days.'[75] As the British officer closest to the French high command, Wilson 'expressed grave doubts as to whether we could count on the continued resistance of the French army and nation' before US forces were able to make a difference, something he expected to take 12 to 18 months. The War Cabinet understood that Pétain 'could not absolutely rely on his men'. Wilson could not confirm an incident 'amounting almost to mutiny', but there was a 'good deal of unrest'. Soon the British would be asked 'to take over a further section of the line on the Western Front. A case …which it would be very difficult to resist.' Macdonogh agreed that there was 'a strong feeling in France that we ought to hold more of the line'. Wilson said the French were 'good comrades' who would not press their case while the Messines offensive, and the actions which were to follow, were in progress.[76]

Wilson's views carried weight. He had been in regular contact with Lloyd George since joining *GQG*.[77] The issue lay dormant in the latter half of 1917 but re-emerged when it became clear that Third Ypres had failed to meet its objectives. Despite British losses, the French once again pressed the BEF to take over more line. On 6 December Wilson, as British PMR, and Milner met Foch and Weygand:

> He [Foch] does not yet realise how badly we are off in recruiting though I let him know rather vaguely that we were in straits… He was angry with Haig for the waste of life and upset at Passchendaele and at Cambrai, and he said that these individual efforts were fatal and upset the general plan, as for example our taking over French line which now we appeared incapable of doing.[78]

---

72   Jeffery, *Wilson*, p. 188; Wilson took up his post on 17 March and stepped down in late June 1917.
73   Foch was appointed French Chief of Staff on 15 May, two days after Pétain became C-in-C. See Greenhalgh, *Foch*, pp. 225-226.
74   Wilson diary, 4 June 1917. French troops in several sectors of the front refused to take part in further offensive action, although they did not refuse to fight in defence of their positions. Pétain spent the summer attempting to restore the army's morale.
75   TNA CAB 23/3/3: War Cabinet Minutes 6 June 1917; for the most recent assessment of the French 'Mutinies' of 1917 see Greenhalgh, *French Army*, pp. 201-216.
76   TNA CAB 23/16/1: War Cabinet, 8 June 1917; Hankey considered Wilson's report on the morale of the French army of such 'very great secrecy' that he restricted it to one manuscript copy.
77   Woodward, *Lloyd George*, p. 196.
78   Wilson diary, 6 December 1917, and *passim*.

Wilson canvassed views in a bid to resolve the issue. Esher told him Clemenceau 'was furious with the English' and he went to see him at once. At a 'memorable and stormy meeting':

> The old man was difficult. He raged against the English and then fastened on Haig and in a minor degree on Robertson. He told of the [French] War Cabinet this morning in which Pétain said that unless he was given 200,000-300,000 men from the interior for some works to dig backward trenches and put up wire and unless we (English) took over the line to Berry-au-Bac ... he – Pétain – would not be responsible for his front. This, said Clemenceau, had a very great effect on the War Cabinet.
> Clemenceau then undertook to:
> a. Get the 200,000 men from the Interior
> b. Make the English take over to Berry-au-Bac
> OR
> c. Resign

Wilson employed diplomatic balm and eventually 'I got the old man a little quieter'. Despite the histrionics, Wilson had been struck by the French Première's argument: 'When all allowance is made it is perfectly clear that we must handle this business of relief and of the future with the greatest care and consideration...Before leaving old C. I told him to submit the whole case to Versailles [in other words to Wilson and the other PMRs] and not to London and I think he will.'[79] Haig thought it 'quite impossible for us to take over any line, that our troops are exhausted, that we have been fighting all the summer and up to now, that the French have done nothing, that we have sent 5 Div[ision]s to Italy, that D.H. won't take over more than to the Oise. All this will be very difficult.'[80] Wilson sent Amery to London 'with a rather anxious message' to recruit Milner's, and the Prime Minister's, support.[81] He made another visit to Haig, who was 'very nice to me ... I begged D.H. and more particularly Kiggell with whom I can speak with greater freedom, to look at the question of the relief of the French from as broad a standpoint as they could, as otherwise there would be trouble, but I did not make much impression, I am afraid.' Nonetheless, Wilson had convinced the Prime Minister, who ordered Haig and Robertson to 'lay the case before Versailles. I will get the French to do ditto. I am sure it is wise.'[82] Robertson's response was to tell Wilson that: 'This extension of the line is a d ___ d nuisance. Haig certainly ought not to go anywhere near Berry-au-Bac.' Robertson said the BEF was 'played out' and needed rest.[83] Haig and Robertson both resented the interference of Versailles. Haig preferred to deal directly with his French opposite number; a practice he maintained into 1918. Haig and Pétain met but failed to agree a way forward. Haig, who apparently arrived at the meeting with 'no papers or figures', said he could extend his line

79   Wilson diary, 13 December 1917; Hankey, *Supreme Command* (vol. II), p. 753.
80   Wilson diary, 14 December 1917.
81   BLO, Milner diary, 15 December 1917.
82   Wilson papers, (2/11/3), Wilson to Milner, 16 December 1917.
83   Ibid., (2/1A/6), Robertson to Wilson, 16 December 1917.

by no more than two divisions by mid-January 1918 'and under no circ[umstance]s could he do anymore! It is clear that my talk did not do any good,' wrote Wilson.[84]

Having secured Lloyd George's support, Wilson persuaded Clemenceau to let the PMRs decide this important issue provided that 'he was prepared to accept the Versailles decision as final. He asked who Versailles was and answered it himself by saying "Nous: Wilson" he then thought a little and finally said, "Yes I will agree to that proposal."' Clemenceau then asked Wilson to dictate what he wanted to say: 'This is an epoch making step because it really calls Versailles into being as the Supreme advisory (military) body and as the Supreme executive body also. I told the Tiger that I thought well of him and liked him and he said he liked me too!' Unsurprisingly, considering he knew Wilson was sympathetic to the French request for British help, Clemenceau 'said that when first he spoke to me ... he was hostile to Versailles but that now he admitted that he was entirely wrong.'[85] Wilson thought the first report Haig submitted to Versailles was a 'feeble defence' of his position and asked for 'much more information.'[86] Wilson suggested Haig send two officers to Versailles to help him develop the British case, 'as otherwise, I am afraid we shall be swamped.' Haig refused, saying there was so much information it would be easier to examine it at GHQ. In other words, the C-in-C was not willing to dance to Wilson's tune.[87] Wilson continued to worry away at the problem, including working on the issue on Christmas Day.[88]

The PMRs produced their recommendation in Joint Note 10 (JN10), a compromise extending the British line 14 miles beyond Barisis to the left bank of the River Ailette, between the Ailette and the Laon-Soissons road 'the exact points to be fixed by the Commanders-in-Chief.'[89] The note also allowed for the British to support the French if an attack further south meant they had to move forces there. The French would support the British if the latter were attacked and the junction between the Allied armies was threatened. In a detail of significance for the future, it excluded the prospect of French forces moving deeper into the British sector, for example around Ypres, or *vice-versa*. The recommended extension fell well short of Berry-au-Bac, the French preference, and Weygand made clear he thought it inadequate, pointing out that the French held 520 kilometres of line, a burden 'which was more than they could bear.'[90] As the date for the Third Session of the SWC approached it was far from certain that the C-in-Cs would support the Wilson compromise. Robertson warned Haig that while 'the Versailles people' were no doubt doing their best 'they cannot help being a probable source of mischief unless we responsible people have made up our minds on all points *beforehand* and are in accord with the French.' Wully recommended that he and Haig confer with Foch, Pétain and Pershing, ahead of the main meeting in order to be 'in a position to get done what you want done without

84   Wilson diary, 17 December 1917; Haig diary, 17 December 1917 in Robert Blake, *The Private Papers of Douglas Haig: 1914-1919* (London: Eyre & Spottiswoode, 1952), p. 273.
85   Wilson diary, 17 December 1917.
86   Ibid., 18 December 1917.
87   IWM, Wilson papers, (2/7A/1) Wilson to Haig, 18 December 1917, and (2/7A/2) Operations, GHQ to Wilson, 19 December 1917.
88   Wilson diary, 25 December 1917.
89   TNA WO 158/57: Joint Note 10, 10 January 1918; the extension proposed was, roughly, the equivalent of 2.5 British divisions, Callwell, *Wilson*, (vol. II), *n.* p. 57.
90   TNA CAB 25/120: 'Supreme War Council: Papers and Minutes,' Minutes of a meeting of the Military Representatives, 7 January 1918.

the interference of the young men at Versailles.' The PMR's compromise had been reached as a result of Wilson's war games 'their panacea for everything.' It would all be 'very funny if it were not such a nuisance, not to say serious.'[91] Wilson was not the only senior soldier who could play a political game.

While Robertson and Haig considered their tactics for the SWC conference, Lloyd George continued to cast around for ways to limit their power. On 13 January Amery asked Wilson's opinion 'of a proposal to make Joffre C-in-C and me as his CGS!'[92] Wilson apparently put a stop to this short-lived notion by telling Milner 'that in my opinion we cannot have a Generalissimo but that if this was tried it would make it still more impossible if he was given a foreigner for Chief of Staff.'[93] The Prime Minister's anxiety over the issue of the French line is illustrated by the fact that he wrote to Wilson on consecutive days asking why the PMRs had settled on the Laon-Soissons road compromise: 'Another wire from L.G. wanting more information about our taking over the line. It is clear that he finds it difficult to get his Cabinet to agree to Versailles and go against Haig and Robertson.'[94] On the same day Wilson saw Foch who was allegedly:

> Rather contemptuous of L.G. who he says seems afraid of everyone, of Haig and Robertson, of the Trades Unions and of the Irish. Then he told me of Robertson's little plot to square [sic] the pitch of Versailles. R. is trying to get up a meeting of Haig, Pétain, Pershing, Foch and himself before the Versailles meeting so as to be able to say at that meeting that all was already settled! Foch much amused.[95]

Wilson, who warned Milner that the French were 'getting cross' about the unresolved issue, had begun to see it as a personal contest between himself and the Haig-Robertson alliance.[96] Lloyd George had to decide whom to support.[97] In the end, he backed Wilson, but then did nothing to ensure Haig and Pétain obeyed. Once in the role of CIGS, such apparently black and white issues took on a more nuanced tone for Wilson himself.

When the heads of the British, Italian and French governments met for the first meeting of the Third Session of the SWC on 30 January, Haig and Pétain had not resolved their differences. Days earlier Haig had reported to Robertson that relations with Pétain were 'good'. The CIGS noted: 'I only hope that he [Pétain] will represent them as being equally good when we come to the discussion of the extension of the front. I daresay this will be difficult for him because his politicians wish for you to take over more front.'[98] Robertson's fears were well founded. Wilson recorded that Haig agreed to his idea of the Allies taking an active defensive position in 1918 and to the principle of creating a reserve force: 'He went on to show that by the autumn his present 57 Div[ision]s would be reduced to 30! Such was the state of the manpower; he was also far from nice to the Americans saying they would be no use till 1919.' Then, in order to illustrate

91   LHCMA, Robertson papers, Robertson to Haig, (7/7/78), 12 January 1918, (original emphasis).
92   Wilson diary, 13 January 1918.
93   Ibid., 14 January 1918; see also p. 218.
94   Ibid., 17, 18 January 1918.
95   Ibid., 18 January 1918.
96   Ibid., 20 January 1918.
97   Ibid., 23 January 1918.
98   LHCMA, Robertson papers, Haig to Robertson, (7/7/81), 20 January 1918 and (7/7/82), Robertson to Haig, 21 January 1918.

how vital it was that the BEF took on more French line, Pétain 'showed that he would have to reduce by the autumn to the tune of 25 Divisions <u>if he had no fighting</u> and by 50 divisions if he had some fighting.' According to Wilson:

> This was all too much for L.G. who said he was absolutely dumbfounded that 77 Divisions were going to be wiped off in this manner & that he really could not accept these figures … all this is extraordinary.
>
> About three weeks ago Haig gave evidence before the War Cabinet & said that if he was the German C-in-C he would <u>not</u> attack because it would be so hopeless an undertaking. A week later (about a fortnight ago) he wrote an official letter to say that in view of the critical situation which now existed the Divisions now in Italy must be at once brought back. Yesterday Haig told us that he was not afraid of any Boche attack. Today Haig told us that he was going to lose 27 Divisions & the position is very critical. The man is a FOOL. The real fact seems to me to be that if we allow the conduct of the war to rest in the hands of Haig, Pétain & Robertson we shall be beaten by the Boches. This is a serious state of affairs, & I think L.G. must take some action.[99]

This 'absolutely desperate picture of the future manpower situation' was painted 'in an apparent attempt to frighten Lloyd George away from his "Eastern" schemes and towards increasing the flow of recruits to the British army'.[100] Wilson thought so, and had reminded Robertson of the confusion created by Haig's recent manpower statements:

> I asked him why Haig claimed to have 'defeated 131 Divisions' with less than half that number & why - that being so [-] he was now afraid of being attacked by 50 or 60 Divisions & called for the Divisions now in Italy to be returned to him. I asked him also why[,] if Haig claimed to have caused 900,000 casualties with a loss of 600,000 he was now afraid of being knocked out by numbers. Robertson said that all that was 'very stupid'.[101]

When the first meeting ended, in an effort to get in first and prevent his adversaries combining to carry their point, Wilson advised Lloyd George to keep military advisers out of the meeting until required:

> As regards Haig and Robertson he does not know what to do. I told Milner later that if it would help them to solve the problem I would resign with pleasure…this Haig is the same man who in his Dispatch a month ago claimed to have 'defeated 131 Divs with less than half this number!'[102]

---

99   Wilson diary, 30 January 1918, (original emphasis); TNA CAB 28/3, War Cabinet, IC (Allied Conferences), Vol. III, IC 40 (SWC), '*Procès-Verbal* of the Second Meeting of the Third Session of Supreme War Council,' 30 January 1918.

100 Woodward, *Lloyd George*, p. 257.

101 Wilson diary, 28 January 1918.

102 Ibid., 30 January 1918.

Lloyd George watered down Wilson's suggestion. For future meetings, the permanent attendees would be the three prime ministers, three war ministers, four PMRs, Haig and Pétain and Robertson and Foch, as C-in-Cs and CoSs respectively. Clemenceau, also stung by the generals' dire warnings, 'begged me to use all my power to get LG to get more men and I told him I was always working in that direction.'[103]

The conference accepted JN10, and Wilson's proposed extension to the mid-point between Barisis and Berry-au-Bac, but not without a strong rearguard action from Haig with, perhaps surprisingly, his Prime Minister in support. Haig had given a clear warning that, if he 'had to extend his front [beyond Barisis] he could not be responsible for the security of his line'. Conscious of the political fall-out at home if he overruled Haig and disaster ensued, Lloyd George argued that the BEF held a line which covered indispensable ports and valuable coal mines, British troops received far less leave than their French comrades and had 'borne the brunt of the fighting during the past year.' While approving JN10's recommendations 'in principle' Haig won the caveat that the timing and other details would be left to the C-in-Cs.[104] Wilson considered this a victory too.[105] In fact, 'not one additional yard of trench beyond Barisis had been taken over' when the German Offensives began on 21 March.[106]

This meeting also created the Strategic Reserve and the EWB to control it, and is discussed later in this volume. The agreement to place a strategic force under the authority of Versailles represented a significant victory for Wilson and was an important building block in the path to Allied Unity of Command. The fact that no Strategic Reserve was in place when the German Spring Offensive began on 21 March reflected the reality of the manpower crisis facing the British and French, and the limits of Wilson's authority.

American Expeditionary Force

One of the main planks of Wilson's strategy document of 20 October 1917 was the need for the Allies to go on the defensive in the west while they waited for the arrival of sufficient American forces to make a difference.[107] Wilson expected a German offensive in the spring, long before the AEF could have a significant impact. As a result, he devoted a lot of time to attempting to persuade the Americans to get their troops into the British line quickly. Wilson, as his diaries reveal, found the task frustrating and, in terms of getting the Americans to do Britain's bidding, ultimately fruitless. His diplomatic skills were tested to their limit, but he was successful in brokering a key agreement between the BEF and AEF.

The United States of America entered the war on 6 April 1917, but it was clear that this knight in shining armour would not be taking the field any time soon. As early as 17 May the General Staff warned the War Cabinet that it was 'clear that we cannot expect a considerable USA Army to be in the field in any theatre of war for a long time to come.' According to Tom

---

103 Wilson diary, 31 January 1918.
104 TNA CAB 28/3: War Cabinet, IC (Allied Conferences), Volume III, IC 43 (SWC), '*Procès-Verbal* of the Fifth Meeting of the Third Session of Supreme War Council,' 2 February 1918.
105 Wilson diary, 2 February 1918
106 Woodward, *Lloyd George*, p. 260 and Sir J.E. Edmonds, *Official History of the War: Military Operations France and Belgium 1918*, Vol. I (London: Macmillan, 1935), pp. 47-8.
107 CAB 27/8: WP 61, p. 10.

Bridges, by this time British liaison officer in Washington, the American military establishment was even more ill-prepared for a modern industrialised war, on an industrial scale, than its British counterpart had been in August 1914. Extensive training was needed before the AEF would be ready.[108] Bridges estimated that by January 1918 the AEF might number no more than 150,000, with only half a million men in theatre by the end of the year.[109] In June, when commenting on the reported unrest in the French Army, Wilson had estimated, correctly, it would take a year to 18 months for the Americans to make a sizeable contribution.[110]

Nonetheless, Allied leaders made US assistance a priority. On 20 November Lloyd George told General Bliss and the American Mission to Britain that the Allies would soon be outnumbered on the Western Front and it was 'a matter of the most urgent and immediate importance that you should send to Europe next year, and as early next year as possible, as many men as you can spare, to enable us to withstand a possible German attack …'[111] Yet the build-up of American forces in France was 'painfully slow'.[112] There were one million men under arms in the US but a shipping shortage meant they had 'no way to get them to Europe, [and] their clothing and training were often woefully inadequate.'[113] This was one reason the navy and shipbuilding was given priority over the army by the British government's Man-Power Committee. The AEF cadres which were arriving comprised infantry and machine-gun units, with the French and British expected to provide the artillery and transport essential for self-contained effective fighting divisions. The best way to make immediate use of those AEF units which were available, it seemed to Wilson, Haig and Robertson, was to 'brigade' US battalions into experienced British divisions. In this way American soldiers would benefit from the BEF's experience and training, producing an effective force quicker than waiting for fully formed and independent AEF divisions, corps and armies to assemble in France. The added benefit, from the British perspective, was that when the German offensive came the Americans could be deployed in the fight. It might also stave off the need to reduce the strength of divisions from 12 battalions to nine.

By early 1918 Wilson was not the only senior Allied officer to be frustrated with what he considered to be the tardy nature of the American response. In the first week of the New Year he emphasised the need to speed up the numbers of AEF troops being trained in British units. A few days later, at one of his regular meetings with Clemenceau, they discussed 'the Americans who are dreadfully slow in tumbling to the situation and the urgent need of <u>pushing</u> things

108 TNA CAB 24/13/46: 'The present situation in regard to Military Assistance by the United States', General Staff to War Cabinet, 17 May 1917.
109 Woodward, *Lloyd George*, p. 171. At the end of January 1918, the AEF had a ration strength of 160,000 men in France, or 4.5 divisions; this had risen to 1,944,000 (42 divisions) by November, TNA CAB 24/70/55, War Cabinet Memorandum, 'Serial No 19, Notes on the American Army', 13 November 1918.
110 TNA CAB 23/16/1, War Cabinet, 8 July 1917.
111 TNA CAB 28/3: War Cabinet, IC (Allied Conferences), Vol. III, IC 33, 'Procès-verbal of a Conference of the British War Cabinet and Heads of Government Departments with certain Members of the Mission from the United States of America,' 20 November 1917.
112 Jeffery, *Wilson*, p. 212.
113 David R. Woodward, *Trial by Friendship: Anglo-American Relations 1917-1918* (Lexington, Kentucky: University of Kentucky Press, 1993), pp. 118-119.

along.'[114] Wilson recognised that the key was shipping. Unfortunately, according to Sir Joseph Maclay, Minister of Shipping, the Allied effort was uncoordinated: 'He [Maclay] discussed matters with Pershing this morning and came to the conclusion that Pershing was a fool.' Wilson thought the AEF's commander was 'a beaten man already' and 'worried and out of his depth'.[115] Robertson also lobbied Pershing to do more. He told Wilson he thought he had persuaded him to attach AEF battalions to the British for training: 'The French want the same thing and Pershing sees Pétain tomorrow before giving Robertson his final answer. Clemenceau told R. (just as he told me) that he did not care who they went to provided they came over as fast as possible.'[116] Robertson's optimism was misplaced. Wilson saw Clemenceau the following day and found him looking tired and depressed. He said the Americans 'were going to come too late, and that he would be dead very soon.'[117]

Bliss, the recently-appointed American PMR, arrived at Versailles with a contingent of 150 AEF officers on the eve of the Third Session of the SWC. Wilson had a positive, collaborative relationship with Bliss; his diary references to the former US Army CoS suggest none of the tensions he had with Pershing. One reason may have been Bliss's support for the principle of 'unified command', of which the SWC was precursor.[118] Fearing an imminent German attack, they discussed the Americans sending 150 battalions to France, in addition to the two divisions per month which had already been agreed.[119] Bliss favoured incorporating the additional battalions into British brigades; but Pershing did not. To support his argument, Bliss wanted convincing of the speed with which these forces needed to arrive. Confident of his powers of persuasion, Wilson told Bliss he was sure he could convince him and arranged for a demonstration of his War Game.[120] Bliss and his colleagues 'were immensely struck by the whole thing and Bliss told me he had never dreamt of such a thing and that it was intensely interesting and that we had made out an outstanding case for America helping us with every single man possible in every possible shape.[121]

Wilson's triumph was short-lived. Pershing, Bliss reported, was opposed to incorporating the extra infantry battalions and wanted troops to come over with all the elements of fully-fledged divisions. Wilson noted Pershing's rationale as being 'that the Boches could not attack with sufficient force to break us. As I said to Bliss: "What on earth does Pershing know about it".' He and Robertson 'agreed we must force Pershing's hand by going straight to [President] Wilson.'[122] French and British leaders believed Pershing was the barrier to getting American troops into the line. Pershing's obduracy, they believed, was in stark contrast to his President's uplifting promises of help and support. In fact, soon after the US entered the war Pershing received clear instructions that his force was to be a 'separate and distinct' component in the war, 'the identity of which must be preserved'. Bliss had warned the President on 25 May 1917 that

---

114 Wilson diary, 1 and 5 January 1918, (original emphasis).
115 Ibid., 9 January 1918.
116 Ibid., 10 January 1918.
117 Ibid., 11 January 1918.
118 Tasker H. Bliss, 'The Evolution of the Unified Command', *Foreign Affairs*, Vol. 1, (2), 1922, pp. 1-31; Cohen, *Supreme Command*, p. 88.
119 TNA WO 158/57: Joint Note 12, '1918 Campaign', 21 January 1918.
120 Wilson diary, 26 January 1918.
121 Ibid., 27 January 1918.
122 Ibid., 28 January 1918.

instead of a large and well trained American army, the Franco-British alliance wanted plenty of small units they could feed into their own lines to help resolve their manpower problems, although his position softened once he arrived in France.[123] Pershing did his best to adhere to his government's policy for the rest of the war. Wilson, with varying degrees of success, worked hard to modify it. Ignorant of Pershing's orders, on the eve of the Third Meeting of the SWC Lloyd George hosted a conference to establish what co-operation Britain could expect. Pershing and Bliss faced not only the British Prime Minister but also Milner, Haig, Robertson and Wilson. As far as Wilson was concerned, the rough way in which the Haig and Robertson alliance handled Pershing was 'a thing to make an angel cry.'[124] During what, even from the formal minutes, appears to have been a strained meeting, the British challenged Pershing about the 150 infantry battalions and when they would arrive. Pershing stalled, citing US domestic sentiment against American soldiers fighting under another flag, the need to maintain military morale and other reasons in favour of building full American divisions, complete with artillery.[125] According to Hankey, Pershing wanted the troops to be attached for training and was willing to allow them to do their share of fighting. Robertson wanted them mainly for fighting though he was willing they should be trained.[126] Afterwards, Wilson spoke to Pershing and was 'convinced that he would agree to our command if only he is properly handled and if the case is properly put to him'.[127] The next day Lloyd George and Pershing agreed a compromise to bring over the equivalent of three full-strength American divisions with the infantry being trained by the British and the artillery by the French.[128] The British case was not helped by Clemenceau who told Pershing and Edward M. House, President Wilson's representative to the SWC, that while it might be necessary to brigade AEF troops with the French Army and the BEF 'he was of the opinion that if the American troops went in, very few of them would ever come out, and that it would be foolish to expect to build up a great American army by that method.'[129] In his diary a frustrated Wilson condemned Clemenceau as a 'narrow pedagogue.'[130]

Lloyd George's struggle with Robertson dominated Wilson's life for the next few weeks but once in the CIGS role he returned to the vexed issue of American commitment. Matters came to head with the German Spring Offensive. Wilson met the US Defence Secretary Newton Baker and the American Ambassador to London Walter H. Page, and 'explained the present dangerous situation & the urgency of immediate dispatch of Batt[alion]s from America. Not complete Divisions as that stupid man Pershing wants.'[131] They were impressed by the seriousness of the situation and Bliss, with the support of Baker and Pershing, signed JN18 which asked

123 Woodward, *Trial by Friendship*, pp. 57-8.
124 Wilson diary, 29 January 1918.
125 TNA CAB 28/3: War Cabinet, IC (Allied Conferences), Volume III, IC 38, 'Notes of a Conference: Co-operation of the American Army', 29 January 1918.
126 CAC, Hankey diary, 29 January 1918.
127 Wilson diary, 29 January 1918.
128 Ibid., 30 January 1918; TNA CAB 28/3, War Cabinet, IC (Allied Conferences), Vol. III, IC 38 (a), Co-operation of the American Army, 30 January 1918.
129 Seymour, *House Papers*, p. 274; 'Colonel' House was President Wilson's 'alter-ego' and trusted emissary to the European allies, Margaret MacMillan, *Peacemakers: Six Months that Changed the World* (London: John Murray, 2002 [2001]), p. 13.
130 Wilson diary, 31 January 1918.
131 Ibid., 24 March 1918, (original emphasis).

the US government to ship only infantry and machine-gun units during the emergency. Baker told his President that the effect was to postpone the creation of an 'independent American army', and was 'conceded only in view of the present critical situation...we must keep in mind the formation of an American army, while at the same time, we must not seem to sacrifice joint efficiency at a critical moment to that object.'[132] There were further frustrations ahead. As the first phase of the German offensive slowed, it became clear that President Wilson and Pershing, despite their words of assurance, did not believe they had made a commitment to parcelling out the newly arriving American units to the Allies.[133] On 31 March, Lloyd George told Wilson that the American President had agreed to send 120,000 infantrymen a month for the next four months. President Wilson had also asked Britain not to introduce conscription into Ireland, an act which would make his task 'very difficult.' Considering Pershing's recent intransigence, Wilson found the offer 'a little fishy!'[134] He was right to be sceptical. At the meeting at Beauvais on 3 April, when Foch's role was extended to the 'strategic' direction of operations, Lloyd George said he understood President Wilson had agreed to send an additional 120,000 troops a month to France. Pershing said he knew nothing of it.[135]

Sackville-West, the new British PMR, complained to Wilson that he had been unable to get any written commitment from Pershing about future AEF contributions. The American was 'playing the old Pétain-Haig stunt [delaying a decision to await developments], he is shoving Bliss on one side. The man's an ass I think, he doesn't mean business. What Bliss calls the ["]God-damned American programme["] is going to b_____ up the whole show.'[136] Wilson thought Pershing a 'd_____ fool'.[137] The Germans launched their second major offensive on 9 April. Operation *Georgette* opened in Flanders and British forces gave up significant ground.[138] The next day Wilson received an 'alarmist' telegram from Maurice (DMO) 'saying [the] position was very serious & could only be saved by all the French & Americans coming to our assistance.' He also had a 'long talk' with Bliss at Versailles. The American was 'entirely on our side, & ag[ains]t Pershing, as regards employment of American Batt[alion]s, so we can count on the old boy & Tit Willow tells me Bliss is eminently sensible & practical.'[139] Two days later, Haig issued his 'Backs to the Wall' order of the day.[140] Wilson met Plumer, the Second Army commander, at his headquarters and was told that 'if the Boches go on attacking heavily, he cannot hold the line of hills [east of the Ypres Salient] much longer.'[141]

---

132 Baker to President Wilson, 28 March 1918, *United States Army in the World War*, Vol. 2, Department of the Army (Historical Division), (Washington DC: Center of Military Research, 1988), (hereafter *USAWW*), pp. 261-2.

133 Woodward, *Trial by Friendship*, pp. 158-159.

134 Wilson diary 31 March 1918.

135 TNA CAB 28/3/IC 55: Procès-verbal of Beauvais Conference, 3 April 1918.

136 Wilson papers, (2/12/B/14) Sackville-West to Wilson, 8 April 1918; 'Tit Willow' succeeded Rawlinson as British PMR on 28 March 1918.

137 Wilson diary, 8 April 1918.

138 Zabecki, *German Offensives*, pp. 186-189.

139 Wilson diary, 10 April 1918.

140 Sir J.E. Edmonds, *Official History of the War: Military Operations France and Belgium, 1918*, Vol. II (London: Macmillan, 1937), p. 512.

141 Wilson diary, 17 April 1918.

Wilson and Milner, who had just been appointed Secretary of State for War, met Pershing on 23 April to establish exactly what American help Britain could expect.[142] Lloyd George had been told by Lord Reading, Britain's ambassador to Washington, that the White House had reconfirmed the contribution of 120,000 men per month for four months.[143] According to Pershing no such agreement had been made and the three agreed diplomatically that there might have been a 'misunderstanding'. Less diplomatically, in his diary Wilson described Pershing as 'a hopelessly stupid pig-headed man.'[144] Milner said all available transport should be used to bring infantry: 'He considered the crucial moment of the war to be here, and that if the Germans reached Calais and the channel ports, the American divisions would be too late.'[145] Wilson and Milner met Pershing again and the British won something of a victory in getting the Americans to make a formal commitment. In the so-called London Agreement, Pershing agreed to allow six divisions, a minimum of 130,000 American infantry and machine-gun troops, to join the British in May. Pershing told his government that in the four months April to the end of July he expected 750,000 AEF troops to be transported to France.[146] It was a hard-won but important victory for Milner, and Wilson, who complained that Pershing was 'so stupid, so narrow, so pig-headed.'[147]

Thereafter American troops arrived in ever-increasing numbers, but it would be some time before they were ready to enter the front line. In mid-May 1918 Lloyd George established the so-called 'X Committee' of himself, Milner and Wilson, with Hankey, or occasionally Amery, as secretary. The triumvirate met at 11am, before the War Cabinet at noon. Amery described it as a 'very interesting and free and easy gathering.'[148] Most of its meetings took place that summer and 'American co-operation' was regularly on the agenda. At the second meeting, Wilson said Haig believed that despite the large numbers of troops being shipped, only three AEF battalions would be in the British line soon, and for instruction only. Lloyd George, suspecting British unwillingness to use the AEF troops, said he 'had found GHQ, rather inclined to belittle the American battalions.' Wilson countered that Foch felt the same: 'He had four United States divisions practically under his orders, but he was only using one in the battle and only one brigade was at present in the line.'[149] The following day Reading reported that 250,000 Americans would arrive in May, including 180,000 infantry/machine-gun troops. Lloyd George told Wilson to ensure they would be used effectively. Milner summed up the challenge when he reported that 20,000 troops had arrived in April: 'Some of this first lot, however, had been pretty rough, and hardly knew how to handle a rifle. This may have partly accounted for Sir Douglas Haig's reluctance to use them without a good deal of further training.'[150] Lloyd George continued to grumble at both X Committee and War Cabinet meetings about American policy.

---

142 Milner succeeded Derby on 20 April; the latter went to Paris as British Ambassador to replace the ailing Lord Bertie.
143 Woodward, *Trial by Friendship*, p. 160.
144 Wilson diary, 23 April 1918.
145 'Memorandum of General Pershing's visit to the British War Office, and interview with General Sir Henry Wilson, and Lord Milner, 22 April 1918', *USAWW* (Vol. 2), pp. 340-341.
146 *USAWW* (Vol. 2), 'London Agreement, Pershing to War Department, 24 April 1918', pp. 342-344.
147 Wilson diary, 24 April 1918.
148 CAC, Amery diary, (AMEL 7/14), 17 May 1918; X Committee minutes are at TNA CAB 23/17.
149 TNA CAB 23/17/2: X Committee minutes, 16 May 1918.
150 TNA CAB 23/17/3: X Committee minutes, 17 May 1918.

Wilson, as his diary and correspondence indicate, was more sanguine. This less critical approach seems to have been due in part to his relief that American forces were at last available in large numbers, even if they were being formed into Pershing's longed for American Army. At the same time Wilson had more pressing concerns, the growing power of his old friend Foch and the challenges of Unity of Command.

With the shortage of manpower besetting the war weary entente in the latter half of 1917, the need for the Allies to co-operate was greater than ever. The French felt the British were not doing enough to prosecute the war to the full and could and should take over more of their trench lines. The British political leadership, for its part, was unwilling to continue to feed the generals' seemingly insatiable demands for men. Wilson's skills as a soldier-diplomat were put to the test when he arrived at Versailles where he worked to successfully defuse French frustrations while protecting British interests. His relationship with Clemenceau was particularly important and they met regularly over the winter of 1917-18. It is significant that despite the almost permanent presence of Lloyd George's War Cabinet colleague Milner at Versailles during this period, it was Wilson whom Clemenceau turned to when he wanted reassurance about British policy. It is equally significant that Wilson invariably managed to assuage the 'Tiger's' temper. The British finally agreed to take over more French line but the commitment, while significant, was not as extreme as it might have been. Wilson had less success when dealing with the Americans, particularly the AEF's C-in-C Pershing. British hopes that large numbers of American troops would pour into the front-line trenches to fight shoulder to shoulder with the BEF were stymied by President Wilson's determination that his forces would fight as a national army. In fairness to Wilson neither he nor his colleagues fully appreciated this and thus condemned Pershing for obstinacy. Wilson displayed obstinacy of his own on the domestic front when in calling for conscription in Ireland he retained an uncharacteristically myopic view of the politics of the land of his birth. The manpower debate remained an issue throughout 1918 and, as is discussed later in this work, was a major factor in defining British foreign policy after the war. When the tide turned on the Western Front Wilson still felt it necessary to warn the C-in-C to use his resources cautiously. At the end of August the CIGS wrote privately to Haig:

> Just a word of caution in regard to incurring heavy losses in attacks on the Hindenburg Line as opposed to losses when driving the enemy back to that line. I do not mean to say that you have incurred such losses, but I know the War Cabinet would become anxious if we received heavy punishment in attacking the Hindenburg Line WITHOUT SUCCESS.

Haig was furious and quite rightly interpreted the warning as a political face-saver designed to avoid criticism if things went wrong while being able to claim the credit in the event of success: 'What a wretched lot! And how well they need to support me!'[151]

151 Haig (transcript) diary, 1 September 1918 cited in Sheffield & Bourne, *Haig Diaries*, pp. 452-3.

8

Unity of Command

It is now time to turn to Wilson's role in the establishment, development and ultimate application of 'unity of command' on the Allied forces on the Western Front in late 1917 and 1918. In this area of policy Wilson has been portrayed as either an opportunist, jumping on the bandwagon of others to serve his own directionless ambition, or as a willing dupe, moulded by astute politicians with clearer motives and vision than he. In fact, Wilson was the principal architect of the structures which led directly to the establishment of unity of command on the Western Front in 1918, and the appointment of his friend Foch as 'General in Chief of the Allied Armies' or 'Generalissimo'. 'Unity of command' was not a novel concept to Allied military and political leaders in late 1917. The notion had been discussed often during the war, with little of substance achieved.[1] The principle appealed, indeed appeared to make sense, and was cited as one reason German strategy had been so effective.[2] In early 1917, Lloyd George put Haig under the orders of the French General Nivelle for his ill-fated April offensive.[3] Subordinating the British Army to the French was a different principle to having a commander who stood above all armies. Since then, thanks to an absence of clear political authority, objections from senior military figures, and a lack of trust between the Allies, matters had returned to 'normal'. Allied leaders and their senior commanders met from time to time, discussed issues of mutual interest, and then returned to normal business with only occasional, limited, tangible agreement on co-operation and co-ordination. What was not in place was a formal structure for policy making, with either advisory or, more significantly executive, powers. Wilson had been a supporter of closer co-operation between the Allies since at least October 1915. At that time, as Britain's Principal Liaison Officer with the French Army, Wilson wrote to Bonar Law condemning the French-led campaign in Salonika as an 'insane project', and the result of a failure of co-ordination between London and Paris:

> I have been warning you for many weeks about the dangers of strained relations with the French (the <u>only</u> way of losing the war) and the necessity of setting up a machinery

1   William Philpott, 'Squaring the Circle: the Higher Co-ordination of the Entente in the winter of 1915-16', *English Historical Review*, Vol. 114 (458) (1999), pp. 875-898.
2   Greenhalgh, *Victory Through Coalition*, p. 3; Hankey, *Supreme Command*, (Vol. II), p. 597.
3   Woodward, *Lloyd George*, pp. 144-156.

for obviating this pressing danger. However this was not approved but it does not alter my opinion by a hair's breadth. I ask you again to set up a small mixed Committee of the [following]:

2 Foreign Affairs
2 War Office Ministers
2 Cs-in-C

to deal with these problems and to obviate useless and mischievous 'mass meetings', visits of high officials bent on saving reputations.[4]

The intervening years reinforced Wilson's views, but for most senior British soldiers in the winter of 1917-18 Robertson's view prevailed: 'In short the general situation is such that our Allies require a strong military lead, and this necessitates that our forces should be provided with the means for giving this lead.' Robertson's model was not a sharing of authority, it was not unity of command; it was, rather, for Britain's military leaders, and her armies, to replace those of the French as the principal players in the Allied balance of power. In 1918 Britain should increasingly take the strategic initiative.[5] Wilson disagreed. He retained the view that the Allies needed to work more closely and in a more structured way if they were to win. It was not until late 1917, when his credibility with leading politicians rose, that he was able to put his ideas into effect.

The other key figures in the equation were Foch, the French CoS, and Milner, Lloyd George's closest ally in the War Cabinet. As already discussed, Wilson's 'superbly argued case' for 'integrated "Superior Direction"' of war policy was the catalyst for the creation of the SWC.[6] Its 'inter-Allied Staff', although overtly advisory in nature, filled the vacuum of strategic creativity British, and to a lesser extent French, politicians believed prevailed amongst the Allied C-in-Cs. Wilson dominated the work of this Staff in its first three months and continued to do so, through the auspices of his loyal successors, for the rest of the war. He played a leading role in the development and concrete expression of the principle of 'unity of command'; an indistinct and elusive concept until then. Many British colleagues saw Wilson as an uncritical Francophile. This is over simplistic. He admired the French Army and enjoyed good relations with some French soldiers and politicians, but he was not their puppet. Once Foch became commander of Allied forces on the Western Front, rather than being the obedient friend, Wilson was a stern critic, regularly warning his political masters of his fears of renewed French strategic domination. Despite this, Wilson's diplomatic skills - with ready and, usually cordial, access to Foch and Clemenceau - made a major contribution to preserving the Alliance at a critical time in Anglo-French relations. Nonetheless, the CIGS was not blind to the failings of his own colleagues, and at one point recommended that Haig be relieved of his command.

Two fundamentally important Joint Notes, produced like those discussed already by Wilson and his team at Versailles, were instrumental in establishing formal Allied unity of command. JN12 ('Campaign 1918'), is considered in the next chapter. Its underlying emphasis on the need for formal co-operation in the Middle East was approved unanimously by the political

4   PA, Bonar Law Papers, Wilson to Bonar Law, (BL 52/1/10), 3 December 1915.
5   TNA CAB 24/28/42, GT 2242, CIGS to War Cabinet, 'Future Military Policy', 9 October 1917, p. 7.
6   Roskill, *Hankey*, p. 444.

leaders on the SWC.[7] The same body also accepted JN14 ('The General Reserve'), and an 'Executive War Board' to oversee it, with Foch as chairman. The historiography acknowledges the relevance of these two Joint Notes in the ongoing dispute between the politicians and the military over strategic control, but their function as catalysts in Wilson's campaign for a more co-ordinated approach to war policy merits further attention. Their genesis in December 1917 and January 1918, the analysis undertaken in their creation and the arguments developed in their promotion convinced Lloyd George and his cabinet allies of Wilson's broad vision. Just as importantly, he convinced the Allied politicians and senior soldiers that closer co-ordination of strategy, something which had not been achieved successfully in the war to this point, was possible. The work of the SWC secretariat has been passed over briefly in the historiography but closer consideration reveals the multiple challenges facing the Allied supreme command at the start of 1918.

Joint Note 14: The General Reserve

This was the most controversial paper of the 14 produced by the PMRs while Wilson led their deliberations. While there was disagreement about action in other theatres, soldiers and statesmen agreed that France and Flanders was the principal front. As discussed in the previous chapter, the problem of manpower and the linked issue of the British taking over more line from the French, also concentrated minds. Wilson believed that a large, mobile, reserve force was essential if the Allies were to overcome the manpower challenge. Wilson's plan was accepted by the SWC on 2 February 1918. The PMRs said the formation of a General Reserve 'for the whole of the Allied forces on the Western front, both in France and Italy, is imperative'. The politicians were asked to act quickly and to get the views of their C-in-Cs and CoSs on the 'number, situation and command' of this reserve.[8] Wilson's secretariat began work on the subject in November, their war games providing justification for a reserve capable of being deployed to any sector. The second meeting of the PMRs on 8 December agreed the issue of reserves was a key element in deciding Allied strategy for 1918.[9] In January Wilson lobbied for the reserve, pressing Clemenceau, Milner and Lloyd George, with support from Foch. Unsurprisingly, the idea did not find favour with Haig, Robertson or Pétain.

The winter of 1917-18 was militarily and politically fraught for the British supreme command. The campaigns of 1917 had been disappointing and costly for the Allies. In Britain, Lloyd George was unhappy with his generals' apparent obsession with offensives on the Western Front but leading a coalition government he was far from confident of his own political security. France had a new Prime Minister who was determined to win the war but who argued that his British allies could and should bear much more of the burden. As a result, opportunities existed for Wilson to influence strategy, but also for him to fail. Although damaged in the eyes of politicians such as Lloyd George and Milner, Haig and Robertson still had considerable support

---

7   TNA WO 158/57: Joint Note No 12 '1918 Campaign', 21 January 1918.
8   TNA CAB 25/120: 'Supreme War Council, Papers and Minutes', (enclosure 64), Minutes of a meeting of Permanent Military Representatives of the Supreme War Council, (hereafter SWC Minutes) 23 January 1918, 'Schedule B': Joint Note 14: The General Reserve; see also Greenhalgh, *Foch*, p. 287.
9   TNA CAB 25/120: (enclosure 17), SWC Minutes, 8 December 1917; Wilson diary, 8 December 1917.

in Parliament and in the Press.[10] Despite Lloyd George's frustration with Robertson, Wilson continued to believe that the CIGS had a role. On 10 January, he talked to Robertson about 'the vital necessity of having a central reserve under Versailles or under him [Robertson] and Foch. He is much taken with this idea, but why the devil didn't he think of it himself.'[11] The following day he saw Clemenceau, who looked 'tired and depressed' and who feared the Americans were going to come too late':

> I told him of my scheme for a central Reserve under Versailles, which he said at once meant 'under Wilson' to which I agreed, and I spoke long & earnestly to him on this question of 3 Boche attacks, the 3rd being only launched when the first two had used up all Haig's & Pétain's Reserves. This would be fatal & my plan of Reserves under Versailles or under Foch & Robertson is the only possible solution.[12]

These contradictory diary entries, a day apart, one suggesting Robertson, with Foch, should take authority over the reserve, the other accepting the responsibility for it himself, has been interpreted as an example of Wilson's artful deceit of a colleague.[13] An alternative interpretation is that when Clemenceau, who liked Wilson, supported the Versailles option he saw an opportunity to settle a problem while advancing himself. It would have been stranger for Wilson to have rejected Clemenceau's confidence than it was that he accepted it.

Lloyd George wanted to regain control of military policy. He played fleetingly with the notion of calling for the return of Joffre as 'Generalissimo' with Wilson as his CoS. The latter told Milner that he 'had always been in favour of one C-in-C in theory and opposed to it in practice'.. The 'real solution to our difficulties', he said 'lies in the further development of the [sic] Versailles, which the PM himself set up'.[14] He also told Milner of 'my proposal for a Central Reserve under Versailles'.[15] At this stage Wilson was gaining in confidence, even those for whom he had little regard paid him complements. On 17 January, Smuts reportedly told Duncannon 'that if I [Wilson] played my cards properly I would soon decide the strategy of the campaign and that if I had been CIGS for the last 2-3 years the war would now have been over'.[16] With Clemenceau's support in mind, Wilson disposed of the notion that Foch and Robertson, as their nations' respective CoSs, should manage the reserve. He and Foch 'discussed my plan for Central Reserve under Versailles with which Foch agrees, & then he thinks we want some executive power & authority. He thinks my proposal will do very well as a commencement.'[17] Encouraged, Wilson took his proposal to the next meeting of the PMRs, but Weygand 'expressed the opinion that no General Reserve was possible without a single Commander-in-Chief for all the armies to deal with it.' Wilson argued that such an arrangement

---

10 For a discussion of the role of the Press in this period see Stephen Badsey, 'The Missing Western Front; Politics, Propaganda and Strategy 1918', in idem, *The British Army in Battle and its Image 1914-18* (London: Continuum, 2009), pp. 185-209.

11 Wilson diary, 10 January 1918.

12 Ibid., 11 January 1918.

13 Woodward, *Lloyd George*, p. 256.

14 PA, Lloyd George Papers, F/38/3/2, Wilson to Milner, 14 January 1918.

15 Wilson diary, 13, 14 January 1918.

16 Ibid., 17 January 1918 (original emphasis).

17 Ibid., 18 January 1918.

was 'impossible' but as a general reserve was 'highly desirable it was equally desirable to find some other arrangement so as to be able to deal with it'.[18] Thanks to Foch, Wilson's plan suffered only the briefest hiatus. On 21 January, he noted: 'Weygand came to tell me he was sorry he had objected to my paper about [the] necessity of having a Central Reserve & he was now prepared to agree. He had evidently seen Foch!'[19]

This was a critical period in Wilson's career. In the days leading up to the third meeting of the SWC he convinced his allies of his strategic vision while disarming his opponents. The conference would be asked to approve 14 Joint Notes, all of them constructed by Wilson and his team and several of them already facing opposition from his colleagues in the British General Staff, and GHQ. If standing on the defensive in the west, while attempting some form of advance in the east, and the creation of a general reserve were not controversial enough, Wilson was also coming around to the notion of a commander for the Allied reserve, or a 'Generalissimo'.[20] On the eve of the conference Wilson met Robertson:

> We then discussed my paper about reserves and I told him that my original idea of having a small pool under Versailles or under Foch and him would not do and that on working out the battle carefully I had come to the conclusion that all the Reserves <u>must</u> be under one authority. I told him that for the first time in the war I was wavering about a C-in-C. But he said 'We can't do that' so I left him to think over it.[21]

The principle of a general reserve was accepted by 'all the soldiers and statesmen' present at the Versailles summit. What was in doubt was the question of how to command it.[22] Wilson was aware of this problem, but knowing he had the support of Foch, Lloyd George and Clemenceau he seems to have been content to allow his adversaries to appear narrow-minded and un-co-operative. The day before the conference he had a meeting with Haig and Robertson:

> To discuss taking over the line and also the question of Reserves. I was horrified at the ignorance and total inability of Haig, Lawrence and Robertson to grasp the elements of either problem. Futile and childish arguments were brought forward and L.G. afterwards told me he had formed the lowest opinion of all three men... then before dinner a long talk with L.G. and Milner about taking over the line, about the Reserve question, about Palestine. Of course L.G. is longing to get rid of Robertson.[23]

---

18   TNA CAB 25/120: (enclosure 56), SWC Minutes, 19 January 1918.
19   Wilson diary, 21 January 1918; Amery diary, 21 January 1918, in Barnes and Nicholson, *Amery Diaries*, p. 201.
20   This was a more limited role than the one Foch ultimately adopted.
21   Wilson diary, 28 January 1918, (original emphasis).
22   Hankey, *Supreme Command* (Vol. II), p. 769.
23   Wilson diary, 29 January 1918; Herbert 'Lorenzo' Lawrence was briefly Haig's Head of Intelligence and replaced Kiggell as CoS in February 1918, Paul Harris, 'Soldier Banker; Lieutenant-General Sir Herbert Lawrence as the BEF's Chief of Staff 1918', *Journal of the Society for Army Historical Research*, Vol. 90 (361), (2012): pp. 44-67.

Much has been written about the third meeting of the SWC (30 January-2 February 1918), with attention being paid to the debates around JN12 and JN14.[24] For the most part it has been characterised as Lloyd George's successful attempt to wrest control of war policy from the senior commanders, specifically Haig and Robertson, with the latter losing his job in the process. The summation, while accurate, is incomplete. This '"personalisation" of the debate, which coloured (and colours) attitudes and responses to it' has led to a superficial representation of Wilson's role.[25] His diplomatic and persuasive skills, backed up by his well-argued reports, have been overlooked in favour of a simplistic picture of a man with a silver-tongue in the right place at the right time. This is to misrepresent his pro-active, influential contribution. Wilson had an ability to see issues from a different angle, challenge established views and explain them clearly to politicians tired of what they perceived as dogmatic and inarticulate generals.[26] For the first time in the war he had an audience of the highest authority, the British and French Prime Ministers, the French CoS, and the soon-to-be British Secretary of State for War. These men had corresponding views and were willing to listen to his ideas. Wilson's ability to persuade is evidenced by his diary entry for the first day of the SWC meeting. Lloyd George, Milner, Clemenceau, the new Italian Prime Minister Vittorio Emanuele Orlando and his Foreign Minister Baron Giorgio Sonnino met at Wilson's villa.[27] They talked for two and a half hours and agreed on the necessity of a central reserve. Clemenceau, seemingly without concerning himself with where the troops would come, from 'insisted that it must be a big one of – he said – 40 Divisions. He would not hear of my original proposal of 10 or 12 Divisions.' Lloyd George continued to complain about Robertson's attitude: 'L.G. discussing the matter with me later said he found it very difficult to know what to do about Robertson and me, though he said he knew what he wanted.'[28] In February the Prime Minister would finally achieve his ambition, the forced resignation of Robertson and his replacement by Wilson.

After agreeing JN12 on the 1918 Campaign, and 11 of the 12 other Joint Notes, the next day and a half were devoted to the creation of the general reserve and its command.[29] For Foch, 'the necessity of having a Reserve was absolutely indisputable'. It had to be relevant to the whole of the Western Front, from Nieuport to the Adriatic. Command should lie with the Italian, British and French C-in-Cs working together.[30] Robertson agreed in principle with the creation of a reserve but doubted the need for one at present because, he correctly argued, 'most of the Allied troops were needed where they were'. Command of reserves was 'fundamental', and if one had to be created then, as Foch had suggested, it should be directed by the COSs. Its job was to perform those duties which could not be undertaken by one C-in-C acting alone on their

24   Greenhalgh, *Foch*, pp. 286-287; idem., 'Paul Painlevé and Franco-British Relations in 1918', *Contemporary British History*, Vol. 25 (2011), pp. 5-27; Jeffery, *Wilson*, pp. 214-218; Woodward, *Lloyd George*, pp. 253-260; Woodward, *Robertson*, pp. 196-201.
25   Jeffery, *Wilson*, p. 216.
26   Years later, in an otherwise critical profile, Lloyd George praised Wilson's 'lucidity of mind ... It was a delight to hear him unravel and expound a military problem,' Lloyd George, *Memoirs* (Vol. II), p. 1688.
27   Orlando became Italian Prime Minister on 29 October 1917, after the Caporetto disaster. See Cassar, *Forgotten Front*, p. 77.
28   Wilson diary, 30 January 1918.
29   A decision on Joint Note 4 'The Balkan Problem' was adjourned for further consideration.
30   TNA CAB 25/120: 'Supreme War Council, Papers and Minutes', (enclosure 75), 'Procès-verbal of the fourth meeting of the Third Session of the Supreme War Council, 1 February 1918, pp. 2-3.

own fronts. Robertson was as consistent as ever in in his logic. Just as when he had objected to the creation of the SWC and its staff of military advisers, he argued for power and responsibility to lie together:

> Whoever commands the Reserve must be in a position to issue orders immediately the emergency arises. The central controlling body, however, should interfere as little as possible with the Commanders-in-Chief, who were responsible to their respective governments.[31]

The delegates were unable to reach agreement in a debate Wilson described as a 'great fight'. Robertson, he wrote:

> Wanted the command to be given to Foch and himself. I wrote out notes for L.G. showing the duties of the Commanders of this Reserve and how impossible it would be for CIGS to be over here to perform them. L.G. entirely agreed and showed that neither London, Rome or Washington could spare their CIGSs, though Paris of course was different...There remained, therefore, only 2 solutions (as everyone agreed a C-in-C impossible) one was Versailles and the other was some Generals *ad hoc*.[32]

Employing Wilson's notes, Hankey wrote a new proposal to put the reserve under the control of a committee consisting of the British, Italian and United States PMRs with Foch in the Chair.[33] Haig felt the decision 'to some extent' made Foch 'a "Generalissimo"'.[34] The resolution was adopted later that day and thus:

> The long duel between me and Robertson has ended in his complete defeat. The Executive War Board now set up consists of the Mil Reps here, less Weygand but plus Foch. Robertson fought to the last to be on it but was badly beaten. I wonder will he resign? ... Robertson was over-ruled about the 1918 campaign and squarely beaten over the question of Command of the General Reserve. In other words our Cabinet and the Cabinets of all the Allies have backed everything Versailles has advised. This really was a triumph.[35]

Fate of the General Reserve

The controlling body for the Reserve, the EWB, met the next day and twice the following week.[36] Foch, who would have commanded it, and his friend Wilson had good reasons to want it to succeed. The events culminating in the principle of where command of the reserve lay was

31 TNA CAB 25/120: 1 February 1918, p. 3.
32 Wilson diary, 1 February 1918; CAC, HNKY, Hankey diary, 1 February 1918.
33 CAC, HNKY, Hankey diary, 2 February 1918; Wilson diary, 2 February 1918.
34 NLS, Haig (manuscript) diary, 2 February 1918.
35 Wilson diary, 2 February 1918.
36 TNA CAB 25/119: Executive War Board minutes, 3, 5, 6 February 1918.

at the root of Robertson's resignation from the post of CIGS. Wilson took over Robertson's role at the War Office on 18 February 1918. The acceptance of the principle of the reserve and the EWB, with Foch as its chairman, 'constituted a momentous step forward' towards unity of command.[37] It did little, however, to ease Anglo-French tensions over troop numbers and the extent of front line each army held. One of Wilson's greatest attributes was pragmatism, his ability to know when to stand his ground and when to give way. Virtue or vice, this political astuteness deserted him on Ireland, but on other issues it was generally sound. On the matter of the reserve, his own creation, he was prepared to bend with events. Days after becoming CIGS Wilson saw Haig who 'flatly refuses' to hand over any of his divisions to the Reserve and 'says he won't be responsible for his line, and rather than do it he would resign.' Haig was prepared to contribute two divisions from Italy, but as such a move was another point of Allied disagreement there seemed little chance of immediate action. Pétain was 'in much the same mood,' according to Clemenceau, who also favoured using troops from Italy and perhaps expanding the force later: 'I confess I don't agree, and said so bluntly, but I am not in a position to overcome the Tiger, Pétain and Haig.'[38] Haig's argument was that he feared an imminent attack and placing some of his force under another's command would put his defence plans at 'grave risk'.[39] Haig was of course correct; *Operation Michael* was less than a month away.

Apart from pure pragmatism, there are other likely reasons for Wilson's turning away from the reserve. While at Versailles a reserve army under him and Foch gave him power and importance. Now he was at the War Office, he had both without needing to fight another battle with the C-in-C. Haig perceived that 'with his advent to power as CIGS', Wilson's interest in Versailles had weakened.[40] With Robertson vanquished, Wilson made great efforts to work co-operatively with Haig. Finally, as CIGS Wilson had a first-hand view of the pressures on the BEF's manpower. In contrast, Wilson's two closest friends on the Western Front lined up against him. Rawlinson, his successor as British PMR, sided with Foch. He wrote to Wilson four times in a week to press the Versailles case, accusing Haig of a *non possumus* [*Lat.* "we cannot"] attitude' and of negating Versailles' authority by agreeing informally with Pétain that they would each come to the aid of the other if the need arose.[41] This 'mere local adjustment' between commanders was exactly the kind of thing Wilson had warned against when lobbying for a strategic supervisory role for the SWC.[42] Foch, also aware that without a General Reserve to command there was little for the EWB he chaired to do, was 'very bitter' at Haig's refusal to co-operate and wanted the Board's powers enhanced or for it to be wound up.[43] Wilson admitted that Haig appeared to have:

> Gone back to his original position...which, by the way, I think he never left, and refused to ear-mark any divisions for the Special Reserve... it does not seem to me that

37   Callwell, *Wilson* (Vol. II), p. 63.
38   Wilson diary, 25 and 26 February 1918.
39   NLS, Haig (manuscript) diary, 25 February 1918.
40   Ibid.
41   IWM, Wilson papers, Rawlinson to Wilson (2/13A/1) 1 March, (2/13A/3) 3 March, (2/13A/6) 6 March, (2/13A/9) 7 March 1918.
42   TNA CAB 25/120/3: SWC: British Secretariat, Papers and Minutes, 'Matters for Action or Watching by the Minister in Charge', 4 December 1917.
43   IWM, Wilson papers, Rawlinson to Wilson (2/13A/10), 8 March 1918.

it is worth our while bringing the Executive Committee into action for so small a force, unless the French and Italians are prepared to put up substantial forces, which I very much doubt when they see that we produce none.[44]

Accepting the inevitable, Wilson put paid to the body he had fought to establish only weeks before. Although in his diary he continued to argue the rightness of the reserve he recognised that without the co-operation of Haig the cause was lost. Just before the meeting of the Fourth Session of the SWC Wilson had another discussion with the Field Marshal:

> He says he can't and he won't give any divisions to the General Reserve. He explained that he had not enough for [a] GHQ Reserve, and he said that, if I wanted a General Reserve, I must make some more divisions and I must get more man-power … I impressed on him the fact that by refusing to contribute to the General Reserve he was killing that body, and he would have to live on Pétain's charity, and he would find that very cold charity. But I was quite unable to persuade him.[45]

Without the support of the C-in-Cs, the SWC resolved to establish a reserve when feasible. Wilson acknowledged that his was 'a nonsense'.[46] Milner disagreed and warned Lloyd George it 'would look very bad indeed' if the idea were dropped.[47] His protest was academic. Less than a week later, on 21 March, the Germans launched the first phase of the *Kaiserschlacht,* their much-anticipated spring offensive, putting an end to the issue.[48] Failure to reach agreement had convinced Foch that without real executive power, bodies such as the EWB were little more than talking shops. The German attack gave Foch, with essential support from Wilson, his opportunity to gain real authority.

Much attention has been paid in the historiography to Haig's recollection of the events surrounding Foch's appointment as 'Generalissimo'.[49] In the typescript version of his diary for 25 March, Haig stated that he telegraphed for Wilson and Milner to come to France to arrange that 'General Foch or some other determined general, who would fight, should be given supreme control of the operations in France.'[50] This detail is not in the original handwritten (manuscript) version of the diary and Sheffield has noted that no record exists of the telegram. He concluded that: 'The simplest explanation is that a tired and stressed man let off steam in his

44 IWM, Wilson papers, Wilson to Rawlinson (2/13A/4), 4 March 1918.

45 Wilson diary, 13 March 1918; NLS, Haig (manuscript) diary, 13 March 1918.

46 TNA CAB 28/3: War Cabinet, IC (Allied Conferences), Volume III, IC 47 (SWC), '*Procès-verbal* of the First Meeting of the Fourth Session of Supreme War Council,' 14 March 1918; Wilson diary, 14 March 1918.

47 PA, Lloyd George Papers, Milner to Lloyd George, (LG/F/23/3/19), 14 March 1918.

48 The most comprehensive works on the offensive is Zabecki, *German Offensives.* See also, Martin Middlebrook, *The Kaiser's Battle* (London: Penguin, 1978); Sheffield, *Forgotten Victory*; Tim Travers, *How the War Was Won: Command and Technology on the Western Front, 1917-1918* (London: Allen & Unwin, 1992).

49 Elizabeth Greenhalgh, 'Myth and Memory: Sir Douglas Haig and the Imposition of Unified Command in March 1918,' *Journal of Military History*, Vol. 68, (2004), pp. 771-820; Sheffield, *The Chief*, pp. 274-5.

50 Haig diary, 25 March 1918, in Sheffield and Bourne, *Haig: Diaries*, pp. 392-393.

diary, apportioning blame and giving himself the credit he believed he deserved.'[51] Wilson's role in the decision has received less critical attention. His diary adds some credence to part of Haig's version of events, the call to Wilson, albeit with slight differences in timing. Wilson recorded that received a telephone call from Foch at 5.30pm:

> Asking me what I thought of [the] situation, & we are of one mind that someone must catch a hold or we shall be beaten. I said I would come over & see him.
>
> At 7 0'c. meeting at 10 Downing Street … While we were discussing, a telephone from Haig to say 3rd Army was falling back to the Ancre & asking me to go over.[52]

He arrived at Haig's headquarters at 11.50am the next day: 'I told Haig that in my opinion we must get greater unity of action, & I suggested that Foch should co-ordinate the action of both C-in-Cs. In the end Douglas Haig agreed.' Wilson proposed to Foch and Pétain that when the British and French leaders met he would 'suggest that he (Foch) should be commissioned by both Governments to co-ordinate the military action of the two C-in-Cs.'[53] British and French political and military leaders, including Clemenceau, Poincaré, Milner, Foch, Pétain, Haig and Wilson, with General Sir Julian Byng (GOC Third Army), Plumer (Second Army) and General Sir Henry Horne (First Army), convened at Doullens on 26 March.[54] Wilson had a preparatory meeting with Milner and Haig, at which the latter 'agreed to my proposal for Foch to co-ordinate'. Milner and Clemenceau approved this on behalf of their governments. According to Wilson's diary: 'Both Lawrence & Haig are delighted with this new arrangement about Foch. So is Foch & so really is Clemenceau, who patted me on the head & said I was *un bon garçon*.'[55] Clemenceau, like most French actors the Great War drama, had long supported unity of command under a French Generalissimo and knew Wilson, while sceptical, was more open to the idea than Robertson.[56] The difference this time was that Foch would have overarching authority over both the French and British C-in-Cs. Even allowing for a degree of personal aggrandisement, Wilson played a more active role in Foch's appointment than has previously been acknowledged. At Versailles, Wilson used this independence from Haig and Robertson to push his own agenda. Once in the position of CIGS, with Foch as Allied Generalissimo, Wilson's energy and creativity, together with their old friendship, would be put to the test.

Foch as Generalissimo

The new, 'unified', approach to Allied strategy making on the Western Front, combined with a series of major German offensives resulted, inevitably, in strained relations. Haig and Pétain found themselves operating under a new, unfamiliar and evolving system. Neither C-in-C was any longer the final arbiter of how and when to deploy his armies. It is incorrect, however, to

---

51   Sheffield, *The Chief*, p. 275.
52   Wilson diary, 24 March 1918.
53   Ibid., 25 March 1918.
54   TNA CAB 28/3: War Cabinet, IC (Allied Conferences), Volume III, IC 52, 'Memorandum by Lord Milner on his visit to France, including the Doullens Conference, 26 March 1918'.
55   Wilson diary, 26 March 1918.
56   Newhall, *Clemenceau*, p. 392; Woodward, *Lloyd George*, pp. 255-6.

suggest that Foch's authority was 'rarely challenged'.[57] Wilson, whilst defending British interests, injected pragmatism and exploited his rapport with the French leadership. The result was that, unlike in the first 18 months of the war, when Anglo-French relations lurched from one crisis to another, disagreements with the potential to develop into major rifts were defused and smoothed over, albeit not without considerable noise and bluster. Wilson successfully represented Haig's anxieties over Foch's use of his forces, and behind the scenes he became concerned by what he believed were growing signs of attempted French strategic hegemony. He invested energy and personal capital in alerting both Lloyd George and Milner, who became Secretary of State for War in mid-April, to these fears. He also worked successfully to keep Britain's French ally 'on side', particularly in late May and June when the latter's continued commitment to the conflict seemed, at least to the British, problematic. Wilson had his concerns about French conduct, and his relationship with Clemenceau was sometimes fraught, but never reached breaking point. Nonetheless, the Wilson-Foch dynamic, though punctuated by occasional quarrels, remained robust, enabling a greater level of Allied co-operation than had been achieved at any earlier period in the war.

Before the Doullens Agreement was signed, Wilson had already been aware of the less accommodating side of Foch's character. They had clashed at the second meeting of the EWB over the number of divisions each country should allocate to the nascent General Reserve. Wilson noted, with apparent surprise, that Foch had been 'difficult and unreasonable' and had used his casting vote as chairman to overrule the former in favour of his own proposal. Typically, Wilson thought his friend was at fault, and told Foch afterwards 'that we must not make things difficult or the machine would never work.'[58] Over the next year Wilson became familiar with Foch's stubborn self-belief and 'clear-sightedness'[59] Foch, like Wilson, was also a first-rate politician. Henry Wilson's priority after Doullens was to ensure the speedy relocation of French reinforcements to the British front. The BEF was undermanned and facing a major offensive, with more expected. Wilson's abiding fear was that the British and French armies would 'lose contact', the British being forced back on the Channel ports and the French falling back to defend Paris. Such a rift, he believed, could mean the loss of the war. Despite British problems, the CIGS told the War Cabinet meeting of 23 March that while French assistance was 'indispensible' another attack was expected on their front in Champagne and 'we must not make too great a demand upon them until the situation there was clearer.' The Prime Minister, with the benefit of hindsight and conveniently forgetting that he had opposed it at the SWC, countered that if the plan for a General Reserve had been carried out 'it would not have been necessary to have this bargaining process.'[60] The next day Lloyd George complained to Riddell, that 'one of the disasters of the war was the failure to appoint Henry Wilson to high command.'[61] Be that as it may, there was no doubt about the seriousness of the situation. Maintaining a balance between the competing priorities of the two C-in-Cs was one reason Wilson, who took a dim view of Pétain's abilities, favoured Foch as arbiter of strategic goals. When Wilson arrived in France to assess the crisis, Haig warned him that 'unless the "whole French Army"

57   Philpott, 'Foch' in Hughes & Seligmann, *Leadership*, p. 43.
58   Wilson diary, 5 February 1918.
59   Greenhalgh, *Foch*, pp. 517-8.
60   TNA CAB 23/5/63: War Cabinet, 23 March 1918.
61   Riddell, *War Diary*, diary 24 March 1918, p. 320.

came up we were beaten & it would be better to make peace on any terms we could.'[62] Pétain, with Foch's encouragement, ordered 10 French divisions to aid the British, but the question of the size, location and timing of French support dominated Wilson's work for the next month.[63]

The confusion with which the BEF in France reacted to Operation Michael was echoed in London. Wilson briefed Lloyd George, the King and then the War Cabinet, reassuring them that, despite serous setbacks, 'the chances were in our favour now.'[64] Anxious to verify Wilson and Milner's assessments, Lloyd George sent Churchill to France to see Foch and provide 'any form of assistance'.[65] This outraged both Wilson and Milner who both saw it as interference in their areas of responsibility. Wilson caught Churchill aboard his train at Charing Cross: 'He was being sent to Foch by LG! I told him I could not agree & I must have this changed & he must go to Clemenceau not to any soldier.' The Prime Minister told Wilson, perhaps to mollify him, that he wanted Churchill to see Clemenceau because the British Ambassador Lord Bertie was 'no use!' Wilson speculated that Churchill would 'advise L.G. to send Derby to Paris & put him (Winston) into the WO!'[66] Lloyd George subsequently instructed Churchill to 'stick to Paris and not go directing strategy at GHQ'. Regardless, Churchill visited GHQ, and was given a personal tour of the forward areas by Clemenceau. His reports to the British Prime Minister so upset Milner that he called on Wilson at his home:

> At this morning's Cabinet L.G. read out portions of 2 wires rec[eive]d from Winston… Milner referred to this and said he was going to tell L.G. that either he (M.) must have L.G.'s full confidence or he would have to leave the Govt. I agreed with Milner. This sending Winston over – first, with the idea of going to Foch which I killed, & then to Clemenceau is a direct snub to Milner who, after all, represented the Govt at Doullens & has, all along, been the Cabinet member at Versailles.[67]

Churchill had been urging a major French counter-offensive and reported that he was happy with their preparations.[68] Wilson was as jealous as Milner of Churchill's access and anxious to get him back to London: 'He is doing mischief in France.'[69] The next day the Prime Minister, at Churchill's request and following 'a serious misunderstanding' between Foch, Haig and Rawlinson over troop deployment, crossed to France with Wilson in tow.[70] Churchill told them 'Clemenceau wanted Foch's position strengthened. I agreed but not up to C-in-C especially as the Tiger wished this principally to allow Foch to coerce Pétain & not Haig who was working smoothly.'[71] The War Cabinet had already discussed extending Foch's powers to give him the right to issue 'directions or orders, instead of being limited to co-ordination.' Lloyd George had

62   Wilson diary, 25 March 1918.
63   Zabecki, *German Offensives*, p. 152; see Edmonds, *Military Operations France and Belgium, 1918* (Vol. I), p. 549.
64   Wilson diary, 27 March 1918; TNA CAB 23/5/66: War Cabinet, 27 March 1918.
65   Martin Gilbert, *Winston S. Churchill: 1917-22* (Vol. IV) (London: Heinemann, 1975), p. 84.
66   Wilson diary, 28 March 1918 (original emphasis).
67   Ibid., 30 March 1918; BLO, Milner diary, 29 and 30 March 1918.
68   Hankey diary 29 March 1918, Hankey, *Supreme Command*, (Vol. II), p. 789.
69   Wilson diary, 2 April 1918.
70   Gilbert, *Churchill: 1917-22*, p. 102; TNA CAB 23/6/2: War Cabinet, 2 April 1918.
71   Wilson diary, 3 April 1918.

been in favour, but stopped short of making Foch C-in-C. Wilson suggested that Foch probably did not need any additional powers and that it would be 'inadvisable' to change something that seemed to be working well.[72] Woodward has argued that Wilson's motivation in seeking to restrict Foch's powers was 'self advancement' and a desire to ensure his friend did not become too powerful.[73] An alternative interpretation is that Wilson was still coming to terms with the impact of the position of Generalissimo on Allied strategy. Despite his confidence in Foch, he had an abiding fear of French domination of this strategy, one which grew as Wilson's relationship with Clemenceau came under pressure. When Lloyd George and Clemenceau met at Beauvais at the beginning of April, Wilson opposed changing Foch's remit because, he said, he wanted to avoid any opportunity for Haig and Pétain to wilfully 'misunderstand' the Generalissimo's role. He argued, unsuccessfully, that the Doullens remit was stronger than the new proposal 'but the Tiger & LG were in favour of the change...Lloyd George said [the] British public wanted Foch to have real power; did Doullens give this power?'[74] Wilson then drafted the agreement, including the right of either C-in-C to appeal to his government if he believed Foch's orders endangered his army.[75] Haig, who was 'in full agreement' with the proposal, Wilson and Lloyd George all stressed the urgent need for a French offensive.[76] Foch agreed. If Wilson felt he had been defeated in his scheme of 'self advancement', at Foch's expense, it was not reflected in his usually frank diary, the entry for this date concluding: 'On the whole a satisfactory day.' [77] Clemenceau suggested subsequently that Foch should also be made C-in-C of the Italian theatre:

> I am entirely opposed & said so strongly that the Cabinet agreed & wired saying that they did not agree. Foch is 67; he is not popular with the Italians; he has not got a Staff yet; he has not yet by <u>any means</u> got our front in hand, & in consequence I think he would be entirely overloaded.[78]

The War Cabinet's diplomatic response was that they thought it 'inadvisable' to burden Foch with additional responsibilities and that the subject should be discussed at the next meeting of the SWC.[79]

Despite his agreement at Beauvais, Foch failed to honour his promise of a French counter-offensive, nor would he agree to Haig's plea for the French to relieve some of the British line, ideally north of the Somme, or in French Flanders, where another German attack was expected.[80] In a tacit acknowledgement of how the balance of power had shifted, Haig asked Wilson to intervene on the BEF's behalf and the War Cabinet gave the latter 'full powers to

72   TNA CAB 23/6/2: War Cabinet, 2 April 1918.
73   Woodward, *Lloyd George*, p. 289.
74   Wilson diary, 3 April 1918.
75   Hankey, *Supreme Command* (Vol. II), pp. 791-2; the full text of the Beauvais Agreement appears as an appendix to TNA CAB 23/6/4: War Cabinet, 4 April 1918.
76   NLS, Haig (manuscript) diary, 3 April 1918.
77   Wilson diary, 3 April 1918; TNA CAB 28/3, War Cabinet, IC (Allied Conferences), Volume III, IC 55 (a), '*Procès-verbal* of a Conference at Beauvais, 3 April 1918'.
78   Wilson diary, 5 April 1918.
79   TNA CAB 23/6/11: War Cabinet minutes, 5 April 1918.
80   Harris, *Haig*, pp. 466-7.

do what I thought best.'[81] The next day, 9 April, Haig and his CoS Herbert Lawrence told the CIGS they now favoured French support in Flanders. Wilson disagreed and wanted the French to relieve the British right in the Somme sector, but Haig said he was 'afraid of French troops taking over our line in front of Amiens as he says they are fighting badly & would lose Amiens.' Haig had concluded that 'the French have neither enough troops nor stomach for a big attack ...such as Foch was contemplating last Wed[nesday]'. While this discussion was taking place, news began to arrive of the start of the second major German offensive *Operation Georgette*, on a 25 mile front from Ypres south, in exactly the location the British had expected.[82] Wilson then spent two fruitless hours with Foch. The Generalissimo 'simply would not hear' of moving troops to Flanders, nor to supporting the defence of Amiens. All Wilson got was a commitment to put French reserves astride the Somme for deployment further north if required. His mission having failed, all he could do was urge Haig, who was worried that the movement of French forces would hinder his own, to register a note of protest.[83] The British C-in-C castigated Foch and complained that Wilson 'did not help us at all in our negotiations...His sympathies almost seem to be with the French.'[84] Wilson could only urge Haig to make a formal note of his disagreement.[85] It was a reminder to Wilson that his old friendship with Foch had its limitations. Another important outcome of these discussions was that Wilson persuaded Foch to accept Lieutenant-General Sir John Du Cane as principal liaison officer between Haig and Foch.[86] A recent Haig biographer noted that it was unclear whose idea this was, but according to Wilson's diary he suggested it to Haig who did 'not in the least understand the situation yet', on 6 April.[87] Foch originally refused to accept so senior a British officer on his staff, but after Wilson's cajoling finally agreed. A former liaison officer himself, Wilson knew the importance of having a senior figure in such a role, at such a time. At first Du Cane found it difficult to settle in to Foch's HQ, but over time developed a good working relationship with both the Generalissimo and his CoS Weygand.[88]

Foch told Wilson that he wanted a title, the latter first favouring 'Chief of Staff of the Allied Forces.' Wilson consulted Clemenceau, who suggested 'C-in-C of Allied Forces but I pointed out that Foch did not command in Italy nor in any theatre except France so I proposed C-in-C of Allied Forces in France & he agreed.' Lloyd George and Milner also gave their consent.[89] The resilience of the Foch-Wilson relationship is evidenced in latter's congratulatory message: 'A thousand congratulations on your new title, it sounds almost as grand as Monsieur Foch.'[90] Wilson spent April shuttling between London and the front; on each of his four visits he saw

81 Wilson diary, 8 April 1918.
82 Wilson diary and Haig (manuscript) diary, 9 April 1918; Zabecki, *German Offensives*, pp. 186-7.
83 Wilson diary, 9 April 1918.
84 NLS, Haig (manuscript) diary, 9 April 1918.
85 Wilson diary, 9 April 1918.
86 Wilson diary, 9 April and Haig (manuscript diary), 9 April 1918.
87 Harris, *Haig*, p. 470; Wilson diary, 6 April 1918.
88 Elizabeth Greenhalgh (ed.), Lieutenant General Sir John Du Cane, KCB, *With Marshal Foch: A British General at Allied Supreme Headquarters April-November 1918* (Solihull: Helion & Company, 2108), p. xiv, and *passim*.
89 Ibid., 9 and 10 April 1918.
90 Wilson correspondence, (HHW 2/24A/14) Wilson to Foch, 12 April 1918.

Haig and Foch, and Clemenceau three times.[91] Wilson aimed to cajole the French to do more, while attempting to calm GHQ's irritation with their ally. Wilson's actions demonstrated how misplaced was the label of blind Francophilia that had long been attached to him, most recently by Haig himself, and deserves examination. Wilson was exasperated with Foch's apparent refusal to help the BEF, and a perceived absence of foresight in the Generalissimo's strategic planning. Also, he grew increasingly suspicious of Clemenceau's ambitions for France's strategic position. Wilson began a campaign to convince Lloyd George and Milner of this perceived threat, one which coloured Anglo-French relations both for the remainder of the war, and during the subsequent peace process.

His overarching fear was that the British Army, facing relentless pressure, would 'lose contact' with the French. Once separated, the enemy would be able to defeat each Allied force at will. The CIGS attempted to take a broader strategic view of the campaign than, he believed, Foch or Haig were doing. On 10 April, while the impact of *Georgette* was becoming clear, he convinced Clemenceau that if the BEF had 'seriously to retire' it would be 'death' to lose the Channel ports. Instead, they finally agreed, the French should hold the left (north) bank of the Somme making it impossible for the Germans to break through there. He then agreed with Foch that French reinforcements could move into place behind them. Most importantly for Wilson: 'I told Foch of my conversation with the Tiger…[about] vital necessity of covering the Ports and Foch absolutely agreed, so my mind is quite at ease on this most important of all points.'[92] It would not stand at ease for long. The next day Haig issued his 'Backs to the Wall' order of the day.[93]

Wilson continued to brief the War Cabinet on the 'desperately serious' state of affairs in Flanders.[94] His suspicions of French motives grew and he 'violently' opposed Clemenceau's request for Lloyd George to go to Paris. He believed the Tiger 'wanted to interfere' in military matters. Milner went instead, but summoned Wilson to join him 'as soon as possible as I alone can bridge the gulf.'[95] The 'gulf' was caused by British demands for French support for Plumer's Second Army in Flanders. Haig convinced Wilson that without substantial French reinforcements, Plumer's position was precarious.[96] Haig told Wilson he believed Foch 'was taking only a short view of the situation (which comes so oddly from Haig!)', and more French reinforcements were needed. Milner, Wilson and Haig met Foch and Weygand at Abbeville on 16 April. Foch 'brushed aside' British concerns and criticised their tactics as 'not good'. Wilson pressed Foch to flood the countryside south of Dunkirk to impede any German advance, allowing the BEF to shorten its line, but the meeting ended indecisively. Wilson believed: 'What was certain was that our Army would soon be reduced to impotence if the French did not directly intervene & take some punishment off us.'[97] One officer who was unimpressed by Wilson's performance at this critical time was General Sir Herbert Lawrence, Haig's new CoS. After the Abbeville meeting he wondered whether Lloyd George might announce 'some more

91   Jeffery, *Wilson*, p. 224.
92   Wilson diary, 10 April 1918.
93   11 April 1918. Edmonds, *Military Operations France and Belgium 1918* (Vol. II), p. 512.
94   Ibid., 12 April 1918; TNA CAB 23/6/12: War Cabinet, 12 April 1918.
95   Wilson diary, 13 and 15 April 1918.
96   NLS, Haig (manuscript) diary, 14 April 1918, and Wilson diary, 16 April 1918..
97   Wilson diary, 16 April 1918; Greenhalgh, *Foch*, pp. 315-6.

wonderful prophecies of Henry Wilson's.'[98] The next day Foch said he would 'accept battle' in Flanders rather than fall back. In response Wilson wrote a formal note to 'My old friend… anxious that you should see the picture as I see it.' In a direct criticism of what he perceived as Foch's short-sightedness the CIGS wrote that it was essential 'that we face the facts as they really are and that we look a little more into the future than we have been doing.' The Allies faced two choices, stand and fight, as Foch wanted, or shorten the British line in the north where the countryside was being flooded. As Foch wanted to fight, Wilson urged him to 'bring up sufficient forces to defeat all the enemy's attacks' and to ensure that Haig was in 'no doubt' as to his wishes. What was clear was that Plumer could not hold on much longer without reinforcement.[99] It was as clear a message as possible that responsibility for whatever befell the British lay with Foch. In the event the British line, although pushed back, held.[100]

Wilson continued to call for French help. At an Allied conference in Abbeville he demanded the French take an equal share of the 'punishment'. Since 21 March, 60 British divisions had suffered 300,000 casualties while the 100 French divisions had suffered just 60-70,000. 'I pointed out that if this went on … the British Army would disappear and we should lose the war.' Foch agreed to consider Haig's request for the French to help the Belgians north of Ypres. Wilson was dissatisfied: 'The attitude of Foch & the Tiger was difficult & it is clear to me that we must assert ourselves more.' Lieutenant-Colonel Edward Spiers, who was acting as liaison between Wilson and the French War Ministry, told him of a 'dangerous campaign' in the press to deprecate the British Army at the expense of the French: 'We talked it over & I am sure we must assert ourselves more. I will discuss with Milner. We must take over High Policy everywhere, command of the Mediterranean etc.'[101] He repeated this to Milner.[102] These were Wilson's first direct references in 1918 to his worries about French domination of war policy, and his conviction that his government should resist. There would be many more.

Wilson continued to press for an agreed strategy on whether or not, if pressed, the Allied armies should stick together or lose contact, the British covering the Channel ports, the French covering Paris. Wilson asked the First Sea Lord, Admiral Sir Rosslyn Wemyss, for his opinion of what the loss of Calais and Boulogne would mean for the British war effort. His assessment was, wrote Wilson, 'a stupid paper & impossible to make out clearly what the Admiralty think but it is certainly not stated that the Channel is lost so I presume we could still keep our communication.'[103] Wilson persuaded the Prime Minister and Milner that British policy, if it came to it, should be to abandon the ports because the Admiralty believed the Channel would be safe. He noted: 'These are momentous decisions, & although I trust they may never have to be carried out they certainly ought to be determined.'[104] To Wilson's frustration, Foch and Haig both refused to consider the prospect of a retreat and therefore would not plan for one. Foch continued to favour 'fighting every yard but not taking long views… Haig agrees that in

98   Herbert Lawrence to Lady Lawrence, 17 April 1918, cited in Paul Harris, *General Sir Herbert Lawrence: Haig's Chief of Staff* (Solihull: Helion & Company, 2019), p. 127.
99   Wilson correspondence, (2/24A/15), Wilson to Foch, 17 April 1918.
100   Zabecki, *German Offensives*, pp. 204-5.
101   Wilson diary, 27 April 1918; Spiers changed the spelling of his name to Spears in September 1918, Egremont, *Under Two Flags*, p. 81.
102   Wilson diary, 28 April 1918.
103   Ibid., 18, 20 April 1918.
104   Ibid., 24 April 1918.

the last resort we should fall back to the South & I asked him specifically twice & both times he agreed.' Considering the numerous more immediate issues he had to consider, Haig's diary merely noted that Wilson was 'anxious' to know what Allied policy in the event of a withdrawal ought to be.[105]

The May meeting of the SWC was rancorous. Milner described it as 'a dog fight'.[106] Wilson 'at once' raised the question of the Channel ports and insisted on a definitive answer. Haig and Pétain favoured French and British forces remaining in contact, and the politicians agreed unanimously. Wilson's dogged determination to get the Generalissimo to agree a strategy had finally succeeded. The Allies had an agreed policy if the need arose. The fact that Wilson's fears were never put to the test may explain why the historiography has paid little attention to this aspect of the CIGS's work. It illustrates Wilson's ability think strategically while his colleagues concentrated on more immediate problems. The same meeting made Foch 'co-ordinator' of Allied forces in Italy, 'a d_____ stupid thing to do', according to Wilson.[107]

For Wilson, much of May was dominated by the government's evolving policy on Ireland, his concerns about Haig's suitability to remain in command of the BEF and wrangling with the Americans over the use of their expanding force. As prominent was his campaign of resistance to French policy. He told Milner his fears of 'the French absorbing us, our Army, our Bases, our Mercantile Marine, our Food, Italy, Salonika etc, & I warned him once more of this real danger, which would lose us the war.' He delivered a similar message to Churchill. Sackville-West, the new PMR at Versailles, was: 'just as convinced as I am that the French mean to take us over body & soul...Numberless signs of increasing interference.'[108] The Downing Street X Committee of 16 May was dominated by Wilson's fears about French policy. His specific concern was Foch's 'dispersal' of British troops to threatened parts of the French front. Despite British representations, Foch 'insisted on the brunt of the fighting being taken by British divisions. This did not mean that he was not using French divisions, but he did not put the French divisions in until the British divisions had been practically knocked out.' With Milner's support he insisted that at minimum British divisions should be grouped together and not 'scattered about'. Lloyd George's unhelpful response was that he presumed Foch wanted the British to 'break the brunt of the attack' before using French forces. It was important the French were preserved for fighting in the summer:

> Nothing should be done which would handicap General Foch in this respect. For his part he hoped that the French would take a very big share in the battle, as he did not want the British Army to be so reduced that next year we should find ourselves the third Military Power on the Western Front.[109]

105 Wilson diary, 26 April 1918 and Haig (manuscript) diary, 26 April 1918.
106 CAC, Hankey diary, 2 May 1918.
107 Wilson diary, 2 May 1918; TNA CAB 28/3, War Cabinet, IC (Allied Conferences), Volume III, IC 57-59, 'Procès-verbal of the Fifth Session, Supreme War Council, Abbéville, 1-2 May 1918'.
108 Wilson diary, 9, 10 and 12 May 1918.
109 TNA CAB 23/17/2: X Committee, 16 May 1918.

Lloyd George sent Wilson for discussions with Foch and the Generalissimo was eventually persuaded that any British units moved south would be of corps strength.[110] The IX Corps had already moved to a reputedly 'quiet' sector of the French line on the Chemin des Dames. It was then badly mauled in the Germans' first offensive against the French, *Operation Blücher*, which began on 27 May.[111] Wilson saw the King who 'was much upset & ranted about the "brutes of French" & how the British Army was going to disappear.' Milner was shaken by the French performance and did not think 'the French Nation will stand a disaster. "I wish we had our Army back in England" he kept on saying. But we <u>can't</u> so what is the use of saying it?'[112] Milner and Wilson began to doubt French resolve: 'The French have lost Château-Thierry & Villers Cotterêts. This latter <u>must</u> mean that they are not fighting. If this is so, we are done & LG & Milner at once went on that assumption & talked of ____ nonsense [sic].'[113]

The crisis coincided with a meeting of the SWC on 1 June when Anglo-French relations plumbed new depths of animosity and mutual suspicion. Wilson began the day thus: 'I find it difficult to realise that there is a possibility, perhaps a probability, of the French Army being beaten! What would this mean?'[114] Clemenceau and Foch blamed the British for not providing enough men, while Lloyd George questioned French statistics. Nonetheless, Wilson supported the principle that the BEF should be kept up to establishment. French demands for immediate help, including moving troops from Salonika and Italy, echoed British pleas of a month earlier when they were under attack.[115] The ill-tempered meeting, the record of which Curzon said left a 'rather disagreeable impression', ended with little resolved.[116]

Next, Wilson had to arbitrate a dispute between Haig and Foch. The British C-in-C raised a formal protest, under terms of the Beauvais agreement, after being ordered to move three of his divisions south to the Somme.[117] Haig was furious that his exhausted and diminished forces were being used to support what he believed was a lacklustre French performance:

> Our troops are being used up to the last man in order to give the French courage to fight!...But I knew this in Aug-us]t 1914; the Somme battle confirmed my view that most of the French good name [sic] are the result of newspaper puffs! Then came Nivelle's fiasco in spring of 1917, and for the rest of last year the French 'rested'. And now when the result of the war depends on their 'fighting spirit', many of their Div[ision]s won't face the enemy.[118]

110 Wilson diary, 16, 17 and 20 May 1918; Greenhalgh, *Foch*, pp. 345-6.
111 Sir J.E. Edmonds, *Official History of the War: Military Operations France and Belgium, 1918*, Vol. III (London: Macmillan, 1939), pp. 30-31; Harris, *Douglas Haig*, p. 477; Zabecki, *German Offensives*, pp. 217-8.
112 Wilson diary, 27 and 28 May 1918.
113 Ibid., 31 May 1918.
114 Ibid., 1 June 1918.
115 TNA CAB 28/4: War Cabinet, IC (Allied Conferences), Volume IV, IC 64, 'Procès-verbal of the Sixth Session of the Supreme War Council, held at the Trianon Palace, Versailles, 1 June 1918'.
116 TNA CAB 23/6/48: War Cabinet, 5 June 1918.
117 Woodward, *Lloyd George*, pp. 171-2; Greenhalgh, *Victory*, pp. 219-22, Callwell, *Wilson*, (Vol. II), pp 105-6.
118 NLS, Haig (manuscript) diary, 4 June 1918.

As evidence of the seriousness with which the French military position was viewed, the X Committee met twice on 5 June. Wilson was 'absolutely convinced' moving troops south would seriously weaken the British line in the north where an attack was expected imminently. Foch continued to refuse to shorten the British line, but both Wilson and Haig now thought it essential.[119] The CIGS was angry at the French reaction to the latest German offensive and convinced that 'Foch will lose the war if he goes on like this... It's simply d____ nonsense saying he won't "laché un pied" ["let go of the feet", i.e. would maintain contact between the British and French armies] & then run from Chemin du Dames [sic] to Château-Thierry.'[120] Lloyd George ordered Wilson and Milner to 'insist', with Clemenceau's support if possible, that Foch rethink his plans. They were so concerned that they discussed the rate at which troops 'could be transported from France in the wake of a sudden disaster.'[121] Wilson warned Lloyd George that if Foch did not comply and allow Haig to make his own decisions about defending the Channel ports 'then L.G. would get a letter from me to say the British Army would be lost.' At GHQ, Lawrence told them that Foch 'has no plan & is heading straight for disaster,' while Haig said the French were 'not fighting & therefore in his opinion we would be mad to go South & join them, but in addition he thinks it is already late.'[122] The British met Clemenceau and Foch on 7 June and concluded there had been a 'misunderstanding'.[123] Foch 'stuck out for full powers, as Generalissimo, to order troops of any nationality wherever he thought fit and at short notice.'[124] Clemenceau admonished Foch for moving forces from Haig's sector without informing him: 'I never saw old Foch so non-plussed. He simply had not a word to say. Clemenceau said such a proceeding was impossible & must never happen again,' wrote Wilson.[125] The meeting reiterated that the strategic priority was for French and British forces to remain in contact; Foch would never move forces until German intentions were clear and would give notice of doing so. While the issue was defused and Wilson thought the meeting had 'done a vast deal of good & has been well worth the trouble,' it was almost inevitable the new system of unity of command would throw up such disagreements.[126] As one authority has noted, 'matters would have come to a head sooner or later'.[127] From Haig's perspective it was now clear that 'the "Generalissimo" can do what he thinks right with my troops'; as a result he requested his terms of reference be amended to reflect the change.[128]

119 TNA CAB 23/17/7: X Committee, 5 June 1918.
120 Wilson diary, 5 June 1918.
121 TNA CAB 17/8/5: X Committee, 5 June 1918; the possibility of evacuating the BEF was discussed in the House of Commons on 18 June 1918, *Hansard*, <http://hansard.millbanksystems.com/commons/1918/jun/18/mr-bonar-laws-review-of-war-situation> (accessed 6 September 2016).
122 TNA CAB 23/17/9: X Committee, 6 June 1918; Wilson diary, 6 June 1918.
123 BLO, Milner papers, 670 (343-520) 'Record of a visit to Paris, 6-8 June 1918'.
124 NLS, Haig (manuscript) diary, 7 June 1918.
125 Wilson diary, 7 June 1918.
126 Ibid.
127 Greenhalgh, *Foch*, p. 368.
128 NLS, Haig (manuscript) diary, 7 June 1918.

Wilson Loses Faith in Haig

The German March Offensive inevitably had consequences for Haig and his colleagues. It also had repercussions for Derby, a dedicated supporter of Haig and Robertson, whom the Prime Minister eventually decided to replace with Milner, his strongest Cabinet ally. Several of Haig's biographers have considered the matter from his perspective. For the most part, this has been limited to the Field Marshal's diary entries and correspondence with his wife. The abiding narrative is that Haig offered to step down if he had lost the confidence of the government, that the War Cabinet briefly considered his removal but could find no suitable alternative and shelved the idea. This is a fair but incomplete assessment. Wilson's involvement in these events has received little direct attention. Offering formal advice as CIGS, Wilson originally backed Haig's retention, albeit with misgivings. In his diary and in discussion with confidantes he was far less steadfast in his support. His doubts continued for several weeks after the March crisis to the point at which he concluded that Haig should be relieved.

Since his forced resignation as commander of the BEF in late 1915 Field Marshal Lord French had been an implacable enemy of Haig's.[129] The true extent of the first German attack was still unclear when he went to see Wilson 'mad to get Haig out of C-in-C & said all sorts of things.' Wilson told Milner 'that Johnnie French wanted to remove Haig but that I was opposed to it at present.' Privately, Wilson castigated the 'entirely inadequate measures taken by Haig & Pétain in their mutual plans for assistance.'[130] A few days after Doullens, 'Johnnie French went bald-headed for Derby to get Haig recalled.' Wilson told him he thought 'we ought to wait to see how he worked with Foch.' He told Derby the same and also saw his old friend Lieutenant-General Tom Bridges who claimed the Army would give a 'sigh of relief' if Haig was removed.[131] Wilson's reluctance to remove Haig, bearing in mind his almost obsessional criticisms of the C-in-C in the second half of 1916 reveals an interesting degree of pragmatism.

What was clear to Wilson was that action had to be taken in response to the events of 21 March. In looking to make 'scapegoats of the generals' Lloyd George's gaze settled on General Sir Hubert Gough, commander of Fifth Army.[132] This was perhaps inevitable. Ever since the Curragh affair in 1914 Gough and Wilson had been on bad terms. In March 1917 Gough did his best to scupper Wilson's chances of being appointed chief liaison officer at the new French C-in-C General Robert Nivelle's headquarters. In a letter to Sir Clive Wigram, the King's private secretary, he branded Wilson a thorough intriguer' and a 'danger' to the British Army should he be given any power.[133] Less than two days into *Operation Michael* Wilson telephoned Lawrence, Haig's CoS and asked 'if D.H. is satisfied with Gough and he said "entirely".'[134] Gough's card was marked. On the eve of the Beauvais meeting Milner told Wilson he was 'in favour of removing Gough.' Wilson agreed.[135] The next day the Prime Minister told Haig that

129 Holmes, *Little Field Marshal*, pp. 327-8.
130 Wilson diary, 24 March 1918.
131 Ibid., 29 March 1918.
132 Woodward, *Lloyd George*, p. 292.
133 Gough to Wigram, 3 March 1917, in Jeffery, *Wilson*, pp. 188-9.
134 Wilson diary, 23 March 1918; I am grateful to John Hussey for drawing my attention to this point.
135 Ibid., 2 April 1918.

'Gough must go.'[136] Haig supported his Army commander, refusing to condemn him before hearing Gough's defence. Lloyd George, he wrote in his diary, seemed a distrustful 'cur,' and Gough was clearly being scapegoated.[137] In discussion with Wilson he insisted on 'an order to remove him, which I told him we would send. He wants Cavan in [Gough's] place but I told him he could not have him, he must ask for someone else.'[138] Wilson helped Derby write the order summoning Gough home because his troops had 'lost confidence in him'.[139] In fact, Haig's diary entry says he told Gough it was the Cabinet which had decided his fate.[140]

Regardless of the almost inevitable demise of Gough, Wilson's doubts about the British C-in-C himself were exacerbated by his trip to France. Lloyd George had complained to Wilson that Haig was 'not the least grateful' about the agreement to send 120,000 American troops per month to France and was a 'fool'. The CIGS told Lawrence that Robertson was:

> Principally to blame for this disaster because in 2 years of almost absolute power he had never insisted on treating the whole line as one which was a sure sign of inferior generalship, but that D.H. was also to blame for refusing the subscribe some Divs to the Gen Reserve, & that the politicians were to blame for nor producing more men.

Wilson questioned Haig as to why Gough had not defended the line of the River Somme:

> He said he did not know. He seems to me to have lost grip of the situation. He took the most languid interest in the new American scheme for which I gave L.G. full credit. He can't understand why Foch does not attack ... I said I supposed Foch was delaying because he had not got enough guns up yet. D.H. is a very stupid man.'[141]

It seems an unreasonably harsh verdict, considering the stress Haig and his team was under at this point. At the War Cabinet the next day, Lloyd George attacked Lawrence as a:

> Very ordinary person & quite unfit to be Chief of Staff. Suddenly Smuts chimed in & said Haig has proved his complete unfitness for C-in-C. ... There was no doubt that the feeling of the Cabinet was I think unanimously ag[ains]t Haig & the whole of GHQ. There was no question that all confidence is lost. I said very little.

Despite expressing doubts in his diary, Wilson protested that he had already removed Gough and had called for a report from Haig. He 'deprecated further action without further information.' The CIGS was 'ordered to ponder' and make proposals the next day.[142] Despite the pressure from the politicians, Milner told Wilson twice in 24 hours that he was in favour of Haig's removal,

---

136 Wilson diary, 3 April 1918.
137 NLS, Haig (manuscript) diary, 3 April 1918.
138 Wilson diary, 3 April 1918.
139 Ibid., 4 April 1918.
140 NLS, Haig (manuscript) diary, 5 April 1918.
141 Wilson diary, 3 April 1918.
142 Ibid., 4 April 1918.

he refused to be drawn.[143] Haig, aware that his future lay in the balance, offered to resign if the War Cabinet decided it wanted someone else.[144] Wilson recorded that: 'L.G. asked me if I did not think we ought to take Haig at his word but I said that failing some really outstanding personality[,] & we have none[,] I thought we ought to wait for Haig's report.'[145]

Wilson had his doubts but continued to keep them to himself. After a dispiriting conversation with Foch, who thought 'nothing' of Rawlinson and believed Plumer ought to become C-in-C, Wilson observed:

> There is no doubt in my mind that Haig is tired, that he has no desire, that he is almost a beaten man, that he is always turning to a Peace to get him out of his difficulties – he spoke to me about peace 2 or 3 times again today – and that I really begin to think that he had better be relieved.[146]

This was a critical day for the BEF, the start of *Operation Georgette*, but at a time when several members of Britain's political leadership took a pessimistic view of the war, Wilson was unwilling to accept the same from the C-in-C.[147] A week later, with the Flanders offensive in full swing, Wilson thought Haig was 'very passive, & has <u>not</u> got full grip of the situation nor any life and drive. In many ways there is no doubt he ought to be removed but there is no outstanding man to replace him except Plumer & I doubt that change worth doing.'[148] Wilson thus dismissed both the highly competent Plumer, and, by omission, his old friend Rawlinson. It is unclear what Wilson considered necessary to make a 'better' commander than Haig.

Over the next month, apart from candid conversations with Milner, the politician he trusted most, Wilson kept his own counsel. His diary records that he listened to the views of several soldiers and statesmen, all of whom were critical of Haig, but he declined to make a recommendation on the C-in-C's future. He supported Haig's views on Anglo-French strategy, especially the need to avoid the Allied armies being split apart. By the second week in May, with Foch in the ascendant as Allied Generalissimo, Wilson finally decided to recommend bringing Haig home. The precise reasons for the timing and the rationale of this decision, nearly two months after the start of *Operation Michael*, remain unclear. This was a relatively quiet period; the Lys Offensive against the British was over and the first major German attack on the French on the Aisne still a month away. It is possible that Wilson saw the lull as the first real opportunity to act. Wilson's diary noted on several occasions that in the light of Foch's elevation, Haig's role had diminished and thus, by implication, the latter might be content to accept another role. Arguably Wilson was 'rehearsing' this argument to soften the blow for Haig if he had to be removed. Study of his diary and correspondence leads this author to suggest an alternative reason for Wilson concluding that Haig had to go. By May 1918 Milner and Lloyd George were considering replacing Haig with a 'better' general. Wilson had rejected the notion because, in

---

143 Wilson diary, 4, 5 April 1918.
144 Sheffield, *The Chief*, p. 280.
145 Wilson diary, 8 April 1918.
146 Ibid., 9 April 1918.
147 Millman, *Pessimism*, pp. 241-249.
148 Wilson diary, 16 April 1918.

his view, a more suitable officer could not be found.[149] Conceivably, Wilson proposed removing Haig from command of the British armies on the Western Front to prevent Robertson's effective rehabilitation and appointment to the vacant post of Commander-in-Chief of Home Forces. Professional disagreement between Wilson and Robertson took on a personal dimension in early 1918. In the build-up to Robertson's removal as CIGS, Wilson's diary references became critical and disdainful. Once Wilson was ensconced at Robertson's desk he did nothing to help his predecessor find suitable alternative employment, letting him languish as GOC of Eastern Command, the lowly post to which he had been assigned on his forced resignation.[150] The decision to appoint Lord French, who had been C-in-C Home Forces since his return from France in 1915, as Lord Lieutenant of Ireland, freed up his prestigious, and influential, post at Horse Guards.[151] It is clear from Wilson's diary that he was opposed to Robertson replacing French. A press campaign in April 1918 blamed Lloyd George for sacking Robertson and, by implication, imperilling the war effort on the eve of the German offensives.[152] The calls in Fleet Street for Wully to be reinstated as CIGS were seen by his successor as a criticism of himself.

French, who made no effort to disguise his long-standing enmity towards both Haig and Robertson, realised that if he were to go to Dublin, Robertson might succeed him and 'he hates this'.[153] French suggested bringing Haig home to replace him 'otherwise it will fall to Robertson!' Wilson put the idea to Milner who was 'rather taken' with it but told him it was 'for him & L.G. to decide.' Later the AG, Macready, a Robertson supporter, told Wilson he wanted Wully to replace French. Unsurprisingly, his diary entry ended 'What a day for my birthday.'[154] Wilson, Milner and the Prime Minister then discussed French's successor: 'I, personally, favour bringing Haig home. His position now under Foch is very different, his Divisions are dwindling, & he has lost much of the confidence of the Army.' Unfortunately for Wilson's plans, Milner favoured Robertson.[155] The following day Robertson's 'alter-ego' Major-General Sir Frederick Maurice committed career suicide by accusing Lloyd George of lying about the numbers of British troops available to meet the German onslaught.[156] The 'Maurice Affair' is discussed exhaustively in the historiography and need not be repeated here.[157] Its significance for this study is that Wilson and Milner saw Robertson and his supporters as the instigators of Maurice's action.[158] The last thing Wilson wanted was the former CIGS in control of home defence with all that meant for

149 In January 1918, Hankey and Smuts went to France to assess possible alternatives to Haig but could only suggest II Corps Commander Lieutenant-General Claud Jacob, Sheffield, *The Chief*, p. 280.

150 Woodward, *MCWR*, p. 248.

151 French was appointed on 11 May 1918, Holmes, *Little Field Marshal*, p. 338.

152 Woodward, *Robertson*, pp. 206-210.

153 Wilson diary, 3 May 1918.

154 Ibid., 5 May 1918.

155 Ibid., 6 May 1918.

156 Woodward, *Robertson*, p. 208.

157 Maurice, *The Maurice Case*; also, David R. Woodward, 'Did Lloyd George Starve the British Army of Men Prior to the German Offensive of 21 March 1918?', *The Historical Journal*, Vol. 27 (1), (1984), pp. 241-252.

158 Robertson denied any involvement in the affair, something Milner doubted; BLO, Milner papers, Robertson to Milner, 17 May 1918, c.696/350-1, and Milner to Robertson 18 May 1918, c.696/352; Wilson diary, 14, 18 May 1915.

manpower resources in other theatres, particularly France, and Ireland.[159] Even the King, a loyal supporter of Robertson, tackled Wilson about the government's position:

> He deprecated Maurice's action but was loud in abuse of L.G. & of Curzon, who was here yesterday & said Maurice's letter was part of an intrigue. The King said that L.G. was always trying to get rid of Robertson to which I agreed & said L.G.'s efforts to get rid of R. was only equalled by R.'s efforts to get rid of L.G. I told the King what I thought of the whole thing & made no concealment of my feelings. It gave him something to think about.[160]

Wilson kept up the pressure on Milner and Lloyd George to recall Haig, noting on 14 May that it was the first time in a week that he had not discussed it with them. His case, put first on 11 May and repeated to Milner 48 hours later, was that the army had 'more confidence in Plumer'. Plumer was better at organising support services behind the lines, Haig's position was significantly changed since Foch's appointment, and the C-in-C had 'lost grip'.[161] Wilson suspected that, with the fall-out from the Maurice affair still fresh in their minds, the politicians were reluctant to act against Haig:

> Milner is afraid of removing Haig & does not want to appoint Robertson to Home Command & so is in a dilemma ... I realise fully that to remove Haig, even if he is put in the Horse Guards is a serious matter & I told Milner that he would be faced with hostile criticism especially as regards me for people will say that I first got Robertson out & now Haig.[162]

The Prime Minister favoured getting Robertson out of London by making him C-in-C India, in place of General Sir Charles Monro who would take over command of the Home Forces. By implication Haig would stay in post, but this fell through.[163] Wilson then went to see Haig and 'told him I had suggested to L.G. that he should bring him (D.H.) home to succeed Johnnie because of the altered status of C-in-C here. He did not say anything but said the way I was being criticised was hateful.'[164] At first sight this frankness seems odd in a soldier so often accused of mendacity and double-dealing. In fact, what Wilson had to say came as no surprise to Haig who almost a fortnight earlier had been told by his wife that London gossips were discussing him as successor to French.[165] Haig's recollection of the meeting at GHQ was that Wilson seemed 'anxious to do the right thing', and the Cabinet did not 'desire to replace me in France'.[166] Towards the end of the month Milner made clear he wanted Robertson to succeed French. While Wilson believed 'on the whole' that Haig would have been the better choice, with

---

159 Despite pressing matters on the Western Front, the future for Irish politics appears prominently in Wilson's diary for this period.
160 Wilson diary, 8 May 1918.
161 Ibid., 11, 13 May 1918.
162 Ibid., 13 May 1918.
163 CAC, Hankey diary, 15 May 1918; Wilson diary, 16, 17 May 1918.
164 Ibid., 20 May 1918; NLS, Haig (manuscript) diary, 20 May 1918.
165 Sheffield and Bourne, *Haig: Diary*, Haig to Lady Haig, 11 May 1918, p. 412.
166 Ibid., Haig diary, 20 May 1918, p. 415.

Plumer becoming C-in-C 'I don't feel sufficiently strong & clear to <u>really</u> press it.'[167] Robertson became C-in-C Home Forces two days later.[168] 'I confess I don't like it,' wrote Wilson, 'I have no opinion of Robertson as a soldier.'[169] What is clear is that Wilson took a much more sustained and interventionist role in the debate about Haig's future than the historiography acknowledges. As the year progressed Wilson and Haig appear to have worked together reasonably amicably, with little evidence of earlier animosity. In the summer Haig told Wilson 'he had never had such a free hand, never been so little worried & therefore never been so happy as under me.'[170] Rawlinson later reported that Haig had told him 'how much easier he found it with you [Wilson] as CIGS instead of Wullie [sic].'[171]

Wilson's role in establishing the principle, and mechanism, for unity of command of the Allied forces in France and Flanders, was greater than has previously been acknowledged. His was an influential voice in the decision to appoint Foch Generalissimo, working in close co-operation with both Milner and Haig. Once Foch was in post, Wilson continued to perform his soldier-diplomat role, soothing tensions between Lloyd George and Clemenceau while maintaining an, admittedly, often strained dialogue with Foch. Although Wilson and Foch disagreed often and argued robustly, their friendship, and mutual recognition of the invaluable nature of the Alliance, kept the entente together at its most critical point. During the next few weeks Wilson found himself embroiled in the business of the Imperial War Cabinet (IWC), much of it concerning strategy for 1919 and beyond, one which once again exposed Anglo-French tensions. This is discussed in chapter 9.

---

167 Wilson diary, 28 May 1918.
168 Becke, *Order of Battle of Divisions*, p. 7.
169 Wilson diary, 30 May 1918.
170 Ibid., 21 July 1918.
171 Wilson papers, (2/13A/26), Rawlinson to Wilson, 19 August 1918.

9

Wilson's 1918 Strategy

Wilson's views on grand strategy in late 1917 and 1918 were more significant than generally acknowledged. The military theorist Basil Liddell Hart defined 'grand strategy' thus: 'while the horizon of strategy is bounded by the war, grand strategy looks beyond the war to the subsequent peace. It should not only combine the various instruments, but so regulate their use as to avoid damage to the future state of peace – for its security and prosperity.' The 'various instruments' which had to be considered included a state's economic and manpower resources, the balancing of military and industrial priorities, and diplomacy.[1] More recently, Brock Millman refined the definition to a dynamic 'political-military amalgam which seeks to qualify how war aims will be achieved with the means at hand': in short, practising the art of the possible with the future to the fore.[2] Earning the confidence of Lloyd George, Wilson maintained Britain's primary strategic focus on the Western Front. Other theatres were considered from a long-term imperial perspective. Wilson differed from Haig, whose focus was constrained by the nature of his command, in that he had a strategic vision that went beyond France and Belgium. His predecessor as CIGS, Sir William Robertson, took a broader view than Haig, but the pressures on the BEF on the Western Front meant that other theatres took second place, with little attention paid to long term objectives outside the main theatre. Like both, Wilson never doubted that the primary theatre was the Western Front and that the principal enemy was Germany. Where his thinking diverged was in seeing the war more holistically. For Wilson, action in other theatres was not – as it was for Lloyd George – an end in itself. He never believed that 'knocking away the props' from beneath Germany, by eliminating her allies, would lead to victory. Action away from the Western Front only found real favour with Wilson, especially once he was CIGS, if it was designed to frustrate a clear German threat, or if it was likely to protect or strengthen Britain's post-war imperial hegemony.

Several of the Joint Notes produced by the PMRs during Wilson's time at Versailles concerned future war policy. Joint Note (JN)1 was essentially a rewrite of his paper to the British War Cabinet of 20 October 1917. JN12, of January 1918, echoed the active-defensive tenets of JN1. It differed in favouring a 'decisive' offensive in Palestine, where Allenby had achieved unexpected success, or elsewhere in the Middle East. It advocated harassing the Turks, if possible, in

---

1   B.H. Liddell Hart, *Strategy: The Indirect Approach*, 3rd Ed. (London: Faber & Faber, 1954), p. 336.
2   Millman, 'Counsel of Despair', p. 241.

Armenia, and opportunities to disrupt the Central Powers' activities in the Caucasus and Black Sea region were also favoured. These were ambitious goals, but, JN12 specifically ruled out reinforcing campaigns elsewhere at the expense of France and Flanders. This thesis suggests that in compiling JN12 Wilson, always a 'Westerner' at heart, satisfied both Lloyd George's instinctive desire to see the prospect of action in the Middle East, while insisting any such campaign had to be achieved within current resources. It was a difficult balance to strike, but one typical of Wilson's 'political' character.

While the Allies faced successive German offensives in the west in the spring of 1918, Wilson formulated policy for the following year. He believed the war could be won in 1919, in contrast to some of his colleagues who expected the conflict to drag on into 1920. To Lloyd George's irritation, his proposal was for a crushing offensive in the west. Britain would play a subsidiary role to the French and Americans, preserving British forces to protect and preserve her imperial priorities. The fact that his recommendations were never put to the test may be one reason Wilson's contribution to this strategic policy debate has been somewhat overlooked in the historiography.

Joint Note 12: 1918 Campaign

JN12 was a development of JN1. Entitled '1918 Campaign', it repeated the SWC policy that the Allies stand on the defensive in the west, and proposed a 'decisive' offensive in the Middle East, in Palestine or Mesopotamia.[3] Woodward, although allowing for Wilson's influence in its creation, dismissed it as little more than him 'taking his instructions directly from the prime minister'.[4] In fact, it was Wilson who was the architect of this new direction for Allied strategy; one at odds with the War Office and Haig, with Lloyd George the eager listener. David French acknowledged JN12's importance, but again Wilson's role was characterised as that of messenger rather than initiator.[5] Hughes, while agreeing with Robertson's view that advances in Palestine were 'not a threat' to the Ottoman Empire, and thus unlikely to change the course of the war, overlooked Wilson's insistence on the need for unity of action at the strategic and political levels.[6] Jeffery summarised JN12 and observed that it 'very significantly' argued for the whole of the Allied front in the west to be treated as one strategic field of action, but Wilson's contribution was not examined in detail.[7] This chapter fills this historiographical gap and argues that the co-operative strand in the paper, emphasised in the section on a proposed offensive in the Middle East, was of major importance for the future. JN12 focussed on theatres away from the Western Front, embodying Wilson's political and military, or 'grand strategic', vision. He strove to develop a formalised inter-Allied approach to policy making in the west while articulating a framework for Britain's future strategy in a region crucial to its imperial hegemony.

---

3   TNA WO 158/57: Joint Note 12, 21 January 1918.
4   Woodward, *Lloyd George*, pp. 243-4.
5   French, *Strategy*, pp. 189-191.
6   Hughes, *Allenby*, p. 62.
7   Jeffery, *Wilson*, p. 214.

JN12 examined opportunities for 'a decisive or, at any rate, far-reaching success' in any peripheral theatres.[8] The Second Session of the SWC called on the PMRs to consider the nature of the campaigns to be undertaken in 1918.[9] Clemenceau left Wilson and his colleagues in little doubt of what their conclusions ought to be. By this stage in the war, manpower was key and it was essential to ensure sufficient shipping to enable the build-up of American forces in Europe. Clemenceau told the PMRs to ensure 'that the conservation of man-power shall not be overlooked'. The war had become 'largely one of exhaustion. It may be that victory will be achieved by endurance rather than by military decision.'[10] While the final objective remained 'the overthrow of Prussian militarism' Clemenceau instructed Wilson and his colleagues:

> To weigh carefully whether possibly that object may not be brought nearer final achievement by the overthrow, first of all, of Germany's Allies, and the isolation of Germany; whether, in fact, the final overthrow of Germany may not best be reserved until the forces of the Allies, greatly augmented by a fully matured American army, can be focused and concentrated as a climax to the war on this final objective.[11]

Wilson's paper of 20 October 1917 had ruled out an offensive in Palestine because it was too late in the campaigning season, but Lloyd George remained wedded to the idea of significant action there. Encouraged by Allenby's capture of Jerusalem on 9 December 1917, the War Cabinet had directed the General Staff to consider a project for completing the conquest of the whole of Palestine, or, having achieved that, continuing to Aleppo, (350 miles away in Syria). This would cut rail links between oil-rich Mesopotamia (modern Iraq) and the rest of the Ottoman Empire.[12] Robertson's response was that neither operation could be accomplished quickly, nor without severe damage to Britain's position in the west.[13] Allenby, aware that he could expect only meagre reinforcement, wanted to continue the 'step by step' approach he had maintained since taking command of the Egyptian Expeditionary Force (EEF) in June 1917.[14] He calculated that, if opposed by a force of no more than 60,000, he could conquer the majority of Palestine by mid-1918. Robertson said that the main problem facing the British was lack of reliable communications, especially railways. Casualties would be high and 'it is for serious consideration whether the advantages to be gained…are worth the cost and risk involved'.[15] He said the answer depended on whether the conquest of Palestine would put Turkey out of the war. He was clear that it would not, thanks to German domination of the Ottoman army and war policy. As a result, the GS view was that Britain would 'incur a great risk by increasing our liabilities in secondary theatres' and ought to reduce these commitments to 'a defensive

---

8   TNA WO 158/57: Joint Note 12, 21 January 1918, p. 1.
9   TNA CAB 28/3: IC (Allied Conferences) Series, Volume III, IC-36, Supreme War Council 'Procès-verbal of the Second Session of the Supreme War Council, 1 December 1917, p. 10.
10 Ibid., pp. 10-11.
11 TNA CAB 28/3: IC, 1 December 1917, p. 11.
12 TNA CAB 23/4/71: War Cabinet, 13 December 1917.
13 LHCMA, Robertson papers, 'Future Operations in Palestine, CIGS to War Cabinet, (4/5/10), 26 December 1917'.
14 LHCMA, Robertson papers, Appendices II, 14 December 1917, and IV, (4/5/10), 20 December 1917, Allenby to Robertson.
15 Ibid., 4/5/10, p. 3.

minimum and concentrate all other resources in the West.'[16] Robertson urged the Cabinet to come to a decision, 'at once' in order to plan for the coming year.[17] His report was viewed with scepticism by the Prime Minister. A month earlier the CIGS had produced a report which, although it noted Allenby's significant advances in Palestine, said it was uncertain he would take Jerusalem thanks to strong Turkish opposition. Better, Robertson had said, to economise forces in the east in 1918 and concentrate on European theatres.[18] Weeks later Allenby, with no additional troops, had entered Jerusalem in triumph. Lloyd George showed Robertson's report to Wilson 'which amounts to doing nothing there, which I can't agree to.' Wilson went to see Milner who:

> Agrees with me that we ought to push about like the devil in the Caucasus and if possible push on in Palestine... Also we must try to get command of the Black Sea. We really must change in 1918 our puerile, useless, costly strategy of 1916 and 1917.
>
> This past year has been a terrible disappointment. Russia and Italy failing so disastrously. L.G. has today handed over to Versailles the study of all these questions and also of how we shall stand a year hence, of the Ukraine and Caucasus, of what chance we have of beating the Boches in the field in 1918 or 1919.[19]

The same day the War Cabinet instructed the PMRs to report on the 'military and strategical position in the Turkish theatre and South Russia as a whole'.[20]

Over Christmas the War Cabinet asked Robertson for his views on the latest hint of peace negotiations from the Central Powers.[21] Wully was sceptical and reiterated his belief in concentrating all available resources in the west while standing on the defensive elsewhere.[22] By spring 1918 Germany, while slightly inferior to the Allies in infantry, would be considerably superior in heavy artillery and therefore: 'It is so clearly in the enemy's interest to win a decisive success before America can intervene in force that it is only prudent to assume that he will make the attempt.'[23] With a greater clarity than Wilson and his fellow PMRs about the timing of the German offensive, Robertson predicted that 'having regard to the necessity for sustaining the morale of his people, he will not defer his attack till after February.'[24] Robertson recalled the 'very successful' German attack at Verdun in February 1916 and concluded: 'We must be prepared for a great battle, or rather series of battles, early in the coming year...'[25]

The day before Robertson submitted this assessment, which accurately foresaw the events of March 1918, Milner summoned Wilson. Following unofficial peace feelers from Austria, the

---

16 Robertson papers, Appendices II, 14 December 1917, and IV, (4/5/10), 20 December 1917, Allenby to Robertson, pp. 3-4.
17 Ibid., p. 4.
18 LHCMA, Robertson papers, 'Situation in Turkey,' CIGS to War Cabinet, (4/5/9), 15 November 1917.
19 Wilson diary, 31 December 1917; TNA CAB 23/4/82, War Cabinet 31 December 1917.
20 TNA CAB 23/4/82: War Cabinet 31 December 1917.
21 Woodward, *Lloyd George*, pp. 239-240.
22 LHCMA, Robertson papers, 'The Present Military Situation, with reference to the Proposals by the Central Powers,' Robertson to War Cabinet, (4/6/6), 29 December 1917.
23 Ibid., pp. 5-6.
24 Ibid., p. 7.
25 Ibid., p. 9.

Prime Minister wanted Wilson's opinion of the Allies' chances of improving their position if the war went on. 'This is an amazing wire and looks as though much would depend on my military opinion,' he wrote.[26] He met Milner who:

> Wired for me because he & L.G. having no longer any faith in Robertson or Haig wanted to know my opinion. The question seems to be: 'Shall we be in a better position from the military point of view in 12 months & if not why not discuss Peace Terms now.'
>
>   Milner & L.G. want to know my opinion. In addition, Milner told me LG is <u>so</u> angry with Robertson that he proposes to kick him out & put me in. As I said to Milner again – I am opposed to this, though all in favour of L.G. giving me more power at Versailles & reducing R. from the position of a Master to that of a Servant.[27]

The next day Wilson saw Lloyd George and discussed Robertson's assessment which was:

> Very poor... L.G., Hankey and Phillip [Kerr][28] all agreed it was a miserable paper & of no possible assistance to anyone. We talked for hours. I described my present war game at Versailles & our, rough, results & L.G. very much interested... Very friendly to me & very hostile to Robertson & contemptuous of Haig's brains though agreeing to his being a sterling fighter.

Wilson wrote that he told Kerr that he did not want Lloyd George to remove Robertson and make him CIGS 'much better for him to keep R. and gradually give Versailles more power in the large issues.' Wilson then went to see Carson and 'told him of my war game. He was a little distant but nice. He is angry with L.G. for his constant abuse of Robertson; in which he is quite right. A long day, but I think good work, & I hope I may save Robertson. L.G. said he hoped Kigg[ell] was going to be kicked out as well as Charteris & Maxwell & others.'[29] There is no reason to suppose that this comment, which undermines the impression that Wilson wanted Robertson's job at any cost, was insincere. Wilson would have no expectation of anybody reading his private journal, and at this stage he appears to have favoured the idea that Versailles would be the new centre of Allied policy making. Lloyd George and the War Cabinet found the CIGS's response wanting and put the following questions:

1. Could the General Staff foresee a victorious end to the War? If so, when and under what circumstances?
2. Did the General Staff foresee an improvement in the Allied military situation that would achieve better terms than might now be available, and if so, would it be worth the sacrifice?
3. Could the General Staff suggest how the enemy could be prevented from taking control of the resources of South Russia?

---

26   Wilson diary, 28 December 1917.
27   Ibid., 29 December 1917; BLO, Milner diary, 30 December 1918.
28   Philip Kerr, Lloyd George's Private Secretary, 1916-1921, Roskill, *Hankey*, p. 184.
29   Wilson diary, 30 December 1917.

4. Did General Staff foresee, in 1918 or 1919, the likelihood of inflicting a 'defeat that would not leave the military domination of Prussia successful and intact?'[30]

These questions précis the issues facing the British at the beginning of 1918; if there was a prospect of a negotiated peace, should Britain pursue it if military victory was impossible? While these were legitimate questions, it is hardly surprising that, as in his earlier paper, Robertson's response was an uncharacteristic exercise in bureaucratic fence-sitting. He returned to his concerns about manpower and suggested a review of resources devoted to the Royal Navy and home defence. Unless there were significant improvements in recruitment, Britain's 52 divisions in France and Italy were likely to be down to 40 by the end of the year.[31] Robertson's dilemma was that he was determined that all available resources should be devoted to offensive action on the Western Front, because he expected a major German effort there. He knew the Prime Minister favoured decisive action elsewhere, but the War Cabinet had not settled, clearly and unequivocally, on such a policy. Nor was he convinced of their willingness to support the military by turning the screw on recruitment again. When they made up their minds, he would offer his opinion; until then he would not speculate. Wilson dismissed Robertson's contribution on western policy as disdainfully as Lloyd George had his CIGS's advice on Palestine. It was, he wrote, 'a miserable effort and there is no guidance in the paper at all. I hope I shall do much better than that.'[32] Wilson thought he knew what was better; a defensive in the west and the prospect of an offensive in the east. These were given voice in JN12.

As for discussions to end the war, Germany was not interested in a general peace and its conciliatory words were aimed at the Russians.[33] At the time this was unclear, and Wilson weighed into the debate to oppose any suggestion of a negotiated settlement. In late December Lloyd George had sent Smuts to Switzerland to meet the Austrian envoy, Count Albert von Mensdorff, and assess whether there was any substance to the German overtures. The following diary extracts from a three-day period document Wilson's level of access to senior figures and gives a flavour of the febrile atmosphere at this time. On 3 January Wilson met Bonar Law, by this time Chancellor of the Exchequer, who was 'thinking about Peace & the impossibility of improving our military situation.' Bonar Law thought the Germans might give up her gains in Belgium, France and the Balkans if provided with:

> Pretty free hand on the Russian side. I don't believe a word of this, but as I said to Bonar, if she is feeling like that she must be nearly beat & if she is nearly beat, then let us beat her & have done with it…All this peace talk frightens me … Duncannon saw Esher who thinks I ought to be more in London as Milner, Haig and I are the only men who want to win right out.[34]

The next day he lunched with Leo Maxse, editor of the right-wing *National Review*:

30 LHCMA, Robertson papers, (4/6/8), 'War Cabinet to CIGS' and 'CIGS to War Cabinet', both dated 3 January 1918.
31 LHCMA, Robertson papers, (4/6/8), 'CIGS to War Cabinet', 3 January 1918, pp. 5-6.
32 Wilson diary, 6 January 1918.
33 French, *Strategy*, pp. 193-212; Woodward, *Lloyd George*, p. 240.
34 Wilson diary, 3 January 1918.

He was full of L.G.'s treachery in now trying to make peace... it makes me uneasy especially in view of L.G.'s questions as to what we soldiers can do to better the situation in 1918 & if we can't better it [,] would it be better to see what terms we can make now! All this makes me uneasy & suspicious.

One of Wilson's most important relationships in this period was with Clemenceau whose elevation to the French premiership in mid-November provided Wilson with another ally, albeit one initially sceptical of the Versailles body.[35] Wilson called on Clemenceau regularly in November and December and they met privately seven times in January 1918, when Wilson and his fellow PMRs were working on their Joint Notes. While Wilson wrote admiringly of Clemenceau in his diary, it is clear the relationship was mutually beneficial. 'The Tiger' used Wilson to influence the British government. Wilson cultivated Clemenceau as a supporting voice when presenting his ideas to his political masters. Once again it is not surprising that Wilson's British colleagues considered him far too sympathetic towards the French position. The day after talking with Maxse, Wilson was summoned to see Clemenceau who was 'charming as usual'. As for the peace discussions: 'It seems to me to be a stupid thing, & we English who have suffered the least of all in the war should be the last of all the Allies to talk of Peace.' That evening Wilson saw Esher who condemned Lloyd George as 'a fool' over the Smuts mission and doubted the Prime Minister 'lasting much longer'.[36] Macready, acknowledging Wilson's value as a mediator, noted that Lloyd George was 'quarrelling hard with Clemenceau, who was the first Frenchman he couldn't 'twist around his finger.'[37]

JN12: Campaign in the West

The first section of JN12 concerned the Western Front, Italy and the security of Britain. Like Wilson's initial strategy paper, it assumed that Britain was defended against 'all serious invasion' without interfering with forces overseas.[38] In other words, Wilson and his colleagues saw no need to use scarce manpower and other resources to augment home defence. In late 1917, the Home Defence Force stood at just under 401,000, including 190,000 'mobile troops' ready for overseas deployment. This was 69,000 fewer than at the start of the year, but a significant figure and one which continued to be contentious in 1918.[39] Secondly, it had been agreed, after 'the most careful and exhaustive examination, that the safety of France could also be assured'. There was an important caveat:

In view of the weight of attack which the enemy can bring to bear upon this front, an attack which may possibly, in the opinion of the Military Representatives attain a

---

35   They met first in December 1915. Wilson liked 'the Tiger', describing him as a 'real character and personality – one of the few I have ever met,' Wilson diary, 5 December 1915.
36   Ibid., 5 January 1918.
37   CAC, Amery diary, (AMEL 7/14), 6 January 1918.
38   TNA WO 158/57: Joint Note 12, 21 January 1918, p. 1.
39   Woodward, *Robertson*, p. 180.

strength of 96 Divisions, exclusive of "roulement" [rotation], they feel obliged to add that France will be safe during 1918 <u>only</u> under certain conditions.[40]

Allied forces should be 'continuously maintained at their present total aggregate strength and receive the expected reinforcements of not less than two American Divisions a month.' Maintaining numbers in the west was challenge enough; hardly surprising then that there would be no diversion of resources eastwards. That said, the assessment would have been music to the Prime Minister's ears, reinforcing Haig's own confident predictions of 7 January.[41] Robertson was suspicious of Wilson's motives. The day before the SWC met to discuss JN12, he sent his ADC, Lucas, to see Wilson:

> He says Robertson is very much upset at our Resolution 12 'The 1918 Campaign'. R.[obertson] seems to think that I have drafted that paper on purpose to get him kicked out & that by underlining the conditions on which alone we are safe on this front I have thrown the whole onus on him for destroying the paper. The Monument went so far as to say 'of course if you want to get rid of the CIGS...' I told him bluntly that if it wasn't for me he would have been got rid of some time ago & that I could have him removed any day I pleased.[42]

While there was a good measure of bravado in this threat, Wilson clearly felt more confident of his position vis-à-vis the CIGS. Nonetheless, he went to see Robertson:

> He asked why when I <u>knew</u> that our effectives could not be kept up I put in as a condition that the total aggregate of troops now in France must be maintained? I replied that ... I had come to the conclusion that <u>if</u> our effectives were kept up we were safe & if not then we were not safe & that I wanted to fix the responsibility on the Prime Ministers which is where it <u>must</u> rest.
> This seemed to soothe him.[43]

This is a crucial point. Wilson was acutely aware of Britain's manpower crisis. He knew Lloyd George wanted to prevent another costly offensive in the west, but believed opportunities existed in the Middle East. With typical Wilsonian subtlety, JN12 said the Western Front was safe, but only if troop numbers were maintained, with none to spare for other theatres. Robertson was far from 'soothed'. He had already taken exception to Wilson's proposal for a central reserve and an executive body to control it. On 19 December Robertson had warned the War Cabinet that its troops would soon face 'a very formidable attack'.[44] JN12 was a prime example of the government receiving contradictory advice from Wilson, something the CIGS had consistently warned of.

---

40   TNA WO 158/57: p. 1, (original emphasis).
41   TNA CAB 23/5/8: War Cabinet, 7 January 1918.
42   Major C.C. Lucas, nicknamed 'the Monument' for his steadfast support of his chief, Woodward, *MCWR*, p. 339.
43   Wilson diary, 28 January 1918 (original emphasis).
44   TNA CAB 23/4/76: War Cabinet, 19 December 1917.

Less controversially, JN12 called for a 'substantial progressive increase' in artillery, machine guns, tanks and aircraft, and trained personnel. Significantly, these should be effectively co-ordinated between the Allied armies. Co-ordination was also essential to strengthen the defence 'particularly in the sectors most liable to a heavy attack'. Repeating the call for inter-allied co-operation in Joint Note 8 (Transportation)[45] the politicians were urged to improve and co-ordinate rail transportation across the Allied front. In line with Wilson's familiar refrain, the whole Allied front should be 'treated as a single strategic field of action, and the disposition of the reserves, the periodic re-arrangement of the point of junction between the various Allied forces on the actual front, and all other arrangements should be dominated by this consideration'.[46] In one sentence the PMRs highlighted the manpower-related problems which had dogged the Allies for months, the length of the British line and the contentious issue of an inter-Allied reserve. It was also agreed that if the Italian Army could be reformed, retrained and re-equipped with artillery before 1 May 1918, that front was safe also. Again, co-operation was the watchword, with the PMRs recommending improved rail transportation between Italy and France 'to secure strategic unity of action over the two theatres'.[47] If these criteria were met, the enemy could not, in 1918, 'gain a definite military decision in the main theatres which would enable him to break finally the resistance of any of the Allied Powers'.[48]

If Germany could not win in the west in 1918, what of the Allies? JN12 concluded that unless something 'improbable and unforeseeable' happened, such as the internal collapse of Germany or Austria-Hungary, or if Russia revived as a serious military contender, there was no possibility of the Allies achieving a 'final, or even a far-reaching decision' in 1918. Wilson scotched Haig's optimistic hopes for major success with another large-scale offensive around Ypres in the late spring or early summer. Although American forces were increasing, they would not make a fundamental difference in the coming year. Likewise, skinning the British armies in the 'secondary theatres' of all men apart from those needed for local defence would not make 'a sufficient difference in the relative position of the opposing forces to justify the hope of attaining such a decision'.[49] The paper then took on a more positive tone and urged the Allied General Staffs to plan in case 'an unexpected favourable development should furnish an opportunity for vigorous offensive actions'. The defensive posture in the west should not be 'merely passive in character, but be worked out definitely and scientifically, with the intention of gaining the maximum from any opportunities offered'. A supporting paper said the likely increases in forces available to the Central Powers imposed 'an expectant attitude' on the Allies until the AEF 'can really come into line'. It repeated that this approach was 'far from being passive' and involved taking every opportunity to take the fight to the enemy while planning for a future offensive. Some basic principles would apply. No territory would be abandoned; any enemy attack would be halted and counter-attacks undertaken. Commanders were also urged to plan diversionary counter-attacks.[50] The Allied C-in-Cs were advised to 'prepare plans of joint operations' to meet any concerted enemy offensive. Testing the extent of their new-found authority, the PMRs

45   TNA WO 158/57: 'Supreme War Council: Joint Notes', Joint Note 8, 8 January 1918.
46   TNA WO 158/57: Joint Note 12, 21 January 1918, p. 1.
47   Ibid., pp. 1-2.
48   Ibid., p. 2.
49   Ibid.
50   TNA WO 158/57: 'Annexure to Joint Note 12,' 21 January 1918, pp. 1-2.

felt it was 'highly desirable' that any schemes should be sent to the SWC 'which would assure the co-ordination of this combined action'.[51] Notwithstanding the opportunities presented by enemy action, rather than an overt Allied offensive strategy, the PMRs concluded that with the Russian collapse the Allies faced 'a fundamental, though not permanent, change in the conditions upon which their strategy has to be based'. A change in the 'balance of forces' would not be achieved until 1919, with the addition of the Americans and the 'progressive exhaustion of the enemy's staying power'.[52] Wilson succeeded in getting his colleagues to support his proposals: 'A great success this morning. We had a meeting of Mil Reps ... on my 1918 note. It was passed with quite insignificant alterations in 3 places. A real victory.'[53]

JN12, as might be expected of a policy document to be considered by Allied statesmen in plenary session at an international conference, was short on detail but a file of analytical reports backed it up. These are of relevance for this study because Wilson's staff produced them all. As a body, they are integral to understanding Wilson's contribution to British strategic thinking in the final months of the war. Despite this, apart from a brief résumé of one of the papers in the relevant volume of the *Official History*, they have received little attention in the historiography.[54] At the turn of 1917-18 Wilson's team played several 'war games' and examined strategic and operational questions from the Allied and enemy perspectives. A third group considered manpower, communications and logistics issues.[55] Wilson demonstrated the war game to a string of visitors, beginning with Robertson on 10 January, who was 'a good deal knocked about by what he saw'. Wilson put this down to the fact that 'he has a broken staff and so has GHQ, and I have a very good one all of whom have been for years in the line and all of whom know their business.'[56] He showed the game to Pershing two days later, to Smuts who 'really <u>was</u> pleased', and the American PMR Bliss on 27. Wilson's friend Lieutenant-General Sir Alexander Godley (then GOC II Anzac Corps) was 'simply delighted' with the performance he saw.[57] Herbert Lawrence, who had just succeeded Charteris as Head of Intelligence at GHQ, asked for a demonstration. 'Just imagine!', wrote Wilson, 'And GHQ has never played one!'[58] On the eve of the third meeting of the SWC 'I played the War Game this morning before L.[loyd] G.[eorge], Milner etc and Hereward [Wake] and Bertie Studd did very well. Everyone <u>really</u> impressed.'[59] The next day's audience was less appreciative: 'Haig, Lawrence, Davidson,[60] Maurice and others came and we played our War Game for them. Haig was frankly bored and

---

51   TNA WO 158/57: 'Annexure to Joint Note 12,' 21 January 1918, p 2.
52   Ibid.
53   Wilson diary, 21 January 1918; Amery diary, 21 January 1918, in Barnes and Nicholson, *Amery Diaries*, p. 201.
54   TNA CAB 25/68: 'Military Action to be taken in 1918 – plan of', 17 enclosures, January-February 1918; Edmonds, *Military Operations France and Belgium 1918* (Vol. I), pp. 79-80.
55   The teams comprised 'A' Allied Branch, 'E' Enemy Branch, 'M' Material and Manpower Branch; IWM, Wilson diary, 3 January 1918; see Chapter Two, 'Wilson's Paper', p. 54.
56   Wilson diary, January 1918.
57   Ibid., 12, 16, 27 January, 4 February 1918.
58   Ibid., 10 January 1918.
59   Ibid., 29 January 1918.
60   Major-General Sir John 'Tavish' Davidson, Head of Operations at GHQ.

read some memorandum he had in his hand, and Lawrence never uttered. Tavish showed a little sense. Haig I find stupider every time I see him.'[61]

Haig had already condemned Wilson's reliance on the war game as 'laughable but for the seriousness of it...'[62] His irritation appears to have been directed against Wilson and his colleagues rather than a contempt for the war game concept. One study has described Wilson's use of the war game as 'novel'.[63] In fact, known as 'Kriegsspiel', it was used widely in the pre-War German Army and was a feature in British General Staff exercises as early as 1905.[64] Haig organised a war game as part of a Staff Ride, while Director of Staff Duties.[65] Wilson's exercises, informed by intelligence data provided by the War Office, influenced the reports which accompanied JN12 submitted to the SWC at the end of January 1918. One of the most significant, produced by 'E' or 'Enemy' Branch, considered a western offensive from the German perspective.[66] This paper said German divisions had begun transferring from Russia and Italy sooner than expected and there were now known to be 169 on the Western Front with the actual total 'possibly' 185. These were opposed by 166 Allied divisions. The 'maximum German effort', an attack by 110 divisions, would be possible between 1 May and 1 June over a 55 kilometre front. By 1 July, the Germans would have a superiority of 37 divisions and 400 heavy guns.[67] Woodward dismissed the war game as 'interesting though hardly fruitful' and said Wilson was 'wide of the mark' in suggesting 1 May as the best time for a German offensive.[68] In fact, the report by 'E' Branch was typically nuanced. It said that the major German offensive would best be postponed to May or June when 'the greatest superiority is attained and the weather is suitable' with preparations being started immediately. However, if preparations 'are already to some extent in hand, it is possible that the offensive might commence on 1 March, provided that severe weather does not cause a postponement or preclude preparations meanwhile.' At the beginning of March sufficient forces would be available, offering an advantage of five divisions but an inferiority of 600 heavy guns. The enemy position would continue to improve such that it would be: '...open to the Germans to commence their offensive on 1 March, but from a purely military point of view it would be better to postpone it to 1 May when they have a superiority of about 20 divisions over the Allies.' American arrivals were slower than expected and only 10 divisions would be in place by 1 June; it had been calculated initially that there would be 15

61   Wilson diary, 30 January 1918; Amery diary, 30 January 1918, in Barnes and Nicolson, *Amery Diaries*, p. 202.
62   Haig diary, 14 January 1918, in Sheffield and Bourne, *Haig: Diaries*, p. 372.
63   Chris Baker, '"Embusqués of the worst type, living among the fleshpots of Paris": The British Permanent Staff at the Supreme War Council', *Stand To!*, (100), June 2014, p. 112.
64   Robert T. Foley, 'Preparing the German Army for the First World War: The Operational Ideas of Alfred von Schlieffen and Helmuth von Moltke the Younger', *War & Society*, Vol. 22 (2), (2004); Matt B. Caffrey Jr., *On Wargaming: How Wargames Have Shaped History and How They May Shape the Future* (Newport, R.I.: Naval War College Press, 2019); Brown, *Logistics*, p. 29.
65   Harris, *Men Who Planned the War*, p. 22.
66   'The General Situation with Notes on a German Offensive in France', submitted 1 January 1918, updated 28 January 1918, in TNA CAB 25/68: 'Military Action to be taken in 1918 – plan of'.
67   TNA CAB 25/68, 'Military Action to be taken in 1918 – plan of' 'The General Situation with Notes on a German Offensive in France', Appendix Z, 1 January (revised 28 January) 1918.
68   Woodward, *Lloyd George*, p. 243 and p. 251 (n. 103); John Charteris, *Field-Marshal Earl Haig* (London: Cassell, 1929), pp. 301-3. See also John Hussey, 'Henry Wilson's Versailles War Game: January 1918', *Records, Journal of the Douglas Haig Fellowship* (No. 20, 2018), pp. 1-32.

divisions available by 1 July. On that date, the Germans would have 96 divisions in reserve, their maximum possible complement in 1918 and 'it would be to their advantage, <u>other things being equal,</u> to postpone their great offensive there until they can be certain of delivering a smashing blow'.[69] In other words, Wilson did not incorrectly predict June or July as the date of the major German offensive as Haig's first biographers claimed, nor 1 May as Woodward concluded.[70] Instead, he hedged his bets and produced evidence which showed it was possible from the beginning of March, with an increasing advantage for the enemy until the end of June. It was a view held by Robertson and the General Staff and supported by his friend Rawlinson.[71]

Where Wilson and his colleagues were wrong was the likely location of the offensive. Three potential sectors were identified. The first, between Bethune and Arras, would 'secure advantages far superior to those to be gained by an attack elsewhere'. An attack there, due to the short distances between this sector and the BEF's bases at the Channel ports, would give 'immediate and possibly decisive results'. Other sectors offering a 'reasonable chance of success' were south of St Quentin between Reims and Ville sur Tourbe or between Nancy and Luneville, west of Strasbourg. It was concluded that the German attack would take place between Bethune and Arras, with subsidiary or feint attacks east of Reims and/or near Nancy to draw in Allied reserves. In fact, the first blow of the German 'Spring Offensive', was struck from just south of Arras, to La Fère, south of the Somme, in the direction of the important rail centre of Amiens.[72]

JN12: Eastern Theatres

With no hope of victory in the west in 1918, JN12 then considered possible action in other theatres 'which may enable us to secure a decision far-reaching in its effect upon the political situation in the Near East and in Russia, both during and after the war, and valuable in paving the way towards a subsequent definitive decision against the enemy's main armies.'[73] This section focussed, predictably enough considering the British Cabinet's long pre-occupation with matters in the Middle East, on proposals for campaigns against the Ottoman Empire. The PMR's ruled out offensive actions in the Balkans, reiterating the position outlined in their Joint Note 4, conceding the possibility of giving ground but preserving the integrity of mainland Greece and, if possible, the port of Salonika.[74]

Wilson argued that Ottoman forces in the Middle East had dwindled to '250,000 men at the utmost', were overstretched and in a state of 'almost complete material and moral exhaustion'.[75] Thus, opportunities existed in either Palestine or Mesopotamia 'to inflict such a crushing series of defeats upon the Turkish armies as would lead to the final collapse of Turkey and her elimination from the war and would…have the most far-reaching result upon the general military situation.' It might allow the Allies to link up with resistance elements in Romania and

69   TNA CAB 25/68: 'Military Action to be taken in 1918 – plan of', Appendix Z, p. 2, (original emphasis).
70   G.A.B. Dewar, & J.H. Boraston, *Sir Douglas Haig's Command 1915-1918*, 2 vols. (London: Constable, 1922), (Vol. II), pp. 76-7.
71   CAC, Rawlinson journal, (RAWLN 1/9), 13 January 1918.
72   Zabecki, *German Offensives*, p. 119.
73   TNA WO 158/57: Joint Note 12, 21 January 1918, pp. 2-3.
74   Ibid., p. 3.
75   TNA WO 158/57: Joint Note 12, pp. 3.

Southern Russia. Even without such a 'crushing' series of victories, Germany would have no choice but to reinforce Turkey, diverting resources from the Western Front. Such a success, even if limited, would 'definitely liberate the Arab regions of the Ottoman Empire from the Turkish yoke'.[76] To this point the actions proposed resembled a re-hash of the standard 'knocking away the props' debate which had never strayed far from the British agenda.[77] Hughes characterised the fall of Jerusalem on as the next step in Lloyd George's 'way of redirecting strategy and diverting troops from France'.[78] In fact, the PMRs rejected any suggestion of diverting troops from the Western Front to do the job. While favouring offensives in the east they accepted that 'in view of the potential menace to the Western Front' there could be 'no question of a transfer of troops on any considerable scale from the Western to the Eastern theatre of operations.' Allied forces in Palestine and Mesopotamia were already superior enough 'to justify the hope that successful operations can be carried out with these forces providing they are maintained at full strength.'[79] There might be opportunities for 'minor reinforcements' by moving 'superfluous' cavalry units from France, curtailing British operations in East Africa, raising new units in India or in the French colonies. If the enemy made no serious offensive in the Balkans, and the organisation of the Greek army made sufficient progress, one or two British divisions might transfer from the Salonika front.

When JN12 was debated at the SWC Clemenceau, in a fine example of political grandstanding, said he supported the Western Front element of the proposal but not that concerning the Middle East. Disregarding Wilson's overt assurance in his paper about no additional troops for the theatre, Clemenceau: "Insisted that the security of the Western front overrode all other considerations...He protested against embarking on this Eastern adventure, when so dreadful a danger was imminent near to Paris itself.[80]

Lloyd George agreed and asserted that the British government had 'no intention of diverting forces from the Western front or in any way relaxing its efforts to maintain the safety of that front, which it regards as a vital interest of the whole Alliance.'[81] The key Allied operational challenge was not dislodging Turkish forces, but following up any initial success by converting 'their retreat into a rout and final annihilation'. For this they would need to build railway infrastructure complete with rolling stock, plus the opening and improvement of coastal bases for supplies. The PMRs accepted that the effort required was 'a great one' but upon it depended 'the whole prospect of achieving any decisive result for the Allied cause in 1918'. Thus: 'Looking upon the resources in material and technical skill possessed by the Allies, not only in Europe, but in Egypt, India the British Dominions, and the United States, the effort should not be

---

76   TNA WO 158/57: Joint Note 12, pp. 3.

77   Plans for securing the Gallipoli Peninsula to allow British warships access to the Dardanelles and the Sea of Marmara were first discussed by Churchill in late August 1914, Martin Gilbert, *Winston S. Churchill, 1914-1916*, Vol. III, (London: Heineman, 1971), esp. pp. 200-204.

78   Hughes, *Allenby*, p. 60.

79   TNA WO 158/57: 21 January 1918, pp. 3-4.

80   TNA CAB 28/3: IC (Allied Conferences) Series, Volume III, IC-40, Supreme War Council 'Procès-verbal of the Second Meeting of the Third Session of the Supreme War Council, 31 January 1918, p. 13.

81   Ibid., *'Procès-verbal* of the Third Meeting of the Third Session of the Supreme War Council, 1 February 1918, p. 25.

beyond the compass of our powers.'[82] Avoiding any detailed suggestions as to how this enormous logistical challenge might be met, the Note called for an improvement in supply lines via the Suez Canal. It identified the importance of aviation in any campaign in the region in 1918. The Allies had air superiority and 'the necessary measures should be taken to maintain and, if possible, increase it'. Strategic air bases would have to be created in Cyprus and the Aegean and the organisation of naval air services for concentrated strategic offensives, were 'essential elements in any scheme of serious operations against Turkey.'[83] The basis of this note was a study by Amery.[84] It suggested that the best way to assist anti-Bolshevik forces in Southern Russia would be by defeating the Turks in Palestine and gaining control of the Black Sea. While Wilson and his colleagues – Amery had no combat experience – can be reasonably accused of over-simplification, if not naïveté, in their blithe assumptions about military operations, they were on safer ground with the political elements of the proposals. Military action alone was not sufficient, the PMRs believed. They were 'convinced of the necessity that strategy and policy should go absolutely hand in hand'. What was needed was 'a definite, co-ordinated and vigorous political offensive both among the non-Turkish races of the Ottoman Empire and among the Turks themselves'. Conscious of the tension which existed between Britain and France over their individual spheres of influence in the region, the paper warned that:

> Any lack of coherence on the part of the Foreign Offices [of the Allied powers] in dealing with the political problems directly or indirectly connected with the Near Eastern situation, any evidence of mutual jealousy or of individual self-seeking, will be bound to prejudice not only the future settlement but the actual military operations.

This element of JN12, central as it was to Wilson's philosophy of the fundamental importance of effective inter-Allied co-operation, has been overlooked in the historiography and therefore merits reproduction in full:

> The aspects upon which stress has been laid in the preceding paragraphs emphasises the need for the most energetic co-operation and the closest co-ordination not only of the Allied Military forces in Palestine, Mesopotamia and Armenia, but also of the Allied Naval and Air forces along the whole coast of Asiatic Turkey, of the local Governments in Egypt, India, Cyprus, or from whatever country materials, supplies or labour can be furnished, and not least, of the Allied Foreign Offices. It is essential to the success of the offensive against Turkey that it should be envisaged not as a series of disconnected operations, but as a single co-ordinated scheme whose object is to eliminate one of the Enemy Powers from the War.[85]

It was a theme Wilson continued to pursue, and which dominated his strategic plan for 1919. The SWC's acceptance of this strategy represented a triumph for Wilson. When the delegates

82 TNA WO 158/57: Joint Note 12, 21 January 1918, p. 4.
83 Ibid., pp. 4-5.
84 TNA CAB 25/68: 'Military Action to be taken in 1918 – plan of', 4 January 1918, 'The Turkish and South Russian Problem'.
85 TNA WO 158/57: Joint Note 12, 21 January 1918, p. 5.

moved to approve the resolution, Robertson intervened to say that he 'did not agree with some of the statements made in Note 12 of the Military Representatives, or with some of the inferences drawn in regard to a campaign against Turkey'. 'Wully' was aware of the risk he was running by making this intervention, acknowledging he was not a member of the SWC. Nonetheless he felt compelled to say that the entente 'ought to adopt a defensive policy in all secondary theatres, and to keep no more troops there than were necessary'. He also believed that the resolution in favour of 'a decisive offensive against Turkey' was 'not a practical plan and that to attempt it would be very dangerous and detrimental to our prospects of winning the war.'[86] He objected in vain and the Joint Note was accepted. As has already been discussed, the German Spring offensives made JN12 irrelevant, but it remains a valuable indicator of Wilson's strategic thinking.

86   TNA CAB 28/3: IC (Allied Conferences) Series, Volume III, IC-40, Supreme War Council 'Procès-verbal of the Third Meeting of the Third Session of the Supreme War Council, 1 February 1918, p. 25.

10

Victory and Aftermath

After his influential role in the establishment of Allied Unity of Command Henry Wilson spent much of the second quarter of 1918 negotiating with French and American commanders over troop allocations and strategic priorities; a frustrating and sometimes fruitless endeavour. By mid-1918 the German effort in the west was losing impetus and in July Lloyd George asked his military advisers for their views on Allied policy for 1919. In Wilson's absence Lloyd George quizzed the Deputy CIGS (DCIGS), Major-General Charles 'Tim' Harington. The Prime Minister was irritated to hear that Foch was already planning western offensives dominated by AEF divisions. Whilst Lloyd George reacted predictably, considering his sustained fixation with the dream of winning the war by offensives in the east, Foch's thinking was firmly based on JN12. This had advocated sitting on the defensive in the west in 1918 while awaiting the arrival of the Americans. Now the Germans had shot their bolt it was logical that Foch, with full support from Haig, would plan for a new offensive, with a new army, in 1919.

The hapless Harington, who had only been in the job for two months, volunteered that the General Staff was considering a major offensive on the Western Front of up to 70 divisions, 20 of them British, involving large formations of tanks. Lloyd George asked if operations in other theatres had been considered: 'He asked if the General Staff were sure that the Germans were not going to break off operations on the Western front and go elsewhere, for example to Russia... Would they merely go on hammering at the Western front, or would they follow the German lead?' Had they considered 'knocking out' Austria or Turkey? Would it not be possible to get rid of Germany's Allies before concentrating on Germany herself? According to the Prime Minister, if the Americans concentrated a great Army on the Western Front next year, 'it might be possible for our Army to follow out its traditional rôle of operating on the outskirts of the war area.' Was anybody studying this? Harington assured him they were.[1] In fact, as Lloyd George well knew, since he arrived at the War Office in February Wilson had spent time studying options for outlying theatres. Operations aimed at either hampering the diversion of German resources to France and Flanders, at minimum cost, or/and protecting British imperial interests, had been high on the agenda. The fifth and final major German offensive on the Western Front, *Operation Marneschutz – Reims*, had begun on 15 July, only to grind to a halt a few days later. It meant that Wilson could finish his new strategy paper, 'British Military Policy, 1918-1919',

---

1   TNA CAB 23/17/19: X Committee, 1 July 1918.

a detailed analysis of which throws new light on Wilson's independence of thought and broad strategic vision.[2]

Strategy for the Western Front

Lloyd George was 'bitterly disappointed with Wilson's purely "Western Front" attitude and described his report as simply "Wully *redivivus*" [reborn].'[3] The Prime Minister was over-simplifying a detailed and closely argued document. In proposing and outlining the details of an Allied offensive on the Western Front to win the war in 1919, its strategic scope went further than he acknowledged. Wilson was inclined to consider military strategy from a broader political perspective. His predecessor, reasonably enough considering his role and the priorities during his time at the War Office, saw the world through a military lens with the political context often relegated to the periphery. It was why Lloyd George deprecated Robertson's seemingly myopic focus and warmed to and encouraged Wilson's apparently wider vision. But, as his 1919 policy paper illustrated, Wilson was not a Lloyd George stooge. The second paragraph summarised his purpose:

> The nearer we get to the end of the war the more necessary is it to keep in mind the ultimate aspects of the situation from the British side, so that the policy of our war aims and the strategy of our war effort may harmonise in securing for the British Empire the best possible position at the dawn of peace.[4]

In other words, strategic planning for the next 18 months needed to be undertaken with the *post-bellum* outcome in mind. Winning the peace was as important as winning the war. As Rawlinson noted after being briefed by the CIGS: 'Henry is looking at all the fronts and wants to hold as many cards as possible when the time comes for discussing peace terms.'[5]

Wilson considered what was, he acknowledged, an increasingly unlikely outcome to the German offensives. If the enemy did drive a wedge between the Allied armies, the British would have to abandon the continent while the French were likely to be defeated. If this happened, Britain and the USA could continue what would become a 'maritime and economic war,' with land operations in the Middle East. Alternatively, assuming 'as we may', that the Germans had been fought to a standstill, the 'immediate pre-occupation of the Allies' must be to prepare for the 'decisive phase and if necessary to detach troops to other theatres without misgivings.' To do this, Wilson recommended a series of offensives with the limited objectives of pushing the Germans away from Channel ports, the strategically important Bruay coal mines, the Amiens communications hub, and Paris. This 'margin of safety' had to be established before the end of the 1918 campaigning season and would need every man and gun. Despite knowing that the Prime Minister and Milner favoured significant operations away from the Western Front,

2   TNA CAB 25/85: Supreme War Council, British Secretariat, Papers and Minutes, 'British Military Policy, 1918-1919', 25 July 1918, (hereafter CAB 25/85).
3   Hankey diary, 30 July 1918, in Hankey, *Supreme Command* (Vol. II), p. 830.
4   TNA CAB 25/85, p. 1.
5   CAC, Rawlinson journal, (RAWLN 1/9), 30 June 1918.

Wilson stated: 'There is therefore no possibility of sending any divisions to operate in other theatres until this aim is accomplished.'[6]

An abiding theme of this work has been an emphasis on the overarching concern for Britain and France during the final two years of the war – the manpower shortage. As a result, the fulcrum of Wilson's report swung on timing; or as he termed it, the 'choice of the moment for supreme effort'.[7] Should the Allies make this effort in 1919 or in 1920? Wilson argued that all rested on the strength of the AEF the following summer. The War Office estimated that by June 1919 there would be 80 US divisions in France, although a shortage of officers and equipment would limit the number available for offensive action.[8] Sackville-West at the SWC had reported that the balance of forces would be 181 Allied divisions facing 170 German, a superiority of 400,000 men. This could be boosted by another quarter of a million if 'Allied intervention in Siberia has materialised sufficiently to reconstitute an effective Eastern Front in Russia - even partially'. While this force might not be considered 'overwhelming' for offensive purposes the impact on German morale of large numbers of high quality and enthusiastic American troops would be significant. In any case:

> Arguments against deferring the crisis to 1920 are so strong as to be irresistible. The war weariness in Great Britain, the exhaustion of France and Italy, and the impatience of America, who will by that time have been at war for over 2 years will oblige us to strike in 1919 or to stop the war ... all enthusiasm for the war is dead.'[9]

Equally, the Germans must not be allowed to consolidate in Russia and Asia and Wilson therefore had 'no hesitation' in saying that the culminating period for supreme military effort on the Western Front should be no later than 1 July 1919. To prepare for this major offensive, he recommended bringing as many British units as possible back from 'out-theatres' and their replacement with Indian divisions. These were hardly the instincts of a committed 'easterner'. The 1919 offensive would need 43 British divisions, a considerable reduction from the 59 available in mid-1918. This echoed Lloyd George's determination that British divisions would be significantly reduced by the autumn; the present levels, he believed, were untenable.[10] Artillery and machine-gun units would be expanded, and the cavalry reduced.

Wilson's scheme, which he shared with Haig and Foch, involved an 'Allied Tank attack' on a 50-mile front by 70 infantry and eight cavalry divisions, supported by 10,500 tanks. The British would contribute 20 divisions and 3,000 tanks, plus 7,300 mechanical tractors with supplies.[11] Wilson's plan failed to impress Haig, who wrote on his copy 'Words! Words! Words! Lots of Words! And little else.'[12] In fairness to both, Haig had just attended a meeting with Pershing, Pétain and Foch to plan for taking the offensive in a few weeks and was unlikely to have been

---

6   TNA CAB 25/85, pp. 4-6.
7   Ibid., p. 6.
8   The authorised strength of AEF divisions was 28,000 officers and men, compared with a BEF division of 18,000 men, including artillery and support units, Mark Ethan Grotelueschen, *The AEF Way of War: The American Army and Combat in World War I* (Cambridge: Cambridge University Press, 2006) p. 325.
9   CAB 25/85, pp. 7-9.
10   TNA CAB 23/17/25: X Committee, 26 July 1918.
11   TNA CAB 25/85: pp. 26-7.
12   Sheffield and Bourne, *Haig: Diaries*, p. 434.

able to give much thought to paper plans for a year hence.[13] Foch, Haig remarked, was 'a great believer in "Tanks"'.[14] Likewise Wilson, along with most of his colleagues, had little idea of Foch's plans for taking the offensive, nor expectations for their subsequent success.

Wilson was left in no doubt of his political masters' disdain. The day after Lloyd George had dismissed it as 'Wully reborn', it was torn apart by the Imperial War Cabinet (IWC).[15] Milner, normally Wilson's ally but as an arch-imperialist a longstanding supporter of 'eastern' initiatives expressed surprise that the Western Front had returned to the strategic debate 'in great strength'. He had the gravest doubts of an Allied victory there in 1919 because 'the Western Front was a candle that burned all the moths that entered it.' As far as he was concerned 'it was now out of the question that we could play the great role on the Western Front.' Wilson was encouraged by the Australian Prime Minister W.M. 'Billy' Hughes who thought 'we must smash the Boches in France'. Smuts also doubted an Allied victory in 1919, 'time, space & season have nothing to do with these strategists!', wrote Wilson, disdainfully.[16] According to Hankey, the view of the meeting was that 'we were running the risk of shattering the American Army next year, as we shattered our own Army in 1916 and 1917, without achieving a decision.'[17] Lloyd George condemned the soldiers for always expecting the government to supply whatever number of troops they asked for. He questioned the cost of the proposed 1919 offensive and 'could not find a syllable as to income or wastage'. Wilson said he could not address the issue of 'income' [numbers of new troops] because he was unclear whether the government intended to conscript Ireland; as for losses, he estimated 25,000 per month.[18] He noted:

> I was able to knock him [Lloyd George] about rather severely by showing that the paper itself & the graphic gave the whole of the information. Practically all the PMs ie L.G., Borden, [Sir Robert Borden, Prime Minister of Canada] Hughes (but not so much), Smuts, Massey [William F. Massey, Prime Minister of New Zealand] & Milner are of opinion that we can't beat the Boches on the Western front, & so they go wandering about looking for other laurels.[19]

Two days later, Milner told Wilson that Lloyd George found him 'too much "Western Front" in his ideas and too much like Robertson.'[20] Wilson's recollection was that 'L.G. was beginning to suspect me of being a "Wully" which of course is nonsense.'[21]

Future Strategy and the 'out-theatres'

Where Wilson's paper differed from his earlier recommendations was the secondary role he assigned to some long-standing priorities. In the first quarter of 1918 the War Cabinet had

13   Greenhalgh, *Foch*, p. 407-9.
14   NLS, Haig (manuscript) diary, 24 July 1918.
15   TNA CAB, 23/44A/7: Imperial War Cabinet (IWC), 31 July 1918.
16   Wilson diary, 31 July 1918.
17   Hankey diary, 31 July 1918, in Hankey, *Supreme Command* (Vol. II), p. 830.
18   TNA CAB 23/44A/8: IWC, 1 August 1918.
19   Wilson diary, 1 August 1918.
20   Hankey diary, 2 August 1918, in Hankey, *Supreme Command* (Vol. II), p. 831.
21   Wilson diary, 2 August 1918.

been concerned about the future of the Italian front. In July, the CIGS concluded that a German offensive in Italy was possible later in the year. He recommended improving transport communications and establishing a reserve by sending three or four British divisions to augment the three already there. There were no proposals for Allied offensive action. At the IWC, Lloyd George and Smuts questioned Wilson on options for an Italian offensive, but he stood his ground. The weather would have deteriorated by the time the additional divisions arrived, and in 1919 effort had to be concentrated on the Western Front.[22] As for the Balkans, Wilson had no fears of an attack by the Central Powers, but again he opposed a large scale offensive because it would be 'handicapped by the interminable political jealousies between Italian, French, Greek and Serbian interests.'[23] In Palestine he favoured 'active defence', pointing out that German advances in Persia and Southern Russia meant she was forging a route to the valuable resources of the east without needing Egypt, the Suez Canal and Syria. This region continued to be a major cause of concern for the British long after the armistice was signed.

The regions in which the Allies needed to concentrate what resources they could spare from the west, according to Wilson, were those which had recently been under the influence of Imperial Russia. Acknowledging that he was 'trenching [sic] on the domain of policy, which is beyond the bounds of my responsibility,' he did so because the 'ultimate security of the British Empire depends on the extent to which British policy and British strategy are made to harmonise in defence of British interests.' What was needed was a political and military strategy to create 'neutral zones' and 'Buffer States' that would help safeguard Britain's vital interests 'for years to come.'[24] In southern Russia, especially in Transcaucasia, between the Black and Caspian Seas, the Germans were making significant inroads.[25] Wilson had similar fears for Persia and parts of Mesopotamia, all of strategic importance due to their oil and other natural resources, and their proximity to Afghanistan and India, the jewel in Britain's imperial crown. The Germans controlled the Black Sea and were now heading towards the oil centre of Baku on the Caspian. If they achieved this, they would control the railways 'up to the very borders of Afghanistan.' Wilson argued that this made it essential for Britain to consolidate in Mesopotamia, Persia and take control of the Caspian: 'Indeed it is not too much to say that both with a view to winning this war and to securing the safety of India for the next generation we should devote our efforts to this theatre rather than to Palestine.'[26]

He recommended bolstering local forces using limited numbers of British and Allied troops to hamper German expansionism. A linked priority was to force Germany to keep divisions in the east by encouraging anti-Bolshevik forces to re-establish an Eastern Front, and distracting German resources.[27] This element of the report encapsulated the challenge the War Cabinet had wrestled with in recent months, the development of a cohesive Allied policy for Russia. The proposal found favour with Lord Milner. He told the IWC he would prefer it if the French and the Americans provided the bulk of the forces in the west in 1919, allowing Britain to move up

---

22   TNA CAB, 23/44A/8: IWC, 1 August 1918.
23   CAB 25/85, pp. 15-17.
24   Ibid., p. 31.
25   Rob Johnson, *The Great War & the Middle East: A Strategic Study* (Oxford: Oxford University Press, 2016), pp. 235-40.
26   CAB 25/85, p.18.
27   William Philpott, *Attrition: Fighting the First World War* (London: Little Brown, 2014), p. 308.

to 15 divisions elsewhere: 'If practically the whole of the Germany Army was contained on the Western Front, this reserve should be able to achieve a great deal.' Hughes, one of the few IWC members who still believed in victory in the west, pointed out that those with the largest forces in that theatre would dominate the peace: 'From this point of view it was very undesirable to leave France and the United States to finish the war on the Western Front.'[28] While agreeing this was a legitimate concern, Wilson was not advocating such a risk. As usual he wanted to hedge his bets and ensure British effectiveness in both theatres – an unrealistic balancing act. The CIGS had already ordered Lieutenant-General Sir William R. Marshall, the commander of the British Mesopotamian Army, to establish a line of communication between Baghdad and Baku and had sanctioned a small force to take the latter city.[29] This action was successful and the port was taken, and held, on 4 August 1918.[30]

The other key opportunity Wilson saw for reviving the Eastern Front was encouraging anti-Bolshevik forces in Siberia and in Northern Russia. These ideas were not new to the 1918-1919 strategy document. Wilson and the War Cabinet had been discussing interventionist policies since before the Treaty of Brest-Litovsk formally ended the war between the Central Powers and Bolshevik Russia on 3 March 1918. The fear in London was that the new Russian revolutionary government, which was not in control of the whole of the former Tsarist Empire, might ally itself with the Germans. At best, it was feared, Germany would dominate Russia and its economy, making it a vassal state.[31] Wilson believed the answer was encouraging, funding and arming anti-Bolshevik forces, and sending them limited military support. On Siberia Wilson and the War Cabinet favoured encouraging Japan to enter the war. The SWC had already agreed JN16 which recommended Japanese intervention in Siberia to seize the strategically important railway between Vladivostok and the Chinese city of Harbin. The idea was that a Japanese force would assist anti-Bolshevik elements and protect the region from German incursions.[32] The result, it was hoped, would at minimum force the Germans to keep significant troop numbers in the east; at best, it would protect the British Empire from the threat of a resurgent Germany.

Wilson stuck to this thesis into the summer of 1918. He stated that: 'The resurrection of Russia can only be brought about by Allied intervention in Siberia and the re-creation of an Eastern Front.' To Wilson's frustration, his 'cousin', as he referred to the US President in his diaries, disagreed. Worried about American public opinion and concerned that it might be difficult for the Allies to contain a Japanese army once it was in Siberia, President Wilson was reluctant to give his approval. The Japanese refused to get involved unless invited specifically by the US.[33] In May, Wilson told the Japanese Military Attaché in London that 'from a military point of view the Japanese Army could not intervene too soon nor go too far & that I was always

28   TNA CAB, 23/44A/7: IWC, 31 July 1918.
29   TNA CAB 25/85, p. 21.
30   F.J. Moberly, *Official History: Military Operations The Campaign in Mesopotamia: 1914-1918* (Vol. IV), (London: HMSO, 1927), pp. 204-10; see also Douglas Boyd, *The Other First World War: The Blood-Soaked Russian Fronts 1914-1922* (Stroud: the History Press, 2017 [2014]).
31   John Fisher, *Curzon and British Imperialism in the Middle East: 1916-1919* (London: Frank Cass, 1999), pp. 268-9.
32   TNA CAB 25/120: (Nos 1-150), Supreme War Council, Papers and Minutes, 'Joint Note 16, Japanese intervention in Siberia,' 19 February 1918.
33   TNA CAB 28/4: War Cabinet, IC 66, *Procès-verbal* of the Third Meeting of the Sixth Session of the Supreme War Council, 3 June 1918; for a detailed discussion of this aspect of the war see Paul E.

impressing this on my Govt. & hoped the Jap[anese] GS would do the same to their Govt.' The same day, according to Wilson, the War Cabinet discussed Russia, and whether the British should occupy Archangel, Murmansk and Vladivostok and if they should 'blow up the [Russian] Baltic fleet'. How this was to be achieved is unclear. There is no record of the discussion in the War Cabinet minutes for that date, although Hankey typically avoided recording strategically sensitive material.[34] The SWC meeting in early June approved an Allied force to protect the northern Russian ports of Murmansk and Archangel from German occupation with the British Major-General F.C. Poole in command. Wilson was actively involved in these X Committee policy debates with the Prime Minister and Milner. Lloyd George displayed a strategic insight greater than his more 'gung-ho' colleagues and, like President Wilson, cautioned against 'the danger of setting Russia against us. This was one of the cases where a mistake might prove fatal. If Germany once got the gigantic man-power of Russia into her hands the Allies would be bankrupt.'[35] Over time Wilson began to see the sense in the Prime Minister's argument and in the immediate post-war period was amongst the first to conclude that Russia was a lost cause. While there was an overarching logic in Wilson's commitment to protect Britain's imperial interest, the lack of a co-ordinated Allied strategy in the outlying theatres made progress difficult. Manpower was short and working with disaffected local groups with their own agenda was problematic. Wilson was casting about for ideas because, as is clear from both his recommendations for future strategy and his diaries, in the summer of 1918 he was not convinced that the war would end in Germany's total defeat. He was worried that even if the Allies won on the Western Front it was:

> Difficult to see how we could force such terms on the Central Powers as would loosen their hold in the East or close the road to Egypt and India. Unless by the end of the war democratic Russia can be reconstituted as an independent military power it is only a question of time before most of Asia becomes a German colony, and nothing can impede the enemy's progress towards India.[36]

It was in Britain's vital interest, he argued, to reconstitute Russia as an armed and independent state, strong enough to withstand future German aggression: 'If the war closes without this being accomplished the future of the British Empire will be seriously menaced.'[37] While Poole's adventure in North Russia fizzled out, a Japanese force did intervene in Siberia in August 1918, but this ended as 'a failure and a sideshow'.[38] By then Wilson had bigger priorities; the collapse of the German forces on the Western Front and the imminent end of the war. In the peace negotiations that followed, many of the fears he had stressed in his policy document would come to the fore.[39]

Dunscomb, *Japan's Siberian Intervention, 1918-1922: 'A Great Disobedience Against the People'* (Lanham, MD: Lexington Books, 2011).
34   Wilson diary, 11 May 1918; TNA CAB 23/6/31: War Cabinet, 11 May 1918.
35   TNA CAB 23/17/15: X Committee, 19 June 1918.
36   CAB 25/85, p. 29.
37   CAB 25/85, p. 31.
38   Dunscomb, *Japan's Siberian Intervention*, p. 56.
39   MacMillan, *Peacemakers*.

Peace – of a kind

With the end of the war in the west in November 1918 there were British troops in Belgium, France, Germany, Italy, Greece, Austria-Hungary, Serbia and Bulgaria – as well as in the pre-war imperial garrisons.[40] In addition, the British army had men in the former Ottoman territories of Turkey, Jordan, Palestine, Mesopotamia, and the Arabian littoral. There were also forces in various parts of Africa, India, Egypt, Persia, northern Russia, Siberia in the east and in the Trans-Caucasus region around both the Black and Caspian seas. By any measure, this was operational over-stretch. The reasons were understandable. The war had destroyed three extensive and long-standing empires, those of Austria-Hungary, Russia and the Ottomans. The relatively new German empire was also about to be dismembered. Europe was in chaos with smaller states declaring self-determination and long-suppressed ethnic tensions resurfacing.

A particular area of concern was Russia and the outlier territories of the former Tsarist empire. In mid-1918 Wilson had been an advocate of opposing Bolshevism in Russia, both as a hedge against similar revolutionary upheaval elsewhere, including Britain, and to maintain an eastern front against Germany. By the turn of the year his view was beginning to change.

On the eve of the Great War British foreign policy had focussed on the promotion and preservation of trade routes, the security of India with the attendant defence of that artery of empire the Suez Canal, and the exclusion of rivals from Egypt, Afghanistan and the Persian Gulf. Persia itself, where oil had been discovered as recently as 1908, was another logical priority.[41] As CIGS Wilson was acutely aware of the pressures on manpower and as the war approached its end on the Western Front his attention turned to considering how Britain might dominate the peace. 'War imperialism', as one authority has called it, meant that in early 1919 the British Empire had reached its apogee, covering 25% of the earth's landmass and one quarter of its population. It was also the beginning of its inexorable decline.[42] Britain had fought, amongst other aims, to retain these areas of influence. While this had been achieved, the cost in lives and treasure had been enormous. Britain's empire had grown, but old rivalries, particularly with France, had begun to re-emerge.

No sooner had the guns on the Western Front fallen silent than Wilson prepared a paper for the War Cabinet which considered 'the war after the war'. His specific concern was that the Germans might hold on to their territory and influence in Russia. While this was an important consideration, Wilson had little if any expectation that either France or the USA would view the issue with similar concern. Anti-Bolshevik forces were unreliable and unpredictable and the cost to Britain of any strategically significant action would be enormous and unsustainable. As a result, the best policy was an orderly withdrawal by the time of the signing the formal Paris peace agreement, which was expected in the summer of 1919.[43] The debate continued with both Milner and Winston Churchill, who succeeded him as War Secretary in January 1919, favouring ongoing action in Russia to prevent the success of Bolshevism. Churchill was

---

40   Keith Jeffery, *The British Army and the Crisis of Empire, 1918-1922* (Manchester: Manchester University Press, 1984), p. 13.
41   Johnson, *The Middle East*, pp. 13-14.
42   Jeffery, *Crisis of Empire*, p. 1 and *passim*.
43   TNA CAB 24/70/11: 'Memorandum on our present and future military strategy in Russia', 13 November 1918, pp. 1-4.

eventually forced to accept Wilson's judgement that the invasion and occupation of Russia was not 'a practical military proposition'. Instead Britain ought to offer support, short of direct military intervention, to anti-Bolshevik forces and withdraw from key locations such as Murmansk and Archangel as soon as conditions allowed.[44] Events in northern Russia continued to be a thorn in the side of British strategy even after the Paris Peace Conference had concluded its business. In August Wilson wrote to Sackville-West at Versailles emphasising his determination to pull out the remaining British forces in the region. For his pains his old friend Henry Rawlinson found himself managing the departure of the northern forces.[45] Wilson told him that the anti-Bolshevik leadership was interested only in British financial and material support 'and there is no doubt that Lenin and Trotsky and those around them are far abler men.'[46]

The southern part of the former Tsarist empire was an even more complicated region for British policy-makers. In Trans-Caucasia, three emerging states, Armenia, George and Azerbaijan were seen as strategically important, as was Transcaspia, a vast region to the east of the Caspian Sea.[47] These territories were close to Mesopotamia and Persia and were seen as offering a gateway to India should they fall under the control of anti-British interests. They, together with embryonic states in Europe, had been given hope of self-determination by the last of US President Woodrow Wilson's 'Fourteen Points' which spoke of 'mutual guarantees of political independence and territorial integrity to great and small states alike.'[48] The speech outlined his war aims and favoured peace terms, and dominated the Paris Peace Conference a year later. Unsurprisingly, the tenor of the US aims sat uncomfortably with the imperialists in the British and French governments, but they did encourage independence movements in the former Austro-Hungarian, Russian and Ottoman empires. Lord Curzon, a former Viceroy of India, became British Foreign Secretary in October 1919. His imperialist instincts were second only to those of Milner. His enthusiasm for British intervention in the Caucasus and in the neighbouring Middle East saw him become a '*bête noir*' for Wilson's War Office, frequently demanding troops to support his expansive policies – troops Wilson insisted the country could not afford.[49] Those on the ground sided with Wilson, seeing the region as beyond redemption. General George Milne, in Command of the Army of the Black Sea saw those in control in the Caucasus as 'illiterate and dishonest demagogues of the worst type…with the one idea of making hay while the sun shines.'[50] Milne had spent the latter half of the war in the thankless role of GOC of the British forces on the Salonika front. His new command was even more dispiriting, defending British strategic interests over a vast area stretching from the Dardanelles

44 TNA CAB 24/75/85: Future Military Operations in Russia', 24 February 1919; see also note on same subject by CIGS, 19 February 1919, in *MCHW*, pp. 83-6.
45 Prior & Wilson, *Command*, p. 392.
46 Wilson to Sackville-West, 6 August 1919, and Wilson to Rawlinson 1 September 1919 in *MCHW*, at pp. 118-120 and 122-3; Wilson diary, 29 August 1919.
47 Modern Turkmenistan and its neighbours.
48 President Wilson gave his famous 'Fourteen Points' speech to the US Congress on 8 January 1918. It outlined his war aims and peace terms, and dominated the Paris Peace Conference a year later, MacMillan, *Peacemakers*, pp. 21-23, 27-8 and *passim*.
49 Jeffery, MCHW, p. 70; Fisher, *Curzon and British Imperialism* offers an excellent account of this subject.
50 Milne to Wilson, 22 January 1919, Jeffery, *MHCW*, p. 77.

via Anatolia to the Trans-Caucasus and the Caspian Sea.[51] Milne urged Wilson to withdraw British troops from the Caucasus as soon as possible:

> I am fully aware that the withdrawal of British troops would probably lead to anarchy but I cannot see that the world would lose much if the whole of the inhabitants of the country cut each other's throats. They are certainly not worth the life of one British soldier. The Georgians are merely disguised Bolsheviks led by men who overthrew Kerensky and were friends of Lenin. The Armenians are what the Armenians have always been, a despicable race. The best are the inhabitants of Azerbaijan, though in reality they are uncivilised.[52]

In the Middle East it was a similar story. The war had not been over a week when Allenby noted 'it looks as if there will be a lot of police work to be done in Europe and Asia before the new little nations settle down, or they will all be tearing each others eyes [sic].' As C-in-C of the Egyptian Expeditionary Force, Allenby's area of responsibility stretched from Egypt and around the Eastern Mediterranean littoral to Turkey. The British and French shared responsibility for the strategically important Dardanelles and Bosphorous sea routes between and Black and Mediterranean seas and occupied Constantinople while the defeated Ottoman army was disarmed and dispersed.[53] The Anglo-French entente was under particular strain in this region and Wilson sent his old friend Lieutenant-General Sir George 'Tom' Bridges to keep an eye on the situation. Bridges was a highly experienced liaison officer, having served in this capacity in Belgium before and in the early years of the war and subsequently in the US. Bridges described his new and thankless task as being 'Head Housemaid to the Near East'.[54] Allenby's observation on the tensions in the region were particularly prophetic: 'Politics in Palestine & Syria are not going to be too easy in the future. Jews, Arabs, French, Italians, English & other nations, all think they have special interests & special claims & rights; and every known religion asserts itself and adds knots to the tangle.'[55] There was also the small matter of the enforcement of the terms of the German armistice and the attendant allied occupation of the Rhineland to consider. Small wonder then that Wilson's primary concern was the future size of the army.[56]

When the war ended Wilson continued to play a central role in the British government's policy-making process.[57] In the years building up to the Great War, during it and in the months after the armistice was signed the key issues facing British policy-makers - including Sir Henry Wilson - were the same: the security of the British Empire, the Anglo-French alliance, military manpower, and the future of Ireland. The transition from war to peace was never going to be easy. Wilson understood this and although he favoured the establishment of a long-service

51   Brian Holden Reid, 'George Francis Milne', *ODNB*, 2011.
52   Milne to Wilson, 22 January 1919, Jeffery, *MHCW*, p. 79.
53   Sir J.E. Edmonds, *Official History of the War: The Occupation of Constantinople: 1918-1923* (Uckfield: Naval & Military Press, 2010).
54   Tom Bridges, *Alarms and Excursions: Reminiscences of a Soldier* (London: Longmans, 1938), p. 279. Bridges' memoir reads like a Boys' Own adventure story.
55   Allenby to Wilson, 16 November 1918, Jeffery, *MCHW*, p. 61.
56   The British army in November 1918 stood at 3.8 million men. By the end of 1919 it had been reduced to 890,000, Jeffery, *Wilson*, p. 231.
57   Ibid., p. 229.

voluntary army he believed in the continuation of conscription while the victorious powers decided the fate of the world. He was not alone amongst British political and military leaders in having predicted the restoration of Anglo-French colonial rivalries. Indeed, there had been many occasions during the war when Lloyd George, William Robertson, Lord Milner and Wilson himself had baulked at French actions in Macedonia and the Middle East. Similar scenes had been played out in Parisian corridors of power when perfidious Albion had jealously guarded its interests in Egypt, Persia and Mesopotamia. Early in 1919 Wilson and Churchill, in close consultation with Sir Douglas Haig and other senior soldiers, came up with a scheme to retain an army of occupation of 1.2 million men, sustained by conscription.[58] Lloyd George dismissed the figure as 'fantastic' and was subsequently lambasted with typical Wilsonian invective as a 'stupid fool. He knows nothing about it & I have not seen a sign of real statesmanship in any of LG's work.' This type of scribbled outburst was common in Wilson's diary, but in this case it revealed a growing tension between the CIGS and his Prime Minister. The honeymoon period was over. Lloyd George was eventually persuaded to accept Wilson's plan, but the respite was only temporary.

That spring Wilson wrote to his old friend Admiral Sir Walter Cowan to stress the need for Britain's overseas commitments to be radically curtailed and limited to Britain's 'storm centres'.[59] He vented his frustration to Cowan mid-way through the Paris Peace Conference while the world's politicians were putting on a show marked by bickering and grandstanding. The admiral was commanding British forces in the Baltic and wrote to the CIGS that 'chaos prevails at Riga, the Bolsheviks are murdering etc'. He wanted advice and help to restore order at the latest post-armistice flashpoint in Europe. Wilson complained that on November the previous year the War Cabinet agreed that the allied powers ought to agree their policy on Russia before any other decision were made. 'The Russia problem has <u>never</u> been discussed although I, certainly & probably others, have urged its imperative importance over & over again. It is a monument to the incompetence of the Frocks.'[60] The indecision of the politicians meant that:

> My whole energies are now bent on getting our troops out of Europe and Russia, and concentrating all our strength in <u>our</u> coming storm centres, viz. England, Ireland, Egypt and India... Since the statesmen can't or won't lay down a policy, I am going to look after & safeguard our own immediate interests, so that when all the hot air now blowing about League of Nations, Small States, Mandatories, turns to the icy cold wind of hard fact, the British Empire will be well clothed & well defended against all the bangs and curses of the future.[61]

Wilson continued to counsel politicians on the need for Britain to withdraw from its many, extended, and very expensive commitments across the Middle East and the fragmented former Tsarist Empire. Conscious of Mesopotamia's strategically vital geographical location Wilson soon added it to his list of priorities. In August, while lobbying for a realistic financial settlement for the army, he argued that its size should be greater than before the war because

58   Wilson diary, 17-21 January 1919.
59   Callwell, *Wilson* (Vol. II), p. 182.
60   Wilson diary, 12 April 1919.
61   Callwell, *Wilson*, (Vol. II), p. 182.

'our own dangers in Ireland, Egypt, Mesopotamia & India were much greater than in 1914.' He instructed his DMO Percy Radcliffe – known as 'P de B' – 'to work out what forces are required to keep these 4 storm centres quiet.' A few days later Wilson was angered that the Foreign Secretary Arthur James Balfour had written to the Prime Minister to 'say if we withdraw from Caucasus there would be massacres. Considering that we begin to withdraw on 15th this is a scandalous thing for A.J.B. to do. I went to see Curzon at H. of L. & told him if we did not remove A.J.B. we would <u>never</u> make peace nor end anything.' Churchill also wanted to delay the evacuation of British troops, but Wilson was against it.[62] The Cabinet agreed to withdraw from northern Russia and to stick to the Caucasus programme, despite wavering from Curzon who was 'very anxious about the massacres which will take place when we withdraw which we begin to do on the 15th. I am not so gloomy about the size of the massacres but in any case it is impossible for us to remain.' He put the annual financial cost of maintaining the force there of £50-60,000:'Nor could we find the men as we have not enough to garrison our own empire.' The priority, Wilson was clear, was to direct all available resources to 'keep our storm centres quiet'.[63]

With the benefit of hindsight Wilson's was a sensible and pragmatic position. British foreign policy, however, was a complex multi-dimensional puzzle beyond the powers of the Chief of the Imperial General Staff to resolve. The fact that the Middle East continues to be of 'paramount importance to the world' bears testament to that fact.[64]

62   Wilson diary, 7 and 11 August 1919.
63   Ibid., 12, 13 and 15 August 1919.
64   Johnson, *The Middle East*, p. 286.

Bibliography

Primary Sources

Bodleian Library Oxford

H.H. Asquith Papers
Viscount Milner Papers

Churchill Archives Centre, Churchill College, Cambridge

Viscount Esher Papers
Lord Hankey of the Chart Papers
General Lord Rawlinson Papers

Imperial War Museum

Roger Beadon Papers
Viscount French of Ypres Papers
Field Marshal Sir Henry Hughes Wilson Papers
C.R. Woodroffe Papers

Liddell Hart Centre for Military Archives

Brigadier-General John Charteris Papers
General G.S. Clive Papers
Launcelot Kiggell Papers
Major-General Sir Frederick Maurice Papers
Field Marshal Sir William Robertson Papers
Sir Edward Spears Papers

The National Archives, Kew

CAB 21 SWC reports and letters
CAB 23 War Cabinet minutes
CAB 24 Cabinet memoranda
CAB 25 SWC records

CAB 27 War Cabinet and Cabinet, miscellaneous committees
CAB 28 War Cabinet: Allied conferences, minutes and papers: IC series
CAB 42 War Council: Minutes and papers
CAB 43 Imperial War Cabinet: Minutes and Papers
WO 106 Directorate of Military Operations and Military Intelligence
WO 158 Military Headquarters: Correspondence and papers
WO 163 War Office, Army Council minutes and reports

National Library of Scotland

Earl Haig Papers

Parliamentary Archives

David Lloyd George Papers
Andrew Bonar Law Papers

Published Primary Sources

Amery, LS, *My Political Life, Volume Two: War & Peace, 1914-1929* (London: Hutchinson, 1953)

Barnes, John and Nicholson, David, (eds.), *The Leo Amery Diaries, Vol. 1, 1896-1929* (London: Hutchinson, 1980)
Beckett, Ian F.W., (ed.), *The Army and the Curragh Incident 1914* (London: The Bodley Head for the Army Records Society, 1985)
_____ (ed.), *The Memoirs of Sir James Edmonds* (Brighton: Tom Donovan Editions, 2013)
Blake, Robert, (ed.), *The Private Papers of Douglas Haig: 1914-1919* (London: Eyre & Spottiswoode, 1952)
Boraston, J.H., (ed.), *Sir Douglas Haig's Despatches (December 1915-April 1919)* (London: J.M. Dent, 1919)
Brock, Michael & Eleanor (eds.), *H.H. Asquith: Letters to Venetia Stanley* (Oxford: Oxford University Press, 1982)

Callwell, C.E., *Experiences of a Dug-Out, 1914-1918* (London: Constable, 1920)
_____ *Field-Marshal Sir Henry Wilson: His Life and Diaries*, (2 Vols.) (London: Cassell, 1927)
Charteris, John, *Field-Marshal Earl Haig* (London: Cassell, 1929)
_____ *At GHQ* (London: Cassell, 1931)
Churchill, Winston S., *The World Crisis* (single volume edition) (London: Thornton Butterworth, 1931)
_____ *World Crisis: 1916-1918*, Vol. III (London: Thornton Butterworth, 1927)

Dewar, G.A.B., & Boraston, J.H., *Sir Douglas Haig's Command 1915-1918* (2 Vols.) (London: Constable, 1922)
Duff Cooper, Alfred, *Haig*, (2 Vols.), (London: Faber & Faber, 1935-6)

Dutton, David, (ed.), *Paris 1918: The War Diary of the British Ambassador, the 17th Earl of Derby* (Liverpool: Liverpool University Press, 2001)

Esher, Viscount Reginald, *The Tragedy of Lord Kitchener* (London: John Murray, 1921)

Esher, Oliver Viscount, (ed.), *Journals and Letters of Reginald Viscount Esher (Vol. IV), 1916-1930* (London: Ivor Nicholson & Watson, 1938)

Farr, Don, *The Silent General: Horne of the First Army* (Solihull: Helion & Company, 2009 [2007])

Farrar-Hockley, Anthony, *Goughie: The Life of General Sir Hubert Gough* (London: Hart-Davis, MacGibbon, 1975)

Fay, Sir Sam, *The War Office at War* (London: Hutchinson, 1937)

Foch, Marshal Ferdinand (translated by Colonel T. Bentley Mott), *The Memoirs of Marshal Foch* (London: Heinemann, 1931)

French, Field Marshal, Viscount of Ypres, *1914* (London: Constable, 1919)

Greenhalgh, Elizabeth, (ed. & trans.), *Liaison: General Pierre des Vallieres at British General Headquarters, 1916-1917* (Stroud: History Press for the Army Records Society, 2016)

_____ (ed.), Lieutenant General Sir John Du Cane, KCB, *With Marshal Foch: A British General at Allied Supreme Headquarters April-November 1918* (Solihull: Helion & Company, 2108)

Gough, General Sir Hubert, *The Fifth Army* (London: Hodder & Stoughton, 1931)

_____ *Soldiering On* (London: Arthur Barker Ltd, 1954)

Hankey, Lord, *The Supreme Command*, 2 Vols. (London: George Allen & Unwin, 1961)

Hughes, Matthew (ed.), *Allenby in Palestine: The Middle East Correspondence of Field Marshal Viscount Allenby* (Stroud: Sutton Publishing for the Army Records Society, 2004)

Huguet, General [Victor J.M.], *Britain and the War: A French Indictment* (London: Cassell, 1928)

Jeffery, Keith, (ed.), *The Military Correspondence of Field Marshal Sir Henry Wilson: 1918-1922* (London: The Bodley Head for the Army Records Society, 1985)

Jones, Thomas, *Whitehall Diary: Volume 1: 1916-1925* (London: Oxford University Press, 1969)

Lady Fingall, Elizabeth Burke Plunkett, *Seventy Years Young: Memories of Elizabeth Countess of Fingall* (Dublin: Lilliput Press, 1991 [1937])

Lloyd George, David, *War Memoirs of David Lloyd George*, 2 Vols. (London: Odhams, 1938)

Riddell, Lord, *Lord Riddell's War Diary 1914-1918* (London: Ivor Nicholson & Watson, 1933)

Maurice, Nancy, (ed.), *The Maurice Case: From the Papers of Major-General Sir Frederick Maurice* (London: Leo Cooper, 1972)

Morris, A.J.A., (ed.), *The Letters of Lieutenant-Colonel Charles à Court Repington* (Stroud: Sutton Publishing for the Army Records Society, 1999)

Newhall, David S., *Clemenceau at War*, (Lewiston, NY: Edwin Mellen Press), 1991

Repington, Lieutenant-Colonel C. á Court, *The First World War, 1914-1918,* 2 Vols., (London: Constable, 1920)

Robertson, Field Marshal Sir William, *From Private to Field-Marshal* (London: Constable, 1921)

_____ *Soldiers and Statesmen* (London: Cassell, 1926)

Scott, Douglas, (ed.), *Douglas Haig: The Preparatory Prologue – Diaries and Letters 1861-1914* (Barnsley: Pen and Sword, 2006)

Seymour, Charles, (ed.), *The Intimate Papers of Colonel House: Into the World War – April 1917-June 1918,* Vol. III (London: Ernest Benn, 1928

Sheffield, Gary, (ed.), *From Vimy Ridge to the Rhine: The Great War Letters of Christopher Stone DSO MC* (Ramsbury, Marlborough: Crowood Press, 1989)

Sheffield, Gary, (ed.), *In Haig's Shadow: The Letters of Major-General Hugo De Pree and Field Marshal Douglas Haig* (Barnsley: Greenhill, 2019).

Sheffield, Gary & Bourne, John, (eds.), *Douglas Haig: War Diaries and Letters 1914-1918* (London: Phoenix, 2006 [2005])

Spears, Edward, *Liaison 1914: A Narrative of the Great Retreat* (London: Cassell, 1999 [1930])

Spears, Edward, *Prelude to Victory* (London: Cape, 1939)

Sykes, Sir Frederick, *From Many Angles: An Autobiography* (London: Harrap, 1943 [1942])

US Army (Historical Division), *United States Army in the World War, Vol. 2* (Washington DC: Center of Military Research, 1988).

War Office, *Statistics of the Military Effort of the British Empire during the Great War 1914-1920* (London: HMSO, 1922)

Williams, Charles, *Pétain* (London: Little, Brown, 2005)

Wilson, Keith, (ed.), *The Rasp of War: The Letters of H.A. Gwynne to the Countess of Bathurst, 1914-1918* (London: Sidgwick & Jackson, 1988)

Woodward, David R., (ed.), *The Military Correspondence of Field-Marshal Sir William Robertson, Chief of the Imperial General Staff, December 1915-February 1918* (London: Army Records Society, 1989)

Wright, Captain Peter E., *At the Supreme War Council* (London: G.P. Putnam's Sons, 1921)

Official Histories

Becke, A.F., *History of the Great War Based on Official Documents: Order of Battle of Divisions, Part 4, The Army Council, GHQs, Armies and Corps 1914-18* (London: HMSO, 1945)

Edmonds, Sir J.E., *Official History of the War: Military Operations France and Belgium 1914,* Vol. II (London: Macmillan, 1925)

_____*Official History of the War: Military Operations France and Belgium 1916,* Vol. 1 (London: Macmillan, 1932)

_____ *Official History of the War: Military Operations France and Belgium 1918,* Vol. 1 (London: Macmillan, 1935)

_____ *Official History of the War: Military Operations France and Belgium 1918*, Vol. 2 (London: Macmillan, 1937)

_____ *Official History of the War: Military Operations France and Belgium,1918*, Vol. 3 (London: Macmillan, 1939)

_____*Official History of the War: The Occupation of Constantinople 1918-1923* (Uckfield: Naval & Military Press 2010 reprint of 1944 edition)

_____ & Davies, H.R., *Official History of the War: Military Operations, Italy: 1915-1919* (London: HMSO, 1949)

Falls, Cyril, *Official History of the War: Military Operations: Macedonia*, 2 Vols. (London: HMSO, 1933 and 1935)

Moberly, F.J., *Official History of the War: The Campaign in Mesopotamia 1914-1918*, Vol. IV (London: HMSO, 1927)

The War Office List (London: HMSO, 1932)

Secondary Sources

Biographies

Ash, Bernard, *The Lost Dictator: Field-Marshal Sir Henry Wilson* (London: Cassell, 1968)
Ash, Eric, *Sir Frederick Sykes and the Air Revolution – 1912-1918* (London: Frank Cass, 1999)

Bonham-Carter, Victor, *Soldier True: The Life and Times of Field Marshal Sir William Robertson* (Aylesbury: Frederick Muller, 1963)
Birdges, Tom, *Alarms and Excursions: Reminiscences of a Soldier* (London: Longmans, 1938)

Caffrey, Matt B. Jr., *On Wargaming: How Wargames Have Shaped History and How They May Shape the Future*, (Newport, Rhode Island.: Naval War College Press, 2019)
Cassar, George H., *Kitchener: Architect of Victory* (London: William Kimber & Co, 1977)
_____ *The Tragedy of Sir John French* (Newark: University of Delaware Press, 1985)
_____ *Asquith as War Leader* (London: Hambledon Press, 1994)
_____ *Kitchener's War: British Strategy from 1914 to 1916* (Dulles, VA: Potomac Books, 2004)
Collier, Basil, *Brasshat* (London: Secker & Warburg, 1961)

Egremont, Max, *Under Two Flags: The Life of Major-General Sir Edward Spears* (London: Phoenix, 1998 [1997])

Fisher, John, *Curzon and British Imperialism in the Middle East: 1916-1919* (London: Frank Cass, 1999)

Gilbert, Martin, *Winston S. Churchill: 1914-16*, Vol. III (London: Heinemann, 1971)
_____ *Winston S. Churchill: 1917-22*, Vol. IV (London: Heinemann, 1975)
Grigg, John, *Lloyd George: War Leader: 1916-1918* (London: Faber & Faber, 2011 [2002])

Gollin, A.M., *Proconsul in Politics: A study of Lord Milner in opposition and in power*, (New York: Macmillan, 1964)

Greenhalgh, Elizabeth, *Foch in Command: The Forging of a First World War General* (Cambridge: Cambridge University Press, 2011)

Griffiths, Richard, *Marshal Pétain* (London: Constable, 1970)

Harris, J.P., *Douglas Haig and the First World War* (Cambridge: Cambridge University Press, 2008)

Harris, Paul, General Sir Herbert Lawrence: Haig's Chief of Staff (Solihull: Helion & Company, 2019)

Holmes, Richard, *The Little Field Marshal: A Life of Sir John French* (London: Cassell, 2005 [1981])

Hughes, Matthew, *Allenby and British Strategy in the Middle East 1917-1919* (London: Frank Cass, 1999)

James, David, *The Life of Lord Roberts* (London: Hollis & Carter, 1954)

Jeffery, Keith, *Field Marshal Sir Henry Wilson: A Political Soldier* (Oxford: Oxford University Press, 2008 [2006])

Jenkins, Roy, *Asquith* (London: Collins, 1964)

Keiger, J.F.V., *Raymond Poincaré* (Cambridge: Cambridge University Press, 1997)

MacPhail, Sir Andrew, *Three Persons* (London: John Murray, 1929)

Mead, Gary, *The Good Soldier: The Biography of Douglas Haig* (London: Atlantic Books, 2007)

Morris A.J.A., *Reporting the First World War: Charles Repington, The Times and the Great War* (Cambridge: Cambridge University Press, 2015)

Prior, Robin, and Wilson, Trevor, *Command on the Western Front: The Military Career of Sir Henry Rawlinson 1914-1918* (Barnsley: Pen & Sword, 2004 [1992])

Reid, Walter, *Architect of Victory: Douglas Haig* (Edinburgh: Birlinn, 2006)

Rose, Kenneth, *Superior Person: A Portrait of Curzon and His Circle in late Victorian England* (London: Weidenfeld & Nicolson, 1969)

Roskill, Stephen W., *Hankey: Man of Secrets, Vol. I, 1877-1918* (London: Collins, 1970)

Sheffield, Gary, *The Chief: Douglas Haig and the British Army* (London: Aurum Press, 2011)

_____ *In Haig's Shadow: Brigadier-General Hugo de Pree and the First World War* (London: Greenhill Books, 2019)

Smythe, Donald, *Pershing: General of the Armies*, (Bloomington: Indiana University Press, 1986)

Taylor, Rex, *Assassination* (London: Hutchinson, 1961)

Terraine, John, *Douglas Haig: The Educated Soldier* (London: Cassell, 2005 [1963])

Woodward, David R., *Field-Marshal Sir William Robertson: Chief of the Imperial General Staff in the Great War* (Westport: Praeger, 1998)

General Volumes

Adams, R.J.Q. & Poirier, Philip P., *The Conscription Controversy in Britain, 1900-1918* (Columbus: Ohio State University Press, 1987)

Badsey, Stephen, *Doctrine and Reform in the British Cavalry 1880-1918* (Aldershot: Ashgate, 2008)

Beach, Jim, *Haig's Intelligence: GHQ and the German Army 1916-1918* (Cambridge: Cambridge University Press, 2015 [2013])

Beaverbrook, Lord, *Politicians and the War: 1914-1916* (London: Oldbourne Book Co, 1960)

Beckett, Ian F.W. & Corvi, Stephen J., (eds.), *Haig's Generals*, (Barnsley: Pen & Sword, 2009 [2006])

_____ *The Great War* (Second Edition) (Harlow: Pearson Education, 2007)

Beckett, Ian, Bowman, Timothy & Connelly, Mark, *The British Army and the First World War* (Cambridge: Cambridge University Press, 2017)

Beckett, Ian F.W., *A British Profession of Arms: The Politics of Command in the Late Victorian Army* (Norman, Oklahoma: University of Oklahoma Press, 2018)

Bidwell, Shelford, and Graham, Dominick, *Firepower: The British Army Weapons and Theories of War, 1904-1945* (Barnsley: Pen & Sword, 2004)

Boff, Jonathan, *Winning and Losing on the Western Front: The British Third Army and the Defeat of Germany in 1918* (Cambridge: Cambridge University Press, 2014 [2012])

Bond, Brian, *The Victorian Army and the Staff College 1854-1914* (London: Eyre Methuen, 1972)

_____ (et. al), *'Look to Your Front': Studies in the First World War by the British Commission for Military History* (Staplehurst: Spellmount, 1999)

Bourne, J.M., *Britain and the Great War 1914-1918* (London: Arnold, 1989)

_____ *Who's Who in World War I* (London: Routledge, 2001)

Bowman, Timothy & Connelly, Mark, *The Edwardian Army: Recruiting, Training and Deploying the British Army, 1902-1914* (Oxford: Oxford University Press, 2012)

Douglas Boyd, *The Other First World War: The Blood-Soaked Russian Fronts 1914-1922* (Stroud: History Press, 2017 [2014]).

Brown, Ian Malcolm, *British Logistics on the Western Front 1914-1919* (Westport, CT and London: Praeger 1998)

Buchan, John, *A History of the Great War*, 4 Vols. (Boston: Houghton Mifflin, 1922)

Cassar, George H., *The Forgotten Front: The British Campaign in Italy, 1917-1918*, (London: Hambledon Press, 1998)

Cohen, Eliot A., *Supreme Command: Soldiers, Statesmen and Leadership in Wartime* (London: Simon & Schuster, 2003 [2002])

Cruttwell, C.R.M.F., *A History of the Great War 1914-1918* (Oxford: Clarendon Press, 1934)

Dunscomb, Paul E., *Japan's Siberian Intervention, 1918-1922: 'A Great Disobedience Against the People"* (Lanham, Maryland: Lexington Books, 2011)

French, David, *British Strategy and War Aims: 1914-1916* (London: Allen & Unwin, 1986)

_____ *The Strategy of the Lloyd George Coalition, 1916-1918* (Oxford: Clarendon Press at Oxford University Press, 1995)

_____ & Holden Reid, Brian, (eds.), *The British General Staff: Reform and Innovation 1890-1939* (London: Frank Cass, 2002)

Figes, Orlando, *A People's Tragedy: The Russian Revolution* (London: The Bodley Head, 2017 [1996])

Gardner, Nikolas, *Trial by Fire: Command and the British Expeditionary Force in 1914* (Westport Connecticut: Praeger, 2004)

Gilbert, Martin, *Churchill and America* (New York: Simon & Schuster, 2008)

Gooch, John, *The Plans of War: The General Staff and British Military Strategy c.1900 – 1914* (London: Routledge, 1974)

Greenhalgh, Elizabeth, *Victory Through Coalition: Britain and France during the First World War* (Cambridge: Cambridge University Press, 2005)

_____ *The French Army and the First World War* (Cambridge: Cambridge University Press, 2014)

Grieves, Keith, *The Politics of Manpower* (Manchester: Manchester University Press, 1988)

Grotelueschen, Mark Ethan *The AEF Way of War: The American Army and Combat in World War I* (Cambridge: Cambridge University Press, 2006)

Guinn, Paul, *British Strategy and Politics: 1914 to 1918* (Oxford: Clarendon Press, 1965)

Handy, Charles, *Understanding Organizations,* 4th Ed. (London: Penguin, 1993 [1976])

Harris, J.P., *Men, Ideas and Tanks: British Military Thought: 1903-1939* (Manchester: Manchester University Press, 1995)

Harris, Paul, *The Men Who Planned the War: A Study of the Staff of the British Army on the Western Front, 1914-1918* (Farnham: Ashgate, 2016)

Horne, Alistair, *The Price of Glory: Verdun 1916*, (London: Penguin, 1993 [1962])

Hughes, Matthew & Seligmann, Matthew, (eds.), *Leadership in Conflict 1914-1918* (Barnsley: Pen & Sword, 2000)

Jeffery, Keith, *The British army and the crisis of empire: 1918-1922* (Manchester: Manchester University Press, 1984)

_____ *Ireland and the Great War* (Cambridge: Cambridge University Press, 2002)

Johnson, Rob, *The Great War & the Middle East: A Strategic Study*, (Oxford: Oxford University Press, 2016)

Jones, Spencer, *From Boer War to World War: Tactical Reform of the British Army 1899-1914* (Norman, Oklahoma: University of Oklahoma Press, 2012)

_____ (ed.), *Courage Without Glory: The British Army on the Western Front 1915* (Solihull: Helion & Company, 2015)

_____ (ed.), *At All Costs: The British Army on the Western Front 1916* (Solihull: Helion & Company, 2018)

Kitchen, Martin, *The German Offensives of 1918* (Stroud: Tempus, 2001)

Liddell Hart, B.H., *The British Way in Warfare* (London: Faber & Faber, 1932)

_____ *Strategy: The Indirect Approach*, 3rd Ed. (London: Faber & Faber, 1967)

Lloyd, Nick, *Loos 1915*, (Stroud: The History Press, 2008)

_____ *Passchendaele: A New History* (London: Viking, 2017)

Lowry, Bullitt, *Armistice 1918* (Kent: Kent State University Press, 1996)

MacMillan, Margaret, *Peacemakers: Six Months that Changed the World* (London: John Murray, 2002 [2001])

McCrae, Meighen, *Coalition Strategy and the End of the First World War: The Supreme War Council and War Planning, 1917-1918* (Cambridge, CUP, 2009)

Middlebrook, Martin, *The Kaiser's Battle* (London: Penguin, 1978)

Millman, Brock, *Pessimism and British War Policy: 1916-1918* (London: Frank Cass, 2001)

Neillands, Robin, *The Great War Generals on the Western Front: 1914-1918* (London: Robinson, 1999)

Neilson, Keith, *Strategy and Supply: The Anglo-Russian Alliance, 1914-17* (London: Routledge, 2014 [1984])

Phillips, Gregory D., *The Diehards: Aristocratic Society and Politics in Edwardian England* (Cambridge Massachusetts: Harvard University Press, 1979)

Philpott, William James, *Anglo-French Relations and Strategy on the Western Front, 1914-18* (London: Macmillan, 1996)

_____ *Attrition: Fighting the First World War* (London: Little Brown, 2014)

Prete, Roy A., *Strategy and Command: the Anglo-French Coalition on the Western Front 1914* (London: McGill-Queen's University Press, 2009)

Rogan, Eugene, *The Fall of the Ottomans: The Great War in the Middle East, 1914-1920* (London: Allen Lane, 2015)

Sheffield, Gary, *Forgotten Victory: The First World War: Myths and Realities* (London: Headline, 2001)

_____ *Command and Morale: The British Army on the Western Front, 1914-1918* (Barnsley: Pen & Sword, 2014)

Sheldon, Jack, *The German Army on Vimy Ridge 1914-1917* (Barnsley: Pen & Sword 2008 [2013])

Showalter, Dennis, *Instrument of War: The German Army 1914-18* (Oxford: Osprey, 2016)

Simpson, Andy, *Directing Operations: British Corps Command on the Western Front 1914-18* (Stroud: Spellmount, 2006)

Stevenson, David, *With Our Backs to the Wall: Victory and Defeat in 1918* (London: Allen Lane, 2011)

Strachan, Hew, *The Politics of the British Army* (Oxford: Oxford University Press, 1997)

Terraine, John, *The Western Front 1914-1918* (London: Hutchinson, 1964)

_____ *To Win a War: 1918 the Year of Victory* (London: Cassell, 2000 [1978])

Travers, Tim, *How the War Was Won: Command and Technology in the British Army on the Western Front, 1917-1918* (London: Routledge, 1992)

_____ *The Killing Ground: The British Army, the Western Front and the Emergence of Modern War 1900-1918* (Barnsley: Pen & Sword, 2009 [1987])

Turner, John, (ed.), *Britain and the First World War* (London: Routledge, 2014 [1988])

Tyler, J.E., *The British Army and the Continent, 1904-1914* (London: Arnold, 1938)

Williamson Jr, S.R., The *Politics of Grand Strategy: Britain and France Prepare for War 1904-1914* (Cambridge, Mass.: Harvard University Press, 1969)

Woodward, David R., *Lloyd George and the Generals* (Newark: University of Delaware Press, 1983)

_____ *Trial by Friendship: Anglo-American Relations 1917-1918* (Lexington, Kentucky: University of Kentucky Press, 1993)

Zabecki, David T., *The German 1918 Offensives: A Case Study in the Operational Level of War* (Oxford: Routledge, 2006)

Book Chapters & Published Articles

Adams, R.J.Q., 'The National Service League and Mandatory Service in Edwardian Britain,' *Armed Forces & Society*, Vol. 12(1), (Fall 1985): pp. 53-74

Badsey, Stephen, 'The Missing Western Front; Politics, Propaganda and Strategy 1918', in idem, *The British Army in Battle and its Image 1914-18* (London: Continuum, 2009), pp. 185-209

Baker, Chris, '"Embusqués of the worst type, living among the fleshpots of Paris": The British Permanent Staff at the Supreme War Council', *Stand To!*, (100), June 2014, pp. 110-114

Beckett, Ian F.W., 'The Nation in Arms', in Beckett, Ian F.W., & Simpson, Keith, (eds.), *A Nation in Arms: A Social Study of the British Army in the First World War* (London: Tom Donovan, 1990 [1986]), pp. 1-36

_____ 'King George V and his Generals' in Hughes and Seligmann, (eds.), *Leadership*, pp. 247-264

Bliss, Tasker H., 'The Evolution of the Unified Command', *Foreign Affairs*, Vol. 1 (2), (1922), pp. 1-31

Clarke, R.J., '"Fit to Fight?" How the Physical Condition of the Conscripts Contributed to the Manpower Crisis of 1917-18,' *Journal of the Society for Army Historical Research*, Vol. 94 (370), Autumn 2016, pp. 225-224

Curragh, Brian, 'Henry Wilson's War' in Jones, Spencer, (ed.), *Stemming the Tide: Officers and Leadership in the British Expeditionary Force 1914* (Solihull: Helion & Company, 2013), pp. 70-88

Dean, Terry, 'General Sir John Steven Cowans', *Stand To!*, 108, (2017), pp. 26-32

French, David, 'Watching the allies: British intelligence and the French mutinies of 1917', *Intelligence and National Security*, Vol. 6 (3), (2008), pp. 573-592.

Foley, Robert T., 'Preparing the German Army for the First World War: The Operational Ideas of Alfred von Schlieffen and Helmuth von Moltke the Younger, *War & Society*, Vol. 22 (2), (2004), pp. 1-25

Fraser, Peter, 'The British "Shells Scandal" of 1915', *Canadian Journal of History*, 28 (1983), pp. 69-86

Gardner, Nikolas, 'Command in Crisis: The British Expeditionary Force and the Forest of Mormal, August 1914', *War & Society*, Vol. 16 (2), (1998), pp. 13-32

Gregory, Adrian, '"You might as well recruit Germans": British public opinion and the decision to conscript the Irish in 1918', in Adrian Gregory and Senia Pašeta, *Ireland and the Great War: 'A War to Unite Us All'?* (Manchester: Manchester University Press, 2002) p. 113-132

Greenhalgh, Elizabeth, 'Myth and Memory: Sir Douglas Haig and the Imposition of Allied Unified Command in March 1918', *Journal of Military History*, Vol. 68, (2004), pp. 771-820

_____ 'Paul Painlevé and Franco-British Relations in 1918', *Contemporary British History*, Vol. 25, (2011), pp. 5-27

Harris, Paul, 'Soldier Banker: Lieutenant-General Sir Herbert Lawrence as the BEF's Chief of Staff 1918', *Journal of the Society for Army Historical Research*, Vol. 90 (361), (2012), pp. 44-67

Hussey, John, 'Henry Wilson's Versailles War Game: January 1918', *Records, Journal of the Douglas Haig Fellowship*, (no. 20, 2018), pp. 1-32

Justice, Simon, 'Vanishing Battalions: The Nature, Impact and Implications of British Infantry Reorganization prior to the German Spring Offensives of 1918' in LoCicero, Michael, Mahoney, Ross, & Mitchell, Stuart, (eds.), *A Military Transformed?: Adaptation and Innovation in the British Military, 1792-1945* (Solihull: Helion & Company, 2014) pp. 157-173

Lockwood, P.A., 'Milner's entry into the War Cabinet: December 1916', *Historical Journal*, Vol. VII (1), (1964), pp. 120-134

Millman, Brock, 'Henry Wilson's Mischief: Field Marshall [sic] Sir Henry Wilson's Rise to Power 1917-18,' *Canadian Journal of History*, Vol. XXX, (1995), pp. 467-486

_____ 'The Problem with Generals: Military Observers and the Origins of the Intervention in Russia', *Journal of Contemporary History*, Vol. 33 (2), (1998), pp. 291-320

_____ 'A Counsel of Despair: British Strategy and War Aims, 1917-18', *Journal of Contemporary History*, Vol. 36 (2), (2001), pp. 241-270

Philpott, William, 'Britain, France and the Belgian Army' in Brian Bond et. al., *'Look to Your Front': Studies in the First World War by the British Commission for Military History* (Staplehurst: Spellmount, 1999), pp. 121-136

_____ 'Haig and Britain's European Allies', in Bond, Brian and Cave, Nigel (eds.), *Haig: A Reappraisal 70 Years On* (Barnsley: Leo Cooper, 1999), pp. 128-144

_____ 'Squaring the Circle: The Higher Co-Ordination of the Entente in the Winter of 1915-16', *English Historical Review*, Vol. 114 (458), (1999), pp. 875-898

_____ 'Marshal Ferdinand Foch and Allied Victory' in Hughes and Seligmann, (eds.), *Leadership*, pp. 38-53

_____ 'The Supreme War Council and the Allied War Effort, 1939-40', in Chassaigne, Philippe & Dockrill, Michael, (eds.), *Anglo-French Relations 1898-1998: From Fashoda to Jospin* (Basingstoke: Palgrave, 2002), pp. 109-124

Prete, Roy A., 'French Strategic Planning and the Deployment of the BEF in France in 1914', *Canadian Journal of History*, Vol. XXIV, (1989), pp. 42-62

Roberts, Pricilla, 'Tasker H. Bliss and the Evolution of Allied Unified Command, 1918: A Note on Old Battles Revisited', *Journal of Military History*, Vol. 65, (2001), pp. 671-696

Rubinstein, William, D., 'Henry Page Croft and the National Party 1917-22', *Journal of Contemporary History*, Vol. 9 (1), (1974), pp. 129-148

Simkins, Peter, 'For Better or for Worse: Sir Henry Rawlinson and his Allies in 1916 and 1918', in Hughes and Seligman, (eds.), pp. 13-37

Sheffield, Gary & Spencer, John, 'Soldiers and Politicians in Strife' in Liddle, Peter, (ed.), *Britain and a Widening War 1915-16: Gallipoli, Mesopotamia and the Somme* (Barnsley: Pen & Sword, 2016), pp. 83-99

Spencer, John 'Friends Disunited: Johnnie French, Wully Robertson and "K. of K.," in 1915', in Jones, Spencer, (ed.), *Courage Without Glory: The British Army on the Western Front 1915* (Solihull: Helion & Company, 2015), pp. 80-102

Wilson, Keith M., 'National Party Spirits: Backing into the Future' in Hughes & Seligmann (eds.), *Leadership*, pp. 209-226

Woodward, David R., 'David Lloyd George, A Negotiated Peace with Germany and the Kulhmann Peace Kite of September 1917', *Canadian Journal of History*, Vol. VI (1), (March 1971): pp. 75-93

_____ 'The Origins and Intent of David Lloyd George's January 5 War Aims Speech', *Historian*, Vol. 34 (1), (1971), pp. 22-39

_____ 'Did Lloyd George Starve the British Army of Men Prior to the German Offensive of 21 March 1918?', *The Historical Journal*, Vol. 27 (1), (1984), pp. 241-252

_____ Review of *Wilson*, *Journal of Military History*, Vol. 73 (2), (2009), pp. 665-666

Index

Milton Keynes UK
Ingram Content Group UK Ltd.
UKHW051627031023
429589UK00007B/34